REVISION

WRITING LIVES
Ethnographic Narratives

Series Editors:
Arthur P. Bochner & Carolyn Ellis
University of South Florida

Writing Lives: Ethnographic Narratives publishes narrative representations of qualitative research projects. The series editors seek manuscripts that blur the boundaries between humanities and social sciences. We encourage novel and evocative forms of expressing concrete lived experience, including autoethnographic, literary, poetic, artistic, visual, performative, critical, multivoiced, conversational, and coconstructed representations. We are interested in ethnographic narratives that depict local stories; employ literary modes of scene setting, dialogue, character development, and unfolding action; and include the author's critical reflections on the research and writing process, such as research ethics, alternative modes of inquiry and representation, reflexivity, and evocative storytelling. Proposals and manuscripts should be directed to abochner@cas.usf.edu.

Volumes in this series:

Erotic Mentoring: Women's Transformations in the University, Janice Hocker Rushing

Intimate Colonialism: Head, Heart, and Body in West African Development Work, Laurie L. Charlés

Last Writes: A Daybook for a Dying Friend, Laurel Richardson

A Trickster in Tweed: The Quest for Quality in a Faculty Life, Thomas F. Frentz

Guyana Diaries: Women's Lives Across Difference, Kimberly D. Nettles

Writing Qualitative Inquiry: Self, Stories, and Academic Life, H. L. Goodall, Jr.

Accidental Ethnography: An Inquiry into Family Secrecy, Christopher N. Poulos

Revision: Autoethnographic Reflections on Life and Work, Carolyn Ellis

R E V I S I O N

Autoethnographic Reflections on Life and Work

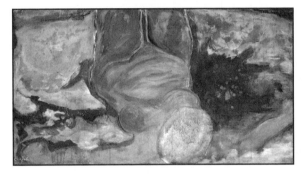

Carolyn Ellis

Left Coast
Press Inc.

Left Coast
Press Inc.

LEFT COAST PRESS, INC.
1630 North Main Street, #400
Walnut Creek, CA 94596
http://www.LCoastPress.com

ISBN 978-1-59874-039-4 hardcover
ISBN 978-1-59874-040-0 paperback

Library of Congress Cataloging-in-Publication Data

Ellis, Carolyn, 1950–
  Revision : autoethnographic reflections on life and work / Carolyn Ellis.
     p. cm. -- (Writing lives : ethnographic narratives)
  Includes bibliographical references and index.
  ISBN 978-1-59874-039-4 (hardback : alk. paper) — ISBN 978-1-59874-040-0
  (pbk. : alk. paper)
  1. Ethnology—Authorship. 2. Ethnology—Biographical methods. I. Title.
  GN307.7.E437 2009
  305.8—dc22
                        2008042276

Printed in the United States of America

⊖™ The paper used in this publication meets the minimum requirements of American
National Standard for Information Sciences—Permanence of Paper for Printed Library
Materials, ANSI/NISO Z39.48–1992.

09 10 11 12 13 5 4 3 2 1

Contents

For

Laurel Richardson

Norman Denzin

Arthur Bochner

My three muses who laid the groundwork and paved the way—
and for all our students who have taken up the journey.

Sokrates: Please assume, then, for the sake of argument, that there is in our souls a block of wax, in one case larger, in another smaller, in one case the wax is purer, in another more impure and harder, in some cases softer, and in some of proper quality . . . Let us, then, say that this is the gift of Mnemosyne (Memory), the mother of the Mousai (Muses), and that whenever we wish to remember anything we see or hear or think of in our own minds, we hold this wax under the perceptions and thoughts and imprint them upon it, just as we make impressions from seal rings; and whatever is imprinted we remember and know as long as its image lasts, but whatever is rubbed out or cannot be imprinted we forget and do not know.

—*Plato,* Theaetetus *191c (trans. Fowler)*

Acknowledgments

I love writing but I also love finishing a writing project and anticipating comments and feedback from new and older readers alike! It is with deep gratitude that I acknowledge my friends, colleagues, and students who have assisted with the completion of this book. First, those who read and commented on every page: Thanks to Laurel Richardson for always asking the right questions and getting to the heart of the matter; to Lisa Tillmann for her superb editing skills and probing observations about what it means to do ethical research; to Judy Tanur for pointing out just the right word to use and helping me to reconstruct history by jogging my memory; to Mitch Allen for being supportively critical, having a sense of humor, and being willing to take risks; to Arthur Bochner for his incisive feedback and editing genius and for caring as much about my work as he does his own.

I have dedicated this book to my three muses: Arthur Bochner, Norman Denzin, and Laurel Richardson. They are the three readers I keep in my mind as I write. I ask how they will interpret what I say, what questions they will ask, and how they will prod me to think deeper and wider. Then I ask if I have met their standards of excellence. I want to thank them for believing in the interpretive project; for paving the way with their words and actions; for acknowledging that scholarship should be caring, meaningful, and concerned with justice; and for being good friends as well as colleagues. I'd also like to thank Tom Frentz, H. L. (Bud) Goodall, Marilyn Myerson, Ron Pelias, Chris Poulos, and Karen Scott-Hoy for good conversations over the years about my work. My department chair, Kenneth Cissna, and my colleagues at University of South Florida deserve recognition for providing a supportive atmosphere of collegiality that encourages creativity and risk-taking.

I also acknowledge all the graduate students from University of South Florida who have inspired me and made me feel that the work I do is worthwhile. I want to thank, in particular, Tony Adams, Robin Boylorn, Christine Davis, Laura Ellingson, Mary Poole, Carol Rambo, Lisa Tillmann, and Jillian Tullis Owen, whose work and conversations directly inspired some of the ideas in this book. Additionally, I express my gratitude to Michael Arrington, Deborah Austin, Julia Barnhill, Korrie Bauman, Leigh Berger, Rachel Binns, Matthew Brooks, Dionel Cotanda, Keith Cherry, Elizabeth Curry, Elissa Foster,

Joan George, Andrew Herrmann, Barbara Jago, Christine Kiesinger, Yvonne Kline, Tori Lockler, Cara Mackie, Cris McRae, Valerie Macleod, Jeanine Minge, Judy Perry, Steve Phalen, Penny Phillips, Gina Rathbun, Patrick Santoro, Kendall Smith-Sullivan, Linda Vangelis, Deb Walker, and Zhong Wang, whose work also contributed to this project.

Thanks to Kelly Clark/Keefe for painting *Mnemosyn,* which graces this book's cover. I appreciate Judy Perry's help with endnotes, references, and the index; Andrew Herrmann's assistance with references; and Rachel Fudge's copyediting and guidance through production. Mitch Allen, once again, was a superb publisher.

Grateful acknowledgment is made to the following journals and presses in which the previously published articles in this book first appeared: AltaMira Press—A Division of Rowman and Littlefield Publishers Incorporated, Blackwell Publishers, *Journal of Contemporary Ethnography,* Pearson Education Publications, *Qualitative Inquiry, Symbolic Interaction,* Sage Publications Incorporated, *The Sociological Quarterly,* Temple University Press, and University of California Press. Complete citations are included in the references and in endnotes.

I acknowledge permission to reproduce materials for which they hold copyrights from the following: Bochner, A. P. (2005a). Interpretive and narrative on the Ellis study. In J. Paul (Ed.), *Introduction to the philosophies of research and criticism in education and the social sciences* (pp. 268–273). Upper Saddle River, NJ: Pearson Education, Inc., reprinted with permission from Pearson Education, Inc.; Kleinman, S. (1993). Culturally speaking: Carolyn Ellis' "There are survivors." *The Sociological Quarterly, 34,* 731–733, reprinted with permission from Blackwell Publishing.

My gratitude goes to all those who are characters in my book, especially my family from Luray and the mountain people with whom I now share my summers, as well as friends who have found their way into my stories. It's not easy being my family and friends, because you never know when you'll appear in one of my stories. I apologize if I have said anything that you would have preferred left unsaid, if I failed to include you when you thought your role should have been honored, or if I neglected to give you an opportunity to respond when you had something to say. Recognizing how messy writing about intimate others tends to be, I have wanted to treat all your stories with love and care, while at the same time present your life as complex and many-sided, as I have tried to do with my own character. My goal has been to balance my ethical responsibilities to participants with my truth-telling obligations to readers while accepting the risks and taking on the burdens that come with writing intimately about myself and my relationships with others. I look forward to continuing the conversations and thinking more deeply about all of the issues raised in this book.

Finally I want to thank my family—Art, Buddha, and Sunya—who remind me every day of the preciousness of life, the wonder of love, and the exhilaration of scampering up and down mountains. Thanks for sustaining me with affection and joy while I climbed this one.

Introduction

Reflecting on Meta-Autoethnography

I dream I am in the shower. Though drenched by the water spraying over me, I am partially clothed. Shadows dance on the translucent shower curtain that surrounds me. When I squint, the shadows slowly come into focus and, to my surprise, I recognize the moving shapes as my doctoral students. They pay no attention to me, seeming not to see me, not yet anyway. I move between panic that the students shouldn't see me like this and calm that surely they will understand why I must be here. But what if they don't? What if I'm not supposed to be here? How do I hide my embarrassment that they have seen me, their professor, in this compromised situation? What happens to their confidence that I can be trusted to guide them, to push limits yet respect necessary boundaries? Why am I in a shower in a public place anyway? Even I don't know. Is it public if I can see them but they can't see me? Have they just not glanced my way? Or are they pretending not to see me to save my face and theirs? I wonder what I should do. Do I squat down and hide from sight, concealing my half-naked body? Do I get out of the shower quickly, my wet clothes dripping on the floor, hoping someone will hand me a towel? Or do I turn my back, take off the rest of my clothes, and shower "properly," assuming that I must finish what I started and others will respond as they must?

I awake without resolving any of these issues.

Writing a Simple Book

"I want you to gather your published stories into one volume so that readers will have access to them," Mitch Allen, publisher of Left Coast Press, says to me. "Sounds simple," I say.

"It is. A few months—that's all it should take."

I become excited, forgetting that there is no *simple* book.

"I want you to pull together the book you were supposed to write when I gave you the contract for *The Ethnographic I*," Mitch says. "Write an intro on 'what is autoethnography' and then give a dozen examples of your writing that showcase autoethnography."

"I'll want to write a story that links the pieces," I muse.

"That's fine, but keep the emphasis on the published stories. The stories should carry the book," Mitch advises.

I nod. It sounds so easy.

But it wasn't. Now three years after that agreement, I'm still working on this "simple" book. Once I started introducing the stories, I found I couldn't repackage them quickly. Too much had happened since I had written them. As with most books, this one took on a life of its own.

The complications began with "There Are Survivors," a story about the death of my brother Rex. As I reread the story, I started to think about how I would tell the story about that loss now, more than twenty-five years later, and I wondered how my feelings had changed. What held my attention was how I had portrayed my mother after Rex's death—as cold, detached, distant, unwilling to acknowledge my grief. Since that watershed event of my brother's death, so much had happened. My father died suddenly a few years after my brother. My mom grew old, she and I developed a close and loving relationship, and my siblings and I cared for her during the last year of her life in 2002 when she was bedridden. Likewise, students had responded to my story of loss with their stories and critics had commented on what I had written. Could I leave this portrayal as I had written it in 1993, fifteen years before? I decided that I could not. I felt it important to question and challenge my earlier versions of events in my life, revising and rethinking what I'd written from the perspective of the present.

This book could not be a simple collection of my stories.

Adding Meta-Autoethnography

Revision: Autoethnographic Reflections on Life and Work begins where *The Ethnographic I*—a novel about the practices of doing and teaching autoethnography—left off. In *Revision,* my purpose is to re-present, re-examine, and re-vision some of the stories I have published about the life I have lived and the autoethnographic projects I have conducted, which are integral parts of each other. To accomplish this, I wrap a larger "story of the stories" around segments of my reprinted narratives and the interpretive materials that originally accompanied them. I write new tales into the gaps. I include and react to voices of other scholars and students whose responses and critiques were evoked by my work. I show how I have sometimes resisted critiques that I felt tried to impede the development of autoethnography, choosing to forge ahead without responding or taking in the criticism too deeply. Other times I have entered into conversations that challenged me to develop autoethnography in a fuller and more complex way and reinterpret or question the meaning of the original stories I had written.

To connect the past to my life now, I add current reflections, narrative vignettes, and analyses, which I call *meta-autoethnographies,*[1] that fast-forward these stories to the present. These are occasions in which I revisit my original representation, consider responses, and write an autoethnographic account about autoethnography. My meta-autoethnographic treatments provide opportunities to alter the frame in which I wrote the original story, ask questions I didn't ask then, consider others' responses to the original story, and include vignettes of related experiences that have happened since I experienced and wrote the story and now affect the way I look back at the story. My goal is to turn the narrative snapshots I have written in the past into a form more akin to a video—a text in motion[2]—one in which I drag and drop in new experiences as well as revised interpretations of old storylines, then reorder and thus restory them. This text becomes one in which I tack back and forth between now and then, where "now" sometimes changes character and "then" moves from denoting the distant past to representing the more near past to sometimes referring to several points in time and memory.

As I reconstruct and revise a portion of my life story, I seek to provide a framework that marks and holds the scenes in place, at least for this moment, one that moves from beginning to end and circles back to the beginning again. My goal is to model "a way to reflectively make sense of experience—using hindsight to follow the thread back into the labyrinth" and to move readers to "contemplate similar ways of accessing [their] own lives" (Birkerts, 2008, p. 22).

As an autoethnographer, I am both the author and focus of the story, the one who tells and the one who experiences, the observer and the observed, the creator and the created. I am the person at the intersection of the personal and the cultural, thinking and observing as an ethnographer and writing and describing as a storyteller.

As an autoethnographer, I tell a situated story, constructed from my current position, one that is always partial, incomplete, and full of silences, and told at a particular time, for a particular purpose, to a particular audience. I am well aware that all of us constantly reframe and restory our lives, attempting to arrive at a version that presents these lives as changing, yet continuous and coherent (Baerger & McAdams, 1999; Bochner, 1997; Carr, 1986; MacIntyre, 1981; Smith & Sparkes, 2006). Our versions change as we age and have new experiences—"we are constantly having to revise the plot as new events are added to our lives" (Polkinghorne, 1988, p. 150)—as others respond to the stories we tell and tell their own, as the world around us evolves, and as we devise new frames for making our diverse experiences meaningful (Baerger & McAdams, 1999; see also Smith & Sparkes, 2006). Thus, reexamining the events we have lived through and the stories we have told about them previously allows us to expand and deepen our understandings of the lives we have led, the culture in which we have lived, and the work we have done. This review provides new possibilities for understanding ourselves and keeps us from remaining stuck in the interpretations we have settled on in the past. Laurel Richardson (1997) says that "writing stories about our 'texts' is . . . a way of making sense of and changing our lives" (p. 5). To persist in revising the stories we have told over the course of our lives opens us to the narrative challenge to continue to compose a life story for ourselves that is worth living.

Still, the opportunity to reexamine our texts is one rarely available to us in academia (but see Richardson, 1997; Tillmann-Healy, 1996; Tillmann, 2008; Zaner, 2004, 2007). We are not encouraged to reanalyze work that we have done before. More often, reviewers and critics take on the task for us, often for the purpose of proving us wrong. It is hard enough to publish our books and articles the first time. How do we convince editors and publishers that our story needs retelling and reanalysis? Or, even more difficult, that they should use their page limits to publish our original version along with our revised one?

This book project offered the perfect opportunity to do just that.

"Hey, Mitch," I write in an e-mail. "I have finally finished a draft of my book, but I should let you know that the project has gotten bigger—both in scope and length—than we talked about initially."

"Your book is longer than I expected? More complex than I asked for? I'm shocked. That never happens ☺," he writes back. "I've suggested in the past to some authors that we eliminate the vowels and save 25% that way, but no one has picked up on that idea before." Then, "I'm sure we'll figure out a way to deal with it. Send what you have by e-mail."

I'm relieved. If Mitch is joking around, he can't be too worried. But then he hasn't seen the manuscript yet. I write back, "You asked for it. Here it comes. But can we at least keep the 'I's'? This seems reasonable given the nature of this work."

"So I ask you for a compilation of papers and I get a new research genre instead," Mitch writes back the next day. "Meta-autoethnography. It doesn't roll trippingly off the tongue, but it does express what you're doing. The introduction is brilliant. And I promise we'll keep all the 'I's.'"

Storying the "I"

After working for a year as a social worker subsequent to getting my B.A. degree, I went to graduate school. Educated as a sociologist, I taught in an M.A.-granting sociology department the first fifteen years of my career. Then midcareer I changed my home department to communication studies to work with Arthur Bochner and to mentor Ph.D. students who were doing ethnographic research.

Thus I view and tell about my social and relational world through a sociological and communicational lens, one positioned between humanities and social sciences. I identify as an ethnographer interested in studying personal and social life. I call myself a writer—not a reporter—which means I focus on the construction of stories and their meanings rather than on the collection, organization, verification, and presentation of evidence.[3] Desiring that my work assist people in their day-to-day lives, I do not subscribe to neutrality; instead I believe in being involved in and caring about and for those in my studies. My goal then is to produce accessible and evocative literary and analytic texts that are the product of an ethnographer's eye, a social worker's heart, and a novelist's penchant for stirring up emotional response.

I did not always write this way. Initially I wrote traditional sociological prose as I had been taught in graduate school. I happened onto autoethnographic writing through a series of life circumstances, which I detail later in this book. Once I did, my life and work changed for the better. I discovered a deeper interest in teaching and scholarship, and I also discovered that I love to write. As I honed my own voice, I found that writing helped me to understand and work through issues in my life and to better comprehend other people's actions and meanings and the cultures in which we lived. The stories I constructed integrated my life and work, connected my life to the lives of others, and came from my heart as well as my head. I asked readers to make similar connections (see, for example, Ellis, 1993, 1995a, 1998).

I often write about epiphanies of loss and trauma that have occurred in my personal life. Sometimes I include traditional social science analysis with my stories when I feel that the integration of ways of knowing will help me know more and convey better (see, for example, Ellis, 1998). Sometimes I do not, and I can be rather insistent that sociologically enriched stories take their place alongside of or stand in for traditional analysis and theory (see, for example, Ellis, 1995c). Sometimes my writing turns the spotlight on the lives of others, but I have come to view myself and my actions and interactions as part of whatever community I seek to describe (see, for example, Ellis, 1995b). My role as an ethnographer and the issues, especially ethical ones, that arise in writing about others often come to the forefront (see, for example, Ellis, 2007a). Mostly I write stories about experiences I have had that I think have sociological and human interest for readers. In my writing, I attempt to integrate physical bodies, feelings, talk, motives, actions, and face-to-face interactions. Though my focus often is on emotionality in the context of relationships and families, I also am interested in how these micro-events play out in and teach us about macro-structures and processes. I care deeply that my stories have the potential to impact and improve social conditions. I make the case that this can happen through examining lives one at a time and encouraging voice person by person, as well as through an explicit focus on social justice or connection with an interest group, ideology, or party politics.

My stories feature dramatic plotlines, scenes, dialogue, and character development. I judge my work by how effectively I take the role of others and develop their characters as well as how successfully I probe and interrogate my own identity, motives, and actions. Literary tropes help make these stories more engaging and evocative. Narrative truth guides me, by which I mean that I try to convey experience in a way that evokes for me and my audience a sense of the significance and meaning the experience had for me and might have for them (Bochner, 2002b, p. 86).

At the same time, I know experience cannot be captured fully; once it happens, it can only be interpreted from limited and partial perspectives. Nevertheless, it is important to be able to story ourselves, to have a story to tell, and to tell it as well as we can. These goals are facilitated by making ourselves vulnerable, considering the truth of our account from multiple perspectives and points of view, and keeping ourselves open to the evolving meanings of what we tell and write—its movement—even while having to "fix" the story for the moment (Davies & Davies, 2007).

To story ourselves does not mean to describe the way it "really" happened; instead it means to "seize hold of a memory as it flashes up at a moment of danger" (Benjamin, 1968, p. 257). It means to "see and rediscover the past, not as a succession of events but as a series of scenes, inventions, emotions, images, and stories" rewritten by the author within the conditions set by the author. In turn, as the story is being produced, it affects the author's reexperience of what happened (Denzin, 2008a, p. 118; see also Ulmer, 1989). The story and the "I" in the story come into being in the telling (Jackson & Mazzei, in press).

Stories are what we have, the barometers by which we fashion our identities, organize and live our lives, connect and compare our lives to others, and make decisions about how to live. These tales open our hearts and eyes to ourselves and the world around us, helping us to change our lives and our world for the better. Stories tell about our lives; they also become a part of our lives (Rosenwald & Ochberg, 1992, pp. 1, 8).

An important part of my life story is concerned with developing autoethnography as a perspective and method. I often write *about* autoethnography, as I'm doing in these pages. For example, I have explored the definition, fit, use, and value of autoethnography (Ellis, 2004). In particular, I have focused on how to write from an ethic of care, where the focus is on protecting those we write about from undue harm (Ellis, 1995, 2007a). This goal is particularly crucial, given that those who are characters in our stories or participants in our autoethnographic research projects often are intimate others who are recognizable.

I also write about *how to do* autoethnography, seeking methodological approaches that help us present issues in our lives, such as meaning and emotionality, that aren't easily addressed by orthodox social science (see, for example, Ellis, 2004). Autoethnographic approaches are flexible, reflexive, and reflective of life as lived; they do not follow a rigid list of rule-based procedures. Often they are multivoiced and include interaction among researchers and participants in the research context as well as stories participants bring to the project (see, for example, Tillmann-Healy, 2001).

Helping others write their stories has been the center of much of my teaching and Ph.D. mentoring. I hope this book continues that practice. I seek to provide a book that can be used by scholars interested in autoethnographic approaches—their history, development, application, and accompanying ethical issues—and in teaching them to students. I write for those who are passionate about thinking "with" stories as well as "about" them (Frank, 1995). I write for an invisible college/collage of colleagues around the globe who desire to create their own stories. I write for all who seek to learn about their lives through reading about the lives of others. I write for those who just can't resist a good tale. My hope is that you find some good tales here.

Autoethnography offers the potential to expand scholarship about human experience. At the same time, it can assist us in our pursuit of happiness and living fully;

provide companionship and coping strategies for dealing with personal disappointments, traumas, and losses; and help us understand, reframe, and live through collective natural and human-made disasters that increasingly seem to be part of our lives. Thus, I also write for all of us who seek to understand our lives, become more aware of what we think and feel, and live a more ethical and caring existence.

Effective autoethnographies are not victim tales; on the contrary, writing autoethnography well produces survivor tales for the writer and for those who read them. Accomplished autoethnographers do not proclaim how things are or how life should be lived, but instead strive to open up a moral and ethical conversation with readers about the possibilities of living life well. I hope this book stimulates readers to continue that conversation with stories of their own.

Revisioning the "I"

Part 1, "Growing Up in a Rural Community, Getting an Education, and Finding My Place in Community Ethnography," begins with a description of my day-to-day life as a child in the small town of Luray, Virginia, and the issues I confronted in writing this autoethnographic account. I describe race relations in this town in the 1960s, focusing on a personal incident that changed my life and provided support for my transition out of Luray and into the College of William and Mary. I contextualize the event from the perspective of living in an integrated urban neighborhood in 2007, where racial conflict takes place and affects me personally. This part ends with a description of the ethnographic study of isolated fishing communities that I began at the College of William and Mary and completed as a dissertation at SUNY Stony Brook. I focus on the ethical issues that I confronted when I later returned to the field, after having published *Fisher Folk: Two Communities on Chesapeake Bay*.

Part 2, "Becoming an Autoethnographer," describes the transition from working as a more traditional community ethnographer to becoming an autoethnographer, once I had tenure at the University of South Florida. I focus on the living and writing of *Final Negotiations*, an autoethnographic story I published about the loss of my partner Gene. Then I discuss the responses I got from critics on this story, and, in turn, the reactions critics received from me.

Part 3, "Surviving and Communicating Family Loss," showcases stories of family loss. The experiences I describe prompted me to write about my life, and these stories are the results of some of my earlier writing endeavors. Included are stories about the loss of my brother Rex, my mother's aging and my caregiving of her, and a pregnancy termination I coconstructed with my partner Art. For each of the three narratives, I write meta-autoethnographic reflections and vignettes that reflect back on my experiences, showing how I interpret and live these experiences now. My hope is that these stories resonate with readers and open up conversations about emotions in romantic and family relationships.

Part 4, "Doing Autoethnography as a Social Project," presents autoethnography more directly as an avenue for helping us understand narratively and conceptually a larger relational, communal, and political world of which we are a part and that speaks to critical engagement, social action, and change. In this part, I write about situations that are difficult in a communicative sense—some might say they are communication breakdowns. The first story describes and analyzes speaking with a lisp, which leads to reflections on the category of minor bodily stigmas. In showing my interactions with a dying friend, the second story emphasizes the difficulty of communication across the boundaries of the communities of the dying and the living. As I write about the personal and communal grief associated with the tragedy of September 11, 2001, I reflect on racial profiling and on how Americans might live post–September 11th without resorting to discrimination. I learn to be "with" my mother who is bedridden and dying and "with" Ground Zero, situations where finally there is nothing more to say and nothing more to see. The last story raises ethical issues in connecting autoethnographic performance to community practice, when research and practice goals may not be the same.

Part 5, "Reconsidering Writing Practices, Relational Ethics, and Rural Communities," includes brief reflections on the process of writing and revising my stories and the types of meta-autoethnographic reflections included in *Revision*. Making ethical decisions in research is a vital part of the writing that took place in this text. Thus I include a story on what I tell students about doing research ethically. The final chapter contains vignettes written at and about our second home, a small, rural, mountain community in the southeastern United States. Thus, I end by coming full circle: as a person living in a small mountain community, trying to understand how those in the community make sense of their lives and how I, in turn, make sense of mine; linking my life and work back to my family and how I was raised; and introspecting about the ethics of the critical ethnographic and autoethnographic work I do and the person I have been and have become, now almost forty years after leaving Luray.

In writing autoethnography and meta-autoethnography, I attempt to integrate the complex, sometimes contradictory, components of my life and scholarship—personal with the professional; family with academia; work with play; heart with head; homogeneous small town with cosmopolitan urban life; literary writing with social science observation and critical analysis with compassionate care—into a meaningful and coherent story: one that frames, yet continues to honor, the diversity of the concrete details in a life being lived; one that stays open to revision and re-visioning. This context—looking out over beautiful mountains and sittin' a spell on the porch and talkin'—provides a place where conversations about family, race, politics, illness, loss, ethical behavior, and the everyday keep on happening in the living of life as well as in my mind and on the page.

PART ONE

Growing Up in a Rural Community, Getting an Education, and Finding My Place in Community Ethnography

CHAPTER ONE

Goin' to the Store, Sittin' on the Street, and Runnin' the Roads

Growing Up in a Rural Southern Neighborhood

I still think of this place, Luray, Virginia, as "home," though I moved away in 1969. Has it really been forty years? Its strange familiarity, when I visit there, mesmerizes me as I feel "of" it and "outside" it at the same time. I walk on Main Street where the Five and Ten used to be, drive through Fairview—my old neighborhood—and past my high school. I am drawn to the high school football field, where I stare at the sign on the building dedicated to my brother, reading the words over and over: "Rex A. Ellis Memorial Field House." I make the run between the two Tastee Freezes, and then up to Wal-Mart, which opened about fifteen years ago and quickly led to the demise of the few department stores on Main Street. Now only churches and banks occupy the center of town. I talk to familiar strangers I see in Wal-Mart about who they are, how many children and grandchildren they have, what year they graduated high school, when I left town, and what's happened in Luray since 1969. I try to imagine how I would have turned out had I, like so many of my classmates, stayed in Luray. Then I have to remind myself how much of this community I continue to carry with me.

Born in 1950, I grew up in a farming area on the outskirts of Luray, a small town of about three thousand people situated in the middle of the Blue Ridge Mountains. I lived with my parents, Arch and Katherine; my mother's sister, Florence; my older sister, Judi; and my younger brother, Rex. My older brother, Arthur,[1] left home to go to a local college when I was only four years old. My neighborhood provides the center of my earliest memories. After school, and in the summers, I spent most of my time playing with the kids who lived along the half-mile stretch of my country road, named Fairview. So did my brother Rex. My sister, Judi, stayed closer to home until she began to concentrate her attention on boyfriends from school. For Rex and me, though, Fairview was our world.

Fairview: The Neighborhood

The neighborhood kids often played softball or baseball in the open fields that stretched between our houses. We had deep red bruises on our hands to prove it, since baseball gloves were too expensive for most of us. Later, when my brother and I put up a basketball net—a misnomer since after the first week there never again was an actual net, just a rusting hoop—we played basketball outside our garage almost every afternoon. H-O-R-S-E, where players had to match shots of their opponents, was our favorite game, since even a quarter-court energetic "man-to-man" game presented the danger of running into the garage door just behind the basket.

Not all our time was consumed by organized sports. To ease any sense of boredom, we also played games of fantasy and challenge for long stretches in the massive sand pile that occupied the front "yard" of our property. The sand pile changed daily as the men in my father's big trucks hauled in the sand and took it away; sometimes the mound temporarily grew to the size of a small house. There we built castles and roads for our toy trucks and action figures—pretending we were contractors like my father—and competed for "king of the mountain," wrestling and falling without harm, caught in the arms of the soft brown sand. Just as good was the large "junk" yard behind our garage, where my father stored lumber, gravel, and old tractor and truck parts. Unsupervised, the neighborhood kids played hide-and-seek there, raced over piled-up lumber, swung on ropes, built playhouses with castoff lumber, and chased each other in "you're it" and "follow me" games. Later, we built clubhouses in the attic over the garage in which my father's men repaired equipment. Sometimes these hidden-away places became opportunities for same- and cross-sex explorations in games of "house" and "doctor," but mostly they provided opportunities to run out our incessant child energy.

Occasionally we took our hide-and-seek games to the cornfields nearby, though then we had to deal with the wrath of Jack, a farmer and my cousin. "You're destroying the corn," he'd yell from his pickup as he drove slowly up and down the stretch of Fairview Road that fronted his field. Then he'd threaten to get his gun, though he never did. At this, we'd run as far away from him as we could, moving quickly in a tiptoeing motion, and trying not to ruffle the corn stalks. Out of sight, we'd squat quietly in the far side of the field, our fingers over our lips, shushing others, and holding back our own laughter. Part of the fun was the adrenaline rush of hiding from Jack and not being sure about the seriousness of the threat he made.

If the weather were bad—rainy or just too hot—we'd play board games. My friend Janet and I set up a Monopoly game on a card table in her unfinished basement where we wouldn't be disturbed. When the game was in danger of ending because one of us was going broke, the other person loaned money to be paid back later when the recipient was more solvent. Then we got the idea of making more money. We traced the Monopoly money onto white sheets of paper, gave it a value, and distributed it equally to each other and the bank. The object was to have fun and pass time, not to win. Besides, who wanted to give up Broadway and Park Place, once you had built hotels on them? Sometimes games lasted all summer. They ended only when we tired of them or each other, or more likely when school started in the fall.

All these activities were fun, but the pursuit that consumed most of our time was "goin' down the road," as we called it. Almost every day, the neighborhood kids walked or rode bikes for hours on end along the country road that connected our houses. At first, the girls and boys stayed in same-sex groups. But before each day was over, we'd all usually meet up somewhere. Barefooted and paying little attention to the hot pavement or our stumped and bleeding big toes, we chased each other, found a field of grass or a forest of leaves to lie in, sat together on the side of the road, or simply walked from house to house and back. In the heat of summer, we went to "The Creek," where we devised rope swings that dropped us into the deep end of the rocky, cool water. But most often our destination was Ruth's Fairview Grocery, our favorite hangout.

The Store

About a third of a mile from my house, "The Store" formed the nexus of the Fairview community. It provided a safe space for kids to play, a meeting grounds for men to talk about farming and the weather and to play cards, and a convenient place for all who lived in the neighborhood to pick up staples and items forgotten at the town grocery store.

The Store was an eight-hundred-square-foot brick-fronted building. A rusted tin roof and tin-covered sides were painted a deep red to match the brick. Inside the one-room store, a large wooden plank counter ran the length of one side, covered by displays of tobacco and packages of peanut butter and cheese nabs. An old-fashioned pull-arm cash register sat in the middle alongside empty space for lining up your purchases. Boxes of candy and snacks, cigarettes and cigars, chewing tobacco, loaves of white bread, cereal, canned goods, and a few supplies, such as toothpaste, detergent, matches, and car oil, covered the single row of shelves in the front of the store. Beside the counter was a horizontal ice cream freezer. A meat counter holding a hand-operated meat slicer occupied the rear of the store. Behind it were boxes of dry goods needed by farmers, such as overalls and rubber boots, as well as sprays and ointments useful for their horses and cattle.

The place I always headed to first was the tall glass enclosure just inside the front door. As a child, I would lean against the short, horizontal drink cooler in front of the glass enclosure and point high to the penny candy, nickel candy bars, chewing gum, and Life Savers protected behind the glass. Once I had my candy, I'd open the lid of the cooler—with "Drink Coke" emblazoned on it—grab a bottle of icy-cold pop, stand back from the melting ice crystals that covered the bottle, and admire the hiss that came from popping the top under the bottle opener on the front of the cooler. I loved the first big gulps of the sweet, brown liquid, and the way the bubbles sizzled on the way down, tingling my tongue and slightly burning my throat. No doubt I enjoyed the caffeine and sugar high as well.

Sometimes my father stopped by The Store to talk and buy "cloth" bologna, juicy, thick-sliced, fatty meat wrapped in a cloth fiber that was coated with wax. Dad took the bologna home to my Aunt Florence, who lived with us and cooked our meals. Aunt Florence made a cut in each slice so it wouldn't curl up, dipped it in water, rolled it in flour, and then fried it in Crisco. With added Miracle Whip on two slices of Wonder Bread, bologna was one of our favorite lunches. Dad's favorite purchase, though, was what came to be called "Arch Ellis cheese," sharp cheddar cheese cut from a round with a black or yellow rind. Dad often unwrapped the block of cheese from its white waxed paper and ate it with sardines or raw oysters on Saltine crackers with lots of pepper while standing in the store. Since he liked the cheese warm and sweaty, not cold from the cooler, the owners often kept some on a shelf especially for him.

In the winter, we sat for hours on old bus seats, patched with electrical tape, around the wood- and coal-fed potbellied stove in the center of the room. Warming our hands, we listened to the fire crackle and stove pipe rattle as it belched smoke through the roof. We unbuckled our plastic galoshes and watched melting snow disappear through the cracks of the uneven floorboards, which sometimes swallowed the pennies and nickels we dropped as well.

In the evenings, this space was transformed as the men in the neighborhood gathered to play cards. They constructed a table by laying a piece of plywood on barrels and played "Set Back"—a simple high/low bidding game—from the bus seats pulled around the table.

In the summer, we dangled our feet off the store's front porch, swigging pop and eating ice cream, and listening to the talk of the adult men who sat on empty kegs or perched their feet on sacks of feed on the porch. When Mr. Fox rode up on his white horse, Ruth would bring him his chewing tobacco. If we grew bored, we chased each other around the parking lot, careful to stay out of the clutches of old Sam—an ancient-looking, wrinkle-faced man—whose shaking hand extended his cane to hook little girls when we ran by. We squealed and resisted, fearing his trembling hand almost as much as we dreaded the slobbery kisses he'd bestow on our cheeks as he pulled us onto his lap and tried to hold us there. Nobody ever tried to stop him; nor did they scold us, unless we ran though the store or hit each other too hard in one of our paper-rock-scissors games. When I interviewed Ruth in 2007, she said, "I didn't have any problems with you kids. You had good times. Oh, you picked on each other and all, but that's all. I knew all of you. I think that made a difference."[2]

When we arrived at The Store, our hands were filled with wet sacks and cartons of empty pop bottles to trade for their two-cent deposit. When we left, our hands were filled with bags of penny candy we had purchased and our fingers covered with the sticky ice cream and pop we had consumed. Bottle collecting was one of the few ways we had of making money. We extracted most of the pop bottles from among the worthless beer cans, cigarette butts, and wrappers that littered the ditches along Fairview Road. People then didn't have much consciousness about littering and assumed the kids would pick up the returnable bottles. I can still see my brother Rex pulling his little red wagon down the road collecting bottles.

I begged my parents for the empties that collected at home. They usually complied, forgoing the opportunity to return them during their weekly grocery shopping. I also got pop bottles from the men who worked in my father's construction business. Peg Leg Les, Moon, Gil, John, Slim, and Billy called me "Pickles"—I don't remember why—and, in addition to their empties, they often gave me money to bring them a cold drink from the store and a nickel or dime for my efforts. Happy to oblige, I loved to walk to the store and besides, I had money then for my own purchases and also could lay claim to the men's next round of empties.

I went to The Store almost every day, sometimes twice or more. It gave me something to do and offered the possibility of seeing my friends also walking along the road or hanging out at the store. "I'm goin' to tha store," I'd yell into the house and take off whether anyone replied or not. My mother and my aunt liked getting me out of their hair and didn't care where I was as long as I stayed in the neighborhood. All the kids had lots of freedom and nobody in the neighborhood ever seemed to worry about our safety or about what we were doing. If we got in trouble—which we rarely did—our parents were bound to find out from the many relatives living along the road.

Ruth, my first cousin—though she was twenty-five years older than I—inherited The Store from her father, my uncle, and from the time she graduated high school she worked behind the counter every day from early in the morning until late at night. Since she didn't have a car, she walked to work, though someone usually stopped to give her a ride in the morning and the last person in the store drove her home at night. Sometimes Ruth hugged us tightly and we loved the feeling of disappearing into her ample bosom. With her easy style, Ruth trusted us to tell her how many pop bottles we had in our bags and cartons, and she paid us our nickels and dimes without checking the count. She let us serve ourselves; sometimes we didn't pay until we were leaving and then we just told her the total of what we had eaten and what we had in our bags. If Ruth was busy waiting on other customers, we'd leave our money on top of the cash register.

A day's collection of bottles, buttressed by my weekly allowance of thirty-five cents, fifty cents when I was older, bought a bag full of penny candy. I loved watching Ruth fill my paper sack with the goodies I pointed out to her: waxed lips and waxed bottles (I drank the sweet syrup inside, then chewed the sweetened, waxy coating until it hardened and broke into pieces in my mouth), taffy, peanut butter cups, caramels (a deal at two for a penny), Mary Janes (my favorite), Tootsie Rolls, and bubble gum (to entertain my tastebuds, massage my mouth muscles, and make my companions laugh when I tried to blow the biggest bubble ever and it burst all over my face). I also bought pop—a six-ounce Pepsi, or occasionally a Mountain Dew—sometimes even a creamsicle or fudgesicle, a popsicle, an ice cream sandwich, or maybe a Nutty Butty—a frozen cone of vanilla ice cream rolled in nuts and topped with hard chocolate. After picking out candy, my friends and I would socialize in the store, reaching our hands time and again into our individual stashes, and sometimes trading with each other. We made sure to save plenty for the walk home, depositing the paper wrappers alongside the rest of the trash on Fairview road.

Unfortunately, the exercise I got from walking (and playing sports) did not cancel out the calories of the candy and ice cream I ate. A pleasingly plump child, I was unaware of the connection between my weight and my consumption of sweets. Surprisingly, no one pointed out that I weighed too much, perhaps because I was similar in size to other family members and kids in the neighborhood. I have not lost my love for sweets now almost fifty years later, nor my few extra pounds, and understanding the connection between sweets and weight hasn't changed my behavior all that much. I still think a day without ice cream and/or candy is not much worth living.

Get Your Nose Out of That Book

When no other kids were around, or if I had just made my weekly trip to the small town library, I stayed at home and read. I'd throw my legs over the arms of the big crushed-red-velvet chair in the living room and lose myself in a Nancy Drew mystery or a love story. I read much of what the library had to offer in those categories, and I had little notion of classics or good literature. I just knew I liked a good story. I often ignored my aunt when she'd command, "Get your nose out of that book and go outside." Other times I'd take her command as permission to visit my friends who lived nearby, and I'd disappear for the rest of the day. Nobody cared as long as I was back at suppertime.

At night, I'd snuggle down under the heavy layers of covers that kept us warm in the cold bedrooms that often had frost on the inside of the windows in winter. Then I'd read my book with a flashlight long after the hour I was supposed to have turned off the light. That is, until my aunt would yell, "Turn off that light and go to bed." Aunt Florence had to go through the room my sister and I shared to get to hers. Because the door between our rooms was swelled and heavy from the clothes that hung on a nail on the back of it—we didn't have closets—it didn't shut tightly. Thus, Aunt Florence always knew when there was a light on—any light. So then I started listening to the earphones of my little transistor radio, which got only one station. The voice from New York City faded in and out, often blending with the static. I'd hear mention of Central Park, Radio City Music Hall, Rockefeller Center, the Statue of Liberty, and the Empire State Building. I'd dream of the bright lights and excitement of Broadway and fantasize how life must be in a big city. "One day I'm going there," I said to myself.

The Family Business

In the summer, my mother sometimes dropped us off at the town swimming pool where we swam and played pinochle all day. Other times I'd ride with my father in whatever shiny new pickup he had bought that year. Though I loved to go with him to his many construction jobs, I sometimes grew bored waiting for him to complete his business. One time I had to wait so long, I peed on his seat. As I watched the pee gather between my pinched thighs and threaten to overrun my legs, I panicked, then grew angry. "It was all his fault," I said to myself, "for keeping me waiting so long." I rolled down the window, got out into the sunshine, hoped the seat would dry, and decided not to tell him. He was too busy to notice when he returned to the truck.

It didn't occur to me to take this opportunity to learn the business—construction was "men's work." But I enjoyed watching my father supervise the other men and organize so much activity—pouring foundations, hauling sand and stone, building roads, and, later in his career, constructing houses. He loved his job and I was proud of him. It seemed important to do something you loved.

Pedro (pronounced as though the first syllable rhymed with "seed"), our little rat terrier, loved to accompany my father each day. He rode perched on Dad's shoulder so he could see out the window in the truck. While my father talked to customers or his employees, Pedro explored the surrounds. Dad got so caught up in his work that sometimes he forget about Pedro and arrived home without him. "Where's Pedro?" my mother asked him. "Gosh dang it, not again," he'd say. Everyone in Luray knew Pedro, so often my mother already had been called by someone, who said, "Arch left Pedro at my house, but don't worry, he's safe." Mom reminded my father where he left Pedro, and Dad headed back out to retrieve his buddy. When he was nine years old, Pedro died crossing a busy intersection to "go see his girlfriend," my father said, with tears streaming down his face. He loved little Pedro, and so did I. I've had the companionship of four rat terriers since Pedro and wouldn't dream of being without at least one.

Sometimes I spent the day riding along with one of my father's employees who hauled sand, dirt, or peach orchid gravel from the quarry in a dump truck. Each load of gravel cost my father five cents. Though I paid no attention when I lived in Luray, every time I go home now, I am bothered by the big brown hole in the Blue Ridge Mountain skyline that the excavation of the rock created. After four or five loads, this activity too got repetitious. There was a lot of waiting—waiting to be loaded, waiting to unload, waiting for the gravel to be raked and spread, waiting while the men got instructions—before the old trucks rambled their way back down the bumpy back roads. While driving, the men took occasional drinks from pints of cheap whiskey in brown bags hidden behind the seats. They made me promise not to tell my parents or anyone, and I didn't (until now).

My mother was secretary—CFO, really—of my father's business. She occupied an office attached to our house during the early morning when the men started work and for a few hours after that answering the phone, doing paperwork, and collecting payments. Sometimes I wondered who she was talking to, especially when she would giggle but not say much to whomever was on the other end of the line. Sometimes then I'd just sit in front of her and wait for her to get off the phone. Sometimes then she'd give me some change from the cash she collected and pocketed, and I'd forget about the phone call temporarily as I made my way to The Store. After lunch until about four in the afternoon, Mom watched her soaps on the TV in our living room. Then she reappeared in the office when the men who worked for my father—at times a dozen or more—came to the office to turn in their time and receipts.

Many Fridays, my father met the men in the office with a fifth of Old Granddad whiskey and they took turns swigging from the bottle sitting on the desk and "chasing" it with a big gulp of pop. The men all seemed to like and respect my dad. Much to my mother's dismay, my father often loaned his workers money before payday and got them out of jams. Of course, I realize now he also made a large profit from their sweat and labor. As the men's faces grew redder, my mother disappeared into the house. At first, I liked being with the men, including my father, who had worked so hard all week, and I thought it was nice that my father socialized with them. As they drank, they got happier and happier, louder and louder. But after a while, the friendly conversation became repetitive and more argumentative. My dad ceased being his usual warm, affectionate, and easygoing self and began slurring his words and being unsteady on his feet. I usually went back into our home at those times, dreading the time he would join us. Often when he did, he displayed an awkward combination of confrontational behavior and need for love and affection.

During such times, sitting blurry-eyed in his chair, he often complained that nobody loved him enough. At those moments, he was right; he wasn't lovable in that state. I prayed he'd fall quickly into a deep, snoring sleep in his La-Z-Boy, before he and Mom got into an argument. Their arguments—loud and vicious, occasionally physical— scared me. One time my mother locked herself in the bathroom to get away from him. Another time, my younger brother Rex stood between my mother and father and, in a loud voice, told my father to leave our mother alone. Standing in the corner watching, I was surprised when my father immediately calmed down. My brother couldn't have been more than twelve then and I thought he was awfully brave.

As much as possible when my father was drinking, I'd make myself scarce and go off with neighborhood friends, usually meeting them away from my house. They understood because many had the same situations in their homes and, in some cases, their circumstances were much worse. I spent many Friday evenings stepping over my best friend's father, who slept naked on the living room floor, covered by a sheet. We'd pretend he wasn't there and take the opportunity to look at the porn magazines he kept under his mattress in his bedroom. I could hardly blame him for getting drunk on Friday nights as soon as he got his paycheck. If I had had to work every day in the tannery, immersed in vats of chemicals with disgusting sights of animal flesh and fat and smells of rotting animal entrails, I would have wanted to get drunk too. On Saturday evenings, he'd sober up just enough for his wife, who cleaned houses for a living, to take him to the bootlegger's for more booze, and my friend and I would go along for the ride. We'd giggle in the backseat and make fun of her dad, who usually was still a little drunk and slurry. In retaliation, he'd make lewd gestures toward us, as though he were going to grab our adolescent breasts, though he never did.

My Aunt Florence, who never married, lived with us during my entire childhood. I swear she was the spittin' image in looks, voice, and actions to Granny on *The Beverly Hillbillies*. Florence did all the housework while my mother worked in the office, and she served as disciplinarian for the kids, setting the rules and yelling when we didn't follow them. The hardest rule she had, other than no lights on after bedtime, was no eating after supper, another reason trips to The Store for snacks were necessary. I always felt I had two mothers, which was good and bad. The good part was that I had relatively few chores to do since they did them all; the bad part was the multiple number of confusing role relationships that had to be negotiated in my family every day. Triads, as Simmel (1950) noted, are more complicated with many more possibilities and entanglements than dyadic relationships.

We ate supper at five on the dot during the work week. Our meal consisted primarily of starches—white Wonder Bread and a combination of potatoes, pinto beans, rice, and macaroni. In the summer, we added fresh vegetables from our garden. On Saturday afternoon, we had hamburgers, which we fried as soon as Mom brought the meat home in her weekly grocery purchase. The burgers were accompanied by the freshly baked homemade cakes and pies my aunt made each week. I can still smell and taste the leftover pieces of flaky dough she baked for the kids—pure lard and flour. On Sunday we had our big meal at noon after church and then we had fried chicken, old Virginia ham, or roast beef, all the Southern fixings to go with it, and more pie.

In summer, we stayed outside in the evenings as long as we could, playing games in the yard followed by chasing lightning bugs when dark descended. The TV was turned on after supper whether anyone was watching it or not. In the winter, we all huddled in front of the TV as soon as supper was over and stayed there until we went to bed. I loved to cuddle on my father's lap, as he lay back in his La-Z-Boy, even after I got too big to fit comfortably. Dad always decided what we'd watch, which meant we were exposed to a steady diet of Westerns, such as *Gun Smoke* and *Maverick*, or *Perry Mason*, or comedy shows, such as *The Beverly Hillbillies*. Some episodes we watched over and over. Though Dad quickly began to snore, tired from his long day at work, he would wake up if we even thought of changing the channel. We kids did our homework at the kitchen table in full view of the TV.

On Saturday morning, my father went to the bank to get money to pay the men who worked for him. Before doing the week's grocery shopping, my mom counted and folded in half the cash he brought home in the leather money sack, inserting it into small pay envelopes. I'd help her write the names of the employees and number of hours on each envelope. Then I'd meet the men at the door when they came to get paid, waiting for a pat on the head and some change from their envelopes.

Street Smarts

On Saturday evenings, Mom took the kids to town. She parked on the street and sat there with a girlfriend while we shopped in the Five and Ten store or at Robinson's General Clothing Store, and then went to the movies. Mom's favorite activity was sittin' on the street, or sitting anywhere. We loved that she didn't mind waiting for us while we were in the movies, and we didn't mind going to town early. But we hated it when she made us go early to other places, such as church. It was never clear why she felt we had to arrive everywhere we went at least an hour early. It is not a habit I picked up, though I am a stickler about being on time.

My mom was not physically affectionate in those days and sometimes she'd get mad and not speak to us or our father for days. But we could always count on her to take us to town. She showed her love by making sure we had enough money to buy what we needed and most of what we wanted in the stores. Saturday evenings before the movie presented a good buying opportunity. Though my father usually went to the Moose hall or out with his drinking friends on Saturday, occasionally he would stop to visit with us on the street. When he did, we'd often hit him up for money.

One night I wanted to buy a pocketbook. My mother gave me $1.50. "Ask your father for more when he comes by," she said. "Tell him you only have a dollar and maybe he'll give you more." When I approached my father, he said, "Here's fifty cents, but you should go to Mr. Robinson's," the only Jewish merchant in town. "Now don't pay full price. You have to 'jew' him down." When I asked how, he said, "Show him how much money you want to pay. Tell him that's all you have. Hold back some of it. Keep it in your pocket."

Nervously I entered Mr. Robinson's store. I walked around on the uneven wide plank floors, picking up the dusty plastic pocketbooks that randomly covered the large timber tables. I watched Mr. Robinson, a stooped-over, wrinkly man who talked with an accent, as he followed me around waiting for me to buy. I clutched a dollar and twenty cents tightly in one hand, and checked that the eighty cents was still safe in my pocket. "Do ya find vat ya vant?" he asked, picking up whatever pocketbook he thought I was looking at, and singing its virtues. Shaking my head each time, I finally took a deep breath and said, "I only have $1.20." "Which wan do ya vant?" I pointed at the one marked $2.00. Mr. Robinson looked puzzled for a minute and then said, "Okay, you are a good customer, one dollar twenty."

Mr. Robinson carefully wrapped my purchase in white tissue paper, put it in a used plastic bag, and handed it to me. I nodded, hardly able to contain my glee, as I thought about how smart my father was. I tried to ignore the twinge of guilt I felt for having told a lie. "I always jew people down," my father said, when I returned to the car and proclaimed that his advice had worked. I learned what it meant to "jew" someone down way before I learned what it meant to be a Jew. Was it just a coincidence that the first person I "jewed" down happened to be the only Jewish merchant in town?

Even today, I find myself fairly conservative about money and make sure to always hold some back. I love to bargain and I find buying a car an interesting challenge. I no longer talk about "jewing someone down" and cringe when others do, since I have now learned what it means to be Jewish and how much discrimination Jewish people have endured historically.

In writing this story, I was reminded of buying something else from Mr. Robinson. The details are vivid and I wonder why this event made such an impression on me. I am in first grade. It is Sunday; yes, I'm sure it is Sunday. I break one of the buckled straps on my black canvas shoe. "You'll just have to miss school tomorrow," my mom said, "until we can get you another pair." She was surprised when I started to cry and told her I didn't want to miss school. The next morning my father took me to Robinson's as soon as it opened, bought me shoes, and took me to school. I'm sure he didn't pay full price then either.

This story stands out in my memory because it was the first time I realized we didn't have much money. I owned one pair of shoes and had only a few dresses to wear to school. Later, when I was a teenager and my father began building houses, we had more resources, bought more things, and had more opportunities. For example, my parents regularly bought new Cadillacs and Ford pickups and paid my way through college.

On Saturdays, after we shopped, my mom gave us the requisite quarter for the movie—the reduced price for the early show—and another quarter with which we could buy popcorn, pop, or candy. Chocolate-covered Sugar Babies were my favorite. The movies that played on the single screen usually were Westerns or horror flicks. We didn't mind that we sometimes watched movies we already had seen. Often we stayed for a double feature and sometimes we watched the same movie twice the same night. What we saw wasn't as important as the opportunity the theater created for meeting up with friends there, catching the eye of a potential romantic interest, or sittin' with a new crush.

After the movies, I was sometimes surprised that my mom was parked in a different spot, and I wondered where she went and what she did while we were in the movies. Though those thoughts reappeared often, I forgot them temporarily when Mom offered money for hamburgers and cokes from the greasy spoon diner on Main Street. Topped with melted American cheese, plenty of Kraft's mayonnaise, tomato, and lettuce, these pressed-flat burgers on grease-soaked, griddle-toasted buns were my favorites, even better than the ones we had at home on Saturday afternoons.

On Sundays, we went to a small Lutheran church in the country, about two miles from our house. Sometimes my dad came with us, but often he did not, especially if Saturday night had been a big drinking night. Though attended by fewer than fifty people each week, this church was the center of my social life until I was about fifteen. I loved the hayrides, dinners, parties and games, summer Bible school, and Bible camp, though I didn't much enjoy going to church and Sunday School.

At fifteen, I got my driver's license and my father bought me a used red Chevy convertible with a sun-cracked, plastic back window that I could never see through. One of the first in my cohort to have a car, now I could attend school activities and visit friends from town. I'd pick up girlfriends from my class and drive back and forth between the two Tastee Freezes in town, hoping to meet boys who might be out cruising as well. With my newfound mobility, I no longer accompanied my mother to town on Saturdays or spent as much time at The Store or with the kids in the neighborhood.

Now the center of my world moved to school. Some of my peers there had parents who had traveled, had managerial jobs, and had gone to college. A few came from places outside Luray. For example, the parents of one of my best high school friends were born in Germany.[3] From these friends and their parents, all the fiction I devoured, what I was learning at school, and the late-night New York radio station, I began to put together a sense of a world outside the confines of my upbringing in Luray. I also began to question who I was, what I believed in, and whether I wanted to be like everyone else in Luray.

My romantic relationship with a Black male schoolmate, the topic of the next chapter, both stimulated and resulted from some of this questioning.

Meta-Autoethnography: Conveying the Feeling World[4]

This story about my childhood moves slowly and gently, without a specific destination in mind, mostly describing feelings and scenes—some particular, many not—that float through my memory. I write these tales, where not a lot happens and not much is said, to evoke a rural life where stimuli don't overwhelm and life unfolds sometimes at a snail's pace. In these stories, I place myself back in my neighborhood and recall my friends and family members, the laziness of summer and the fun of wiling away the days playing sports, the routine of going to town on Saturday, and the intrigue of learning new things and figuring out the world around me. As I call up these memories, I taste my aunt's southern cooking and the sweet candy I bought from the neighborhood store; I smell the newly mown hay, then get a mild scent of cheap liquor and a powerful whiff of the town tannery; I hear the laughter of my friends, ignore again the sound of adults telling me to get my nose out of a book, and experience my father's trucks and tractors starting up under my bedroom window at 7:30 a.m. sharp; I feel the sun on my arms, the pain of stubbed toes as I walk the neighborhood roads, the wind on my face as I ride my bike, and the coolness of the creek water as I jump from a rope swing. Reliving these senses stimulates me to recall the overall feeling of growing up in Luray, what Birkerts (2008, p. 13) calls the "'feeling world' of my childhood."

I did not, however, begin the process of writing this story with a description of the day-to-day "feeling world" I convey now; it took several years and many revisions to arrive at this account. Thus, I think it is important to comment on how this story came into being (see Woolf, 1985; see also Carlson, 2007) so that readers understand better the account I include here and how it fits into the theme of *Revision*.

In the first version of this chapter, I focused on several traumatic events of family alcoholism, infidelity, deceit, and betrayal I experienced as a child, an approach often used by autoethnographers and memoirists in portraying their childhoods.[5] Though anxiety producing, this writing was therapeutic and rewarding insofar as I examined difficult events in my childhood. In doing so, I gained a greater understanding of my past and I was able to identify more closely with the difficulty my students experience in telling their childhood stories. Additionally, constructing these tales broke through a barrier that had prevented me from previously composing stories about my early life, which was my belief that I didn't remember my childhood well enough to write about it. The original stories I wrote gave me confidence that I could re-create my early life and prompted me to remember and construct other everyday, less dramatic aspects of that time period as well. I began to think about how meaning resides in the mundane details of everyday life, in addition to the tragic ones, and I questioned whether these traumatic episodes were reminiscent of the way I lived my childhood on a daily basis. I came to feel that daily life contains the trauma at the same time trauma circles in and through the events and feelings and that it was important to focus on how trauma is contextualized by daily life as well as on how it sometimes interrupts that life.

Though these initial stories had been important for me to examine and write about, they did not necessarily need to be told to others. I did not want to reduce and freeze the whole of my childhood and family relationships into those few traumatic moments, especially when so much had happened in the fifty years since then, which many of the stories in this book will detail. This decision came partly from feeling that I could not justify exposing these family secrets when doing so might bring pain to family members and sully memories of our family, especially since I did not seem to be crippled by these events or need to tell them to move on with my life. I was uncertain that publishing these stories would bring healing to me beyond what had occurred in the writing I had done privately about them. Moreover, I was not convinced that these stories would give readers, who I fear have gotten somewhat desensitized to tales of trauma, more insight into their own lives. Did it make sense then to inscribe these stories in a book, which might then engrave them in my readers' minds? Is this the way I want to remember my childhood and family? Would it represent the "truth" of my childhood? Might not publishing this account make these events loom even larger in my life, magnify rather than minimize them? Henry (1971, p. 438) says "[t]he secret of sanity is to exaggerate the good of the world." By magnifying the trauma, wouldn't I run the risk of dwelling in it, sticking in the muck? For me, at this point in my life, that's not where I want to live. For me, at this point in my life, this is not the story I want to tell. I do not want or need to lose myself (and/or my readers) in moments of chaos and trauma.

This does not mean that I have ignored the traumatic moments in this account (or that others should do so). Remnants of the original stories linger within and between the lines of the stories I do tell, complexifying my relatively happy portrayal with hints— some subtle and some more direct—of ambiguity, conflict, and suffering. This is how I remember living most days in Luray—not as existing within the trauma, but as coexisting with trauma. In describing this coexistence, I try to bring forth the pace and rhythm

of my everyday world, celebrate the ordinary, and find the extraordinary in it (Tollifson, 2003; see also Quinney, 1991, 1996). As they experience my story, I want readers to
settle into the sounds, smells, and sights of their childhoods, and the everyday mundane
world—what Henry (1971, p. 447) calls the "alleviating conditions" that get children
through trauma and help them survive.

My intention in this chapter has been to introduce my family of origin and the town
in which I spent the first eighteen years of my life. My mother will continue to be a main
character in the family story in this book as will my brother Rex, whose death in 1982 first
inspired me to write narratively to cope with my loss. In many of the stories that follow,
family and small-town socialization will continue to play an important role. These chapters will invite readers directly into the immediacy of particular scenes, dramatic action,
vivid conversations, and forward-moving plots. With the exception of the last story in
the book, which—like this one—is an original work written for this book, the main
stories in the chapters were published some time ago and the meta-autoethnographic
commentaries examine and revise these stories from my perspective now.

CHAPTER TWO

Talking Across Fences

Race Matters

Luray: My Town

Homogeneity was cultivated and demanded in Luray, which was isolated from the rest of the world by the Blue Ridge and Massanutten Mountains. Ours was a small working-class community in which telling stories provided an important way to pass the time. The stories I heard and told repeatedly concerned values, feelings, getting through day-to-day life, and deviance or difference. Rarely were abstract theoretical or philosophical issues discussed, and political economy, culture, or society were never mentioned. Abstract discussion brought the response, "You think you're better than everybody else talking that way. Quit puttin' on airs," while political subjects usually were met with the simple statement, "Politicians and government are crooked." That was all the locals considered necessary to say.

Townspeople often shared stories about their lives—memories of the past, descriptions of present events, and dreams of the future. Illness and health issues always stimulated a lively conversation. Friends and acquaintances compared illness sites, doctors' orders, prescriptions, and home remedies. Frequently we talked about the local environment, especially the weather—how it felt, what was predicted, especially if it called for rain or snow, or was unseasonably hot. Other times we talked about the local lives of others. Day-to-day concerns and crisis events dominated: what the neighbor was doing—where he placed the garbage, how he painted the house, how she dressed when going to town, and when the yard was mowed; who had her hair done this morning, was seen coming out of the liquor store, or was driving a new car; and who died, lost their minds, went broke, found a new love, got engaged, or started a new business. Juicy gossip regarding violation of community norms—who was cheating on a spouse, who got "pissy-assed" drunk and spent the night in jail, lost a job, or had a brawl—was shared with enthusiasm.

Television brought in the outside world, but how much could be learned from game shows, murder mysteries, Westerns, soap operas, and sitcoms, the shows that most people watched? News programs were usually categorized as being about "those crazy city folk and politicians 'down in the country'" in Washington, D.C.[1] Locals did not think that the national news, which they saw on Washington channels, impacted us, unless the news meant money would be taken out of our pocketbooks in the form of higher taxes. Then some townspeople might complain, but we never thought to try to do anything about the problem. A good complaint was thought to be all regular people could do.

Few people that I knew in Luray read newspapers, other than the weekly *Page News and Courier*, a local paper distributed for a nickel on the street corner near the town's red light every Wednesday, and the *Daily News Record*, a paper delivered by mail from nearby Harrisonburg. Though my family got both papers, usually my mother was the only one to read them and she concentrated on the obituaries and traffic citations. The only other reading materials in our home were Bibles—an old family Bible on the coffee table and several smaller ones we had won at school—our current schoolbooks, a set of Childcraft children's books, and, when the kids were in high school, a set of World Book Encyclopedias bought from a door-to-door salesman.

Sometimes while living at home I longed to know what was going on outside the confines of this small town, though I didn't do much to find out. Now that I've lived outside, sometimes I think fondly of the simplicity of staring out my mom's front window to see that, as she would say, "Indeed, the neighbor is washing his car again and he just washed it two days before. Next thing you know, he's gonna wash the paint right off the fender."[2]

But growing up in Luray was not confined completely to this rural simplicity. Under the surface lay more sinister stories of race relations in the 1960s in small southern towns.

The Other Side of the Fence:
Seeing Black and White in a Small Southern Town[3]

Hurrah for Luray. Hurrah for Luray. Someone's in the stands yelling hurrah for Luray. One, two, three, four. Who you gonna yell for? Luray, that's us. Hey, rah, rah.

Memories flood my body as I hear the familiar football cheer burst forth from the bleachers. With "hurrah" pronounced as "who-ray" and rhyming with "Lou-ray," the jingle is too catchy to resist. I join the small group of Luray High School fans, who sing along enthusiastically, waving their outstretched fists in rhythm. No one seems to mind that the band plays out of tune: "Hurrah for Luray . . ."

I wonder, where are the cheering crowds? The loud and roaring band? The rows and rows of bleachers I remember? Tonight there are only twenty band members and fifty or sixty fans seated in the three sets of five-row-high bleachers, similar to what you would expect to see at a neighborhood league softball game. Because the population of Luray has not changed in the twenty-five years I have been away, I assume that my memory is confounded by the way I perceived Luray when I was an eighteen-year-old girl who had not traveled beyond the mountains that surrounded and protected our small Virginia town.

From 1964 to 1969, I attended Luray High School and played clarinet in the band at football games. Tonight I have returned, for the first time, to a high school game. I have come to participate with my family in the halftime dedication of a new field house honoring my younger brother Rex, who died at the age of twenty-nine in an airplane crash in 1982 (see Ellis, 1993, and Chapter 6 in this book). From auctions, raffles of guns, and donations of money and labor, Rex's classmates have raised $25,000 over the past twelve years to pay for the building, which will house team locker and meeting rooms at Bulldog Field.

Many local people yell out greetings as my family and I head out to the fifty-yard line for the halftime ceremony. "Carolyn, Carolyn, remember me?" a voice from the crowd inquires above the rest. Recognizing a former classmate, I smile as I turn toward him. Most people from high school expect me to remember their names no matter how many years I have been away. High school was a memorable time for them; many said it was the best time of their lives. Though I remembered that time fondly, some of those recollections were now lost among the memories of my many years of college and graduate school.

"Hi," I say, extending my left hand over the fence that separates the playing field from the spectators, and grasping the hand that hesitantly teaches out. "Let's see," I begin, a little embarrassed, "I certainly remember you, but I can't think of your name." Usually this introduction got me off the hook and the name and appropriate details were supplied immediately. Not this time.

"Well, I'm not Grady," the man says, looking at me expectantly.

"I know you're not," I reply, wondering what is meant by his response.

"I'm not Kevin," he continues, smiling and raising his eyebrows, and when I don't respond, "or Anthony."

"No, no, I don't mean that all Blacks look alike," I burst forth, placing my hand gently on his arm, as I finally understand he has just named almost all the Black males in our graduating class. Suddenly the fence between us is too symbolic. I want to go around and stand beside him, but I feel I should not leave my family as we wait for the halftime ceremony. "I just . . ."

"I'm Bobby," he interrupts, and I wonder whether I should even be referring to Blacks; we never did in high school—not *to* them anyway, just when we talked *about* them.

"Oh, that's right," I respond, snapping my fingers and nodding my head as though his name had been on the tip of my tongue. "How are you?" I leave my hand on his arm. Fragments of race stories that took place in Luray flicker through my mind. I think about how different Bobby's life must be from that of the urban, educated Black professors and students I interact with now.

"I'm okay," Bobby says. "Got divorced. Grady's paralyzed." I respond viscerally to the name. "Kevin is dead. And Anthony is unemployed, living with his mother and his two children. His wife left him."

"Oh, that's awful," I acknowledge. "Kevin's dead? What happened?"

"He was shot."

"Oh." Sensing our limited time, I do not ask for the details. Instead, I move to Grady, hoping Bobby does not detect that I am more interested in him than I am in the others. If he does notice, maybe my curiosity does not surprise him. After all, this is a small town where most people eventually know most of whatever has gone on. I wonder, why do I care anyway? How easily I recede momentarily into being a Luray girl concerned about small-town gossip.

"I heard Grady had a car accident," I say, and Bobby nods his head affirmatively. "Several years ago, somebody at our twentieth reunion told me." I always hoped to run into Grady at one of our reunions, but none of the Black students ever attended.

"How is he?" I continue. "Can he walk at all?"

"With crutches, a little now," he answers.

"Where is he?"

"Lives with his mother."

"His mother," I repeat, and get a visual image of Grady's mother and the house in which they live. At the same time, I glance over at my family: my eighty-year-old mother, in a wheelchair recuperating from gallbladder surgery; my older brother and his wife and two grown sons, all of whom live in Luray; my sister and her husband from Mississippi; and my partner Art, who has accompanied me from Tampa, Florida, where we live together. Exchanging smiles with Art I feel a link to my outside world. I remind myself that my main consideration tonight is to be available to comfort my mother if she becomes upset at this occasion honoring my deceased brother.

"Hey, good to see you," I say to Bobby, as I nod toward my family and step away. I wish we could talk longer. I have more questions, especially about Grady.

In that moment, I experience the contradictory pulls of several worlds—my family and our losses, the high school and small town of my childhood, and the urban university community in Florida that I now call home—the world I always am anxious to return to when I visit my family. The bond to Luray, vibrating from participating in this scene from my past, surprises me. I was sure I had left this connection behind. My feelings remind me that I am still a part of this community. I wonder, how much of this community is still a part of me? How much have the choices I made in my life been impacted by my experience of small-town life? How different is my life from their lives?

As I reach the fifty-yard line, lights suddenly illuminate the dedication engraved on the building—"Rex A. Ellis Memorial Field House"—signaling the beginning of the ceremony. Emotion wells up in my throat, and I cannot bear the pain of feeling the loss of my brother. Instead I concentrate on the fragments of high school recollections running through my head. The conversation with Bobby, the cheers, the smells of autumn, the chill in the air—the whole scene transports me back to high school and then to the brief romance I had with Grady during the late 1960s, a relationship that challenged my taken-for-granted, small-town socialization and started my move away from Luray.

Black and White Relations in Luray

When I entered high school in the mid-1960s, Luray was a typical, segregated southern town. Most Blacks lived in West Luray, referred to by White town residents as "Colored Hill" or "The Hill." I never thought to inquire what Black people called it. About half a mile from Luray proper, Colored Hill separated the town from the lucrative Luray Caverns area, our main tourist attraction. Lined with houses and churches, Main Street extended through The Hill for about a third of a mile. Off on the hillside, dirt roads connected many houses occupied by Blacks. The small public school for Blacks was located down a paved road in the same area.

Whites often made fun of Colored Hill. Each summer, when I got a dark suntan, my mother would say, "I'm going to drop you on Colored Hill, you little darkey," or my older brother would tease, "Can't tell you from the jungle bunnies on The Hill." This talk occurred so commonly that I never thought much about it—that is, until I got to know Grady.

My parents warned that if I walked on Colored Hill, "the Coloreds would get you," which I interpreted to mean kidnap, rape, or something more horrible. For my parents, "the Coloreds" was the public, polite term for "niggers," a word they also used and I occasionally criticized. I remember walking on Colored Hill only once, and then with a girlfriend. I believe I was returning home from visiting on the other side of town and was in too much of a hurry to wait for our ride. Whatever the situation, I convinced myself it was necessary to walk there. Curious, yet fearful, I walked quickly, looking straight ahead as though I had somewhere to get to quickly. When nothing out of the ordinary happened—people I passed just looked and nodded—I felt surprised and relieved. But I lived in fear for days after that someone would tell my parents they had seen me there.

After we got driver's licenses, my girlfriends and I drove up The Hill every night of every weekend, from the town Tastee Freeze to the Tastee Freeze near the Luray Caverns, looking for boys to talk to and flirt with—White ones, of course. Groups of Black males often stood on the corner, occasionally nodding discreetly in our direction. We pretended to pay them no mind except to speed up. After we got past, we sometimes exclaimed in disgust, "Do you believe that?" and then gave away our contradictory purposes by giggling, proud we could attract their attention.

A large Baptist church with peeling paint and a dilapidated porch stood in the middle of The Hill. Almost every night, groups of older, church-dressed Blacks in dark suits and white shirts or dark dresses and frilly hats gathered in front. As I drove by quickly, I wished I could see what went on inside the church that drew so much attention; I also wondered about life inside the rundown white houses with the big inviting porches.

In 1967, when I was a sophomore, our White school was partially integrated when four Blacks, two girls and two boys, were sent to our school from West Luray School. The administrators, forced by law to integrate, chose the students they thought would fit in best. When we were completely integrated, six Black males and four Black females were part of our cohort of ninety-eight students, the largest class in the history of Luray High School.

Grady was one of the first four. Because he sat beside me in homeroom, we talked a lot and I quickly got to know him. I liked him immediately. I found him mysteriously attractive and often watched him from a distance.[4] His coal-black color frightened yet attracted me. At six feet five inches, he was the tallest person I knew. When he walked, his long lanky legs and arms, shoulders, and torso seemed to be held together by rubber ball socket joints. He moved with long strides as though dancing, his arms swinging, his shoulders rolling, his head bobbing, his hips swaying. Except on the basketball court, he never appeared to be in a hurry.

Everybody liked Grady—he was so laidback and nonthreatening. And there were few, if any, problems with integration—that I knew of anyway—except for occasional grumbling among parents at the mere thought of their children going to school with "the Coloreds." Because of his basketball prowess, Grady helped smooth the transition and even became a town hero of sorts. Until that time, our basketball team almost always finished last in its division. After Grady arrived, he and several other Black males dominated the game. During the three years Grady played, we were first in our division, we won the State Championship his sophomore year and came in second his senior year, and we were undefeated for two years in a row. Home games, previously attended by fewer than a hundred people, became "the event" in town; rarely was there a vacant bleacher seat. Many people attended out-of-town games as well. When Grady graduated, he was honored as an alternate high school All-American.

That was on the basketball court. Off the court, attitudes toward Blacks continued much the same. The Black boys were still "the Coloreds" or, in private, "niggers," still from Colored Hill, and still to be avoided.

"I hear that some of the White girls are kissing Black boys after the basketball games," my father said sternly one day. I did not respond, just shrugged my shoulders. Of course they were. I had not done so, but only because I did not have access to center court like the White cheerleaders did. "If I ever found out one of my daughters was kissing the Coloreds, I'd disown her," he threatened. Still I said nothing, although his harsh words, unusual for my father, reverberated through my head.

That day I felt, perhaps for the first time, that I existed in a world apart from my parents. I had been brought up racist enough to understand some of what my father felt. But already my friendships with Grady and the other Black students had changed my mind about my parents' taken-for-granted beliefs, common throughout White Luray, that Blacks were inferior, dangerous, and to be avoided. Although I still believed the races should not "mix," by which was meant to have sex and marry, sometimes I wondered whether I was so sure even of this. I felt angry, initially at the town and later at myself, that I had never before thought to question these beliefs.

After integration, the relationship between Blacks and Whites grew more complicated. Sometimes the Black boys also drove from Tastee Freeze to Tastee Freeze, and now my girlfriends and I waved back instead of pretending to ignore them. After all, were we not schoolmates? Sometimes we spoke briefly when they coincidentally ended up in the same line at the same time as we were ordering our cheeseburgers with lots of chili and double fries loaded with ketchup. But that was all, just talk.

Face to Face with Prejudice

During our last year in high school, our class raised money through bake sales and raffles to pay part of the cost of a senior trip to Florida. We chartered a bus that drove all night to St. Augustine, then spent several nights at Daytona Beach and a day at Cypress Gardens before driving back during the night to Virginia. About one third of the class, including two of the Black males (Kevin and Grady) and two Black females, came along. On the bus, the Black girls sat together and, at first, so did Grady and Kevin. Soon, however, we switched seats, and Grady and I sat side by side while Kevin sat with another White girl. I knew Grady's brother was dating a White woman, but it had never occurred to me that I might become involved with a Black man. I had heard of only one other interracial couple in Luray, and they saw each other in secret. My parents would kill me. Not to mention how my White boyfriend of several years, who was waiting back home, would react. But, I rationalized, I was not dating Grady, just sitting beside him. I was thankful that the senior trip provided liminal space where nothing seemed quite real; the darkness on the bus contributed to that atmosphere.

On the beach in Daytona, the chaperones were lenient about letting boys and girls socialize together until lights out. The first night, most of us went for a walk. Immersed in a conversation about his experience of being Black in a White world, Grady and I wandered away from the group and sat on a pile of rocks.

"You always remember you're Black," he said. "People's responses remind you."

"What was it like growing up?" I asked.

"Awful. We had no money. My father left when I was a baby, so I was raised by my mother and grandmother, like a lot of Black kids. Then my mother remarried. My stepfather didn't like me. Once I woke up and he had a butcher knife at my throat."

"What did you do?" I asked, unable to picture the event as I thought about how well my parents had provided for me.

"I ran outside. In the freezing cold, with no shoes on, few clothes. I got frostbite on my toes."

"What had you done?"

"Nothing. He was drunk. And he was always jealous that my mother loved me and my brother more than him. That's all. Just jealous."

"We better go back in," I said, noticing that everyone else had disappeared. What will people think about the two of us out here in the dark alone together? I desperately wanted to stay on the beach with Grady. I do not recall the initial attraction as particularly sexual; instead my desire to be with him came from wanting to understand the story of his life and from the exhilaration I experienced in the mystery and adventure of the experience.

I led the way into the room where the other students had gathered. Although nervous, I felt I had nothing to be embarrassed about because our time together had been innocent. What I felt did not matter when all eyes turned on me and all voices stopped at the same time. I had never felt such hostile attention before. Grady, who had, hesitated before walking into the same treatment a few moments later.

Suddenly I knew viscerally a little of what it must feel like to be Black in a White world. In that one silent yet loaded moment, I felt as though I were Black and I knew the power of prejudice. My peers had tolerated my talking to Grady in public; in private was a different matter, especially because it connoted a sexual, intimate association. The hostility only increased my desire to know more about Black experiences and opened up new levels of communication between Grady and me as we later analyzed what had happened and how we felt.

Grady went home to basketball; I went home to my boyfriend, the town banker's son. Without explanation, I no longer wanted to see him so often. Without explanation, I often disappeared from my parents' home without telling them where I was going. Later my brother Rex would tell me that my mother worried that I was seeing a married man. No, Ma, much worse in your view, I wanted to say but couldn't.

I met Grady whenever I could, which was no easy matter in a small town. Occasionally I called his house; he never called mine. Or I would see him as I ran the Tastee Freeze shuttle, nod at his sign, then follow him discreetly at a distance to an isolated part of town, where I would get into his car and talk, occasionally sharing inhibited kisses. One night we held hands, and I gently rubbed his arm, hairless and well oiled, exclaiming that he had the smoothest skin I had ever felt. We lay our arms side by side and compared color. How strange that the shade should make such a difference in our lives, we agreed. We kissed passionately that night, his full lips engulfing my pencil-thin ones, our passion no doubt fueled by our revelations to each other. I liked it and was repelled and turned on by the fear I felt—the fear of discovery and the excitement of difference and unfamiliarity confounded by the burden of all the myths about Blacks that had permeated my childhood. We talked about how our kisses felt "strange" and laughed at the intimacy of our revelations.

That was as far as our physical relationship ever went. Inexperienced sexually, I was scared of going to hell for making out with anyone. With Grady, I also was scared of the consequences of being discovered with a Black man. Just being with him provided adventure enough.

One night I parked my car in the school parking lot and Grady picked me up. The next morning, my father asked where I had been. "With friends," I replied nonchalantly, but my heart constricted inside. "Why was your car parked at the schoolhouse?" he inquired, watching my face closely. Given that my father was more probing than usual, I feared he knew more than he was saying.

"Because I was riding around with Jeanie and June," I lied. "How'd you know about my car?"

"The police checked it out and someone told me they heard it mentioned on the short-wave radio."

"I see," I replied, remembering that few things are private in a small town.

A few nights later, Grady urged me to come to his house. "No one will see you, and you won't have to worry about where to park your car."

When I protested, he argued, "My mother won't care. My brother brings his girl-friend." Against my better judgment, but feeling that I should be able to meet his mother and see where he lived, I agreed.

Culture Clash: "You Shouldn't Have to Put Up with This"

Darkness is just beginning to fall when I turn down the quarter-mile dirt lane to Grady's house. Waiting outside, Grady says, "Come in. I have to shower. Just got home from playing basketball."

His mother, an attractive, large, and dark woman, opens the door to the kitchen. A rectangular yellow Formica table sits in the middle and appliances, including a washer and dryer, line two sides. White porcelain dominates. Grady introduces us, and his mother greets me in a very soft voice, "Come in." I feel welcomed. From behind her flowing dress and apron, a kerchiefed head leans around her right side. Other than her head, this little old lady is completely hidden from sight. "And this is my grandmother," Grady says, pointing to the red-and-white-checkered head.

"Nice to meet you," I say to the blue-checkered skirt tail that follows the disappearing head.

"Hurumf, hurumf," she replies in a surprisingly gruff voice for such a little woman. As Grady's mother shuts the door and turns around, the grandmother turns also, keeping herself completely hidden from me, muttering over and over, "Hurumf, hurumf!" It is not difficult to decipher that she does not approve of my being there.

"Come with me," Grady says. "Sit there until I shower," he directs, pointing to a worn-out deep maroon couch pulled out from the wall in the living room. "I'll only be a minute. Then we'll go out." I sink low into the fluffy couch.

The room is sparsely decorated with fake velvet furniture similar to the furnishings in my own home; there is just less, and it is more worn. The rugless wooden floors and picture-less gray-white walls add to the sparseness.

As darkness falls, it feels eerie to be sitting alone in this silent, unlit Black family's living room. Where are Grady's mother and grandmother? After a few minutes, I am relieved to hear the sound of voices start up in the kitchen. Grady's mother's quiet voice speaks reassuringly, "It's okay. Nothing's wrong. Go on home."

Then an angry loud Black man's voice responds, "What do you mean, go home? *This is my home, and I'm coming in.*"

"Get out of here," I hear, and I assume the gruff words come from Grady's grandmother.

I wonder what is going on but am not unduly alarmed. Suddenly Grady bounds out of the bathroom wearing only his gym shorts and carrying a towel in his hand. "You better get down," he says as he hurries past. "He's got a gun." Before I can respond, Grady disappears through another door, leaving me confused and emotionless.

It is darker now. The male voice from the kitchen escalates; I strain to hear the quiet voice responding. The experience is surreal, made more so by sudden popping sounds, three in a row. Then silence. Still I sit on the couch. Noting the open windows and curtains blowing, I say to myself, in slow motion now, "Those were gunshots. I guess I ought to get down. He could shoot through the window." I feel like I am watching a suspenseful television show and imagining that I am a character.

I crouch on hands and knees behind the couch, then sit down, slouching to be lower, my head buried sideways in my neck and shoulder, my elbows under my hips. Participating in this drama now makes my part more real; my body starts to tremble, and my breath catches in my throat. The arguing voices start up again. Through it all, I hear Grady's mother's soothing quiet voice, the same tone with which she had greeted me, "It's okay. It's okay." I do not hear the grandmother now, but I am relieved that at least the man did not shoot Grady's mother. The male voice gets louder. His slur reveals that he is drunk.

Two more shots ring out hollowly, and I almost convince myself that they sound like shots from a cap pistol until I get a whiff of gunpowder. I imagine a crazy Black man waving a pistol and threatening to kill Grady's mother—or Grady. Where is Grady? Why is he not here protecting me? Time slows down. More and more, I am conscious of how sluggishly my thoughts are being processed and of how much my senses are being assaulted by the foreign odor of gunpowder. What if I am killed at a Black man's house? What will my parents think?

I sit behind the couch, still slouched, for what seems like hours. Silence takes over everything. Then, suddenly and quietly, Grady's mother touches me on the shoulder. Relieved, I start to speak, to ask what has happened and where Grady is. "Shh," she says quietly with her finger on her lips, her face near mine, eyes wide open with pupils enlarged and surrounded in white. She motions me to come with her. Totally trusting, I follow her through the door that Grady had escaped behind earlier. Good, maybe she is taking me to Grady. He will know how to get me out of this.

I am now in what appears to be Grady's bedroom. "Stay here," she commands and then walks out the door. The small room contains only a twin bed and a small dresser. The screen hangs out the window, and the curtains blow freely. I sit down beside the door facing the window and realize there is no place to hide. Suddenly I reach up and turn off the light. The man outside could shoot me through the open window, I think, feeling my heart speed up. With that, I lie down on my side, propping my head on my hand.

I remain motionless for a long time. There is no sign of Grady, who I presumed had jumped out the window. I consider locking the door but do not. Why should I? Anyone who wants to can enter through the open window. I also am afraid to move, even an inch, until this woman tells me it is all right. I do not know the rules here—or if there are any.

Finally the door opens and Grady's mother reappears. "Come with me," she instructs in a whisper. Standing up, I quickly grab onto her arm. We walk through the living room and out the back door. I hold on tightly with both hands, then link my arms through one of hers, to ensure that she cannot get away. Her arm is thick and strong. We walk in rhythm, a slow cadence. She offers no explanation of where we are headed.

"Who is he? The man?" I ask.

"My ex-husband," she answers.

"Has he done this before? Shot a gun—at you, I mean."

"Oh, yes, many times," she says without emotion.

"Why don't you call the cops?"

"I have. They don't do anything. Besides, he would be gone before they got here."

"But they have to do something," I say. "He can't be allowed to come here with a gun and threaten to kill you."

"Yes, he can," she says matter-of-factly.

"But it's not right," I respond. "You shouldn't have to put up with this."

"There's nothing to do," she says in a monotone. I feel close to and appreciate this woman, who endures this horrible life yet risks it to escort me, a White girl she does not know, to safety. Tightening my grip, I ask where she is taking me.

"To the end of the lane."

"I can't leave without my car," I declare.

"He might be back there, between the cars. We can't risk it," she says.

"I have to risk it," I say, thinking of explaining to my parents why I have come home without my car, skipping over the problem of how I would get home in the first place. "If he doesn't kill me, my parents will."

"We'll see," she says. "Just keep walking for now."

Hearing a rustling in the bushes, we stop and hold our breath. A Black man steps into our path.

"Grady?" I ask tentatively, letting out the air I had been holding in. "Thank God."

"Are you okay?" his mother asks.

"Yes, are you?"

"Yes, but I think he's still at the house. You have to get her out of here," she says, nodding toward me.

"Okay, Ma. I will."

His mother turns and walks back toward the house; Grady and I continue walking down the lane toward the main road. "Take care of yourself," I say to her, quietly over my shoulder.

"Grady, I have to get my car," I plead.

"I know," he replies, and I understand that he understands that if I do not get my car, we will both be in trouble. "But not now. Let's wait." His caution reminds me that at the moment, there is more immediate trouble.

"Who is he?" I ask.

"My stepfather. The one who held the knife to my neck. Ma divorced him because he's a drunk. Never should have married him in the first place. He's done this many times before. Wants her to take him back. Threatens to kill her if she don't."

"Can't something be done?"

"What?" he asks. "The cops don't want to get involved. No use in calling. For them, it's just Colored people acting up."

"What a world you live in," I reply. "Did you jump out the window?"

"Yes, he would have killed me. I don't think he would kill Ma. But he's tried to kill me many times."

"Would he kill me?"

"I don't know."

"Would it matter one way or another that I'm White?"

"Only in that he'd think he had something on you."

"Grady, I have to get my car." I am adamant.

"It's risky."

"I know, but I can't go home without it."

"Okay, come with me, but be very quiet." We turn and walk back to the house, my heart beating wildly. Grady holds my hand and leads the way. We stand for a long time at the edge of the house. Finally we move slowly around the corner toward my car. Grady holds out his hand for my keys, then darts between the cars to the driver's side and gets in. I jump into the passenger's side, with visions of a Black man popping up in the backseat and holding a gun to my head. The engine starts and we drive down the road. I turn around and scan the backseat. Whew, there is no man. When I look down the road, there is no man running behind us waving a gun. I turn back toward the front, and there is no man jumping in front of the car daring us to run him down. We do not turn on the lights until we reach the hard surface road. When I hear the sound of pavement, I finally am conscious of breathing.

"Where are we going?" I ask.

"To the church?" Grady asks.

"Yes, I want to talk." We drive to the nearby Baptist church, our favorite parking spot, and talk for a while about Grady's life with his stepfather. Now I am more fascinated by and more fearful of the life Grady leads.

"How will I get you back home?" I ask when we notice it is almost 11 o'clock, my curfew. I do not want to travel down that lane again tonight—or ever.

"Let me out at the dirt road," he instructs. "I'll be all right."

When I arrive home, I am glad everyone is asleep because I am too shaken to participate in cover-up conversation. Early the next day, the phone rings and, frowning, my mother hands it to me. An unfamiliar female voice says, "I'm Grady's brother's girlfriend. Grady's stepfather took down your license number. He's going to make trouble. I thought you should know."

"Thank you," I say.

"Who was that?" my usually unquestioning mother demands to know.

"Nobody you know," I say, realizing she is aware something is wrong. Then I walk out the door, panicked, but realizing there is nothing I can do.

A few days later, without hearing from Grady's stepfather or from Grady, I leave for my first year at the College of William and Mary, determined to study race relations. The same day, Grady leaves to attend a college in West Virginia, where he has a full basketball scholarship. Grady and I correspond haltingly by letters for about a year but are unable to rekindle our excitement and exploration long distance through written words. I hear that he does well in basketball but drops out of college without getting a B.A. degree. After William and Mary, I go to graduate school in New York and become a sociologist.

I never see Grady again.

Reflections on Community and Racism

Standing on the other side of the fence from Bobby, a member of my high school graduating class, I feel lost momentarily. Looking for a way to go around, worried about whether I should have mentioned race to an African American man from Luray, looking back at my family, I wonder, where do I belong? Where are my loyalties and commitments? I glance across the fence at Bobby and I think, this community is racist; it violates one of my most deeply held values. Then I turn toward my family and Rex's friends and I think, this community is family; these are some of the strongest ties I ever had. Fragmented, I am confused by my contradictory thoughts and feelings. The haunting familiarity and disturbing distance brought on by attachment to and estrangement from my memories swirl through my consciousness.

For the moment, the alienation I feel toward my working-class family and this rural community absorbs me. Talking to Bobby has reminded me of the racial attitudes I experienced while growing up in Luray, attitudes that do not seem to have changed substantially in the twenty-five years I have been away. I feel angry about the way in which people here insisted that everyone abide by their narrow set of beliefs and values. Why did it take me so long to figure out that their small-town values need not be mine, that there were ways to live life other than theirs?

Yet, I remind myself, I did get out. Social experiences that contradicted the values and attitudes I was expected to manifest, such as the one with Grady, provoked me to escape the confines of Luray's local culture. I went off to college "to study race relations," I said. College life offered ideas and experiences that challenged my small-town assumptions and offered opportunities to learn about and explore in a relatively safe environment different ways of being in the world. Sociology, in particular, provoked my imagination and led to reflections on self, other, and social life. Sociological reflection moved me further and further away—emotionally, psychically, and geographically— from the world of Luray and my family. Only later would I wonder whether Grady found college as hospitable. What had the experience been like for him?

Standing on the fifty-yard line, I redirect my thoughts to the dedication ceremony now in full swing. One by one, Rex's friends speak of Rex, the town of Luray, and the importance of this new building to the football program and the community. "Rex always gave of himself to others," a friend says into the mike. "He was active in the community, a standout athlete, and a good friend to many. We want to honor him with this building."

Next, Rex's old football coach, who used to let me sneak into the boy's locker room in high school to play Ping-Pong on the only available table, speaks. "If it was third down and you needed a few yards, you always gave the ball to Rex." I feel proud. (Only later do I wonder, if Grady had been killed in a tragic airplane crash, would he have been honored as well? Unfortunately, I knew the answer was no.) My older brother moves to the mike to give his prepared speech. He stands silently for a moment, then says simply in a cracking voice, "On behalf of my family, we thank the Luray community." My normally composed and controlled brother walks back to the family without saying more.

Engulfed now by my loss (and theirs), anesthetized only slightly by time, I experience my grief communally for the first time. The fragments of anger, resentment, and sense of superiority I have harbored all these years—and experienced deeply just a few minutes earlier—begin to disintegrate. As my habitually superior stance crumbles, I experience closeness, compassion, and, most of all, identification with these people who, like me, struggle to create a meaningful world in which to live. I cannot stand apart from this community in this moment as I did when Rex died twelve years earlier. Nor do I want to.

I care deeply about the people in this small town who have gone to so much effort to honor Rex. They are part of me; I am one of them, no matter that I have lived away from Luray for more years than I lived there. At the moment, I welcome the feelings of meaning and membership this inclusion provides.

Reflections on Community and Sociology

After this event, I am able to think about Luray in more complex ways, and I realize that my unidimensional stereotyping of people who live there is a mirror image of the unidimensional values this community offered me and against which I rebelled. My sociological perspective, which initially provided escape, now helps me to reconnect to the same world I fled.

My relationship with family, local community, and sociology seems a particularly ironic one. I could not have accomplished becoming a sociologist without my family's support, and thus my family helped me become someone they barely recognized (Myerhoff, 1978, p. 93); by making me feel secure and important as a child, my family and community gave me the foundation to believe in myself and pursue my dreams, which included becoming "not them." Becoming a sociologist had "freed" me from the Luray I resisted; now it places me in a position from which I am able to develop a critical understanding and appreciation of their ideals and my relationship to them.

Thus I have come full circle. When I left Luray, I used sociology to make the strange, wider world become more familiar (Rorty, 1982, p. 203); now, returning to Luray helps me "remystify" this familiar local scene so that it appears stranger and more complicated than I had come to believe (Sherwood, Smith, & Alexander, 1993). Through this process, the local community becomes part of—not separate from—the mysterious social world I have sought to understand for most of my adult life.

Without condoning racist attitudes, I think I can now stop blaming Luray, a small town frozen in time and place, for what it did not do, much as I stopped blaming my parents some time ago. As a result, my relationship with Luray, similar to my relationship with my family, now takes on a refreshingly new complexity and open-endedness. From the perspective of locals, this community gave me what it could. From their worldview, the set of beliefs they imposed on me made sense. Many of them, my family included, did not recognize the possibility of thinking and feeling otherwise, and so how could I expect them to teach me to think and feel otherwise?

Through education and mobility, I have had a luxury many people in Luray have not had: By traveling through many worlds, I have been exposed to diverse people and ways of thinking. By becoming a sociologist, I have had the opportunity to examine many beliefs as well as more choice to design who I have become. As a sociologist, I recognize that I cannot escape the social forces that sociological theories say act on everyone else (Gouldner, 1970, pp. 54–55). I too have been constrained by time, location, and the culture of my small-town upbringing, but it, in turn, has been affected substantially by the urban, academic, feminist, countercultural environment to which I fled.

What personal choices have I made as a result? I have chosen to put career above other institutions, rebel against traditional family life, remain childless, and live in a relatively anonymous urban community. Is this environment better than the one I left behind in Luray? Fortunately, it does not have the scrutiny, routine, prejudice, rigidity, and narrowness of Luray. But my community also does not surround me with mutual aid, friendliness, caring, safety, and kinship (see Vidich & Bensman, 1958). I live in a place defined mostly by career, not community; a place where I always feel stimulated but, as a result, always lack for time; a place where not even a tragic death would engender a building with my name on it (although donating substantial money might); a place where I do not know the names of all the people who live across the street; a place where I have become fearful of taking out my garbage after dark; a place where I am happily and regrettably "not bothered" and "not recognized" except at my university office.

I cannot return to Luray now except to visit, nor would I want to. I do not fit. But I value many lessons I learned there, my ties to the people who still live there, the role this community played in who I have become, and the mysteries still to be investigated. I also value the affinity I developed there for the meaning to be found in good conversation and stories of concrete experience.

For the moment, then, one fence disappears.

Meta-Autoethnography: Reflections on "The Other Side of the Fence"

I wrote this story in 1990 and published it in 1995, more than twenty-five years after the experience took place in 1969. Subsequently, I received two significant reactions to what I had written. Both gave me insight into the complexities of race, opened up questions about the content of my story and the ethics of writing about others, and offered examples of how those included in a story might respond.

Assume Those You Write About Will Read What You Have Written

"Carolyn, I'm teaching a class on racism to 200 students this summer and wondered if you would be able to give a lecture?" an e-mail from Sandy, a Black professor in psychology at my university, reads. The year is 1995.

"Sure," I respond, "especially if I can speak from a paper I have just finished on interracial relationships."

Sandy readily agrees, and I send her my recently published story, "The Other Side of the Fence."

A few days later, Sandy calls. "I just read the article you sent," she says. "Carolyn, you aren't going to believe this. A few months ago, I bought a mountain cottage in Luray."

"My Luray?" I ask.

"Your Luray."

"Sandy, how could that be? Luray is almost a thousand miles from Tampa."

"I know. I have friends who have a summer home there and, after visiting, I decided I wanted one too. I plan to spend next year, my sabbatical year, there as well as summers. But your depiction of the racism in Luray makes me wonder if that's really where I want to be."

I teach Sandy's class that spring. Then I meet her in Luray during the summer and introduce her to local friends. She becomes friends with the parents of one of my best high school friends in Luray, even spending the night with them several times when snowfall makes her feel unsafe in her mountain cabin. The next time I meet Sandy back in Luray, she informs me that she has given my published article to this family and has had many discussions about it. "Your friends defended the town," she says, "and described it as less racist than you pictured it. They told me I would be welcomed anywhere in Luray." She also shows the article to a Black female supervisor in the school system, who says, "I knew Mr. Ellis, Carolyn's father. I never thought he felt that way." The supervisor was very hurt, Sandy reports, and I feel shame for having exposed my father as well as shame for my father's racial attitudes.

"Should I not have shown it to her?" Sandy asks, when she sees my frown.

"It's a public document," I reply. "You can show it to anyone you want."

"Have you shown it to your mother or your brother?"

"No, I haven't, and I'm not sure I ever will. I know that doesn't coincide with my beliefs about race or your expectations about what I should do, but I would hope you don't show it to my mother," I say, as we pull into my mother's driveway where I have brought Sandy for the first time.

"Isn't that dishonest and cowardly behavior?" she asks.

"Yes, it is, but confronting my mother won't change her attitudes and most likely will harden them. I do try to change my family's beliefs about race in subtle ways, such as questioning their language and response to images on television. The other day my mother asked me if some newscaster was Black or White, and I said, 'If you can't tell, what difference does it make?'" Despite my rationalizations, I was embarrassed that the taboos of Luray (and my family) still had such hold over me more than twenty-five years later.

"Don't worry, my mother will be nice to you," I say as we enter my mother's home.

"And don't worry, I won't tell her about your story," she replies. Sandy seems comfortable meeting and talking with my mother and my mother is gracious and welcoming.

Taking Your Story Back to Participants and Getting Their Reactions

"Have you seen Jesse [the pseudonym I used for Grady in my original story] since all this happened?" a student in my undergraduate personal storytelling class asks. It is the year 2000. Students often ask this question when they read my story, and I'm always a little uncomfortable when I respond.

"No, I haven't. I always hoped to see him at high school reunions, but he never attended. None of the Black students did."

"Did you ever try to find him?" another student inquires.

"I've thought of trying to find him when I visit my mother in Luray, but I'm not sure where to look. I thought of going back to his mother's house, but I'm not sure I'd know how to find it, or if I'd feel comfortable going there. Besides I want to spend all my time with my mother when I am in Luray." Similar to my rationalizations to Sandy about why I didn't show this story to my mother, these reasons sound hollow.

That all changes in February 2004 when my sister-in-law sends me a newspaper clipping from the *Page News and Courier*, my hometown newspaper. In Section B, listed under "Black History Month Special," is a two-page article headlined with "Integration pushes

Luray High School to its first state title in '67" (Collins, 2004). A picture of the 1967 Luray High School State Championship team shows the team running down the court. Leading the way is Grady, arms pumping, muscles bulging, his lanky form the tallest on the court. "Arrington . . . would hit his head on the backboard going up for rebounds . . . In rebounding drills, he could grab the ball with two hands at a height of 11 and a half feet," the article reads (p. B2).

I turn to page two and there is a recent picture of the 1967 starters, appearing considerably older. Four players and the coach stand along the back. My eyes are drawn to the man in front seated in a wheelchair. Grady is no longer lanky and muscular. His hands lie still in his lap. He is no longer bounding into the air. I stare at his picture. I recognize the twinkle in his eyes, the smile on his face. Yes, that's Grady. I eagerly read the article to find out what has happened to him.

He was working at Joshua Tree National Park when he was in an automobile crash that left him paralyzed, the article reads. Now he works at Mammoth Cave as a supervising park ranger. Grady gives praise to his family, especially his wife, for sticking by him, and he says he remains positive and proud, which is apparent from the expression on his face.

A few months later, I look up Mammoth Cave on the web. When I see Grady's name listed as an employee, I e-mail the general address. "I am trying to locate Grady Arrington," I write. When Grady replies, we exchange a few e-mails, I tell him about the paper I have written, and then I send him a copy. He writes back that he likes it and that my descriptions dovetail with what he remembers happening. I want him to say more. I always want the people I write about to say more, even if what they have to say is not what I want to hear. We continue to exchange brief e-mails and talk a few times on the phone. We are, of course, like strangers, but we seem to enjoy the contact. He tells me about his wife; I tell him about my husband. We talk about our work and exchange photos. Grady sends me a letter about a scholarship that has been set up in his honor at Luray High School. Glad that things *have* changed in the twenty-five years since I lived in Luray, I send a check for $100 and continue contributing each year. I am invited to Grady's retirement party though I do not go. I invite him to visit me though he does not come.

But we do continue talking on the phone periodically during the next few years. We reminisce about high school and talk about the shooting of Martin Luther King. I tell him it's hard for me to remember that day, and that I am not sure I understood the significance of it when it happened. He says he didn't either. "We were isolated from so much in that little town," I say. "Yes, but I also felt protected there," Grady responds. "I didn't have to fear retaliation." He tells me that he thinks that protection is why there are so many interracial couples and biracial children now in Luray.

I think about the article I read in the local newspaper, which mentioned the role of the basketball team in integration (Collins, 2004, pp. B1–B2). "[Integration] was a very easy transition," Grady said there. "There was no hatred that I can remember. We [the White and Black players] had always played together."

"We just didn't go to school together," said another Black player.

"It wasn't like other places in the Deep South," said a third Black player. "In my time at Luray High School, I never experienced any nastiness."

A fourth said that though Luray was a segregated community, it wasn't a "nasty segregation."

I wonder about the way the Black players remember integration. It's true there wasn't violence or expressed hostility and hatred. But signs of racist attitudes were ever-present in the segregated housing, the rules about interracial contact, the movie theater where Blacks continued sitting in the balcony long after they legally could sit anywhere they pleased, the annual Black minstrel shows where the White male leaders of the town dressed in blackface and acted in disparaging stereotypical Black roles. It was apparent in the way Whites talked behind closed doors. It was apparent in the low-wage jobs most Blacks had and in the poverty within which most of them lived. The Blacks didn't ask for more. In the parlance of the times, the Blacks in Luray "knew their place" and acted accordingly, isolated from influences that might have altered and radicalized their racial identity development.

I believe it's also true that the Black basketball players, more than most Blacks, were protected from racist attitudes because they became the town heroes, at least while they were playing basketball.

As Grady and I correspond in 2006, he asks me for a copy of the book that contains the story about him. I tell him I am including the story in a book I am writing now and ask, "Would you like to respond to what I have written?" When he replies affirmatively through e-mail, I send him a series of questions but tell him to write anything he wants. In the first draft, he gives me the pseudonym of "Judy."

"I think it's time we came out of the closet," I write back. "I think you should change 'Judy' to 'Carolyn' and I'd like to change the pseudonym 'Jesse' to 'Grady' in this version of the story." Agreeing, he later includes my story and his response in an autobiography he types with one finger, which he sends to me for feedback. He entitles his work "Da Man."

Grady's Response

I was surprised to know that after thirty-five years, a summer romance had made such an impact on Carolyn. The story made me feel proud and humbled that she would take the time to write about our relationship. My parents read our story and agree with all of the accounts depicted in the story. They were pleased and surprised to know someone had cared about a relationship their son had during the summer of 1969.

One part of our story tells about my stepfather shooting up the house and I jumped out the window, leaving Carolyn to fend for herself! Unknown to Carolyn, my stepfather and I had a very strained relationship where he had shot at me several times in the past. I left when my stepfather started shooting, because I believed it would be safer for

Carolyn if I was not there. I really didn't think he would have shot her, but she could have got hurt trying to defend me. After all was done I recall the part where Carolyn was leaving the house with my mother and I jumped out of the bushes to let her know I was alright. My wife's reaction to this was "I would still be whupping your ass for scaring me when you jumped out of the bushes!" I really admire and respect Carolyn for going against the thoughts of her family and friends to date me.

Several years later when my niece was old enough to help paint my mother's house, she found the holes in the ceiling from that night. My mother explained to my niece that her grandfather had shot up the house one night when Uncle Grady had Carolyn over.

Dating Carolyn was an experience that changed my outlook on the race relationship in Luray. She opened my eyes to the good and the bad in all races. At the time I was very naive about the consequences of an interracial relationship, until Carolyn told me that she would be disowned if her father found out we were dating.

The race relationship in Luray has not always been on good grounds. The town of Luray is divided into an east side and west side. The whites live in the east side and the blacks live in the west side of town. The east and west is divided by a traffic light. In my neighborhood of Blainesville, the children that I played with in the afternoon would get on separate buses in the morning for school. At the time, this made me feel very uncomfortable and it hurt my feelings. Once the schools were integrated, life in Luray changed for the better. I feel that today Luray's race relations has changed the attitude of many of the residents. Today, the blacks and whites live anywhere they want in this small town. There are many interracial families in this small town, and interracial dating seems to be common. Race never had an adverse impact on my life, because I was a star athlete on a winning basketball team; I was widely accepted by all races.

On April 9, 1990, I was involved in a single-car rollover, which left me a quadriplegic. This accident changed me and my family drastically. I rely on my wife for 90 percent of my basic care and livelihood. I have two children and three grandchildren who have helped me to live a full and productive life. Twenty months after my accident I returned to work at Joshua Tree National Park, California. On December 1, 1991, I transferred to Mammoth Cave National Park, Kentucky, where I am the fee operations supervisor.

In 2005 I was honored with a scholarship in my name at Luray High School, Virginia. This award came about because of my many accomplishments in playing basketball during high school and college. I have given three scholarships to date to student athletes.

After thirty years with the National Park Service, I will retire June 1, 2006, and reside in Cave City, Kentucky, with my wife and family.

Story Interlude: Reflections from the Neighborhood

As I complete this book in 2007–2008, I look out the window of my study at my integrated Tampa cul-de-sac, on which we have lived for over sixteen years. Black families live on both sides of us and across the street. One of them has lived here for over ten years, the second for two. The third, a family from the Caribbean, moved in last summer and has quickly become the scourge of this middle- to upper-middle-class neighborhood. For almost a year, the entryway to their home has been decorated with a toilet, a large and broken-down chair and sometimes a couch, a castaway grill, and an old vacuum cleaner, among other unusable items.

In September 2006, their furniture is repossessed. I watch as the current man of the house—there have been two—dances around, fists in the air, dreadlocks flying. "I will beat your ass for doing this in front of my children," he threatens over and over, getting into the faces of the White men who come to retrieve the stained and torn furniture. "I don't care if they take it. I'm getting new furniture anyway," his wife says to my husband and me, when we walk to our mailbox to get our mail. The White men leave and return with the police.

The man and woman argue viciously with each other in their driveway and with men and women who arrive in strange cars at all times of the day and night. A five-year-old staying at their house shows up one morning at my door crying that she has been locked out. I take care of her for a few minutes, then quickly take her home, fearing they will accuse me of kidnapping her. The mortgage business they run illegally out of their residence attracts all kinds of visitors, who regularly park on the lawn, or more accurately the weeds, sand, and trash, and sometimes mistakenly knock on our door. Cars full of women and children arrive throughout the day, making it appear that the woman also runs a babysitting business, though perhaps she just has a large extended family.

I don't like all this activity, but I can put up with it. I can feel for this woman who is trying to make ends meet the best way she knows how, and for the kids who can't have an easy life. But it's the outhouse smell of their drain field that I can't stand. Raw sewage seeps through their yard, threatening four feet from our property line to drain into our garage. It's been that way now for ten months. The other neighbors on our cul-de-sac street—most often the White families—gather and talk about the horrible smell from the sewage and unsightly junk in the yard, and all of us—the other Black families included—agree we want them gone.

I complain to City Code enforcement. A female employee there is sympathetic until she comes to visit my neighbor. On my third call to her, she says, "You are harassing these people. They're going to fix it. Besides I didn't see any sewage when I was there."

"I am looking at the sewage right now," I say, my voice rising in exasperation.

"I am hanging up," she says. "I will not tolerate being yelled at."

I shift to a quiet and calm voice and ask her to listen to my story. I feel I am a schoolkid and the teacher is threatening to call my mom if I don't behave. When she then begins to speak, I say quietly, "I understand." At that, she screams at me, "I listened to you; now you listen to me and don't interrupt." I listen quietly as she defends our neighbors and tells me she has reported to the Health Department that the problem has been resolved.

I hang up and tell my husband Art what happened. "She is Black, probably from the Caribbean," I say, "like our neighbors. I feel discriminated against because I sound White, but I guess Black people feel this kind of discrimination all the time."

My empathy doesn't solve the problem. I call the County Health Department many times about the sanitary problem. They say it is a disgrace and a felony not to fix it. Two White men and a White sheriff visit my neighbor, make threats to her and promises to us, but months go by and the problem remains. Some of our friends say they don't want to return to our house because of the stink. We stay indoors most of the time.

The woman from the house with the sewage problem comes to our door. When Art answers, she accuses us of harassing them for calling the Health Department. She and Art argue. As she walks away, she yells at my husband to kiss her "Black ass," and pats her behind as she says it. "It's too big," Art yells after her, and with those words, I know we will hear more from them. The next day the man with the dreadlocks comes to our door. Prepared, I audiotape his threats. He screams at Art, "I'll beat your ass if you insult my wife again. I'll beat your ass if you come on my property or so much as look this way." Art remains silent, as he and I have agreed is the best response. After that, we stay inside whenever this man is outside, because we do not want to deal with him again. We wonder, without any evidence, if he has anything to do with the recent break-ins in our neighborhood.

In the beginning, Art and I talk about whether we could have done anything differently. "Did we jump too quickly to calling the Health Department rather than trying to talk to these neighbors?" Art asks.

"Maybe you're right. But they didn't fix the septic, and I was scared the sewage would run into our house."

"They are poor," Art continues. "They can't afford to fix the drain field, and I'm not sure we gave enough consideration to how hard it is to get by when you're poor."

"Is there anything we can do now to change our interactions with them?" I ask, thinking of the difficulties of negotiating with people whose first reaction is to scream. I ask that question of Robin, a Black Ph.D. student, with whom I will co-teach a course in "Race, Class, and Emotions." Tears form in my eyes and in hers when we both admit there's probably no way to mend this fence.

A few weeks later, I am resigned that nothing else would have worked either. "Given that the problem still isn't fixed, I don't think anything else would have worked," I say.

Art agrees. "They just don't have the money."

"Then they shouldn't have moved into a house and neighborhood they couldn't afford," I say.

"It's as much the fault of the lenders as theirs," Art responds.

I nod, then say, "But she works for the lenders. She's a mortgage broker."

I find it easier to be empathetic about subprime loans and ghetto living conditions when the problems are abstract and not in my neighborhood.

Not wanting to give up, I organize a petition to the Health Department about the septic problem and get it signed by all the families on the street. No matter their color, everyone is horrified by the way this family lives.

"It's in the courts," the Health Department officials finally say. "But it will take a long time to be resolved." We don't have a long time. Summer is just around the corner, and with summer come mosquitoes and the threat of hepatitis, dysentery, and other diseases if the mosquitoes drink from their "pond." Aren't septic systems what separate us from third-world countries?

"Call your county commissioner," the man at the Health Department says. "We've done all we can do. I'm sorry. You shouldn't have to live this way." I'm appalled that government can't do more. But what do I want? Do I want this woman to be thrown into jail because she can't pay her bills?

Sometimes we think of moving, though we love our house and until now have loved our neighborhood.

I talk often with the White neighbor on the other side of this family. She and I stare at this family from our mutual office windows, while we talk about what this family is doing. When we discuss how often the man with dreadlocks washes his white Cadillac, given the septic problem, I have flashes of my mother watching her neighbors. I have more understanding and compassion for my mother now, and I wonder if I am becoming her.

After my White neighbor and I complain, we wonder aloud if we are just protecting our turf. We say it is a class problem, not a race issue, and feel better. Then, one day my White neighbor asks the man with dreadlocks to move his trash can off her yard. When he doesn't, she asks again. "Yes, Massa," he says. "What's the matter? Am I not movin' fast enough for you, Massa?" Apparently *he* sees this as a race issue.

I concentrate hard not to see this family as representing Black people. I tell myself not to see this family as representing what will happen if our neighborhood becomes predominantly Black. I sing the praises of my other Black neighbors, but I find myself counting when I walk my dogs: nine homes, six White, three Black on our cul-de-sac—I feel relieved; but on the cul-de-sac next to us, I count thirteen homes, nine Black, four White.

I ask an older White man on the cul-de-sac next to our street, "Who bought the big house for sale on your street?"

"A landscaper," he replies. Then, "Don't worry. He looks like us." He knows, and I know, that this is code for "White." His wife elbows him. "Well, that's what she wanted to know," he says. I'm offended that he should say that. How dare he think like that and include me? Then I wonder, *is* that what I wanted to know?

"No use calling the newspaper about the septic problem," one of my White neighbors responds to my suggestion. "They can't do anything because this family is Black and poor and we're White middle-class." I don't respond. The comment reminds me of the words of a neighbor at our summer home in the mountains, who said, "The response in Florida after the hurricanes would have been swifter if the people affected had been

Black like they were in New Orleans after Katrina." I didn't respond then either, but Black faces looking out from the water, on top of houses, crowded in the Dome, and on the bridges of New Orleans still haunt me.

Yet I find myself uncomfortable when I am the only White person on the neighborhood streets in Tampa, or in the nearby stores and parks, which happens often now. When I walk my dogs, I notice that Black people occupy almost all the cars that drive by. I note the coloring of the community. I have a race consciousness that is different from the one I had in Luray, where there were fewer than 2 percent African Americans and no other minorities large enough to count. In 2007, Tampa is 26 percent African American and 19 percent Hispanic or Latino[5]; the number of Hispanics is rising[6]; and Whites have moved south and north of the area in which we live. Orlando Patterson says that repeated polls show that Whites say they are comfortable living in neighborhoods that are no more than 25 percent black and that Blacks prefer to live in neighborhoods that are at least 40 percent Black. The result, the near isolation of Blacks from the private life of the White majority, is what Patterson calls the "last race problem" (Patterson, 2006).

Is my newly formed race consciousness a product of the feud with my neighbor or a result of the coloring of my community? Or both?

How far have things really come since 1969 when at eighteen my Black boyfriend's father intimidated me, and my own father threatened to disown me if I kissed the Black basketball players after they won a game? How far have I come?

Sometimes I think about building a fence.

* * *

Not wanting to leave the story at this point, I read what I have written to my "Race, Class, and Emotions" class. I am nervous, afraid of how I will appear, afraid of how they will interpret it.

"I was really hoping he wouldn't have a Cadillac," said Robin, my Black co-teacher. "I kept saying to myself as you read, 'Please, not a Cadillac.' That's just too much."

"At what point did this become about race?" asks a Black woman student.

"Good question," I respond. "Because it certainly wasn't in the beginning. We just wanted the problem solved. I think race entered when the woman told my husband to kiss her Black ass. Things went downhill from there."

"I would have felt the same as you, and I would have done what you did," said another Black woman, "if sewage was running into my yard. I would have been pissed." Her words make me feel justified in my thoughts and actions. Then she continues, "Yet if I were your neighbor, I would have felt that you were being racist, and reacting as you did because I was Black." Her simple analysis helps me to see the different sides of this situation more clearly.

* * *

One night during the summer of 2007, about a year after the sewage first bubbled into the yard, the inhabitants of this house moved out during the middle of the night. The house sat vacant for another five months—the toilet still on the front porch—before a Black neighbor finally bought it from the bank, repaired the drain field, fixed it up, and sold it in spring of 2008 to his nephew and his wife, a young, middle-class Black couple with three children. We immediately developed a friendly relationship with our new neighbors and also have gotten to know the people who fixed up the house and the real estate agent who sold it. All of them live in our neighborhood.

CHAPTER THREE

Investigating the *Fisher Folk* and Coping with Ethical Quagmires

"You should go to college," the guidance counselor said after I did well on an achievement test in the tenth grade. Excited, I went home to sell this idea to my mother, figuring that then she'd sell it to my father.

"How much would it cost?" my mother asked.

"A lot," I said. "Maybe two thousand a year, including books, room, and food."

"We'll find a way. I'll talk to your father." She did, and it was settled: I was going to college. Given that my parents had only elementary school educations, this was a big step for me, and for them.

A few days later I sought more information. A list of college majors on a form in the school guidance office piqued my interest. What would be my major in college? I recognized "social work" and thought that might be interesting since I cared about helping people in need. The word *sociology* followed. What's that? I wondered. At home, I looked up "sociology" in my dictionary. Attracted by the emphasis on social behavior in face-to-face interaction, relationships, and groups, I decided that was what I wanted to study. I never wavered from that decision, even when, in graduate school, sociology turned out to be something different from what I expected.

Getting an Education

I left home in 1969 to go 150 miles away to the College of William and Mary, where I had gained early admission. My situation with Grady had shown me ways to think other than the small-town values instilled in me from childhood. I anticipated more change once I left home. But initially the foreign atmosphere of a college campus led me to hold on to my familiar small-town values. I went to church every Sunday and kept "deviant" activities, consisting of drinking alcohol a few times and staying out late, to a bare minimum. I spent most free time in the library studying, committed to doing well in this competitive environment.

Having been an all-A student in an undemanding high school, I was not prepared for the rigors of college. In the middle of the first semester, I called my mother, crying, because I had gotten 26 (out of a possible 100) points on my first biology test. Sympathetic and protective, she said, "Don't worry. You'll just come home." This made me feel better, though I already knew there was no coming home in spite of the difficulties. Already, I was hooked on learning and on the excitement and freedom the college atmosphere provided.

By the time I was a senior, I had figured out how to do well in college and was no longer intimidated. After taking a course in world religions, I had stopped believing in religion and the Christian God (and announced it to my family). If one religion made as much sense as the other, then perhaps none of them made sense. I had broken up with my high school boyfriend, whom I had continued to date for another year in college, tried out a number of relationships, and experimented with drugs. Taking seriously the social construction of reality I learned in sociology classes, I was on a mission to reconstruct myself, which meant moving as far away from small-town values as I could.

Because of my experience with Grady, I chose race relations as my concentration. In my first course in sociology of race, my professor, who was from Japan, taught the demography of Black-White relations with graphs and statistics. I lost interest quickly. Even a readings course in the "Black Family" couldn't renew my passion after my plunge into demography, which ignored the heart, soul, and lived experience of race.

None of that got in the way of my desire to major in sociology, and I took the maximum number of sociology classes allowed by the university. Because of my interest in "helping people," therapy, and the individual, I also took psychology classes. But I couldn't find myself—indeed, I couldn't find people in general—in the experimental labs, rat mazes, and behaviorist theory I was introduced to in psychology classes. I don't recall anyone in my psychology classes ever talking about helping anybody.

But some of the sociology classes spoke to me. Early on, I found social psychology and was introduced to writers like Erving Goffman (1959, 1967, 1971, 1974), who excelled in describing the surface and deeper structures of what people do and say in everyday public interaction. Along with countless other wannabe sociologists, from the time I read Goffman's *Presentation of Self in Everyday Life*, I was mesmerized by his insights and hoped I had a Goffmanian eye. Goffman's work gave me a new way of seeing both others and myself. It wasn't until much later that I would grow critical of aspects of Goffman's perspective, especially how his distanced-observer focus privileging the view of the beholder of social life neglected the self-identification and subjectivity of the person being watched.[1]

Having been exposed, albeit briefly, to ethnographic study in my sociology classes, I quickly decided this was the kind of approach I wanted to take. To be with people, watching and participating in their lived experiences, seemed preferable to a statistical or textual study. In search of a real-world situation in which to practice my sociological eye, I chose to study an isolated fishing community in the Chesapeake Bay, which I called Fishneck, for my undergraduate honor's work. There I concentrated on how isolation impacted community members' lives and values. I would continue this study for my M.A. thesis and Ph.D. dissertation later in graduate school.

Before graduate school, I spent a year as a social worker in Virginia. As I had thought, I liked helping people and thought I was pretty good at it, but the bureaucratic structure and workload, plus the demands of being at work from eight to five, dampened my enthusiasm considerably. Missing academia, I applied to SUNY at Stony Brook, hoping to study social psychology with Gene Weinstein. I knew of Gene's work from Larry Beckhouse, one of my professors at William and Mary and one of Gene's former students. For me, Gene's work on altercasting, presentation of self, and interpersonal competence epitomized a Goffmanian eye (Weinstein, 1969; Weinstein & Deutschberger, 1963).

Once again, the transition was difficult. The contrast between the worldly experience of social work and the abstract discourse I encountered in my graduate classes at Stony Brook in 1974 was hard to reconcile. I learned early on that my sentiment that sociology should "help people" was best left unexpressed publicly. My socialization "took," and soon I shared the hierarchical notion that it was important to separate sociologists (the knowers) from social workers (the doers). Still I continued to wonder whether sociology shouldn't strive to open people's eyes to the world and assist us in living better lives. For the most part, I could not connect my life to what was being taught in classes. How could those outside this academic tribe connect their lives to what we were doing? The reality was that few scholars included connection to lived life as one of their goals.

By the time I got to graduate school at Stony Brook, I had made a break from small-town life. I became an "experience junkie," wanting to try everything that had been unavailable to me in Luray. I collected other people's life experiences as comparison points. I celebrated being different from those in my hometown community, who became "other" to me (Ellis, 1995b). The social and political climate of the 1970s made "being different" a relatively easy task, though it encouraged college students to be like each other.

I wanted to blend in with other students, who came from many locations and had led lives different from mine. Like them, I wore the outfit of the day—faded, tight bell-bottomed (the more belled the better) blue jeans, preferably bought from an Army/Navy store; accessorized with a drab tee-shirt or nondescript sweatshirt, army-green cloth backpack, and, of course, leather work boots; all accentuated by my long and straight, stringy blond hair with a paisley bandana tied around my forehead. The image was completed with the constant presence of my second rat terrier, Poogie, who was always at my side, inside and outside of classes.

The students formed a subculture and, for the most part, shared values as well, values that were not always consistent—the importance of education and career, living a meaningful and authentic life, doing one's thing and letting it all hang out, telling it like it was, and participating in a youth movement that included sex, drugs, and radical politics.

As frequently happens when working-class youth go to college, I felt alienated from my past and became someone my parents hardly recognized (Rodriguez, 1983; see also Casey, 2005). Upset by my changes—in religious values, the way I talked, my dress and appearance—my mother viewed my unshaven armpits and hairy legs as signs of my final demise. After reprimanding me for my "unclean" ways, she told me, "You're just like that Patty Hearst." Most likely, my family felt similarly to the working-class mother of academic Carolyn Leste Law, who said, "Education destroys something" (Law, 1995, p. 1; Casey, 2005). I went home regularly to visit my parents and stayed in touch by phone, but I kept myself removed, more concerned about how I was feeling than about what they might be going through. My life revolved around graduate school, not my family and hometown community. I was determined to shed my small-town, southern influences.

Still, similar to the experience of other working-class college students, graduate school in some ways continued to be a foreign environment to me (Lubrano, 2004). I was intimidated by the elite intellectual repartee I encountered there, which celebrated abstract thinking and knowledge of macro-political issues. I did not have a developed academic vocabulary in which to express myself, nor was I knowledgeable about political issues. I also was not accustomed to calling on higher authorities as I talked: "Marx said . . ." "According to Weber . . . or Durkheim . . . or Simmel . . ." "In the *New York Review of Books* . . ."

The only higher authority we had called on as I was growing up had been God (in church), and occasionally my father (when I was in trouble). Instead, I was accustomed to calling on my feelings and everyday experiences, and comparing them to the experiences of those around me, whom I always watched carefully, especially if they were different from me. Given my background, people around me in graduate school often seemed different (though we wore the same clothes and professed the same values), so I never lacked for things to watch.

I felt I had to learn to think and talk like other academics if I wanted to be a full member of this tribe (see Philipsen, 1975). Parallel to trying to fit in with my peer group and rebel against those "over thirty," I now tried desperately to speak like the professors I admired in this Long Island university setting, many of whom were Jewish intellectuals and all over thirty. With my dictionary, and sometimes with close friends, I practiced saying unfamiliar words. In front of the mirror, I rehearsed speaking without the heavy southern accent I had carried from small-town Virginia to Long Island—the accent that always reappeared when I talked to my relatives over the phone. I practiced interrupting aggressively yet politely and speaking assertively. I worked hard to develop a voice that clearly articulated ideas, if not always the sounds I heard. It was only later that I realized that having a lisp in addition to a southern accent also contributed to the problems I had speaking like an "intellectual" and fitting in (see Ellis, 1998; see also Chapter 10).

Writing a Dissertation

For my dissertation, I compared Fishneck, the community I studied as an undergraduate, to Crab Reef, a fishing community in the Chesapeake Bay (Ellis, 1986). Ethnographic participant observation allowed me to live with the people I studied and to participate in, observe, and describe their day-to-day lives. While in the communities, however, I often experienced conflict between remaining uninvolved and distant, as I had been taught in methods classes, and participating fully; between recording only my "objective" observations of the Fisher Folk's actions and speech and noting my sense of their emotional lives, a process that required my engagement. Often distance won out over involvement because of my concern about meeting the requirements of neutrality and objectivity I had learned in my graduate education.

When I returned to the university to write my dissertation, I struggled with the constraints of detached social science prose and the demand to write theoretically in an authoritative and uninvolved voice. I thought I had to write this way to be considered an academic. Yet this kind of thinking and writing did not come naturally to me. I struggled to organize my dissertation around "legitimate" sociological topics—social structure, family, work, and social change. Within this framework, I discussed "hard" sociological concepts, such as personal attachment, locus of social control, reciprocity, public conformity, civic status, individualism, communitarianism, center, and periphery. I found it difficult to capture the complexity of the lives of the Fisher Folk using these categories, and I often felt unsure of the distinctions I was forced to make.

Though I was probably more visible as a character in my study than were authors in most ethnographic texts of that time period, I still largely described "them," the Fisher Folk, interacting with each other, as though I were off in a corner, invisible. In reality, most of what I learned came through my interactions with the people, especially their reactions to me. But those exchanges and the effects my presence might have had on what the Fisher Folk said and did took a backseat. I anguished over speaking too often in the first person, having been told it was "unprofessional" and that readers would then conclude I had not been neutral and distant (see Krieger, 1991).

In my dissertation, I rarely talked about how I felt. I was reluctant to admit how much my own emotional experiences in the communities influenced what I saw and how I framed my study theoretically in terms of "tight" and "loose" communities (Pelto, 1968). For example, I carefully watched how I comported myself in Crab Reef, which was under tight community control, and I felt much freer in Fishneck, which was managed more by family and personal loyalty.

Even during this research, however, I was drawn to stories for conveying lived experience and insisted on inserting vignettes showing specific incidents. In these stories, I could occasionally be present, though I rarely got to speak and almost never showed how I felt. But I knew, even then, that I wanted readers to hear the participants' voices and see them acting. The vignettes breathed life into my more passive telling and categorizing of the Fisher Folk.[2]

Fisher Folk: Two Communities on Chesapeake Bay[3]

The narratives that follow include some of the stories that I interspersed among the theoretical prose, authoritative voice, and distanced descriptions of common characteristics and typical patterns in *Fisher Folk*, the book I published from my dissertation.

Vignette One

The first vignette is an example of stories that demonstrated conceptual ideas. I asked the question: how can values of individualism and communitarianism exist side by side in this community? In this story I show informal mechanisms of work control that functioned to inhibit achievement differences and invidiousness and managed the more visible aspects of competitiveness, yet also allowed the sense of individual achievement and success to flourish. While it is apparent that I am present in the story, I do not include myself as a character.

Generational differences, observed in other fishing studies, were associated with varying acceptable minimum work levels. Younger men said they resented feeling that they were expected to live up to the standards of the older men, who sometimes went out earlier and stayed longer than they did: "Yeah, he and them others stay out just on a chance. And they act like you're common if you don't too. They don't know how to enjoy themselves. They think having a good time is going to church." As a result, young men sometimes tried to convince other watermen that they should go in before the end of the day if the weather was bad or if they were not catching much. If a group could be convinced to quit early, it legitimated breaking of normal working hours. But unless one was willing to risk criticism, he never went in alone. The following was a typical way of ending work early:

"Hey, John [over the CB]. Are you catching anything?"

"Me neither. Want to go in after two more 'licks' and have a beer?"

"Okay. See how Larry feels." (After this exchange, a small group started for the island and the bulk of the fleet followed.)[4]

Vignette Two

The second story elaborates on an attitude or practice. In this case, it shows community members' attitudes toward marriage. Though I am a character, I appear as a researcher watching and asking questions rather than as a full participant.

One Saturday I went to visit a family and found the son, age twenty, hanging out at the dock drinking beer with some friends. He was more dressed up than usual for a Saturday afternoon. When I asked why, he replied, "I got married today." "Where's your wife?" I asked. "Over at her ma's," he said nonchalantly and continued talking with his friends about various topics. No one seemed concerned. There was no celebration, no honeymoon—just the usual Saturday-afternoon beer drinking. The ceremony had been simple. He and his wife had gone to the small church nearby, where almost all Fishneck marriages take place. Only the preacher and two witnesses were present. Many married people related similar experiences: "We didn't tell anyone. Just did it one day," related two thirty-year-old women, both of whom had been married for over fifteen years.[5]

Vignette Three

The third story shows a scene where I become a full participant in community activities, this time clamming. Here the scene is expanded and the description is rich and active.

"What are they doing?" I asked Michael Paul, a waterman who was taking me in his skiff to Net Island, part of the isolated fishing culture I was studying. Nine men, women, and children stood in the water together. Some of the women had on dresses and carried baskets tied to their waists.

"They're rakin' clams," he said, calling me "foolish" (a term of endearment) for not knowing.

"Tell me how," I asked.

"Well, you gits in the water as fur up as your waist. Tie a basket 'round you in the middle. Then you take a clam rake and dig for the clams. If you's really good, you can flip them up with the rake or your toes, but some has to bend over to git them. Can make a lot of money that way."

The next day I met Michael Paul and a thirteen-year-old boy named Jimmy James, who wanted to show me "a better way to clam—treadin.'"

Jimmy James said, "Git ya' on me back, doll. I'll tote you to the skiff so's you don't git yer feet wet."

After Jimmy James deposited me into his skiff, he drove the boat to a shallow area and all of us jumped overboard (including Michael Paul, who was sixty-three years old) and held onto the side of the boat. We were in water about waist-deep and sometimes deeper (I didn't call this shallow!), and dug into the bottom with our feet, hoping to find the prized clams. (Actually I was hoping that I wouldn't find a broken bottle.) It was a contest to see who could find the most and the "biggest one that ever has been." The person who came up with a rock instead had to suffer laughter from others. They tried to teach me to toss the clams with my feet, but I finally decided I preferred bending over to retrieve them, since I was already wet.

We clammed about an hour. Jimmy James found 120 clams, Michael Paul retrieved 60, and I got 30. "Not bad for you," they reassured me. We had 210 clams, which we could sell for $3^1/_2$ cents each or $7.35. Not much for three people, I thought.[6]

Though this last kind of vignette did not occur often in the text, in hindsight it seems to capture my experience in Fishneck and make the Fisher Folk come alive. This kind of scenic writing in which I observe myself in interaction with community members helps demonstrate and open up the more abstract prose with which I described the organization of and change in this isolated community. It also foreshadows the direction my writing would take in the years to come.

Publishing this book in the fifth year of my employment as an assistant professor at University of South Florida in Tampa and getting positive responses and reviews pretty much guaranteed me tenure and freed me to follow my heart and write personally and emotionally in the next project on which I already was working. *Final Negotiations: A Story of Love, Loss, and Chronic Illness* told a story of my relationship with my first husband, Gene Weinstein, and how we coped with his declining health, illness, and dying. Though I was immersed in living that story from 1975 through 1984 and writing about it from 1984 through 1994, issues involved in the writing and publishing of *Fisher Folk* continued to reverberate. It was during this time that I began to intuit how much there was to learn from this study—about the Fisher Folk, about practice and ethics in ethnography, about the relational entanglements between ethnographers and the communities they study, and about my own life.

Emotional and Ethical Quagmires in Returning to the Field[7]

In April 1989, I returned to Fishneck after not having been there for a few years. Though *Fisher Folk: Two Communities on Chesapeake Bay* (Ellis, 1986) had been published in 1986, I did not initially give the people in Fishneck a copy of my book and, without thinking much about it, doubted they would ever know what was in it since most people there did not read. But a few months before my visit, a former professor of mine from the College of William and Mary, who was working on a book on the region and was upset that I had published my book, copied and highlighted some particularly uncomplimentary sections and read them to the Fishneckers.[8] I planned this visit to talk with the people there about the book. I worried how they would respond to some of the private and unflattering things I had written about them.

Here's what happened.

The Return Visit: April 1989[9]

When I arrive at Michael Paul's trailer, I slowly get out of my car and glance around at the usual array of hound dogs guarding the entryway. Michael Paul, in his seventies now, had been my main informant. I remember with fondness his wife who had died, and one of his children who had been shot and killed. I think of the many days I have spent at his house, eating meals, holding infants, planning activities, and conversing in many directions at once from the middle of crossfire conversations.

Knocking loudly on the door, I yell, "Michael Paul, it's Carolyn." The whole neighborhood seems unusually quiet. I guess nobody is home at any of the trailers huddled at the end of this oyster-shell road that looks too narrow and rutted to lead anywhere, except further into the marsh. I dismiss the thought that the Fishneckers might be treating me now as they do strangers—by disappearing from view and remaining silent.

Because nobody is around, I take pictures. I intend to capture change from what this area was like many years ago, although the scene's familiarity disputes the time passing. Exploring the litter-strewn yard, I note the new built-on room attached to the middle trailer and walk toward the hastily constructed and jury-rigged pigpens out back. I feel surprisingly uncomfortable, as though I'm sneaking around and don't belong here. Not knowing how people feel about me now makes me nervous. Hoping that nobody has seen me "snooping" around, I put away my camera and sit on my car hood. My feelings provide a vivid reminder of my dual roles of researcher and friend. That I would risk taking pictures now, after what has happened, saddens me as it reminds me of which role was, and apparently still is, most important.

Suddenly Michael Paul's daughter-in-law, Mimi, a twenty-five-year-old woman I have known since she was a child, appears. Apprehensively, I watch her approach from an old trailer I hadn't noticed hidden by the tall grass behind Michael Paul's. "Cawl, I'll take you to see Michael Paul. He's at the trailer park," Mimi greets me warmly.

"Mimi, great to see you."

"You too, Cawl," she says shyly, pronouncing my name in the Fishneck dialect. Once in my car, she says, "You wrote a book, didn't you?"

"Yeah, why?" I hold my breath.

"Some people don't like it."

"You?"

"Not me child. I don't care what's in no book." Feeling let off the hook, I release my breath. We drive down the familiar road to the trailer park, where one of Michael Paul's sons lives. As soon as I blow the horn, Michael Paul opens the door to the trailer to greet me. Others follow him out.

"It's Cawl," I hear someone say excitedly.

"Hi, Cawl. Where ya' been? How long ya' gonna' stay? I told them you was a comin' today." The questions come all at once.

"How'd you know it was today?" I ask.

"I felt it in my bones," Michael Paul answers.

"Gal, you married yet?" I smile at the question that Michael Paul always asks, and then give my usual reply, "You know better than that. I'm not the marrying kind." It's too complicated to explain that I was married for a short while until my husband died. They wouldn't understand why I married a fatally ill man. Why bring it up now? Still I feel a twinge at blatantly lying.

"I'm still runnin' women," Michael Paul announces proudly.

"That's good, you keep it up," I say, again giving a well-practiced reply.

When Michael Paul's daughter-in-law, whom I don't know well, immediately asks, "Did you write a book?" I realize that my book probably is being talked about by the larger community, not just in isolated pockets. Knowing that she has a sixth-grade education stimulates me to think about how many people here are able to read.

Taking a deep breath, I ask, "Yes, what do you think about it?" I hope I'm ready for the answer.

"Don't know. Ain't seen it yet."

"I'll send you a copy," I say, not knowing how else to respond. Thinking about her reading it makes me feel anxious as I recall some of the personal topics I discuss.

Seeing no reason to avoid the issue, in the car I ask Michael Paul, "What do you think about the book?"

"Write anything you want, child," he says lovingly. Yet, I detect a little distance. Is this because I haven't seen him for so long? Or is he upset too?

"Make it as common as you want," Michael Paul continues. I am jolted by the word "common," which to the Fishneckers always means vulgar.

Softly, Michael Paul continues, "I'll tell you even more things to put in. It don't matter. Professor Jack is doing all this, keeping it all stirred up. He brung some of the book to Minnie and Betty and gave some pages of it to a many others."

"Could they read it?"

"He marked parts, then read it to them over and over and said how mad he was about it."

"What did you think of what he read?"

"I laughed, and he told me it weren't nothing to laugh at. I said I thought it was. I told him that what you wrote was true. I'd heard those stories too."

Wondering what he had read, I try to explain. "Michael Paul, he's only reading a small part of the book. I don't use real names, and I call the place Fishneck."

"That's right," he replies. "Don't you mind now, gal."

• • •

After visiting several people there and getting some friendly responses and some not so friendly, I go to visit Michael Paul's daughter, Minnie. I don't want to avoid her, a common practice in Fishneck when you are upset at someone. I want to know how much emotional damage has been done to her and to our relationship.

On the way I run into Ada, a younger sister who lives with Minnie. "You wrote all kinds of things in that book," she suddenly blurts out angrily.

I am shocked at the confrontation. "Yes, but I didn't identify anybody or the community," I say, feeling like an impostor who has been caught.

"I know all those names though," she replies. My strategy of inventing pseudonyms starting with the same letters as the double names of the Fishneckers and having other similarities in sound had made it easy to keep names straight, but at the cost of making it convenient for Fishneckers to figure out the characters in my story.

"Is Minnie mad?"

"She don't like what you wrote," Ada replies, as I take a deep breath and knock on Minnie's door.

Minnie tells me to come in, but she doesn't get up to greet me. She looks down at her photocopied pages of my book on the table, as she says, "That was a lot of nonsense you wrote. I know you was a writin' 'bout me."

I sit down and pick up the manuscript, eager to see what is outlined in yellow marker. My quick breathing reveals my anxiety as I read silently a passage I have quoted in *Fisher Folk*:

> Two strange boys carried us home and were going to do it to us. I was on the back with one. He unzipped my pants and tried to put what he had in my hand. I screamed and was scared. (Ellis, 1986, p. 25)

I flip through a few pages and the highlighted text glares at me:

> As late as 1978, I asked a woman how she kept from getting pregnant since she said the pill made her sick and gave her a headache. She replied, "I's goes to the bathroom right after I have been with a man. Piss the baby out. Doctor said that's the best thing to do." (Ellis, 1986, p. 28)

I stop reading. Having no idea what to say, I revert to rationality. "How do you know this is about you?"

"Cause you're the only one who could a known that story about us goin' out with boys. Now everybody will know it was us. And it weren't even true. I just told you that mess of stuff."

I wonder now what is the truth and why they would only have told the story to me. I ask, "But if I didn't use your names and it's not true, how will they know it's you I'm writing about?"

"They'll know," she says confidently. "And I didn't say the doctor said to piss the baby out either. I said the doctor told me to piss after I have sex. I thought we was friends, you and me, just talkin.' I didn't think you would put it in no book."

"But I told people down here I was writing a book," I reply feebly.

"But I still thought we was just talkin.' And you said we're dirty and don't know how to dress.

I turn the pages and see:

> Most Fishneck women wore pants and often knee-length rubber boots and layers of unmatched clothing. . . . By age eighteen, many of them weighed two hundred pounds or more. (Ellis, 1986, p. 14)

> Scarcity of plumbing meant baths were infrequent. That combined with everyday work with fish produced a characteristic fishy body odor, identified by outsiders as the "fishneck smell." (Ellis, 1986, p. 14)

The contradiction of caring about these people and knowing they are aware of my descriptions makes me feel sick to my stomach. Understanding now that I have no defense that makes sense in Fishneck, I close the pages. My God, what else did I say? I wonder, as I view these words now through Minnie's eyes.

"You said ten-year-olds were having sex," Minnie continues, answering my unspoken question, now in full gear. "The Island people, you said. Made us sound like whores. I never did it 'til I was 21. I'm not a whore."

"I'm sorry," I reply sadly, head hanging. No longer do I have the desire to defend what I have written. "I understand what you're saying. I shouldn't have said some of those things. If I could do it over, I wouldn't say them. Can I make it up to you?" My words sound as hollow as I feel.

"No, it's already here now," she says, banging on the page. "Burn the book," someone quietly suggests from the background. For a second, I think that might be a solution. We would burn the book together. Good riddance, be done with it.

"But then there are still others," Minnie says.

"You're the only one who knows who I'm writing about," I try again, anything to get out of this psychological space, where I am caught in the trap I have created.

"But that's the point. We know. People say things."

"I care about you," I say, tired of rational argument.

"Well, I did you too. Still do, but you shouldn't a done this." The "did" resonates through my head.

"I said many good things about a lot of people, but Professor Jack didn't read you those."

She continues, "Professor Jack said he was gonna' publish a book and get us all to sign it and say it was right. I ain't gonna' do that. I told him he better not publish anything. I'll get my lawyer if my name is in his book. It's my life, not anybody else's business. Weren't yours, neither."

"I'm sorry," I say, as I get up to go, feeling unwelcome for the first time in the seventeen years I have been coming to Fishneck.

When I glance from face to face, no one meets my eyes. I walk quietly out the screen door, being careful to return it to its proper place on broken hinges.

"Come back, anytime," Minnie suddenly yells out the door.

"Thanks," I say, and look back to see her for the first time looking at me. I am relieved that she still wants to see me, but I doubt if our relationship will ever be the same.

As I drive back to Michael Paul's, I am too shaken up to observe as a fieldworker. With the lack of dual roles comes an unfamiliar feeling of authenticity. My compartmentalization of roles finally has broken down and I am "myself" in this community, simultaneously experiencing self and relationships in all the complexity and ambiguity that authenticity is supposed to entail. I wonder if I have ever felt that way in this community before. Did I feel it when I attended funerals or helped with disasters? Or was I more the distant observer than active participant even then?

After visiting with Michael Paul a while, I say, "Well, I guess I have to go see Betty." Michael Paul's daughter-in-law Betty is often angry, given to yelling and holding grudges, but she and I have known each other for seventeen years and I have never been the object of her anger before.

"Do what you have to, child," Michael Paul says softly, resignedly shaking his head. He often has been the object of her wrath.

Although I want to leave Fishneck now, I feel obligated to face Betty, with whom I have shared meals and friendship. Betty is hanging up clothes in her backyard next door. Instead of returning my hello as I approach, she shouts at the top of her voice, "You wrote that damn mess. I don't want anything to do with you."

Although I expect anger, the fury in her words is mind-boggling. "You've only seen part of it," I say, still determined to make amends.

"I've seen enough. Forty-foot scrapes? Whoever heard tell?"

"Well, I don't know everything. I'd like you to read the book and tell me where I was wrong." My heart pounds, but I feel I have given a good response. It is easier to react to factual errors than emotionally painful descriptions.

"You wrote the book. You're supposed to know. Six hundred people in Fishneck. Where do you think Fishneck starts?"

"Where are the boundaries, Betty? That's a good question," I say, thinking about my discussion of that issue in the book.

"At Benton."

"That's not where I placed the boundaries."

"Then you're wrong."

"Betty, you know if you ask ten people here, you'll get ten different answers to that question."

"You should know the right one," she says bitterly. "You wrote the book. A hundred and fifty houses? You said you was in 150 houses. You ain't been in no 150 houses."

"That's not what I said. I said there were 150 households in Fishneck." I think that Betty still may be right—that I probably did overestimate the number of people I knew in Fishneck.

"You snuck around writin' this book and didn't tell us."

"I did tell many of you."

"Well, not me."

"I'm sorry. I thought you knew."

"You just saw the chance to make money off us and you took it."

"Hum," I chuckle, grunt, and sigh at the same time, rolling my eyes back and tossing my head. "Betty, that's not true. I haven't made a cent and I never will." But she's right in that I used them as an opportunity to advance my career.

"You said all ten-year-olds had screwed."

"No, I didn't," I reply adamantly.

"Such common talk. I didn't know you was like that. Did you screw at ten?" When I don't reply, she demands, "Answer me, did you?"

When I say no, she continues, "Okay, see. Would you want someone writin' this about you?"

"No. But I didn't say everybody had sex at age ten."

"I can show you where you wrote it," she shouts.

"Okay show me." Now I am yelling as loudly as Betty. I follow her as she marches ferociously to her trailer. I didn't write that, did I?

Betty picks up a photocopy similar to the one Minnie had and gestures toward a marked paragraph, "There."

I read the paragraph out loud, triumphantly. It is a description of the geography of the community. "What's wrong with that?" I ask, wondering why this passage is highlighted.

"Plenty," she says. "And you also said everybody screwed at ten."

"Show me," I demand.

She hesitates, flips through the pages. I wait, ready to pounce. "Well, I would if my daughter Amy were at home," she says, now looking embarrassed. Through my anger, I realize—Betty can't read. This simple fact sadly takes away my desire to win the battle, as I think of the advantage I have.

"I might not have the education of you," Betty continues, throwing the manuscript on the table, "but I got common sense."

"I know you do, Betty," I say softly. "I would never say you weren't bright. You know a lot more about many things than I do."

"And I always treated you right. And my daughter is graduating from high school."

"I know. I'm proud of her," I respond. Our mutual celebration is short-lived.

"I don't want you steppin' foot in my trailer again." Betty's voice is still loud and shrill. "You can come see Michael Paul. I have nothin' to do with that. But not here."

When I see tears gather in her eyes, I feel there is still hope. At that moment I understand that I have caused her pain. "I thought we were friends. Can't we still be friends?" I ask. "I care about you."

"I thought we was friends too, but that's over." Both voices are quiet now.

"You won't reconsider?" She shakes her head no. "So there's nothing I can do? You're going to throw a seventeen-year relationship down the drain?" I feel tears form in my eyes. I try to stop them, because I don't want Betty to feel she has gotten the best of me. Being emotional also is not part of my perceived role of researcher. Then deciding that I want her to know I care, that this is a real relationship, a personal one, and that it's okay if she brags later about how she won, I let a few tears fall before blinking them back. I am not surprised when it doesn't work.

"It's over."

"Does your husband feel this way too?"

"I don't control him."

Of course, you don't, I think as I recall how he rarely does anything without her approval. I walk out of the trailer, head down; Betty doesn't call me back. I say hello to her husband, Bob, who gives me a half wave, hoping, I'm sure, that Betty doesn't notice.

"She was really mad, Michael Paul," I say, as I enter his trailer. My tears start to flow, and this time I can't stop them. "I never meant to hurt anyone," I say.

"I know, child," he says, and then sits quietly. I realize he has never seen me upset and doesn't know what to do. Our relationship has always been positive, upbeat, and bantering.

I work to stop crying, just as a young boy arrives to tell me that his mother, Sandy Jill, another of Michael Paul's daughters, wants me to come over. I am careful to go around the back way so that I do not walk across Betty's property. I'm feeling too fragile to deal with her now. "Are you mad at me, too?" I ask as I enter Sandy Jill's trailer.

"Shit, I don't care what you wrote. They told you that stuff—I've heard those stories too—and then they got pissed because you wrote it." She turns to her husband and says proudly, "You should a seen Cawl. She was a yellin' just as loud as Betty. And pointin' her finger at her and shakin' it just like Betty was." Sandy Jill demonstrates. "I loved it. She really stood up to her."

I puff up and feel brave. A moment later, I want to cry again because I have hurt people I care about, and now I hurt as well. . . .

Keeping in Touch

A few months later, I received several letters from Minnie, written by her daughter. One read in part:

> I am sorry for the way I acted that day you come to my home. I hope you can forgive
> me. I also hope we can remain friends. . . . I hope that you will write me back and

forgive me for what I said. . . . Please consider my words I have written I am sorry. Your friend, Minnie

These letters gave me back my "face" (Goffman, 1967) and provided an opportunity for me to give them back theirs—the face of loyal and deserving close friends. I responded immediately with a letter expressing my apologies and several gifts for the families of Mary Jane and Minnie. Mary Jane and other Fishneckers continued to write occasionally. I never heard from Betty again.

I returned to Fishneck in 1991, that time taking my mother and my partner, Art, with me. Betty and her family had moved, and I was glad not to have to see her. Mary Jane and Michael Paul welcomed me as usual. So did Minnie, and I went out of my way to make sure I had some time with her. The quick contact—we stayed only a few hours—and being in Fishneck with my mother and Art reminded me of how much an outsider I was. I lived in a radically different world from the Fishneckers, although theirs continued to have a haunting familiarity.

After we left Fishneck, Art asked if I had noticed the only picture in Michael Paul's trailer. The photograph that had hung on his wall since 1972 immediately came to mind— a picture of Michael Paul and me riding in the back of an old skiff. His arm is draped around me, and we are both laughing. Recalling this picture reminded me of how much I *had* been a part of the Fishneck community.

In July 1993, while working on this story, I called Minnie and Mary Jane, whom I had not talked to for two years. After many wrong numbers, I feared I had lost contact for good. When I finally reached Mary Jane, the excitement I heard in her voice was matched only by my glee at connecting with her. Minnie immediately took the phone to tell me about a personal trauma in her life. She was still suffering, she said, and she really wanted me to know what happened. I hurt for her and wanted to be with her, to comfort her as she told me about her pain. As Minnie and Mary Jane shared the joys—new babies and marriages—and sorrows—poverty, sickness, and death—in their lives, I wondered how much more authentic relationships get. I made sure to tell them some of the intimate details of my life—that I was living with Art, that we might get married. Perhaps that had always been where their feelings of deception and my feelings of inauthenticity lay—in the one-sided revelations. I became excited as I made plans to visit them, thinking that I would ask questions about mothering, loss, and creating meaning—they certainly had enough experience in these areas. This time I would have these conversations because I cared about their lives, to feel close to them, and to relate their answers to my own personal life, not so I could write a book.

* * *

In the years that followed, I sent money and gifts on holidays, and flowers and cards for funerals. I talked on the phone regularly to Minnie and kept up with her life, but Mary Jane and I lost touch. My last visit was in the mid-nineties and then I spent time only with Minnie's family. When Minnie died in 2006, thirty-two years after I began my study in Fishneck, I felt the loss of my closest tie in Fishneck. Though Minnie's husband and grown children encouraged me to visit again and Fishneck continues to occupy a place in my heart, I haven't returned.

Meta-Autoethnography: Questioning Ethics[10]

In this ethnographic story about my return to Fishneck, I became a full participant, and an acting *and* feeling character. I explored the issues and emotions that my research has raised by showing my interactions with community members, including what we did with and said to each other. In that way, I hoped to bring the reader into our conflicts and emotions and let them experience firsthand the ethical issues that arose in the situation. As I'll discuss in the next chapter, I had begun writing personal narratives about losses in my life in 1986, so it was an easy step to merge that kind of writing with my ethnographic study of the Fisher Folk in this piece on returning to the field.

My return to Fishneck raised questions about the way I had conducted the study and about some of the ways ethnography was being done and taught at this time. What do we owe those we study? I asked. How should we treat them? How much do they have a right to know about us, both our personal lives and what we are doing in their lives? Are there ways to write about people that honor and empower them (Richardson, 1992b) rather than "other" them as exotic, overemphasize their differences, make them appear less than us? How can we best follow Michelle Fine's (1994) advice to "work the hyphen" in our studies to "probe how we are in relation with the contexts we study and with our informants," honor blurred boundaries rather than build concrete ones, respect contradictions rather than reify patterns, study self in relationship with them rather than white out any evidence that we were there as feeling participants, learning about ourselves as we learned about them (p. 72)?

My concern with these issues no doubt influenced my narrative writing in all future projects. Though my book on Fishneck made a contribution to the study of organization and change in isolated communities, the story I had to tell would have been very different if I had indulged my intellectual strengths: those concerning emotionality, lived experience, close relationships, sense-making, and creating a meaningful life. Of course, my awareness and examination of patterns, categories, and macroscopic processes in this community helped make my sociological eye deeper and better. Still, I believe I would have made different ethical decisions if I had viewed research then as relational, rather than a project to be accomplished. As painful as it was, returning to the field helped me better understand what was at stake ethically and personally in research, and made it possible for me to become a better ethnographer and teacher of ethnographic practice.

But my ethical story doesn't end here; looking back now, I understand that this story was only the beginning. The same kinds of dilemmas would arise in writing and teaching autoethnography and also later in my return to community ethnography to write the conclusion to this book.

Meta-Autoethnography: Rural Like Me

Writing this story helped me see how much my relationship with my family and small mountain town had influenced my attraction to the Fishneckers as well as how I saw the people there. My upbringing in the Blue Ridge Mountains undoubtedly increased the intrigue I felt regarding the isolated lifestyle of the Fisher Folk and their abbreviated relationship with the rest of the world. How did Fishneckers manage to maintain their isolation? What did they think and feel when they confronted how different they were from people in the surrounding areas or those they saw on television? What did they hope for or dream about? How did they make their lives feel meaningful?

I had similar questions about my own life as I moved from a comfortable and homogeneous small town to the competitive atmosphere of William and Mary, and then to the ethnically diverse wilds of Stony Brook for my Ph.D. Fishneck provided a safe situation to explore adaptation to changes that had similarities to those occurring in my own life. Fishneck provided a place to think about how I was "unlike" those in the mountain community in which I had been raised and "unlike" those in the fishing community, which had a much more tenuous relationship to mainstream America than even the mountain community of my childhood. I didn't reveal these personal interests to the Fishneckers and I had only a hint, at the time, of the connection of this study to my own experience.

Just as I wished I had let myself be more connected to the Fisher Folk, later I would wish I had not been so intent for so long on maintaining emotional and cognitive distance from my family upbringing. Just as I returned to the Fisher Folk more interested in what I could learn from them, later in life, I would return home to Luray much more interested in and engaged by the life I had lived there. Though

I always cared about and kept in touch with family, the symbolic "return" would occur as I coped with the death of my parents, and it would culminate in 2003 when my partner Art and I built a summer home in another small, rural, mountain community located in the same mountain range where I was born.

But before that happened, I still had to finish graduate school, where I would begin a romantic relationship that would have a profound impact on my life and later my work.

PART TWO

Becoming an
Autoethnographer

CHAPTER FOUR

Reliving *Final Negotiations*

While a graduate student at Stony Brook, I began a romantic relationship with Gene Weinstein, the sociology professor I had gone to graduate school to study with. Our relationship was complicated by his illness—he had emphysema—and our status differences, yet it lasted until he died nine years later.[1] One of the many attractions of the relationship was the sociological discussions we had around Gene's kitchen table about social psychology. He and I also spent many hours each week talking about his illness, our relationship, and their intersection, as well as probing emotions and other aspects of sociological inquiry. I was mesmerized by the stories we shared and examined, and the insights I thought we had about emotions. But when I left the kitchen table and went to classes, I encountered a different conversation. The graduate curriculum revolved around building theory, thinking abstractly, and synthesizing the results of empirical studies. I soon learned that sociology was not about personal stories and feelings, but rather it focused on theorizing, generalizing, and manipulating variables.

I finished my dissertation on the fishing communities in 1981, and that same year, I began an academic appointment at University of South Florida. In 1982, Gene came to Florida to live with me, first on a sabbatical, then on sick leave, and finally he retired there. We married on December 25, 1984, while he was in the hospital, where he died on February 8, 1985, during a return visit.

When Gene first arrived in Tampa, we began to work together on a paper on jealousy. Both of us desired to bring the study of emotion into sociology's rational studies of human behavior, and we also sought to understand our own personal and relational experiences of jealousy. Our main source of information consisted of our personal episodes of jealousy buttressed by friends' descriptions of their experiences. When we submitted our work for publication, we played down our introspective method and instead emphasized informal interviews and written descriptions that we had collected from students. Even though our jealousy paper was based on people's stories, the final version was written abstractly, camouflaging informants' everyday experiences. When the reviewers rejected our paper saying we needed quantitative data, we inserted a few statistics from a survey of jealousy we had administered to three hundred students, and the article was published (Ellis & Weinstein, 1986).

Gene and I began to talk about why introspective data had to be hidden in our published article. After all, we knew some things from our own jealousy experiences that we would never know from surveys or interviews of others, such as what it felt like when the jealousy flash took us over physically and emotionally in spite of our rational intentions. Why did social science have to be written in a way that made detailed lived experience secondary to abstraction and statistical data? Our experience with this work led us to ask at the end of the article about the importance of evocative detail, metaphor, and felt emotions in writing and reading about emotional experience. Though our ideas were couched in theoretical social scientific prose, the beginning rumblings of our desire to examine emotions in a more concrete and evocative way became apparent. We wrote:

[T]here is an inherent methodological dilemma facing the researcher in the sociology of emotions, one which forces hard and sometimes unsatisfactory choices. To stay close to the conditions under which emotional responses are evoked, the researcher must attend to the context-based details and specific conditioned associations. But the analysis is often distracted from details and the role of affect as information because the rhetorical conventions of theoretical discourse overemphasize categorical aspects of interpretation. The language is cleansed by abstraction of evocative detail. Compare your response to "extreme, intense pain" with "like a dentist's drill hitting a nerve," as descriptions of the jealousy flash. The latter, appropriate for a literary métier, uses anchoring detail to reduce the distance between subject and arousal (cf. Scheff, 1983). Such details enhance vicarious participation by evoking arousal more directly on the primary, sensory-motor level on which retrieval is grounded. Theoretical discussion attempts to transcend context dependency, but, in doing so, can fatally inhibit developing explanations of what "really" happens in the case of emotion. Perhaps simile and metaphor need to be accepted as an alternative to syllogism in hypotheses about emotion. The problem then is that whether we vicariously experience some emotion would then become the "empirical" test of some theoretical statements. However, we lose reliability as a constraining requirement when personal cogency is elevated to an aesthetic of proof. Research would be judged like poetry. (Ellis & Weinstein, 1986, p. 353)

As we worked on this paper, I was going through several life experiences that made me question the kind of work I wanted to do and moved me toward embracing storytelling and evocative social science. In January 1982, my younger brother was killed in an airplane crash on his way to visit me (see Ellis, 1993). In the summer of 1984, I tore the anterior cruciate ligament and meniscus in my left knee while playing basketball, which demanded surgery. During this time, Gene entered the final stages of chronic emphysema. Flashbacks of my brother's death and my ongoing inability to "get over" my loss were interrupted in real life by Gene gasping for breath while I hobbled as fast as I could to untangle his oxygen hose. In this context, the scientifically respectable survey of jealousy we were working on seemed insignificant.

Instead, I wanted to understand and cope with the intense emotion I felt about the sudden loss of my brother, the midlife crisis I experienced from my body failing me, and the emotional pain Gene and I both felt as he deteriorated. On July 14, 1984, I began keeping notes about these experiences, focusing on Gene's deterioration, our relationship, and coping with illness and dying. These notes were therapeutic for me and I thought sociologically insightful as well. I wasn't sure initially what to do with them; I just knew I had to write them. I continued writing notes about my personal experience for the next two years, including the year after Gene's death.

In January 1985 I was promoted to associate professor at University of South Florida, primarily based on my work on the Fisher Folk. Now it felt less risky to write something other than traditional social science, something that would be engaging, therapeutic, and sociologically useful. Now I could better afford to challenge the boundaries of what counted as legitimate sociology, an endeavor that became my passion after Gene's death a few weeks after my promotion.

In 1986, Candace Clark and I, along with others, started a section in the American Sociological Association called "Sociology of Emotions," which helped legitimate the study of emotions as a proper arena of research. I now had an opportunity to broaden the scope of sociological writing, but soon I was disappointed to see many colleagues follow a "rational actor" approach to emotions research, busily handing out surveys, counting and predicting emotional reactions, observing facial muscles contracting on videotapes, categorizing people, and abstracting generalizations from lived experience. Emotion was in danger of becoming simply another variable to add to rational models for studying social life. What about emotion as lived experience and interaction? I vowed to resist the rationalist tendency to portray people exclusively as spiritless, empty husks with programmed, managed, predictable, and patterned emotions (Ellis, 1991b).

The deaths of my brother Rex and my partner Gene inspired me to study grief and loss. After trying a number of different approaches, I returned to the notes I had kept on my relationship with Gene and decided to analyze my own experience of loss. I was interested in writing from the inside about the bigger picture of the process of loss. The result was *Final Negotiations: A Story of Love, Loss, and Chronic Illness,* written as a narrative autoethnography.[2]

Final Negotiations: Negotiating Hope and Truth

A theme that occurred often in *Final Negotiations* involved negotiating hope and reality along with hope and truth telling so that Gene and I could live the best life possible given the confines of his illness. The negotiations moved from those that occurred dyadically between Gene and me and between Gene and his primary doctor; to triadic discussions among Gene, his doctor, and me; and finally, as Gene became sicker, to dyadic discussions between me as the caregiver and Gene's physician, in which we made decisions about Gene's fate.[3]

The three short stories that follow show these negotiations. The first illustrates our private attempt during "time-out weekends" to deal with Gene's illness and inevitable death. Gene encourages me to practice grieving and experiencing his death, while he takes a rational approach to his illness. The second tells about a trip to a doctor's office during which the doctor discusses Gene's illness in my presence and we begin learning and practicing how to balance hope and reality. The third shows the move from patient-centered negotiations to a coalition between the doctor and me—the caregiver—as we negotiate truth and hope for ourselves as well as for Gene.[4]

Weekend Moratoriums: Practicing Death

Periodically, when we felt overwhelmed by disease and by our disagreements about how to cope, we set aside weekends to deal with Gene's deterioration and impending death. Gene took additional steroids, though they increased the rate of deterioration of his muscles, upset his stomach, and caused other less visible, long-term side effects. Our decision to meet short-term needs with long-term costs scared us but gave Gene a sense of strength. For a while, we did not have to deal with the worst effects of the disease—the coughing, feelings of suffocation caused by mucus plugs, and severe shortness of breath.

For Gene, the process was one of rational, conscious acceptance of his deteriorating health. Pure will, determination, and pushing hard could not defeat the disease and, in fact, sometimes made it worse. With that recognition, he became more loving and sensitive, gaining a renewed sense of the importance of caring and relationships.

These weekend retreats evoked deep emotions in me that I normally tried desperately to suppress. My immersion in mutual self-revelation, at times uncontrollably passionate, was not without consciousness. I experienced wrenching pain as I sobbed—my entire body shuddering with grief—but still I observed myself. As I tried to gain entrée into Gene's world of anguish, I entered my own, positioned as a third-party observer to a world collapsing around and inside me.

During the first of these weekend retreats, Gene tries to pull me out of my agony. To ease my pain, stop my tears, and lighten my heart, he says, "Think of all the good times. Be happy for our love."

"No, let me feel it. I think it's good for me. Just hold me." The loss of emotional control is the most excruciating sensation of my life. I want to get away, deny it; paradoxically, I crave this emotionally pure, but seductive, experience like a masochist craves the whip. Feelings of being a separate entity, alone in the world, fluctuate with spiritual connection to Gene and the universe.

At first, I don't know what I'm experiencing. Like the power of an intense orgasm, the abyss of agony pulls me in, until I am powerless. But, this feeling is different from the physiological release of orgasm that rushes to emotional release. This sensation simultaneously penetrates body, mind, and emotional being. The painful sobbing, moaning, and, sometimes, at the peak, screaming, go on and on, culminating in the internal explosion of the emotional ball that has been building in my gut and threatening suffocation. Then, like spent fireworks falling to the ground, my agony is diffused and I can breathe freely. Immediately, I feel the fluttering of the surviving sparks converging and struggling to be reproduced. The explosion itself triggers and becomes physical release. I go deep into my self, where I have never been before.

"Tell me what you're going through," Gene says, after my sobbing slows. "I want to share it with you. Please, let me be there for you."

I hesitate. Can he stand it? Can I bear telling him? When he insists, the feelings I try to describe come out in short phrases: "The pain. The human condition. Meaninglessness. The deterioration. It hurts—in my heart. I feel so helpless." When the sobbing renews, his strengthening embrace encourages me to continue. "I have so many unanswered questions. What is life about? Why do people die? Isn't there something we can do?"

He doesn't pull back, giving me confidence now to talk between sobs. "I feel grief for every single thing you have lost—that you have trouble walking, that your lungs will no longer carry your booming voice in class, that you run out of breath when we make love. These are my losses, too. I cry for both of us. For the pain I stifle in my heart when I see you struggling for breath, just to walk. For the love I feel when you suffer. For the numbness that comes over me when my pain becomes too great. And, even for the anger, yes, the anger I feel because we don't have a normal relationship."

"What else? What else are you feeling?"

When I hesitate, he says softly, but strongly, "You're experiencing how you might feel when I die, aren't you?"

Can I admit this? To be thinking about life without him seems disloyal. I let myself picture him as an invalid, then as dying, and, finally, for the first time, as dead. The pain tearing through my body means that, for a while, I exist again only as feeling, sobbing. He's going to die. I'm going to die. This is all there is. I find solace in the warm blackness that surrounds me, but then I am drawn back to Gene, holding me tightly, our bodies rocking gently together in a soothing rhythm.

"Hey, open your eyes. I'm still here," Gene says, reminding me of the immediate present. "Touch me. Kiss me. I'm not dead yet. We still have wonderful time together."

I open my eyes to his smile, his strong embrace. I feel relieved; he isn't dead yet. I want to make good all the time we have left. So does he, he says.

He wipes my face. "Do you feel better about my death now?" I shake my head no. "But you just experienced it and you're still functioning. Just like you will when I really die."

"No, I can't imagine it," I say, turning away.

"Yes, you can. Make yourself think about what it will be like," he demands, turning my face back to him. "How will you cope? What will you do after I'm dead? You need to practice this too. Not just death itself."

The slow and drawn-out act of acceptance now contrasts with the quick, immediate emotional release I just experienced. I can't take any more now.

* * *

These weekend moratoriums allowed us to hold his disease at bay, at least its psychological consequences, leaving us to deal only with the physical details of the disease. Only? The physical particulars were present every day. Still, in the cyclical fluctuations between our psychological victories and physical emergencies, we pretended we were living normal lives and became skillful at building and sustaining our illusions.

That worked for a while, but eventually the preoccupation with physical infirmities overtook our happiness once again. Just as we perfected a routine for dealing with the current level of health, the level often dropped. The disease stabilized on a plateau for a while, with small peaks and valleys camouflaging the sudden drop that inevitably occurred, often without warning. It took a while to recognize that this was a permanent decline; sometimes we knew and ignored the warning signals. At each new level, we found ourselves arguing, sometimes viciously, about strategies for coping. Often one step behind, playing catch-up, we failed to understand why our coping mechanisms, which had functioned so well for a while, had stopped working. Then it would again take another time-out weekend to deal with the new reality.

Eventually the cyclical movement from psychological catharsis to physical emergencies would become more unbalanced over time, until finally Gene no longer would have the physical strength to deal with the intensity demanded during these weekends. Emphysema was a vicious progressive disease![5]

Doctors' Visits

Visits to Dr. Silverman, Gene's physician, also provided occasions for confronting and evaluating Gene's illness. The doctor's office was on Park Avenue, yet he made us feel we were being visited by a rural doctor in a horse-drawn carriage. Sentimental and grandfatherly, he held Gene's hand and teared when he had to tell us bad news; but his eyes brightened when immediately afterward he informed us of some new medicine to try or of a success story—a mayor who was working while hooked to a breathing machine—or when telling Gene how far he was above the normal curve given the extent of his emphysema.

"Most people in your condition are home in bed, but look at you, you're traveling around the world," he says to Gene, after hearing about our vacation in the Himalayas.

"See, I'm not a wimp," Gene tells me when Dr. Silverman leaves the room.

"Don't you know that I know that?"

Gene needed the validation. Otherwise, how could he be certain how well he was doing? The same was true for me: How else did I know how hard he was trying to cope? Dr. Silverman understood those needs and recognized that his words motivated Gene and supported our illusions.

Dr. Silverman usually was engaged in several activities at the same time—phone calls from patients in other countries, questions from staff—but we never felt short-changed. Although our appointment took most of a day, we had time to ask questions and hear about the latest findings on emphysema, including the doctor's own research. He responded to Gene as a colleague, not a dying man, asking about his sociological projects and letting Gene take part in the analysis of his disease. Later developing lung cancer himself, Dr. Silverman talked quite candidly to Gene about his own health, quality-of-life concerns, and how to live to the fullest as long as possible.

Still, at every successive visit, Gene was worse. As Dr. Silverman compared the indices of tests measuring breathing rate and lung capacity for us, we could not ignore the downward progression.

During one visit when there is a dramatic drop, Dr. Silverman tries to be optimistic. "But look at what you can still do. And there are some developments; a new drug is being tested in Canada. Let's see if we can figure out a way to obtain it."

Gene listens attentively, hopefully. Then a cloud passes over his face. "But, Doc, it's not a cure, is it?"

"No," the doctor replies, holding eye-to-eye contact with Gene. "There is no cure. Maybe in the future, but not in your lifetime."

Gene's shoulders sag farther into his chair as Dr. Silverman looks away busying himself with altering Gene's many medications. "I think changing your antibiotic will help. Try taking one four times a day, instead of two twice a day."

It took only a few visits to realize that new medications and rearrangements of old ones were of little sustained value. We simply substituted one steroid, one adrenaline, for others. The only time the change mattered was when Gene developed an allergy to an ingredient in one medication. Initially, Gene's improved condition gave us false hope that this medication was a panacea only to let us down again when the allergy disappeared and the labored breathing continued.

* * *

As we settle into Maxwell's Plum after the doctor's visit, the tension dissolves under the influence of champagne and gourmet food. Cost does not concern us. Like new lovers, we hold hands. Like old companions, we talk about death and the shortness of time we have left together. We cry softly as we admit the lowered numbers on pulmonary tests have reaffirmed our worst fears.

Then Gene says angrily, "Why does Silverman pretend there's hope, when there isn't any? Why doesn't he just say so?"

"He does, Gene. He said there was no cure in your lifetime." A pall spreads over our conversation.

"But then he says the shuffling of the medicine will help. It won't," replies Gene, still angry.

"That's true. But think of his position. He wants to be honest, yet not totally depress you or make you feel there's no hope for improvement. So he confronts us with the stark reality of your deterioration, and then gives us a ray of hope to hang on to. It isn't dishonest. He wants to have hope too."

"I guess," Gene replies, softening with resignation. Then, because nothing reminds us of our love in quite the same way as facing the loss of it, Gene connects with my eyes and mouths, "I love you." As the feeling flashes back and forth between us, my fear subsides.

"At least we have each other," he continues, now changing sides. "And who knows. Maybe I'll live longer than anybody thinks. There's always the possibility of a lung transplant."

Sure, I think ironically, but say sincerely, "Anything is possible. I'm just glad to have this time now. I guess our situation is not really worse than others. Everybody will die."

"This champagne is wonderful," Gene says. "Taste it in the back of your throat. It's so full and dry."

So began a tradition of having lunch at Maxwell's Plum after each doctor's visit. Without fully realizing it at the time, the two of us were being socialized into the roles of dying and grieving. I rehearsed how to show Gene love, yet shut out pain and fear; Gene practiced how to face his illness, yet escape living as a dying person.

The doctor's candid opinion, supported by the declining test results, confronted us with the reality of Gene's impending death. We began to relate to the disease much as the doctor had—facing the inevitable and then looking for some reason to be hopeful. Ambivalence as a coping mechanism offered comfort yet left room for reality. These afternoon lunches provided opportunities to integrate hope and reality, a balance that would tip toward reality as the illness took over.[6]

Doctor and Caregiver Collude

"We have to intubate Gene. The conservative treatment isn't working," Dr. Townson, Gene's doctor in Tampa, says quickly and apologetically as I enter the emergency room.

"Might he die?" I ask. The doctor nods yes. "Even if he's intubated?"

"Yes, possibly. But we won't feel guilty about it, not you or me. We are doing everything we can. We'll make it as comfortable as possible. And if he doesn't die now, he will die soon anyway."

After the intubation, Dr. Townson comes to Gene's room. "I hate the tube," Gene mouths. "It hurts." On a pad, he writes, "I think this happened because I wasn't getting enough oxygen."

"No," says Dr. Townson. "Your body can't get rid of CO_2."

With eyes blazing and anger and pain etched on his face, Gene mouths as a statement and a question, "Then I'm dying."

"You're not dying," says Dr. Townson, with an edge of a nervous chuckle. "There are some radical things to try."

Gene mouths to me, "He's not being straight with me." Since Gene already knows he's dying, I wonder why he asks.

When Dr. Townson leaves, I say to Gene, "He doesn't want you to give up hope."

"I just want him to be straight with me."

"It's hard to tell someone he's dying."

"I want the truth."

"Basically he's telling you the truth. They don't know anymore."

* * *

A few days before Gene died, he screamed all night at home that he was being kidnapped. I finally called the ambulance to take him into the hospital. There Dr. Colter, who was Dr. Townson's associate and the doctor on duty, gave him an antipsychotic drug, Haldol. When Gene refused to take it the second time, demanding physical therapy instead so he "could walk again," the following scene ensued:

"You must take your Haldol, Mr. Weinstein."

"See how short of breath I am. They're trying to kill me," Gene says, his eyes beseeching me to do something.

Dr. Colter and I step into the hall. "I don't see Haldol making any difference in his breathing," the doctor says coldly. "Without it, he's going to be back where he was when you brought him in here."

Although aware that pain medication might slow down his respiration and kill him, I ask, "Can you give him Valium or codeine or something to calm him down if he won't take Haldol?"

After consulting with Dr. Townson about my request, Dr. Colter returns and says, "I'm going to go in and make Gene take the Haldol, unless you object. You can stay out here if it would be easier."

"No, I want to be there," I say, following him as the play I am in seems to move into fast-forward. Is this the right thing to do? Though we have stopped Gene from doing things he wants to do, such as driving and buying a new car, this is the first time we have forced him to do anything against his will.

"Mr. Weinstein," the doctor says loudly, as if he is talking to a recalcitrant child or a hearing-impaired person, "here is your Haldol."

"I don't want it. It's killing me," Gene insists, turning his mouth away.

"If you don't take it, I'm going to stick you with it," the doctor threatens, holding the pill and water next to Gene's puckered mouth. I see the doctor as a large face with distorted features, like in a cartoon, when the bad guy balloons and occupies the whole screen. I scream, but no sound comes out.

Gene pleads, "Please don't. You said you wouldn't. You bastard." I try to make a sound, but when I see Gene is about to give in, I hold back and let the drama unfold.

"I didn't say I wouldn't."

"Stop," the sound escapes. "This is awful." I cry out the words, but softly, hoping the doctor won't hear and will continue in his mission.

Dr. Colter keeps going. I am surprised when Gene opens his mouth, whimpering softly. Colter holds the water glass for him while he drinks.

After taking the Haldol, Gene became "sane," calm, and loving during the three days before he finally died.[7]

Meta-Autoethnography: Communicating About Dying

In the process of Gene's disease, he and I continually designed new frames about his illness, and we moved deftly from one definition of the situation to another, attempting to maintain the most hopeful frame possible. We began early in our relationship to live in uncertainty and ambivalence and, following the lead of Gene's doctors, to keep hope and the despairing truth of his physical condition in balance. We tried to live fully in the moment every day, yet take periodic time-outs to discuss how to cope with his physical deterioration and its impact on our relationship, and plan for future contingencies. We felt it was important to feel and show love without constantly being overtaken by the pain and fear of loss, and to live as though Gene were not dying in order to squeeze as much happiness as possible out of our limited time together.

As we moved through the emotional and physical plateaus of the illness experience, our conversations became more and more framed by the reality of his physical deterioration and I became more involved in triadic discussions involving Gene, his doctors, and myself. For a while both Gene and I lived in two realities simultaneously—that he could die and that there was something to try—and we began to shift at about the same pace toward the truthful framing of his illness as terminal. But as reality became too much to bear in its day-to-day physical, emotional, and psychological manifestations, Gene moved more toward hope that something still could be done while I was forced to understand and confront his declining medical prognosis. No longer feeling that I could turn to Gene to help work out how we should feel about all this, yet not wanting to replace his hope with despair, I found myself depending more on discussions with the doctors (and they on me) to decide how to accomplish Gene's dying the best we knew how. While in the end Gene stayed more consistently in the frame of hope, I had to move repeatedly between hope and practicality, since there were things that had to be done and decisions that had to be made. The story I tell of this process presents a far more complex, messy, and processual picture of communication and truth telling than the one-shot doctor-patient studies that take place in doctors' offices and make up most of the literature on patient-provider communication (Sharf, 1993).[8]

As I wrote the stories in *Final Negotiation,* such as the ones in this chapter, it became important that they evoke readers' experiences and be useful for all of us—the ill, their caregivers, and all of us who will suffer illness and loss some day. I also wanted these stories to offer sociological understanding of grief, relationships, doctor-patient communication, caregiving, illness, and dying. While most of the readers of early drafts of *Final Negotiations* confirmed that the stories I wrote helped them understand something about illness and caregiving, many of my colleagues still questioned the value of narrative understanding and therapeutic usefulness in sociology. Indeed, many also were suspect about my claim that writing evocative narratives about oneself contributed to the sociological imagination. Getting to the point of writing *Final Negotiations* the way I felt moved to do was fraught with many roadblocks and critical responses.

CHAPTER FIVE

Renegotiating *Final Negotiations*

From Introspection to Emotional Sociology

I wrote *Final Negotiations* to provide comfort, "companionship in a common venture," and a point of comparison for people in their time of personal tragedy (Mairs, 1993, p. 25). I wrote for myself as an identity- and meaning-making project in which I could come to terms with both my relationship with Gene and the loss of it. Seeking to humanize the academic project, I wrote the book for sociologists. I advocated telling sociology in a passionate way, including emotions in our theories and studies, and making sociology relevant to people's lived lives. Though I did not expect all sociologists to answer this call, I wanted my academic peers to view what I was doing as legitimate sociology. This chapter is about some of the conversations that ensued about this project.

Critics Respond to *Final Negotiations*[1]

Early in my writing process, I sent the first two excerpts included in the last chapter to friends and colleagues. From the lay audience, people dealing with illness, those in the helping professions, and several friends in sociology, I received glowing evaluations about how well written and emotionally expressive these stories were, and how much they were affected by what they read. One sociologist said, "I can never remember being so deeply and emotionally affected by something, time and again. Each time I read about your experiences I am blown away, amazed by how you were able to cope, and in deep admiration of your ability to live and care . . . You are correct in doggedly sticking to your guns, ignoring the chastising of your colleagues and respected 'scholars,' because you have something so much more powerful, so much more moving, so much more important."

But some friends and colleagues in the academy admitted not knowing what to say, feeing "uneasy reading these materials," embarrassed by my "emotional nakedness," as though they had peered into a dimension of my personal life they were not supposed to see. "The writer's calm has to quiet the reader's embarrassment," critiqued a colleague, and "Some things need to be written; they do not need to be read," responded a second critical reader, both assuming that readers need protection. "If you have to do this for therapy, go ahead, but this is not sociology," warned a friend, who felt sociology needed protection. "These kinds of things should not be revealed," warned a sociologist, who assumed that I, the author, needed protection. "The greatest gift that we can give, is the gift of our dispassionate analysis, our coolness, our marginality," added another, in hopes of protecting all of us from the threat of emotional involvement. Even colleagues active in the movement to include emotions in sociology showed concern about what my work meant for the sociological enterprise: "How does what you are saying tell me anything about my own experience? How can this be generalized?" one sociologist of emotions asked.

The intense responses to my work, even the critical ones, signaled that I was on to something important. My vulnerabilities about this project were overshadowed by the challenge of convincing the academic world that introspective ethnography should be included in sociology and could meet the criteria of rigorous inquiry.

Determined to reach sociologists, I spent a year researching and writing a paper on systematic sociological introspection. I developed the idea that introspection was a scientific approach to social science research, and I included narrative excerpts from my unfinished manuscript to demonstrate its value. I claimed that introspection was a social as well as a psychological process, and though it had problems and strengths—just like any other method—it deserved recognition. The multitude of reviewers who responded formally to this work noted the excellence of my writing and seemed interested in my points of view and affected by my narratives. But, for the most part, sociological reviewers argued that introspection did not produce sociology. One wrote, "Your writing reminds one a bit of the poems that some write while on drugs. I kept asking myself what is the significance to a sociological reader of your encounter with Gene's doctor. Does a reader *really* care?" Some wanted the paper to be more scientific and analytic. A few claimed that to consider what I did to be sociology might endanger the sociological enterprise. I wrote and rewrote this paper, responding to these critiques, for example, by substituting interviews with others for my autobiographic materials. I was disappointed with the responses, but suspected that these sentiments illustrated the power of what I was doing, rather than its irrelevance.

The review that caught my attention said that the manuscript was "schizophrenic." "It makes a case for the method, and then turns hard science against it and ends up limply defending its case ... The author is caught between two camps—hard psychological (sociological) science, and interpretive, imaginative, humanistic, phenomenological inquiry.

You can't have it both ways," Norman Denzin wrote. This review probably changed my life; I know it changed the focus of my work. I revised the paper again, omitting the focus on proving that what I was doing was science, and "Sociological Introspection and Emotional Experience" was published in *Symbolic Interaction* in 1991.

Examining this published article now, I see the lingering remnants of my preoccupation with convincing orthodox social scientists on their own terms of the value of detailed, lived experience. Yet I also see a yearning to examine what could be learned from my project about how meaning is attached to human experience. Although some mainstream sociologists—especially women—would be receptive to this work, my move away from orthodox sociology would continue, and I would eventually begin to communicate with scholars from all disciplines who were interested in taking an interpretive stance toward understanding meaning and human life.

Nevertheless, in 1991, "Sociological Introspection and Emotional Experience" offered readers a persuasive sociological rationale for accepting introspection as a legitimate way of doing social science research and for examining what emotions feel like and how they are experienced, including the emotions of the researcher. Along with a second article on emotional sociology (Ellis, 1991b), this work provided justification for those who wanted to study emotions emotionally and suggested that introspective and interactive methods along with narrative writing might provide ways to accomplish this goal. I include portions of this article here to provide historical context for what follows.

Sociological Introspection and Emotional Experience[2]

Sociologists, including symbolic interactionists, have been accused of neglecting emotions in the past (Adler & Adler, 1980; Meltzer, Petras, & Reynolds, 1975; Stryker, 1981). Even now with the emphasis on emotion, sociologists continue to ignore what emotion feels like and how it is experienced. This article argues that sociologists can and should study how private and social experience are fused in felt emotions. Resurrecting introspection (conscious awareness of awareness or self-examination) as a systematic sociological technique will allow sociologists to examine emotion as a product of the individual processing of meaning as well as socially shared cognitions.

In the current resurgence in the study of emotions, social scientists have focused on emotions as socially constructed, culturally influenced, and managed (Harré, 1986; Hochschild, 1983; Shott, 1979). Social constructionists contend that intrinsic to the constitution of emotions are contextual considerations, local moral orders, moral imperatives of display, linguistic practices, shared cognitions, and social roles. Averill (1974), for instance, writes of the "cognitive core" of emotion.

Certainly emotions involve shared cognitions and socially constructed definitions. For example, many authors have demonstrated the sociocultural codes of "possession and property" that are necessary conditions for jealousy (Clanton & Smith, 1977; Davis, 1936; Ellis & Weinstein, 1986). Yet, for this emotion to be felt in any particular case, these cultural beliefs must be subjectively processed.

Few sociologists have examined lived emotional experience, or looked into the details of the process by which people come to feel the way they do.[3] Hochschild (1983), in her insightful study of flight attendants, warns that we must not ignore the subjective aspects of emotions. But she does not go as far as one could in examining the subjective process of feeling management and redefinition of self. Do attendants blindly follow emotion rules? What private arguments or self-dialogues occur as they take on emotions? How do they actually feel? What is the process of feeling management and redefinition of self?

Subjective processing must take into account physiological response, another neglected part of emotional experience (Kemper, 1981; Scheff, 1985). Physiological elements of lived experience often are ignored by "strong constructionists" or regarded by "moderate constructionists" as ingredients to be socially shaped (Armon-Jones, 1986; Hochschild, 1990; Kemper, 1981). Harré (1986, p. 5), for example, is willing to admit only that there might be "'leakages' into consciousness from raised heartbeat, increased sweating, swollen tear ducts, and so on." Yet, the physical act of sobbing uncontrollably after losing a loved one is more than just an adjunct event. It is likely to be an important physiological cue for confirming the authenticity of and thus intensifying the deep grief being experienced. Scheff (1985) suggests further that coarse emotions, such as grief and fear, may even involve internal sequences that impact external expressive signals. Unfortunately, as Denzin (1985) observes, those few sociologists who do examine the biological part of emotions tend to sever the body from the lived experience (see Wentworth & Ryan, 1992, for an exception). But it is important to examine the role of physiological feeling in lived experience, for example, in our embracing of feeling rules, and to look at how people label physiological response or ignore it. Emotional experience, including the physiological, is also essential to the authenticating process as a clue to self-knowledge/self-identity (Hochschild, 1983; Morgan & Averill, 1992).

Emotions result from applying personal interpretations of collectively created rules to the situations in which we find ourselves (David Franks, personal communication). Although "what transpires individually and privately is appropriated from the public-collective realm" (Wood, 1986, p. 197), how the public-collective or social definition gets translated into the "individually realized" is a subject that can be penetrated deeply by introspecting about our own experiences. In introspection, collective symbols become embodied by individuals involved in continued "interpretive apprehension" and transformation of these symbols (Rosaldo, 1984, p. 140). The meaning they take on is a "product of the mental-social complex and known to us only through consciousness" (Cooley, 1926, p. 68). How social actors process or appropriate the public into their personal autobiographies (Sarbin, 1986) to make sense of what is going on provides the private part of our emotion.

In some cases, constructionists are willing to examine emotion as private as well as social experience, but they move quickly to the social part of emotion, playing down its private essence as belonging to psychology.[4] Still, there is nothing unsociological in saying that individually lived experience includes subjective feelings and physiology that play a crucial part in emotions (Kemper, 1981). Examining the private processing of feeling does not have to imply irreducibility or an individualistic orientation (see, for example, Gordon, 1989). Furthermore, to argue that we can know our emotions through introspection is not to counter the importance of context and behavior in determining emotion (Bedford, 1986; Armon-Jones, 1986). Nor does it deny that our knowledge of emotions as well as the sentences we use to describe them are enabled by culture (Solomon, 1984).

Such would be true only for the over-psychological perspective on introspection that deals with experience as if it was a solely internal phenomenon, instead of an appropriation from the public order. Culture, as Rosaldo (1984, p. 150) says, is "the very stuff of which our subjectivities are created." Or, as Mead expressed it, the locus of mind (or the field of which it is part) must indeed be social, but the focus lies within the individual (Goff, 1980).

The first step in studying this fusion of private and social is to acknowledge introspection, whether our own or that of others, as a sociological technique that can provide access to private experiences and generate interpretive materials from self and others useful for understanding the complex, ambiguous, and processual nature of lived emotional experience.

From a Psychological to a Sociological Introspection

Sociological insight has been built on the introspective methods of its forebears in philosophy and psychology (Heidegger, Husserl, Kulpe, Mead, Merleau-Ponty, Sartre, Titchener, Wundt). Yet modern social constructionists have neglected Cooley's affective orientation (Stryker, 1981) and introspective method for Mead's more cognitive emphasis and technique of understanding humans by studying what they do (Charon, 1985). Many researchers examining the development of modern sociology suggest that in the post–Civil War era sociology was trying to prove itself a science and claim scientific legitimacy apart from the physiologically based behaviorism of psychologists (Camic, 1986; Hinkle & Hinkle, 1954; Ross, 1979). Introspection as a method had already been rejected by the behaviorist psychologists as nonscientific (Grover, 1982; Watson, 1913). Grover (1982, p. 206), for example, went so far as to say that "with the advent of Watsonian radical behaviorism in the 1900s, introspection became an embarrassment to those psychologists aspiring to scientific respectability." For sociologists to have embraced introspection then would have hindered the case for sociology as science.

Rosenberg (1988) suggests further that the sociological paradigm of social factism—that sociologists must study social facts that exist outside of individual consciousness—along with the more recent social behaviorist paradigm prevented sociologists from dealing with self-concept, which he defines as the "totality of the individual's thoughts and feelings with reference to the self as an object" (p. 3). The rejection of introspection as a technique, along with the neglect of introspection as an object of study in the form of thoughts and feelings, comes then from the idea that sociology should define as its territory rational action (see Camic, 1986) and social facts (see Rosenberg, 1988).[5]

In theory, the gate in sociology has never been closed entirely to introspection. Some sociological and philosophical traditions closely allied with sociology have maintained that understanding the meaning of one's own experience and empathically interpreting meaning in the experience of others constitute bases for inquiry.[6] Along with ethnographic, feminist, and hermeneutic approaches, social constructionism—including symbolic interaction, phenomenology, existential sociology, and more recently, textual analysis—continue laying the groundwork for investigating emotions, thoughts, and subjective meaning. Yet, social constructionists have not attempted to use introspection in any systematic fashion to understand social life.

Nevertheless, most researchers, and especially social constructionists, use data gathered introspectively at some point in their research, but camouflage them as behavior, questionnaire responses, verbal reports, and laboratory experiment results. Verbal reports, for example, are considered behavior observed by an experimenter, and are sometimes transformed into "latencies and numbers of items correct" (Ericsson & Simon, 1980, p. 216), while introspections are viewed as descriptions of inner states reported by the subject (Boring, 1953; Radford, 1974). While in principle introspection may be a "verboten method," in practice it appears to be prevalent and frequently used as an adjunct to other strategies (Grover, 1982). As Kohut (1959) suggests, researchers have neglected the investigation of introspection because they are reluctant to "acknowledge it wholeheartedly as [their] mode of observation" (p. 465).

This neglect also may come from constructionists' and others' reaction against the psychological view of introspection as implying self-contained internal events. Coulter (1986, p. 122), for example, refers to the "fallacious doctrine of perceptual introspection-ism, which leads us to think that emotions are internal events." Armon-Jones (1986, p. 36) says that "if it were possible to identify emotions via introspection alone, then the notion of 'appropriate context' would be redundant and could not have the explanatory role which the constructionist ascribes to it." The real problem, however, has been the neglect of introspection as a sociological process, one that is compatible with and necessary for the constructionist position. With few exceptions (Denzin, 1971), introspection continues to be a taboo subject among mainstream sociologists.

The psychological approach ignored the socially constructed, processual nature of thoughts, feelings, and introspection. Viewed as process, introspection, like any thinking, is covert communicative behavior. As private, inner dialogue, it is enabled by publicly shared significant symbols, and, thus, is inherently social (Lewis, 1979). Because of the cognitive element in human emotion (Averill, 1974), the same is true for emotions. Psychologists who used introspection presented it as a way to investigate how an individual mind had constructed the world. For example, James ([1890] 1981, p. 185) said: "All people unhesitatingly believe that they feel themselves thinking, and that they distinguish the mental state as an *inward activity or passion*, from all the objects with which it may cognitively deal" (emphasis mine). Psychology de-emphasized the self-dialogue inherent in introspection. It underplayed the impact of shared symbols on our response to our own selves in inner conversation (Lewis, 1979). Excluded also was the role of external norms and social structure.

Introspection then is a social process as well as a psychological one. It is active thinking about one's thoughts and feelings; it emerges from social interaction; it occurs in response to bodily sensations, mental processes, and external stimuli as well as affecting these same processes. It is not just listening to one voice arising alone in one's head; usually, it consists of interacting voices, which are products of social forces and roles. Gagnon (1990), for example, argues persuasively that twentieth-century voices are influenced by the rise of literacy and the reading of novels, access to rapid travel, availability of the photograph, and fantasy consumption.

In the context of descriptive introspection, many psychologists and philosophers argued that the act of self-observation changed the content of introspection. Thus, they said, this meant we interfered with the very life experience we were trying to understand (Dilthey [1900] 1976; McDougal, 1922). The introspective process was therefore thought impossible to study. To remedy this charge, some of its advocates conceived of it as proper only for analyzing the past (Bakan, 1954; James [1890] 1981; Mill, 1879).

Yet, introspection is no more mediated or retrospective than any other method (cf. Peirce, 1958). We cannot study "unmediated" thought using any method. All reflection is of the past. We live in the "specious" present (Mead [1934] 1962). The "I" is never directly observed, since reflection changes it to a past "me" (Stone & Farberman, 1970). Our observation of introspection is part of the introspective process just as interviewer-subject interaction is part of questionnaire responses (see Cicourel, 1974). It is impossible to compare a subject's "natural perception" to her response organized to answer our interview questions; in the same way, comparing "pure" thought with self-observation of pure thought, as the psychologists tried to do, can't be done. These are not different processes to be compared. In actuality, observation of one's own emerging dialogue is a continuing and important part of any introspection as well as being the foundation of role-taking in the theory of the self-control of behavior.

Introspection as a Source of Interpretive Materials

For the most part, social constructionists who look at emotions fail to examine their own responses and, instead, view emotions as feelings that other people have. Even when they use their own experiences, they do so in an emotionally detached way (e.g. Goffman, 1959; Kotarba, 1983), or they hide reactions in an array of participant observation data (e.g. Denzin, 1987). Sociologists, however, can generate interpretive materials about the lived experience of emotions by studying their own self-dialogue in process. Who knows better the right questions to ask than a social scientist who has lived through the experience? Who would make a better subject than a researcher consumed by wanting to figure it all out? That there are problems in this technique is a given; that we have to take precautions in interpreting, generalizing, and eliminating bias here the same as we do with any data we collect is assumed (Ellis, 1989). But the understanding to be gained makes working out the problems worthwhile.

Using self as subject, we can base the researcher's self-introspection on accepted practices of field research and take into account the same issues as we do when studying any "n" of one. Some ethnographers already see themselves as part of the situation they study (Adler & Adler, 1987; Caughey, 1982; Van Maanen, 1988) and many openly acknowledge looking to their own thoughts, feelings, and personal experiences as legitimate and insightful data (cf. Clifford, 1986; Crapanzano, 1970; Hayano, 1979; Johnson, 1975; Krieger, 1985; Reinharz, 1979). This paper moves from ethnographers' use of self-observation as part of the situation studied to self-introspection or self-ethnography as a legitimate focus of study in and of itself (see also Jules-Rosette, 1975; Sudnow, 1978).

Interactive introspection is also part of the introspective technique. Here, the researcher works back and forth with others to assist in their introspection, but the object of study is the emergent experiences of both parties. Interactive introspection provides self-introspection from subject and researcher, since a researcher must introspect about her own responses in reaction to experiences and feelings of respondents (Denzin, 1971).

While interactive introspection resembles an intensive interview, it is more interactive. Here, the researcher and subject work as equal participants and concentrate directly on emotional process (Smith, 1979; Stacey & Thorne, 1985). Brief descriptive accounts and intensive interviews, while compatible with introspection, often differ in their focus on outcome and categories; the process is boxed in as "an experience" (see for example Hochschild, 1983; Thoits, 1990). Although similar to obtaining verbal reports (Boring, 1953; Ericsson & Simon, 1980, 1984; Radford, 1974), interactive introspection differs in that its goal is for subjects to relive their emotion and talk about it as they experience it.

Finally, interactive introspection has some similarities to psychoanalysis in its probing and feedback techniques. However, it differs in that the introspectionist's primary goal is not to help, change, or reach the unconscious of the subject; instead, it is to describe conscious experiences of both subject and researcher.[7]

Introspection, as I am defining it, can be accomplished in dialogue with self, and represented in the form of field notes, or narratives; in participant observation and interviews, depending on the extent the researcher sees herself also as subject in the research process; in interactive dialogue with others; or in reading and analyzing others' journals or free writing, where subjects write nonstop about what they are thinking and feeling and what it means to them (Candace Clark, personal communication; Elbow, 1973).

Systematic sociological introspection permits a look into the processing of everyday emotional life. It will provide a link between one's own experience and the expressions of life (Polkinghorne, 1983) sociologists currently study, such as cultural representations of emotional life on film (see Denzin, 1990), directed interviews of emotion management and display (see Hochschild, 1983), and historical treatments of "emotionology," rules and standards affecting our feelings (Stearns & Stearns, 1986). In addition, introspection may provide a glimpse of the interface between social and biological phenomena (Kemper, 1981).

Introspection will allow us to address previously neglected experiential questions that can be approached by fusing social and personal experience. For example, do we construct new feelings when we change situations (Averill, 1986)? Do people in the same situation feel different emotions? Are some emotions harder to create? Harder to control? Do emotions such as indignation and annoyance actually feel different to us (Bedford, 1986)? If so, how? What are the situational and historical cues that lead us to label them differently (Davitz, 1969)? What is the relationship of felt emotions to behavior? The relationship of felt emotions to feeling rules? Do people feel what we observe them feeling? How do we move from emotional to cognitive reality?

* * *

In this article, I addressed these questions using autobiographical narratives and stories gathered from intimate others in interactive contexts, all of which showed the value of an introspective perspective. I gave examples and noted that introspective accounts may make it possible for researchers to: learn about emotions people might not otherwise acknowledge or admit; explore the role of social context in emotions that appear to be impulsive; emphasize the serial, processual nature of emotions; make visible emotional patterns that often are hidden under what appear to be different practices; disentangle the complexity subsumed under taken-for-granted categories; and examine patterns in emotion work strategies and how and why people manage emotions the way they do.

I concluded in the article:

To bring emotion into the sociological study of human behavior, we have to address the descriptive and analytical task of precisely detailing the moments in the complex process through which it is experienced. Otherwise, it isn't the whole of emotion we are bringing into our sociological studies, but a severed, edited version of emotion. Particular sociologists may well choose not to focus on the private and felt aspects of emotion. But if the field as a whole ignores lived experience, our interpretations of emotions will be as incomplete as was our understanding of social life before we took emotions into account.

Most methods available to sociologists focus on the rational order in the world. Surveys, questionnaires, and laboratory observations of emotional feelings tell us about the surface public self (Goffman, 1959; Hochschild, 1983). Even participant observation and phenomenological study are rational, cognitive searches for order (Douglas, 1977, p. xiii). Without examining the lived experience of emotion in individuals and across collectives, we are forced to talk of spiritless, empty husks of people who have programmed, patterned emotions, and whose feelings resemble the decision-making models of rational choice theorists. Introspection will allow us to study emotions as they are experienced without using models that have rationality built into them.

Introspection permits us to prompt and collect our own and other people's stories about the lived details of socially constructed experience. To stay as close as possible to the details reported, introspection is best presented as narrative text (Ellis, 1991b; Sarbin, 1986; Wood, 1986). Such accounts will provide a stimulus for discussing issues of the relationship between presented text and feeling/thought and for comparing experiences across groups and culture. Since reflexivity—thinking and feeling as a subject about oneself as an object—is so distinctively human, its place in emotion warrants consideration for a systematic study.

* * *

When this article found a home, I felt ready to return to writing *Final Negotiations*. Though less attached than before to traditional sociology, I still questioned at times what I was doing. Why am I writing a kind of sociology for which there are no models? Is this sociology or literature? Fiction or fact? Do I want to write literature and work in the tradition of humanities or be a scientist and try to follow rigorous rules for doing social science? Though unsure, I put aside the questions and just wrote. What came out was more evocative narrative than research report. Ironically, feeling that I didn't really "fit" in science or humanities freed me (or forced me) to begin to develop my own quasi-humanities, quasi-science link (Zald, 1991). This became apparent as I began to reflect on the process of writing *Final Negotiations*.

Writing *Final Negotiations* as Emotional Sociology[8]

It took nine years to construct and reconstruct the story of my relationship with Gene (Ellis, 1995a), to work out satisfactorily a version of what this relationship had been and had meant to me, and to tell a story that cohered both with what I remembered and what my life had become (Crites, 1971). During this time, I moved from conceiving of my project as science to viewing it as interpretive human studies and narrative inquiry (Bochner, 1994), transforming the process of writing the text from realist ethnography to a narrative story and my primary goal from representation to evocation.

Writing about this relationship was so difficult that I kept notes on the writing process in the same way I had written field notes on the actual relationship and illness process. These notes eventually became the basis for telling how I moved from ethnographic data to writing a meaningful story that I hoped would speak therapeutically to a mass audience and sociologically to an academic one.

Writing sociology as an intimate conversation about the intricacies of feeling, relating, and working confronted me with the deficiencies of traditional social science research practices and representational forms for dealing with day-to-day realities of chronic illness and relational processes. From the beginning, I violated many taken-for-granted notions in social science research: making myself the object of my research and writing in the first person infringed upon the separation of subject and researcher (Jackson, 1989); writing about a single case breached the traditional concerns of research with generalization across cases and focused instead on generalization within a case (Geertz, 1973); the mode of storytelling fractured the boundaries that normally separated social science from literature; the episodic portrayal of the ebb and flow of relationship experience dramatized the motion of connected lives across the curve of time and thus resisted the standard practice of portraying social life as a snapshot; and the disclosure of normally hidden details of private life highlighted emotional experience and thus challenged the rational actor model of social performance that dominates social science.

As I wrote and rewrote, I moved closer to telling an evocative and dramatic story and farther away from trying to get all the ethnographic details "right." I *showed* interaction so that the reader might participate more fully in the emotional process, not merely observe the resolution. This meant moving from generalizing about a kind of event that took place to showing one event in particular, such as a doctor's visit, often by condensing a number of scenes into evocative composites. I reconstructed conversations Gene and I might have had, even when I had not recorded them, reading and rereading them aloud until I heard the ring of authenticity, continually questioning my mode of presentation and my motives.

I began to concentrate more on being true to the feelings that seemed to apply in each situation I described than to getting all the "facts" in the exact sequence. More and more I moved away from trying to make my tale a mirror representation of chronologically ordered events and toward telling a story, where the events and feelings cohered, where questions of meaning and interpretation were emphasized, and where readers could grasp the main points and feel some of what I felt.

I also began to advocate research and scholarly writing as healing and to question more deeply the dichotomy of scholarship and therapeutic writing, a critical response from sociologists that I had accepted initially. I stopped being defensive when others accused my work of being therapeutic, and I began claiming that feature as a necessary and ethical part of what I wrote. I made the case that what I had learned from my own struggles for meaning was unique enough to be interesting, yet typical enough to help others understand important aspects of their lives (Abrahams, 1986).

My aims were to extend the boundaries of social science in terms of its goals and what was considered legitimate and to write an honest, evocative, and helpful account that came from the heart as well as the head.

Writing an Honest and Evocative Story

In *Final Negotiations*, I worked from an assumption of "truth" rather than "fiction" (Webster, 1982) and told a story that cohered with the details of personal experience, my notes, and recollections of others (Krieger, 1984). I tried to tell a story that was "faithful to facts" and that stayed as close as possible to what I recall happened (Richardson, 1992a).

The first version of the text poured out of me, uncensored. It seemed important to get it all down and contextualized, so that I might have some sense of "what had been." I wrote with the confidence that I could delete anything at any time. The notes that I kept during the eight months prior to Gene's death and for two years afterward guided my writing. I interacted constantly with them to recall the way events had happened and how I had felt, adding details that came to memory.

As soon as I began to write from these notes, I realized that I could not talk about loss without showing attachment. This led to re-creating my chronological history with Gene by first recording major events during the relationship and then connecting them. Interviews with family and friends; physicians' records and nurses' notes; taped conversations; and diaries, calendars, and travel logs contributed to my systematic recollection of this period. I also had the advantage of many sociological conversations that Gene and I had had throughout the years about our relationship and the illness process.

Over time I allowed myself dramatic license to tell a good story, since it was not so much the "facts" that I wanted to redeem but rather an articulation of the significance and meaning of my experiences. I came to feel that while personal narratives should be based on facts, they cannot be completely determined by them (Bochner, Ellis, & Tillmann-Healy, 1998). I became less concerned with "historical truth" and more involved with "narrative truth," which Spence (1982, p. 28) described as "the criterion we use to decide when a certain experience has been captured to our satisfaction." It is "what we have in mind when we say that such and such is a good story, that a given explanation carries conviction, that one solution to a mystery must be true." Narrative truth seeks to keep the past alive in the present; through narrative we learn to understand the meanings and significance of the past as incomplete, tentative, and revisable according to contingencies of present life circumstances and our projection of our lives into the future (Bochner, Ellis, & Tillmann-Healy, 1997). I tried then, as Merleau-Ponty (1964, p. 59) said, "to give the past not a survival, which is the hypocritical form of forgetfulness, but a new life, which is the noble form of memory."

Telling one's story gives meaning to both the present and past of human experience (Bertaux-Wiame, 1981; Bruner, 1986b; Polkinghorne, 1988) and allows the teller to see that present as part of a "constituted past and a future" (Bruner, 1986b, p. 153). Every biographical and autobiographical account "takes place in the present time, and in relation to the present." For the people who tell their life stories, the "first purpose is not to describe the past 'as it was,' or even as it was experienced . . . , but to confer to the past experience a certain meaning" (Bertaux-Wiame, 1981, pp. 257–258). Meaning is not permanent, "narratives change, all stories are partial, all meanings incomplete. There is no fixed meaning in the past, for with each new telling the context varies, the audience differs, the story is modified" (Bruner, 1986b, p. 153). Memory is an "active, restructuring process" (Linden, 1993). The past is not frozen in the moment of experience.

In addition to constructing a version of what happened in the past, I also was intent on probing my psychic defenses and the emotional complexities of this experience, although I understood that my attempts would be limited by what is possible to know and admit to oneself about oneself. To explore these psychological processes, I used a practice of "emotional recall," similar to the "method acting" of Lee Strasberg at the Actors' Studio (Bruner, 1986a, p. 28). To give a convincing and authentic performance, the actor relives in detail a situation in which she or he previously felt the emotion to be enacted. I placed myself back into situations, conjuring up details until I was immersed in the event emotionally. Because recall increases when the emotional content at the time of retrieval resembles that of the experience to be retrieved (Bower, 1981; Ellis & Weinstein, 1986), this process enhanced the recollection of more details.

In writing about my experience, my goal was to let the reader in on the emotional process. I was more intent on showing ambivalences and contradictions that occurred along the way than on declaring an outcome. As Virginia Woolf (1953, p. 66) stated about de Montaigne's essays, I attempted "to communicate a soul . . . to go down boldly and bring to light those hidden thoughts which are the most diseased; to conceal nothing; to pretend nothing."

I hoped that readers would see my focus on self as an avenue to learn from my candor and vulnerability (Lopate, 1994, p. xxvi). Necessarily, the exposure had to include betrayals, uncertainties, and self-doubt, including doubt about what was actually written. I wanted readers to trust that I had started with what I did not know and discovered what I did know through the process of writing. As an honest writer, I never pretended to have it all worked out, or to suggest that the finished product disclosed the "bare truth."

The moves in and out of these emotional situations were painful yet therapeutic. They allowed me to experience emotionality safely in my office, often reminded by a phone call or a click of the computer key that I was not actually *in* this situation. If the emotionality became too intense, I could stop and return to current time, a safety valve I did not have while engulfed by the actual experience. This "safety" gave me confidence to explore each incident as fully as I could and to pay attention to what was most upsetting and least resolved.

I concentrated on the lone, loud voice screaming inside my head or the raw fear gnarling within my gut. Then, embracing the multiplicity of selves that all human beings harbor, I tried to bring to my consciousness the contradictory and ambiguous thoughts and feelings that I also had felt. Whenever I could, I wrote down what the many competing voices in my head were saying. The experience was similar to a conference call in which I interacted with many speakers at one time.

This introspective homework (Ellis, 1991a) allowed me to enter into dialogues and disputes with myself before creating a discourse in which others could take part. The "plot" of my story, its drama and suspense, consisted of inviting readers to move with me through my defenses toward deeper levels of examination (Lopate, 1994, pp. xxv–xxvi). I wanted my story to "grasp" readers, pull them into its world, and persuade them that they were "in the reality of the story" (Parry, 1991, p. 42).

My open text permitted readers to move back and forth between being in *my* story and being in theirs, where they could fill in or compare their experiences and provide their own sensitivities about what was going on. I attempted to write in a way that readers might feel the specificity of my situation, yet sense the unity of human experience as well (Lopate, 1994, p. xxiii); in a way that they might connect to what happened to me, remember what happened to them, or anticipate what might happen in the future. Though the specific details might have differed, I tried to write about all our lives, because I believed that every person has in him or herself the entire human condition (Montaigne, 1973). I wanted readers to feel that in describing my experience I had penetrated their heads and their hearts. I hoped they would grapple with the ways they were unique and the ways we were similar. Along with Mairs (1994, p. 120), I shared the sense that if "I do my job, the books I write vanish before your eyes," and I invited the reader into "the house of my past," hoping the "threshold" crossed would lead them into their own.

Returning to each event time and again, I felt that it was my responsibility, as a sociological writer, not only to probe feelings but also to try to make sense of the experiences, to find concepts and patterns that might explain how certain actions, even contradictory ones, fit together. Similar to the grounded theory approach (Glaser & Strauss, 1967), I looked for larger schemas within which these events might be contained. Sometimes I could explain situationally or historically why seemingly contradictory details had occurred. Features of culture and social structure, gender and socialization patterns, and structural constraints had affected my experience, and social conventions and commitments had narrowed my vision and understanding of myself (Rosenwald, 1992, pp. 276, 280). I tried to give readers enough clues about these macrosocial forces that they could see the impact and draw their own conclusions.

Sometimes, unlike grounded theory, I let contradictions and seemingly random events stand, willing to admit, after deep exploration, that no explanatory scheme or pattern was readily apparent. I continued to be intent on making sure that lived experience did not get lost under the authority of abstract explanatory concepts. I could only hope that this stance would resonate with readers, who, I had to assume, also sometimes experienced a lack of resolution in or explanation for their thoughts and feelings.

It seemed to me that all of us live with contingency and that to attempt to explain all of it away would be illusionary (see Becker, 1994). "As far as I'm concerned," stated Mairs (1994), "my text is flawed not when it is ambiguous or even contradictory, but only when it leaves you no room for stories of your own. I keep my tale as wide open as I can" (p. 74).

In the telling, I worked constantly to find a balance between honest writing and good sense, between portraying life as intimately and candidly as I could and protecting my relationships with characters in the story and with my readers. Nevertheless, I held firm to a commitment to tell an interesting, evocative story that adequately conveyed the emotionality and complexity of what I felt took place and that resonated true with the experience I thought I had had. I tried to make the story horizontally coherent, in that the events should be cohesive enough to warrant their meaningfulness, and vertically coherent, in that the episodes were warranted by an honest depiction of feelings and thoughts of the characters (Rosenwald, 1992, p. 285).

All stories transform experience (Bateson, 1972; Denzin, 1991; Derrida, 1978). As soon as experience is put into words, it is shaped by language and cultural understanding as well as orientation to an "other." The experience is always more than can be put into the text (Denzin, 1991) and less than the text tries to tell (Goodman, 1994). Life experience is always "larger and more ambiguous" than any account of it can be (Rosenwald, 1992, p. 275). And, the telling of it always involves circular emotional and cognitive understanding and the processes of interpretation that in everyday life blur and intertwine (Denzin, 1984). Each reflection on the experience generates alternative versions of what happened, revised senses of the self, and the values held. The past "appears different at every new turn we take" (Rosenwald, 1992, p. 275).

For me, the question had become not whether narratives convey precisely the way things actually were, but rather what narratives do, what consequences they have, and to what uses they can be put (Bochner, Ellis, & Tillmann-Healy, 1997). "The beauty of a good story is its openness," how readers "take it in" and use it for themselves (Coles, 1989, p. 47).

Working with Passion

In early 1990, as I wrote yet another draft of *Final Negotiations,* I also worked on completing an article entitled "Emotional Sociology" (1991b), in which I continued to advocate for passionate, evocative, and introspective writing. To advance my case that we should study emotions emotionally and feel and care for our selves, participants, readers, and topics of study, I showcased the writing of thick, detailed narratives that concretely described, embodied, and interpreted lived experience of self and others. The power of the stories, I wrote, lay in their ability to elicit "raw" experience from readers, which in turn offered a way to convey such experience to others.

That same year, I had the good fortune of meeting Art Bochner, a seasoned academic writer and communication professor, interested in accomplishing the same goals in social science as was I—to make it more human, useful, and evocative. His reading of "Emotional Sociology" was invaluable for helping me think through not only what I wanted to say but *how* I wanted to—and could—say it.

Of course, our common interest in humanizing social science was not the only curiosity that attracted us to each other. Our relationship emerged in tandem with our joint involvement in developing a research program that embraced autoethnography, personal narrative, and interpretive social science.

Story Interlude: Moving Together
By Arthur Bochner and Carolyn Ellis[9]

Scene: Art and Carolyn stand at two podia. Periodically they join each other at a table in center stage.

ART (*Picks up school newspaper in his office, turns to his student.*): Look, there's a talk being given in the business school today entitled "Systematic Sociological Introspection and Research on Emotions." The author is Carolyn Ellis from the sociology department. Um, I've never heard of her, but the topic sounds intriguing. Let's go.

(Art sits down. Carolyn turns podium toward Art.)

CAROLYN: And in conclusion, what I've done in this presentation is to lay out how one might use a systematic, scientific form of sociological introspection to try to understand the intersection of personal and social aspects of emotions. In my reading from my book manuscript, *Final Negotiations*, about the illness and death of my partner, Gene Weinstein, I have tried to help you imagine what narrative written from introspection might look like—a story with a plot, character development, scenes, and action, which invite you to enter our experience with us, feel what we feel, or imagine what you might feel or have felt in similar circumstances. In that way, you have your own emotions to examine, the best way I know to convey to you what emotions feel like.

Now I'd like to open up this session for questions from the audience. Yes . . .

ART (*Stands and raises his hand; Carolyn nods.*): Dr. Ellis, I really appreciated your talk. Social science does indeed need more heart and emotion. I have only one small point to raise. You seem to accept the terms that orthodox social scientists use to describe their work—objectivity, validity, reliability. This ends up making you sound very defensive. Why not drop all the science talk? Just take it for granted that what you are doing is important. It only distracts you and your readers from the very human sense of suffering and loss you communicate so beautifully. . . . [pause] . . . and another question I have . . .

(Art sits down. As Carolyn walks to her seat, she speaks to the audience.)

CAROLYN: And that's how we met. I gave this talk in the business school in January 1990. I was apprehensive that the faculty there wouldn't be interested in introspection and emotions. I tried to anticipate their objections to my work.

I wondered who this man in the audience asking all these questions could be. They were interesting questions, though I couldn't help but think he was one of those "language is everything" people. Anyway, I was accustomed to defending myself against the accusation that what I was doing wasn't science. But this guy was coming at me from a whole new angle: Why are you being so defensive about your work as science? Certainly it gave me a lot to think about. Besides I also was fascinated with how good looking he was. Who is this person anyway?

ART: I sat in amazement listening to Carolyn speak. When she mentioned her partner Gene Weinstein, I couldn't believe it, since his work on altercasting and interpersonal competence[10] had strongly influenced my dissertation research twenty years earlier. Then, as she continued, I realized how similar she was to me in the way she described what needed to be done to resurrect the social sciences and make them meaningful. I thought, She's giving my talk. Who is this woman anyway? How could we have been on the same campus for the last six years and never met?

Of course, the truth is I was immediately attracted to her passion and energy (to say nothing of her good looks). She seemed to be about the same age as me, give or take a few years, and her talk focused on how she had taken care of a partner who died. I couldn't help wondering: Is she available? Unattached? If she is, is she still mourning her loss? Hmmm, I liked her vitality and sense of humor. I thought I ought to at least give it a shot, go up and meet her, feel out the possibilities. So I waited until the crowd around her dissipated and introduced myself. We walked out of the room and into the parking lot together.

CAROLYN: After talking, we decided to exchange articles we'd published. On Monday, I had a student run some things across campus to Art's mailbox. That day and the next, every time I went to my mailbox, I had another article from Art. Sometimes only an hour apart. Hm, I thought, this is definitely an academic form of flirtation. So I wrote Art a note thanking him for the articles, and added, "I'm certainly glad we found each other." That was my form of flirtation.

ART and CAROLYN (in unison): And as the saying goes, one thing leads to another.

(Carolyn and Art stand.)

CAROLYN (speaking to audience): When Art and I first began talking about our work, we observed how similar our projects were. We both wanted a different kind of social science, a more artful one centered on meanings and stories. I was developing a narrative and conversational style of writing that felt natural and exemplified my way of showing interaction in which emotions are felt and expressed. I was a storyteller at heart. Art had taught and written philosophy of communication and communication theory and as a former college debater had always been most comfortable with a critical, theoretical, and conceptual voice. To a certain extent his was the voice of theory; mine, the voice of story. Though we saw ourselves emerging as partners in a project on bringing the personal voice into social science, we initially relied on our individual strengths to articulate the significance of the project. While I was completing *Final Negotiations* and the story of my brother's death, Art published "Theories and Stories" in 1994. There he outlined in a conceptual voice the five characteristics of a narrative perspective on social science writing.

ART *(elaborates on characteristics of personal narrative, including 1. In a narrative perspective, writing about "others" is problematized and becomes a focus point for social research; 2. an autobiographical voice is encouraged and legitimated; 3. attention is focused on the ways in which narrative practices historically influence accounts of the past and future; 4. new and alternative forms for expressing and/or evoking lived experiences are explored; 5. the image we have of conceptions between writers and readers of social science texts is converted from neutral and distanced to participatory and involved.)*

CAROLYN: Through our work as well as our personal relationship, our two voices—one more storied, the other more theoretical—gradually began to merge. We found ourselves co-constructing what we wanted from our life together, personally as well as academically. What did it take to move these voices into greater contact with each other? This period of our lives, we refer to as *(in unison) "moving together."*

(Both sit down at table.)

ART: When Carolyn and I met, each of us was established as a single, independent person. I had my house; she had hers. She worked in her department; I worked in mine. When we made the decision to be together, we weren't completely sure what that meant. Would she move into my house; would I move into hers? Or would we create ours? My house was in the suburbs, far from campus. I had wanted to be closer to the university anyway, so if a move was to be made to one place or the other, hers seemed the logical home. Her house, though, was quite a bit smaller than mine, only 1,400 square feet. One Sunday, I came over to plan with Carolyn my move into her house.

ART: "Where will I keep my clothes?"

CAROLYN: "Well, the closets are pretty full, but I can probably make room in one of the smaller ones for some of your stuff."

ART: "And exactly which room did you have in mind for my study?"

CAROLYN: "You might be able to squeeze a desk into a corner of my exercise room."

ART: Suddenly, I found myself squeezed between some chairs and a wall, metaphorically expressing what I was thinking: that this would never do. We would both have to move together, create our own new space. It wouldn't be hers, nor would it be mine;

it would be (*in unison*) *ours*, a third space, akin to the space between social sciences and humanities.

CAROLYN: The following year, we moved into a large house with two upstairs studies accessed by separate sets of steps. Two and a half years later, in early 1995, we married. Just before that, *Final Negotiations* was published. Just after that, I moved officially from sociology to the communication department at the University of South Florida, where I could work with Art and with the large number of Ph.D. students who had come to study ethnography, narrative, and autoethnography. This move provided an opportunity to educate graduate students who we hoped would teach other M.A. and Ph.D. students about this perspective.

*   *   *

Looking back now as I finish this manuscript, it is difficult to put into words what my relationship with Art—my partner in every respect of the word—has meant to me personally and professionally. Art read every page of *Final Negotiations*—several times. Not only was he significant in editing my prose and listening to me as I tried to figure out how to focus and end my story, he became part of my story, adding coherence and continuity to my life, and supporting me as I wrote and revised. He helped make it possible for me "to recover a living past, to believe again in the future, to perform acts that have significance for the person who acts" (Crites, 1971, p. 311). And, he did all this without ever expressing jealousy about my relationship with Gene or pushing me to move beyond grief and immersion in writing until it was clear that I was ready to do so.

Not only did Art help me see the value of writing less defensively, he also supported me on an occasion when I crumbled from criticism. A scholar I admired had reviewed my publications for promotion to full professor and had written a formal reference letter to the university and a private letter to me. The review noted that without considering *Final Negotiations*, which was still in progress, my record was sufficient to warrant my promotion, but that with it, my case was tenuous. It's hard to think of a more damning statement. More difficult than the formal evaluation of my work and case for promotion was the private letter to me, which read in part: "For all the raw emotion in this book, important emotions are hiding. . . . [Gene's] love, jealousy, distrust, need for you, your love, devotion, anger, and need of him; these are the feelings that are central. The rest of the world barely exists. But it is the rest of the world, and your feelings about it, that I came to feel increasingly uneasy about. . . . [You describe] a dyadic morality, only you and Gene matter in the world. . . . If it were me, I would wonder whether I took his death from [his children]."

My head throbbed and my pulse speeded up as I hyperventilated upon reading these words. I went home to bed, unable to stop crying and feeling the moral fiber of the life I had lived had been attacked. "Do *you* think I lived an immoral life?" I asked Art, who had come to sit by my side. "Is that what this is about?" he asked, holding me gently as my sobs gathered momentum. He didn't have to say anything else. His being there, his unwavering love and support, gave me the strength to get out of bed the next day and the courage to complete the book without straying from my goals. In conversation with Art, I was able to sort out how to listen to responses to my story, yet stand behind my interpretation without being consumed by wondering if I had "done it all wrong." I learned to deal with critical feedback: to learn what I could about my life and work from these reactions and then to focus on them as a window into people's lives and interpretive procedures, history, and beliefs; to move from a focus on how readers had responded to my work to a focus on what I might learn about *them* and their cultural beliefs from their responses. After making that move, I could get past the problem Nancy Mairs (1994) points out is endemic for most writers: that the "praise counts for so little in relation to even a whisper of blame" (p. 140), and I was able to view all responses—the many positive as well as the negative—as grist for the interpretive mill.[11]

Meta-Autoethnography: Writing a Past/Imagining a Future

In 2007, I gave a presentation at the National Communication Association in a panel on "Writing about the Death of a Spouse." In it I read an edited version of the last three pages of *Final Negotiations* and then commented on it from my current positioning.

Endings: Renegotiating Meaning and Identity[12]

Now I must end this project. For the last few years, any fear I had of letting go came from my fear that this book would not be "good enough" to have justified the many years I worked at finishing it or that it would never get a respectable publisher. Or, if it did, that the book would sit on a shelf somewhere; that is, my life would sit on a shelf. How do I do this well? I wondered, much as I had with Gene's dying and death, and the dilemma I faced with completing this book sometimes seemed almost as ambiguous, unknowable, and overwhelming. As in Gene's death, I feared and, at the same time, craved being done.

In writing my stories, I have not wanted to complain or call attention to the specialness of my personal disaster since I know from this experience, if from no other source, that there is nothing "exceptional" about my life or my tragedies (Mairs, 1993). What I have hoped for is insight, companionship, and comfort during my grief (Hauerwas, 1990). The process of writing and the anticipation of an involved audience have provided that. Personally, I hoped you, the audience, would identify with my plight and gain a heightened emotional sense of what it felt like to live this experience, as well as an intellectual understanding of the contradictions that occurred. In return, I have wanted to offer comfort and "companionship in a common venture" when your time for personal tragedy comes (Mairs, 1993, p. 25) and provide a point of comparison for your life story.

Telling both the relationship and the writing stories has been part of my project to make life more meaningful. I found meaning in my relationship with Gene and in being a part of his living and dying. That we worked so hard to create meaning reveals that it was always in danger of falling apart. When death approached and I needed Gene most to help me frame this experience, he was unable to participate. Nor did I have the safety of our relationship after his death to provide continuity and security to my life.

Thus it makes sense that I took on writing this text. Each telling of my story created new significance to my experience and contributed to personal identity (Polkinghorne, 1988). From writing this, I understand in a profound way that meaning is not permanent, "narratives change, all stories are partial, all meanings incomplete" (Bruner, 1986b, p. 153).

For most drafts of this book, the "Endings" reflected my struggle to find meaning in relationships. Now I focus instead on meaning-making in my academic work. As I rewrite myself in this manner, I am confronted once again with how much of the way we view our lives in the past is contextualized by what is going on in the present. As I work through the final version of this ending, I write out of my relationship with Art, an academic partner interested in meaning-making and intimate connections. It is no surprise that our interaction has had a profound influence on the telling of this story.

This project has given me a way to think and talk about close relationships and knowledge that I did not have when I started. In crossing disciplinary boundaries to join humanities and social sciences, this discourse connects human experience as lived to research on emotions and intimate bonds, permitting my "heart and head [to] go hand and hand," as Art (Bochner, 1981, p. 70) said in "Forming Warm Ideas." By contributing to a larger, collective project that seeks to humanize social science, create a space for experimental texts, and encourage writing stories that make a difference in peoples' lives, I have created for myself the same kind of excitement— only more intense—I felt when I first picked up Goffman's *The Presentation of Self in Everyday Life* (1959) and decided to study sociology. As I wrestle with (and enjoy) the ambiguity, complexity, and contradiction in lived experience, sometimes now I feel I know a great deal about living in relationships and writing narratives; other times, I'm sure I know almost nothing, even about the most basic process. Thus, there is no simple, tidy ending to this book; there is merely a practical one that honors the messiness of living (Marcus, 1994).

June 14, 1991 (Gene's birthday, six years after his death)

I wake up, emotionally exhausted, in the middle of a nightmare. I dream I am about to read a part of this book to a large audience. It is finally perfect. When I open my folder at the podium, my only copy of the final draft with my handwritten corrections is missing. I ruffle through the earlier drafts that are there. I feel the anticipation of the large, waiting crowd. I crawl under the podium, frantically searching.

"I can't find it," I exclaim. "I have lost it, and it was perfect."

"Can't you read an earlier draft?" the moderator asks.

I break down and sob, experiencing the same kind of explosion of the ball of grief as when Gene was dying.

When I tell Art about the dream, he says gently that it is time to be finished with the book, and I agree.

But, like Gene's death, the writing of this story lingered for a long time after the dream. Gene refused to die; this book refused to be born. Even now, in 1994, as I add the finishing touches, I do not feel "finished" with the relationship or the book. As Anderson (1968) writes: "Death ends a life, but it does not end the relationship which struggles on in the survivor's mind towards some final resolution, some clear meaning, which it perhaps never finds" (p. 281). Writing privileges one version of a story, but memories of untold details and alternate story lines still linger.

All this said, I finally am ready to put both the relationship and the book on a shelf, relinquishing as I do the responsibility to resolve the "real" ending.

Negotiations. Are they ever final?

Reflections on Writing about the Death of a Spouse
National Communication Association Convention, November 17, 2007

"What I just read to you is how I ended *Final Negotiations*," I tell my audience at NCA. "Now I speak from a different place, thirty-three years after I began a relationship with Gene, twenty-three years after his death, and twelve years after publishing *Final Negotiations*. I ask again: Are negotiations ever final?

"Negotiating meaning in the face of the inevitable loss of it through death seems to be the ultimate issue that affects our ability to live fully. I have tried to learn to live comfortably 'between' two views. First, that all meaning construction is an illusion; second, that there is some permanent meaning or immortality that transcends our individual lives;

between first, the denial of death and second, the immersion in it. Gene and I learned to live as well as we could in these liminal spaces through rehearsing his death, then returning as quickly as possible to the living of life. His actual death fractured that balance. Often I find myself thrown off kilter again, as I experience accumulated losses and anticipate future ones, and I, like Humpty Dumpty, have to put myself and my theorizing back together again.

"In my life now, my relationship with Gene no longer provides the context for my negotiating identity and meaning. In most ways, I don't work now to sustain my relationship with Gene. I rarely talk to him, because so much time has passed and so many things have happened that he hasn't been a part of, that sometimes it doesn't seem relevant to seek him out in my mind or memory. Okay, well, once in a while I think, Oh Gene, you would have loved all this autoethnography stuff—though you couldn't write worth a damn. And sometimes I reminisce with mutual friends who loved him. But I no longer need or want to make Gene a part of my day-to-day life, which doesn't negate the love I have for him or the pain I felt upon losing him. I don't struggle with the relationship anymore, as Anderson (1968) warns, at least not consciously, though I perhaps have to deal still with leftover remnants that live in me.

"Given the many years that have passed since Gene died, and all that's taken place, I'd say it's healthy to see the world from my current positioning rather than from several decades ago. There are many more pressing identity issues for me now than who I was in that relationship, for example, dealing with my own deteriorating, sagging, and aging body. I don't want so much to carry Gene with me, since I prefer to be fully present with the people who are physically in my life, rather than speaking to a ghost. Though as I say this, I must admit that I do occasionally smile as I sense Gene's spirit in the massage chair in my study, lounging with a pencil in one hand and a joint in the other, asking penetrating questions about my psyche, and then reminding me to play as well as work. Mostly when I think of Gene, though, it's in the context of writing autoethnography and revisiting the writing I've done about the time he and I were together.

"What, I ask myself now, are the long-term effects of having written and published an autoethnography about an intimate relationship? I *needed* to write to deal with the complexities of the relationship—the good and bad—to heal and move on. Autoethnographic writing offered intense self-therapy. From writing, I also learned things about relationships that I carry into my current partnership, and I think that I left behind some unnecessary baggage, though you probably should ask Art for a second opinion. Through writing, I discovered I only want to write stories that give meaning to my life and have the potential to offer meaning to and evoke meaning in others. An additional bonus is that I met Art though my writing, and our partnership was formed around our mutual interest in close relationships and evocative writing as inquiry.

"Thus, I attribute whatever well-being I have about my relationship with Gene and the loss of it to the following: 1) to writing and working through who I was in that relationship, a reworking of the past that allowed me to imagine a hopeful story for my future. Writing permitted me to move on while constructing a sense of narrative continuity; 2) to finding a new conversational partner with whom I construct identity, meaning, and an "us" that works beautifully, and who honored and validated my past; 3) to the conversations I've had with others who have suffered loss, many of whom responded to my writing, and offered comfort and stories of their own. Both of these processes—a new conversational partner and conversations with others about their losses—wed me to living and meaning-making in the here and now; and, finally, 4) I attribute whatever well-being I have about my past to doing work that I think makes a difference in people's lives, thus giving meaning some kind of permanence beyond my individual life and the illusions I try so hard to maintain. Writing academically about my life has given me a sense of wholeness and purpose.

"Thankfully, I no longer dream about the perfect book, the perfect relationship, or worry about my life sitting on a shelf.

"Negotiations. Some are more final than others."

Deeper Reflections on Grief and Loss

In my presentation, when I read aloud the sentence, "But I no longer need or want to make Gene a part of my day-to-day life, which doesn't negate the love I have for him or the pain I felt upon losing him," tears form in my eyes and roll down my face. I am surprised at my emotion. I thought I had this grief "put away." I have never broken down reading my stories at a conference and this presentation wasn't written evocatively. Does my emotion arise because I already am in an emotional space from experiencing the raw grief in Tom Frentz's presentation on the same panel about Janice Rushing (his wife who died a few years before)? Am I feeling my own loss of my friend Janice? My own accumulated loss of loved ones? Am I identifying with the pain of love and loss for everyone at the session? Anticipating my loss of Art, who is in the audience? Or his loss of me? Or more accumulated loss for both of us? Or is my long-term grief about losing Gene less well put together than my text represents?

I, of course, don't have answers to these questions. Nor is the literature on grief very helpful, since little is written about long-term or cumulative grief of twenty-five years.[13] But I do remember that the feeling I had was not all together painful. The emotion reminded

me of the attachment I felt to Gene and the positive memories I had of him. I felt his presence, saying, "Wait just a moment. You can't put me away that easily" (see Rosenblatt,
1996). (And, indeed, I can't, as evidenced by the place he still holds in my writing life.) I
also felt strong bonds to the small audience that came to our session, most of them dear
friends; I was glad for our collective feeling and support. I was particularly happy that Art
was in the audience, sharing this moment with me. From the front of the room, I felt our
strong connection, and though I didn't know for sure what he was feeling, I felt confident
he would be supportive of whatever was going on with me in terms of my continuing relationship with Gene. He always had been exemplary in that regard.[14]

I return to this issue of long-term grief in the next two chapters, which tell and discuss
the story of the loss of my brother Rex, who died in 1982 in an airplane crash two years
before Gene died. Unlike the agonizing slow loss of Gene, the loss of my brother was
unbearably sudden. The grief that followed was intense and long-lasting.

PART THREE

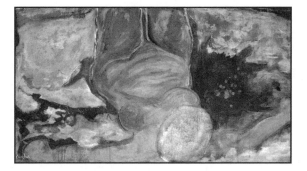

Surviving and Communicating Family Loss

CHAPTER SIX

Surviving the Loss of My Brother

"There Are Survivors": Telling a Story of Sudden Death[1]

I grew up in a small town in the foothills of Virginia, the same place my parents were born and raised. After attending elementary school in one-room schoolhouses, both parents took wage-labor jobs. My mother sewed pockets on pants; my father worked on a farm and then pumped gas. After marriage, my father started a small construction business. Although he never grasped the "abstractions" of a calculator, he could intuitively figure out on the back of a matchbook how much a new house or an addition would cost. As the office manager, my mother organized the business and kept the books, although she never fully understood how taxes worked or how spreadsheets were balanced. By the end of the booming 1960s, their construction business was considered the best in the area, and we went from near poverty level to being able to afford many of the luxuries of life. Still we lived similarly to the working-class families that surrounded us—we bought the same things, only more and newer models, and our talk and stories were about close-to-home events, day-to-day joys, and real-life tragedies.

Arthur, my oldest sibling, was born in 1937. Thirteen years older than I, he was more like a caring and dependable uncle than a brother. Judi weighed only three pounds when she was born in 1948. She seemed fragile as a child and was easily moved to tears. I saw her sensitivity as both her most outstanding characteristic and her most problematic one. She and I slept in the same room and argued constantly about when to turn out the light, who had worn the other's clothes without asking, and whose turn it was to dry the dishes. Coping with a younger, competitive, and less sensitive sister who made top grades and excelled in sports could not have been easy. I was born in 1950, then Rex in 1952.

Rex and I had an intense and complex relationship as children. He and I fought almost every day, but in contrast to my constant verbal irritation with my sister, our fights were physical and short-lived. I sat on top of him, holding his arms spread-eagle above his head. He squirmed as my face drew nearer and I threatened him with spittle dangling from my lips, sucking it in just before it escaped. Although he threatened all kinds of retribution, we ended most episodes laughing. He could have gotten me back during adolescence. But he didn't. All he ever did was win in arm wrestling a few times, just to show me.

Then I tried to outwit him. Often, I "borrowed" his bike when he wasn't looking. My parents didn't think a girl needed to have one. Finally, in exasperation, Rex secured his bike with a lock. That worked fine, until I discovered the lock not completely fastened one day, and I rode off for the afternoon. I convinced Rex I had picked the lock, and he never used it again. When he offered to let me borrow the bike occasionally after that, I stopped stealing it.

I had more academic smarts than Rex, but it never seemed to bother him. Although he followed me by two years in school, he managed to stand out, sometimes as an athlete, a jokester, or a musician. People loved his commonsense approach to life, his charm, good nature, and seemingly unselfconscious ability to have fun no matter what.

Rex cared about me. I knew because I tested him. I used to wash my hair over a washbasin in the bathroom. Once when he came into the room, I held perfectly still, my head listless in the water, and didn't respond to his conversation. When he peered under my hair to see if I was breathing, I opened my eyes and said, "Boo." I never let on I knew he thought I was dead. I felt sorry when I saw his worried expression and never did anything like that again.

Rex accidentally blackened my eye with a baseball bat one day. He cried when he saw he had hurt me. I knew I cared about him then too, because I made sure my mother understood it had been an accident so she wouldn't punish him, and I felt worse about his crying about hurting me than I did about my black eye.

Once I even risked a spanking for refusing to find a switch for my father who, in a moment of anguish, wanted to spank Rex for swimming in a pond in the middle of winter. Rex and I could count on protection from each other.

The Crash

As adults, Rex and I had become great friends. The last time I had seen him, at my parents' home at Christmas a few weeks before, he and I had spent only a few minutes together settling up for my parents' gifts and planning his trip to Tampa.

"I like it when you pick out the gifts," he had said. "Let's do this again next year. I can't wait to see you in Tampa."

"Yeah," I replied. "I'll get your airplane ticket. I know how to get the best rates."

"I tell all my friends you're a professor," Rex said proudly. "It'll be fun to come to your class." Suddenly, I felt nervous about being evaluated by my brother.

* * *

Rex was scheduled to arrive today, Friday, January 13, 1982. Although I was supposed to meet him at 4:30, his plane was just ready for takeoff from Washington when I called the airline at 3:45. Since I had invited several friends to dinner, I was glad for the extra time.

"Hey, what you doing?" my older brother, Arthur, asks when I pick up the ringing phone. I am surprised to hear from him, and, in spite of the lightness of his words, detect worry in his voice. Rather quickly, he asks, "Has Rex gotten there yet?"

"No, his plane has been delayed. Why?" Already I feel alarmed.

"Oh, someone called Mom and said a plane had crashed, and she thought they said something about Tampa. I just want to reassure her that Rex is okay. You know how she worries."

Although he says this nonchalantly, I tense up because I feel how hard he is working to normalize this conversation. Then I speak from inside a numb fog, "Where did they say the plane was headed?"

"Well, she thought they said it was coming from Tampa to Washington."

"Then that can't be it," I respond too quickly, adrenaline now starting to pump. We breathe.

Into the silence my brother says, "But there was confusion because they said it was Flight 90."

"That's his flight number, but Mom probably just got the number wrong." Yes, that's the explanation, I assure myself.

"No," he says. "I just heard the number myself on the radio."

"Did they say Air Florida?"

"I don't know, just that it had crashed into the Potomac."

"Oh, God, I'll call the airline and call you right back."

Flashes of lightning go off behind my eyes. My breathing speeds up, yet I am suffocating. As I dial, my hands shake, and I say aloud over and over, "No, please, God." Struck by the triviality of my everyday concerns, I remember how rushed I had felt getting ready for Rex's arrival and how important that had seemed. Now, if he is only alive, nothing else will matter. Of course he is, I admonish myself. Calm down. Mom has this all messed up. But then how did Arthur hear the same flight number?

I get a busy signal a couple of times before an Air Florida agent responds, "Air Florida, may I help you?"

The familiar greeting comforts me. See, there's nothing wrong, I reassure myself. "Yes, I want information on an arrival time."

"Certainly. What is the flight number?" he asks cheerfully.

"Flight 90."

Now his voice takes on a businesslike quality as he quickly replies, "We cannot give out information on that flight."

"What do you mean you 'can't give out information on that flight'?"

"We can't give out information on that flight," he repeats.

My heart pounds, as I calmly ask, "Did an Air Florida plane crash today?"

"Yes."

"Was it going from Washington to Tampa?"

"Yes," he says, seeming relieved to answer my questions.

"How many flights do you have going from Washington to Tampa today?"

"Two."

"When were they scheduled?"

"One this morning. One this afternoon."

"Did the one this morning make it?"

"Yes."

"Thank you very much," I say softly and hang up the phone, my heart pounding.

Arthur answers on the first ring. "There was a crash," I say. "And it sounds like it was Rex's plane."

"They are saying now there are survivors," says my brother, and I feel hope. He continues, "I'm going to Mom and Dad's. They're pretty upset. They're going to be more upset."

"Okay, yes, go. We'll keep in touch."

Now I am alone, in shock, adrenaline rushing through my body. Numb on the outside, my insides are overstimulated. I tumble slowly through blank space. "Please, God, no," I hear myself moaning deeply from my gut. I move quickly to turn on the television. "Flight 90 crashes," it rings in my ears. "There are survivors in the water being rescued. Look, another head." This is not a movie, or an instant replay. I sit, my arms wrapped around my body, and sway back and forth twelve inches from the TV, breathing deeply and groaning. My eyes are glued to the rescue of the victims from the Potomac, and I search frantically for Rex. "He has to be there," I say out loud. In a daze, I am conscious of myself watching the TV as part of the scene. Reality becomes hazy, and more multi-layered and boundaryless than usual.

A car approaches and I know from the familiar sound that it is Gene, my partner, and Beth, his daughter, home from shopping. When I rush to the door, the fog lifts suddenly and the slow-motion scene I am in slips into fast-forward. "What's wrong, honey?" Gene asks as he steps through the door, drops his packages to the floor, and embraces me.

Quietly and desperately, I say, "My brother's plane crashed."

"Oh, my God," he says calmly. Do something, I want to yell. Make it okay. But I say nothing. His body quivers; his embrace tightens. It feels good to be held and to have told someone. Not just someone. Gene, my anchor. He will know what to do and how to think about what has happened. My body slumps against his. "Oh, my God," he says again.

"It doesn't seem real," I say.

"Death never does," he replies. "But it is." Death? Why is he talking about death? It's just a crash. I cry quietly.

Then like a shot, I remember, "The TV. I've got to get back to the TV. There are survivors," and I break free from his embrace. That's right, he doesn't know there are survivors. That's why he's talking about death. "I'll see Rex being pulled from the river," I say loudly, fists clenched in the air. "Then I'll know he's all right. He had to make it. He's tough. There are survivors," I repeat.

Beth and Gene don't watch the instant replays of the people floundering in the icy water. Why do they sit silently at the kitchen table? They should be helping me look for Rex. They must not believe me. But they don't know him like I do. He can get himself out of anything. Any minute his head will appear. I continue rocking back and forth with my hands clasped together, periodically putting my face against the television screen to get a closer view. But I cannot find my brother in the Monet-like dots and lines. Hope and desperation alternate—hope when a new survivor is sighted, desperation when it is not Rex. There must be more survivors. "Rex, pop up out of the fucking water," I scream.

The announcers talk about the hero who just died saving others. "That must be Rex," I say, feeling proud. "He would do that. That's what he was like." Was? Why am I using the past tense? "He's not dead," I say. "I know he isn't." But if he has to be dead, I want him to be the hero. But then I will be angry that he could have saved himself and didn't. Why aren't Gene and Beth responding to me? They sit, silent, sad, watching me. He's not dead. Quit acting like he's dead. Of course, he's not dead. Not my brother.

Nancy, a friend who was coming to dinner, has heard about the plane crash and calls to give me up-to-date newscasts from her cable channels. Her calls distract me from watching what are now the same instant replays of the same people being pulled out of the same river. Twelve people have survived. Then they announce seven. Then there are five. And one dead hero.

Even I can see that there is no reason now to chain myself to the TV. Instead, I pace and chatter, "Okay, let's see. He has five chances out of seventy-nine, the number of people on the plane. That's about 1/16th possibility that he survived. Not much. But they think all the survivors were sitting in the tail section. He was, I mean is, a smoker. So he was probably in the rear, which makes his chances even greater. But then they think one of the survivors was a stewardess, so his chances are four out of seventy-eight." When all else fails, try probability. Gene and Beth stare at me, still without speaking. When I break down, Gene comes to hold me. But soon I am up, moving around, calculating frantically, like a mad woman.

It is announced on TV that relatives who are waiting at Tampa International Airport have been taken to a special room. They suggest that other relatives come there for up-to-date information and counseling. "Do you want to go?" asks Gene. "I'll take you."

My impulse to go is short-lived. "No, what good will it do? We're getting current information here. Why do I want to be around other upset people I don't know? What can counseling do? I want to be here with you, and where I can talk to Arthur."

Every half hour, I am on the phone with Arthur. It takes at least ten attempts to get through the busy circuits. The Tampa–Virginia lines are being overworked by all the grieving people soothing each other, seeking information, and refusing to believe their worst fears are true. Just like us.

Arthur is with our parents, who, he says, "are a disaster." The news is spreading through Luray, and the phone is constantly busy with people who want to know "Is it true?" and "What's the latest?"

My brother and I do not break down as we share information, of which there is practically none, and what is available keeps getting worse. And worse. Our spirits drop every time we talk, "but I still have hope," I say. "I know he's alive."

Arthur replies, "It doesn't look good, Susie [his pet name for me]." Not him too. It's not like him to give up. I hide my anger, and an inner voice says, He's probably right. Get yourself ready for this. No, no, other voices scream, and I listen to them instead.

Sometimes I feel like laughing when I survey this horrible, surreal scene that plays as a TV suspense show. Then I switch from being an observer to being a participant in the tragedy, and I sob.

"Call the people we have invited to dinner and cancel," I instruct Gene, who wants to help. "I don't want to talk to anyone."

Each time I hear him say, "Carolyn's brother's plane has crashed. It doesn't look good," I cry anew. Glad for the felt sympathy, I also am distressed when Gene's words give reality to the experience.

When I finally plop down, exhausted, at the table with Gene and Beth, we stare silently, and nervous giggles alternate with my sobs and Gene's comforting touches. "Eat something," Gene commands. "You must eat." Is he kidding? I will throw up if I eat, but suddenly I have a craving for the warm, strong taste of Scotch, which I seldom drink. From that day on, every time I experience severe stress I will want Scotch.

"I feel like getting out, going to the mall," Beth says. "I'm not doing anything useful. But I'll stay if you want me to."

"No, go have a good time," I respond, appreciating her concern. Feeling closer to Gene when we are alone, I tell him I am glad he is with me.

Gene takes a rational approach, "What can you do? It's done now."

"I just know he's alive," I insist.

I speak of my parents and the agony they must be going through. I think of the difficulty of Arthur's position. "I am glad I'm not there. But I feel I ought to be there. I wish I were there." My confused thoughts mix with each other in slow motion. Finally I put the big pot of Mexican stew I have made into the freezer. A few weeks later, I will throw it out.

Beth brings us two cat humor books. "We need some laughter," she explains. When she and Gene read aloud and laugh, I smile but don't hear.

"We are sitting around looking at each other, too," Arthur says when he calls at ten p.m. "The airline will let me know when it's official."

"Why are you assuming he's dead?" I ask.

"Because Bev [our cousin] went to the Marriott Hotel in Washington where they announced the list of survivors. He wasn't on there, Susie," he says reverently. Did I hear him right? It is hard to hear from inside the fog, with my heart beating so loudly.

"I don't care," I say after a pause, defiantly. "I won't give up hope."

"I don't think there's any hope left," Arthur says even more softly, and this time I know he's right. I feel closer to him than ever in my life, and understand that he needs me to face reality and help him carry the burden.

I try. "Yeah, I guess you're right. What do we do now? Have you told Mom and Dad?"

"No. I want to wait until I get the official word." I wonder why. But I know. He wants to put it off as long as possible. And he hopes for a miracle, just like I do.

"Okay, I understand," I say, to be supportive of his decision.

Arthur and I talk several times the next few hours, and decide to call Judi, our sister, the next morning. "Why put her through a night of agony?" I rationalize, without acknowledging that I do not want to experience her shock of grief now, which will be raw and unmonitored. Arthur agrees quickly, and then we make other decisions together. We express our love for each other for the first time. Sharing our brother's death brings us closer and makes us aware of what we usually don't say.

I decide to wait a day before going home. "I need to be with you right now," I say to Gene. "When I get home I'll have to be together. I need to collapse and feel your love." In spite of Gene's chronic emphysema, he seems strong and glad to help me. When he offers to come with me, I say, "I'd love it, but it's too hard for you."

During the night, Gene's tight embrace and burly chest, barrel-shaped from the steroids he takes to combat his emphysema, comfort me each time I cry. We make love in the night, quietly, softly, for the attachment.

When the phone rings at three a.m., I jump, still hoping for good news. I am angry, feel sorry for myself, and cry again after I figure out that it is an obscene phone call.

Arthur calls early the next morning, and says Air Florida finally called at three a.m. to tell us officially that Rex was dead. "It's been horrible," he says. "I lay awake all night waiting for the call I knew would come. Mom and Dad were full of hope. At three, Dad came in and woke me—I must have dozed off—and said, 'It's the phone.' I had instructed the officials to talk to no one but me, and I couldn't believe I hadn't heard the phone. I answered knowing what they would say. Mom and Dad stood around me like little kids waiting for the news. They knew by my voice. Everyone started sobbing. Then Aunt Florence came into the room and said, 'He's dead, ain't he?' We all cried together."

Sorry not to have shared that moment, I crave attachment with my family, and even with the pain—I want to feel as much pain as I can. Rex is worth my suffering. At the same time, I am glad to be with Gene, who comforts me.

I am relieved when Arthur says, "I called Judi." Does my relief come from not wanting to take care of her? From the lack of closeness that has characterized our relationship from early on? Or because I now do not have to be the bearer of bad news?

"How did she take it?" What a ridiculous question.

"She started sobbing and couldn't talk. Her husband got on the phone."

"I'll call her now," I tell my brother. "We'll make plans to come to Luray tonight. I need today."

"I understand," he says.

"Hang in there, little brother," I say, using my pet name, and then realize that he is now my only living brother. "I'll be there soon. Then you can lean on me. I know you're holding everyone together." My words feel forced, and I am not sure I will have the strength.

"Thanks," he says. "It'll be good to have you here."

By the time I call my sister, I am numb. Interspersed with sobs is talk of her belief in God. I am glad she has it, but I don't want to hear it now. We make airline reservations for later that day, managing to connect on the same plane from Atlanta to Washington, D.C.

A newspaper reporter calls, identifying himself as a Washington correspondent. Thinking this is an official, I answer irrelevant questions: "When did you last see your brother?" "What was he like?" "He was wonderful, just wonderful." What else could I say? "I can't talk anymore." The reporter doesn't press. "How dare they," I say to Gene as I hang up, and then wish I had said more. Rex would have liked to be in the *Washington Post.*

When some of my colleagues arrive with food, I am still in my housecoat and have not combed my hair or brushed my teeth. Aware that my robe sometimes exposes the curve of my breast, I listlessly pull the sash tighter several times. Finally, I say, "Oh, what difference does it make anyway?" and let it hang. Nothing is sexual now. I have two Scotches, but I can't eat. No one speaks of my brother. I am glad they came.

Because of weather conditions, my plane is late taking off. My brother was just killed in this icy weather—I must be crazy to get on a plane. But I have no options. I take a deep breath and walk past the smiling stewardess. How could she be the same as always? On takeoff, I pretend to be my brother and the plane is crashing and I imagine what it must have been like for him. Eyes closed, I feel the plane diving, then the smack as it hits the water. Then darkness. God, I hope he didn't know what was happening.

My sister's flight is even later than mine. When I get nervous waiting for her at the departure gate in Atlanta, I run to her gate and ask the arrival time. "It should be here in a few minutes," the woman says nonchalantly.

"My brother was killed on the Air Florida flight yesterday. I am connecting with my sister here to go home." Suddenly I have her attention.

"Oh, my, well, don't worry. If it doesn't come in a few minutes, we'll try to delay your departing flight." Hearing my words and seeing the attendant's concern make tears stream down my face. When people show compassion, I feel sorry for myself.

I am relieved to see my sister and her husband walk through the door. She is sobbing and I am near tears as we embrace. Momentarily, my pain increases (or escapes) with hers. At the same time, I feel close to her, glad to be with family. We run to the departing flight, holding onto each other.

Small-Town Death Rituals

What will it be like to see my parents? I take a deep breath, my head swims, and I walk into the house. My dad cries and holds onto me. Already in my caretaker role, I have no tears. My mom's body is rigid in response to my hug. "It's going to be okay," I say. "We'll talk."

"It won't be okay," she says angrily. "He's dead. He's not coming back." I am silenced by the truth of her response.

I ignore the two local ministers I don't know and hug Barbara, my sister-in-law, who whispers into my ear, "They found his body."

"Thank God," I say, feeling great relief and then wonder why. "When?"

"They called an hour ago."

Arthur and I hug each other tightly. The atmosphere feels like death. When the town sheriff and the funeral director stop on their way to Washington to identify and bring back my brother's body, my mother sobs, "Bring my boy home." My grief for her then, and for myself, threatens to take me over. Afraid, I choke it down.

Individual Grief and Community Sympathy

From Saturday evening until the funeral on Monday our house was filled with people. The only quiet time was at night when I would talk to Mom, who lay on the couch in the living room. My father slept beside her in his La-Z-Boy chair. Neither wanted to be in their separate bedrooms.

"Rex brought me a rose in a bud vase the week before he died," Mom says. "When I asked him what occasion it was for, he said, 'Because I love you.'"

Over and over, she describes the details of the last time she saw him. "He came in here, in this room, and asked me for a strap to tie around his suitcase. I can see him now kneeling on the floor and tying it on. Then he hugged me like he didn't want to let go. 'I don't know when I'll be back. Expect me when you see me,' he said."

"My life is over," she sobs, believing it and coming close to convincing me. Every night I listened and asked the same questions so she could tell her story again. Besides, I liked picturing him leaving on a trip and I wanted every detail of the last time she saw him. Maybe she would remember something new, provide a clue to Rex's death, something that would make it all make sense. Finally, when I venture, "I'm upset too," I get no comfort.

"A mother's pain is worse, the worst there is," she says bitterly, her self-absorption offering no place for my grief. In contrast, my father is warm and open in his sadness, receiving my love. We hug and cry silently together, feeling a lot but saying little.

The only time I had for myself was when I showered. I loved feeling the hot water run over my body. As I cried and relaxed, the pain would break through my numbness and a moan from deep in my being would escape. Amazed at the intensity of the pain, I pushed it down. I can't deal with you now. Would I ever be able to? I talked out loud to

Rex, telling him how much I already missed him. "Rex, help me deal with this. Help me comfort Mom and Dad." It was a close, peaceful feeling.

"I am communicating with Rex," I tell my mom, thinking she will like that I am being "religious," even though it doesn't fit into her Lutheran doctrine.

"What kind of religion do you have anyway? You can't talk to the dead," she replies, and I shrug.

* * *

The people came. Three to four hundred of them. They occupied my parents and validated for me how important Rex had been. I became the greeter, letting them in, hugging, listening to them marvel at how I had changed, and then directing them to my parents, who sat side-by-side in their La-Z-Boy chairs. Offering their sympathies, men looked sad and stoically held my father's hand and kissed my mother. Women were more likely to cry openly with my mother and often with my father, sometimes falling in sobs into my parents' arms. Older people comforted, while the younger ones stammered about not knowing what to say. That would come with experience. My mother cried continually and my father wiped tears constantly. I was the dry-eyed director, who craved and feared collapsing into my parents' embrace.

Everyone came bearing food. The smell was sickening. Knowing exactly what to do, several community women took over our kitchen. They served big meals to whoever was there, ignoring that no one ate much. Later in the week, it would take hours to throw away all the uneaten food: green beans cooked with ham hock; whole Old Virginia hams—the real ones, salty, strong, and fat; green and red Jell-O salads embedded with nuts and coconut, made in circular tins with globs of Miracle Whip filling the middle hole; apple pies made quickly from canned apples with dough crisscrossed on the top and too much cinnamon added; sweet pound cakes, chocolate layer cakes with chocolate icing, and yellow cakes with white frosting; big, fluffy white loaves of Wonder Bread; gallons of sweet tea in pickle jars that still tasted and smelled of pickles. Years later I would find containers of instant coffee—the family size—Coffee-Mate, and hundreds of plastic utensils still bundled in plastic wrappers in the cabinets.

Part of the role of greeter was to record who had brought what so that thank-you cards could be sent. My sister and I took turns keeping records. Sometimes I wanted to scream, What a waste of time and energy. Other times I was glad for the task and respected the ritual of acknowledgment.

Mixed in with the mourners came the florists with the flowers we had requested not be sent. Donations for my parents' church also poured in. "What can we do?" everyone asked. Write some thank-you notes, I wanted to say, but didn't. It was not their job. Then go help throw food away, I thought, but again, I said nothing. Proper etiquette dictated that you wait until people insisted—or, better yet, just did something. I had never been involved in a funeral before, but I intuitively knew the rules. They were an extension of the small-town etiquette that I had lived the first twenty-two years of my life.

I helped my mother make up a list of pallbearers. "They should be his best friends," she instructs. "It can't be relatives. They have to be men. There must be six." This is not the time to argue for women pallbearers. This is for my mother.

The Funeral Home and the Funeral

On Sunday I call the funeral director and ask to see Rex's body. Because the body had been in water and because Rex had a bad head injury, we wouldn't have an open-casket funeral.

"Do you want to go?" I hesitantly ask my mother.

"I just can't. But I wish I had his gold chain so you could put it on him. The one I gave him, that he always wore, that he was wearing the day he died."

"Why don't I put my gold chain around his neck? The one you gave me."

"Good," she says, smiling for the first time.

The funeral home. What a place. What a smell—intense flowers mixed with cologne, disinfectants, and just a hint of embalming fluid. It's the only context in which I hate the odor of flowers. I have trouble catching my breath as I enter. Yet I walk ahead of Arthur and Rex's ex-wife into the room containing the casket. I have to see him.

I stand close to the casket as the director opens it. I am not afraid of you. I love you. There he is. Is it him? I have to be sure. I know it is. I dare hope and know it is impossible that they have made a mistake. But it doesn't look like him. His face is swollen and his nose, from being broken, is flatter and much bigger than usual. And that dead color doesn't help either. Then the huge gash on his forehead glares at me from underneath multilayers of pasty make-up. I swallow, and it is *my* head hitting the front seat as we crash.

He is shrouded in polyester, dead clothes complete with clip-on tie, an outfit that would have horrified him. I want to dress him in his own clothes. But my mom has proudly announced she told the funeral director to put him in a new blue suit. No one else is going to see him. What difference does it make anyway?

Arthur stands frozen some distance behind me. In a short while, he leaves. Rex's ex-wife, who also is behind me, looks relieved when I ask if I can have time alone with Rex. I glide my hands over the hardness of his body, remembering his being and adding to my memory now his deadness. I caress his face lovingly and talk softly to him. "I'm going to miss you. I love you." Then I put my necklace around his neck and say, "This is for you. From Mom and me. We love you." And I walk away.

"Can you tell if he died in pain or fear?" I ask the funeral director.

"Not really," he replies. "When a person dies, the muscles relax." Later I realized he had to say that. Was he going to tell me that my brother had the look of utmost fear on his face?

"What is it like to bury friends?" I ask. My way of dealing now is to be the rational field-worker. My brother's is to kid with the director as usual, even making dead people jokes.

* * *

Arthur and I felt as though we were in a conspiracy, directing this event, often from behind the scenes, to make sure things went as smoothly as possible. Whenever we could get away from rituals, we met in the hallway to plan and anticipate problems. I covered when Arthur was with the funeral director, or on the phone with callers—concerned friends, acquaintances, and businesspeople who had heard the news and needed more information, and airline officials. "The airlines are paying for the whole funeral," he tells me. "They told the funeral director to do whatever we wanted."

Even with the planning, we did not anticipate the effect seeing the flag-draped casket would have on my mother on Sunday night when our family went to the funeral home to receive friends. Silently, we walk through the bitter cold weather and into the funeral home. When my mother sees the casket, she screams, "My baby. Oh my baby is dead." She collapses to the floor, while the rest of us stand rooted to our spots. It is like a play rehearsal, and my mother has messed up her lines. In slow motion, we finally help her up and support her, still sobbing, to a chair. My once-powerful and imposing father looks helplessly on, confused, as someone approaches to remove his coat.

Several hundred people have come to pay respects. Arthur and I shake hands or hug each one, thank them for their expressions of sorrow, exchange light talk, smile, sometimes even laugh. "It is God's will." "God will look after him," they say to make us and themselves feel better. I nod. The same sentences are uttered over and over. It doesn't matter. There are no points for originality. We pass each person to the rest of the family seated behind us, the receivers of sympathy. Sometimes I want to be there too, to give in; other times I am glad for the numbing effects of being in control. There are hugs, quiet talk now, and sniffles. Sometimes sobs. Then they stare quickly at the closed casket, hands down and crossed in front, and sign the book. It is important to document that you came; the family should have a record, to know who and how many.

"How are you doing?" I ask Arthur, when there is a lull in the line. "Want a Valium? I had one. It helped. I feel calm and removed, like I am watching this on a movie screen." I want to be protected from my grief.

"No, I'm going to do it on my own," he responds, tightly under control and afraid to change anything.

I want this ritual to be over. Yet I want the people to keep coming, to share their grief with my parents, and to show their love for Rex. When it is done, Arthur and I say at the same time, "We made it through another one."

"The biggie is tomorrow," says my brother. No. The biggie comes after tomorrow when we both have to face the void of life without Rex.

* * *

The next day, Monday, is the funeral. We prepare a big lunch for the minister, relatives, and out-of-town guests. Again people eat little. The funeral parade leaves from our house. A town policeman, my eighth-grade boyfriend, holds up traffic so we can enter the main road. Now he stands, with rigid posture and hat held over his chest, crying openly. I wave and feel tears on my face and love for the small town in which I was raised. I take a deep breath and another Valium. Wonderful numbness settles over me. How I dread the funeral. The icy-cold, windy weather seems appropriate now.

This time my brother holds onto my mother and I support my father as we enter the side door of the funeral home. My brother-in-law and sister take care of Aunt Florence, who has difficulty walking. The curtain is drawn before we approach the casket so that the crowd cannot see our grief. But it is impossible to keep it hidden. Mom screams when she sees the casket, and Arthur holds on tightly as she breaks out into loud sobs. The rest of us cry softly, staring at the casket draped by the American flag, surrounded by the flowers that people weren't supposed to send. I am removed. This isn't what I want. I kiss the casket.

When the curtain is opened, I see that the funeral home is packed. I am glad that hundreds of people stand in the hall and outside in below-zero weather, while others wait in their cars to go to the cemetery. Rex is here, watching with me, like Tom Sawyer. How he relishes all these people. You ham. You would have loved all the media coverage of your death. I smile. And just think, Rex, you lucky stiff, you will never have to suffer through the death of loved ones.

Although the music moves me, I shut it out. This is not the place to break down. My parents' minister makes some abstract statements about God's will and about Rex. I fight back the urge to stand up and ask the minister if I can please say something personal about my brother. I would say it like a Pentecostal minister and we'd all wail together. I want to get in touch with the spirit of my brother. Why is this minister who hardly knew Rex running the show? I sit silently, since I can't risk upsetting the ritual, or my parents. When the service is over, suddenly I jump from my seat and kiss two of Rex's close friends who are helping to move the death flowers to the hearse. We cry openly then and I feel better.

The curtain is drawn again. The casket is removed by the six male pallbearers. The family is removed, led to their cars by the funeral director. Poof! Magically we will appear at the cemetery.

At the cemetery we are seated in front of the magic casket and the freshly dug hole in the ground. When I see Rex's ex-wife standing near, I grab her hand, and bring her to sit with the family. I don't care if it is appropriate. Rex would want her here. My body shakes violently from the cold and wind, as she and I hold onto each other.

The service is brief, and meaningless. After the minister reads scripture, I kiss the casket. "I love you," I say, once again feeling tension between freedom of expression and ritualistic expectation. Even though I dread facing the silence at home, I want this to be over. When it is done, people chat as though they have just gotten out of a play.

Many people come home with us to have dinner. This time they eat heartily and talk, reaffirming kinship ties. I still have no appetite and I say little. As soon as they leave, my mother takes sick and does not have the strength to walk. We put her to bed on the couch and tiptoe around her. Next morning, when she can't stand up, the doctor puts her in the hospital, and says she is in severe shock.

My sister and I write hundreds of thank-you notes, and I am reminded of our childhood relationship when we argue once about who should do what. Then we try to make it better by both insisting on doing everything.

After the Funeral

Rex's friends organize a party. "A better way to remember him," we say. But it isn't what we want either. We want Rex. Okay, the joke is over, Rex, come out of hiding. "If the boy would just send me a sign that he's okay, I would feel better," a friend says. "He left so suddenly." "Yeah, have a drink in Heaven and tell us how it is." But our gayness keeps switching back to serious talk. I have a Scotch, and my feeling breaks through, my sobs catching me by surprise. "I am tired of supporting everyone, including myself," I say to Rex's friends who gather around me. "I don't know why I feel I have to be so strong."

"You don't. Let go," I hear, and I feel a bond with the people who embrace me.

* * *

"Ah, help," my Aunt Helen yells from the bedroom of Rex's house, where we have gone to check on his things. She points to the ripple of the bed, backs off, white, as though she has seen a ghost.

"It's okay. It's a water bed," I assure her. "See," I say, pushing down on the mattress. "It's not a ghost." The smile on my face feels alien.

We open some of Rex's drawers. What an invasion to be looking at another's personal items. "That's what Rex used to tickle his girlfriends," my brother says to my father, who is examining a dildo. My father smiles devilishly—I am glad the thought pleases him—and then he respectfully puts it back in its place. We close the drawers without disturbing anything else, pick up little mementos of Rex, and leave. I am relieved when Arthur says he will go through Rex's possessions later and sell everything at an auction.

* * *

During my last few days at home, I visited my mother often in the hospital. "I'm in shock," she says almost proudly from her quiet, withdrawn posture. Being sick showed how much Rex had meant to her; and for a while she didn't have to cope. "They say I can stay here as long as I want," she announces. "I don't want to go home and face what has happened. I feel safe in the hospital."

* * *

Now it would be happening, a few seconds after takeoff. There is the bridge it hit. Here is how his head snapped forward. Boom. I let my head fall into the seat in front of me. The vivid picture of the gash in Rex's head helps me reenact the scene.

When I see Gene at the Tampa airport, I fall into his arms, overwhelmed by my love and need for him. Then I shudder when I feel his frail body and hear his labored breathing, realizing that one day I will be experiencing his death, too. I hold onto him tightly. He and Rex have been the two most important people in my world.

Gene is totally devoted to me during the next few days and tries hard to ease my pain, but I can't cry or even talk about what I feel. "Let's go see *Ragtime* at the theater. It will get your mind off death," Gene says. When I see a casket in the movie, I recoil, and then cry until the end.

When I get home that night, I lie alone on the couch in the living room, unable to sleep. When I sense Rex's spirit, it scares me, and I retreat into the bedroom, clutching my pillow, to be with Gene.

That was the last time I would feel Rex's presence so strongly. I would always be sorry that I had not stayed on the couch that night. Maybe he had come to say good-bye. Did that really happen?

* * *

I didn't dream about Rex until more than a year after he died. In the first of a series, we are children playing in my father's brown sand pile. Dump-truck mounds of fine, light-colored sand form waves at the points they blend into other heaps of the heavy, moist, darker kind, better for building castles. All the neighborhood kids used to play "king of the mountain" in this basketball court–sized playhouse. When we grew tired of that game, we played hide-and-go-seek, or "drove" our toy trucks that were filled with sand scooped with our pretend backhoes, fantasizing about my father's real trucks and loading equipment.

In the second dream, we are older. Although I don't remember the context—only a dark background highlighting the two of us—I am aware as I look at Rex that he is going to die. But he doesn't know it and acts as if nothing is wrong. I keep my awareness secret because I know Rex hates to be out of control.

In the third dream, I decide that there has been a mistake. Rex has not died. He just went away for a while. Now he is back and we are having a conversation. Overjoyed, I begin to tell him that I thought he had died. But I stop in mid-sentence because I feel confused, unsure of whether the accident happened or not. Then I decide the accident occurred, but Rex survived and has just been in the hospital for a while. Now he is well. Elated, I start to tell him again that I thought he died, and again I stop.

In the fourth dream, Rex is already dead, yet we are together. How can he be dead and not know it, I wonder. Maybe he isn't really dead. What am I going to do? I can't tell him. How can he possibly handle it? How can I? I begin to tell him how horrible I felt when I thought he had died in the crash. I wake up, realizing he is really dead.

Shortly after that, I finally tell Rex in a dream that he is dead. I awake screaming and crying, and I don't dream about him again for a long time. In my dreams, as in my life, there is no other ending.

Meta-Autoethnography: Responding to the Story

There is no ending to life other than death, but the story of a person's life goes on after s/he dies. I continue to try to understand Rex's life and his death and integrate it into the life I'm living. There is no ending other than death, but the multitude of responses to this story encourage me to continue retelling the story and considering what the experience and the story mean to me now.

In "There Are Survivors," I seek to reposition readers of social science research, evoking feeling and identification as well as cognitive processing. As you read this story, some of you may have felt empathy with me, as you would in watching a "true-to-life" movie; some of you may have been reminded of parallels in your own lives, as in reading a good novel. Perhaps reading my work evoked feelings that you could then examine, or led to recall of other similar emotional situations in which you have participated. Hopefully reading this work called into play your sociological imagination (Mills, 1959). Whichever is the case, acknowledging the potential for optional readings gives readers license to take part in an experience that can reveal to them not only how it was for me (the author) but how it could be or once was for them (Ellis & Bochner, 1992; Turner, 1986).

In the next chapter, I present two of these optional readings and my responses to them. The first reading was given by Sherryl Kleinman in a session at the Midwest Sociological Society in 1993 and then published in the same journal issue as "There Are Survivors"; the second was authored by Art Bochner (2005a) and published more than a decade after "There Are Survivors" in an edited collection that featured several articles, including "Survivors," along with responses by scholars from different perspectives. Thus, my story continues to have movement rather than being fixed as the text I wrote and published in 1993 (Davies & Davies, 2007). In this way, I continue to interpret, question, and reinterpret what happened then from my position now.

CHAPTER SEVEN

Rereading "There Are Survivors"

Cultural and Evocative Responses

Culturally Speaking: Carolyn Ellis's "There Are Survivors"
By Sherryl Kleinman[1]

What does Carolyn Ellis's story tell us? First, we get to know Carolyn the individual— her feelings, thoughts, actions, and relationships. But sociologists want to know more. What cultural story does she tell?

I read Carolyn's story this way: she struggles and then comes to terms with the cultural changes and changes in self that have accompanied her social, generational, and geographic mobility. Specifically, Carolyn teaches us about her ambivalence toward conventions in her traditional, religious, working-class family and small-town community. As she alternates between closeness and distance to her family and hometown, we see no less than a struggle over her own moral identity. On the one hand, she wants to be the *Good Daughter* who cares for her parents during a crisis without complaining about the death rituals she finds estranging or the feeling rules she has rejected in her current life. On the other hand, she wants to retain her *integrity of self*; the rituals she'd prefer and the feeling rules she now embraces are also moral matters, central to her current definition of self.

She finds it hard to be a good daughter because her brother's death is not only a crisis for her parents, but also for her. Rex is not a long-lost brother, but a friend. Yet, because she must experience the crisis in the home she was born into rather than in her chosen home, the weight of community bears upon her. To risk "going her own way" at this time is to risk disapproval from her parents and her first community.

For example, we see Carolyn the feminist collide with Carolyn the good girl:

I helped my mother make up a list of pallbearers. There were rules. "They should be his best friends," she [Carolyn's mother] says. "It can't be relatives. They have to be men. There should be six of them." This is not the time to argue for women pallbearers. This is for my mother. (p. 719)

When she looks at her brother in the casket, Carolyn's distaste for the cultural accoutrements of her past becomes clear:

> He is shrouded in polyester, dead clothes complete with clip-on tie. This outfit would have horrified him. I want to dress him in his own clothes. But my Mom has proudly announced having told the funeral director to put him in a new blue suit. (p. 720)

Is she angered by her mother's pride at putting Rex in a suit he'd abhor? What does she do with this feeling of disgust? She engages in emotion work, telling herself that what he wears doesn't really matter:

> No one else is going to see him. What difference does it make anyway? (p. 720)

It makes a difference to Carolyn. In her last look at his body she wanted to see Rex as he fashioned himself, not as others fashioned him. But she decides that for this occasion, her mother's feelings matter more than her own.

A poignant scene of culture clash occurs when Carolyn tells her mother about an experience that she hopes will connect them.

> "I am communicating with Rex," I tell my Mom, thinking she will like that I am being "religious," even though it doesn't fit her Lutheran doctrine. "What kind of religion do you have anyway? You can't talk to the dead," she replies, and I shrug. (p. 719)

Did Carolyn shrug off her feeling? Or was she engaging in surface acting, trying to convince her mother that their differences in religion/spirituality don't matter? Or was she shrugging in order to convince *herself*?

Carolyn wants to break through the feeling rules of the rituals, but she does so only through silent screams. We see this in her reaction to the minister's comments at the funeral:

> I fight back the urge to stand up and ask the minister if I can please say something personal about my brother. I would say it like a Pentecostal minister and we'd all wail together. . . . Why is this minister who hardly knew Rex running the show? I sit silently, since I can't risk upsetting the ritual, or my parents. (p. 721)

Yet she engages in one act of resistance. At the cemetery:

> I see Rex's ex-wife standing near and I grab her hand, and bring her to sit with the
> family. I don't care if it is appropriate. Rex would want her there. She and I hold onto
> one another. (p. 722)

Carolyn's story speaks to me because I too am a baby boom professor who experiences the push-pull of old and new selves when I return to my original community. Yet I also think about differences between Carolyn's account and what I imagine my own would have been. For example, I am struck by the absence of Carolyn's guilt. As I put myself into Carolyn's position—the sister who arranged her brother's flights, the person he was on his way to visit—I felt pangs of guilt. If this were my account, there'd be pages of What If's?, If Only's, and I Should Have's. I'd go over and over my initial calls to the airline, asking myself, Could I have put him on a different flight? And I'd have these thoughts knowing full well that I'm incapable of warding off plane crashes.

Perhaps I'm only revealing my own neurosis. But I wonder if my reaction tells us something about cultural differences between me and Carolyn. I grew up in the guilt culture of lower-middle-class Jews. In that milieu, every thought or feeling, action or inaction is a potential source of guilt. Even one's inherited imperfections—a pale complexion or a crooked nose—can engender guilt. As one gentle Gentile said to me after I talked about this, "My, you were taught to believe that you're responsible for your bad genes!"

Carolyn's story, and stories like hers, can help us understand how culture informs lived experience. In Carolyn's words:

> As social scientists, we will not know if others' intimate experiences are similar or
> different until we offer our own stories and pay attention to how others respond,
> just as we do in everyday life. (p. 725)

Let me return to Carolyn's experiences. In writing drafts of her story, Carolyn found a way to resolve her cultural dilemma. She came to appreciate her first community and her working-class background. She put it this way:

> As an educated person, I value the understanding that comes from abstract thought.
> Yet, I am still connected to my working-class roots where the meaning inherent in
> concrete experience, stories, and dialogue was privileged over the theoretical and
> general. (p. 727)

Ironically, Carolyn's academic self allows her to appreciate her pre-academic life. Her emerging intellectual perspective—her post-positivist self—helps her incorporate elements of her working-class background. She becomes a sociologist of emotions who studies lived experience and communicates through vivid descriptions. By recapturing her emotional memories and making them the object of study she makes sense of herself and her original community.

How many of us who engage in reflexive sociology are invoking identities we thought we'd left behind, such as being a woman, a Jew, a member of the working class? Sociology (read: science) was supposed to be an equalizer, a leveler of identities. But it is not and cannot be. An honest sociology is a sociology created by people who have particular identities and who make the relationship between themselves and their work known to others. By coming to terms with who we've been and want to become, we can also refashion our past identities and bring them consciously into our sociology. Carolyn, for instance, is selective about what she brings from her past. She incorporates storytelling into her sociology, but rejects her community's taboo against expressing strong feelings.

Similarly, feminists are selective about which parts of "feminine" culture they bring into their work. They acknowledge the importance of emotions, yet reject the self-effacing demeanor that femininity prescribes. Feminists can proudly bring emotions into their work rather than apologize for their lack of "objectivity."

Like Carolyn, perhaps some of us who bring our selves into our sociological work write our way to survival. I, for one, hope our efforts breathe new life into sociology rather than merely keep it alive.

Surviving Autoethnography
By Arthur P. Bochner[2]

Carolyn Ellis and I have been partners for more than a decade. Shortly after we met in 1990, Carolyn sent me a draft copy of a book manuscript she had written entitled *Final Negotiations* (Ellis, 1995a). The book described in detail the history of Carolyn's nine-year relationship with Gene Weinstein, who died of emphysema in 1985 (Ellis, 1995a). As I read through the chapter in which Carolyn told the story of her brother's death in an airplane crash, I felt as if all my senses were being pricked. I had never read a social science article in which the researcher wrote from the source of her own grief, openly expressing what it felt like to be stricken so suddenly, refusing to gloss the layers of conflicting feelings, the exciting rush of adrenalin countered by the deadening fog of numbness, the waves of hope and despair, and finally, the struggle first to choke down, then to grope toward an understanding of the meaning of her suffering and loss.

My immediate reaction was overwhelming sorrow. I felt the pressure squeezing in my chest when Carolyn told how her heart was racing when she asked the Air Florida agent for information on Rex's flight. I felt the tightness in my throat, holding back the swell of sadness inside me as Carolyn recounted the television replay—"Then they announce seven. Then there are five. And one dead hero" (Ellis, 1993, p. 715). And I could no longer stifle my tears, which flowed freely down my cheeks, when Carolyn's mother sobbed, "Bring my boy home." I felt as if I had been swept into the experience of sudden loss. It wasn't a place I wanted to be, but the same can be said for Carolyn, her family, Rex's friends, or the people of Luray, Virginia. Carolyn's writing had a raw force that made me feel its truth in my stomach, so close to the bone of reality. The truth wasn't pretty—bad things happen to good people, the course of one's life can turn in a split second, the meanings one attaches to life are never completely secure, some people may never come back from such a blow—but it was something that had to be endured, worked through, and learned from. Others, those for whom one tells a story, need to feel it—the shock, the numbness, the exhaustion, the hope, the resolution, the sorrow—to know its truth. The writer—the teller of the story—needs to write it to work her way through the pain and be transformed by its truth.

As I contemplated the feelings that were running through me, I felt a rush of optimism about the future of social science inquiry. Yes! I shouted to myself. This is what social science is missing! This is what social science needs to become in order to make a differ-ence in the world—daring, honest, intimate, personal, emotional, moral, embodied, and evocative. Here was a social scientist venturing beyond the realm of predictable events and rational actions, revealing life's particularities, bearing witness to the wreckage of human suffering, showing what it might mean to live well while afflicted by loss, inviting her readers to receive her testimony and become witnesses themselves, questioning the subject matter and methodologies of her discipline, refusing to hide behind academic jargon and citations, making us feel the truth of her story in our guts.

When Carolyn and I met to discuss her work, I advised her to take this chapter out of the larger manuscript. "It's too powerful for the book," I said. "The story of Rex's death overwhelms the other story you are telling there. It is what most people will remember first when they finish the book. Besides, you should publish it in an academic jour-nal where scholars can see an example of what social science could be if it embraced narrative, if it made the heart as important as the mind, if it encouraged the goal of empathizing with the sufferings of others, if it were written from inside experience, and if its authority came from the emotions it evokes in its readers as well as the lessons it teaches about human vulnerability, moral choice, and suffering." Although Carolyn felt Rex's death was a significant event in her relationship with Gene, she agreed with me. She took the chapter out of the book and published it in *The Sociological Quarterly* (Ellis, 1993).

As a wounded storyteller, Carolyn offers her testimony as a witness to the pain and suffering of sudden death. She tells her story for your sake as well as for her own. She wants you to enter into dialogue with her and with her story, not to stand outside it as a detached critic but to step into it as if it were happening to you.

Try to put yourself in Carolyn Ellis's shoes. Your brother is coming to visit you. The two of you are close and loving siblings who don't get to see each other nearly as often as you'd like. You anticipate his visit eagerly, knowing it will be a relaxing and fun-filled holiday. You stock up on his favorite foods and buy presents you know he will adore. You chuckle when you realize that he will adore the gifts *because* they are from you. You picture his smiling face in your mind all day as you work furiously to finish projects you know won't get done while he is here. Then the phone rings. There's been a crash. The plane is in the water. Your brother may be dead.

Stop for a minute. Become aware of your body. How do you feel? Numb? Frightened? Sad? Is adrenalin rushing through you? Do you cry? Scream? Think what to do next? To whom do you want to talk? What do you say?

Return to the scene. Recall how you talked to your brother on the phone yesterday. How you thought about him all day, replaying some of the happiest moments of your childhood in your mind. He was alive then; he can't be dead now. He's too young, fresh, full of life. You had no warning, no sign that anything like this could happen. Neither did he. It doesn't feel real. It's too sudden—shocking. Feelings flood your consciousness, overwhelming you. You feel lightheaded, as if you are falling from the edge of a cliff. You sense yourself descending into an abyss of despair. Nothing makes sense. You feel lost, unanchored, adrift in meaninglessness. Life feels so dangerous, death so arbitrary, knowledge so uncertain, loss so painful, the future so unpredictable. You wonder, how can I make sense of this? How can I go on with my life—feel safe and sane again? To whom or to what can I turn?

Take a minute to regain your composure. Return to the present.

* * *

"There Are Survivors" is a work of self-narration, sometimes referred to as autoethnography (Ellis, 2004), in which Carolyn Ellis uses her personal experience to display multiple levels of consciousness and emotionality, connecting and contrasting her own personal suffering, the ways in which members of her family cope with their loss, and the patterns of ritualized grieving she observes when she returns for her brother's funeral to the community in which she grew up. Focusing on her own feelings and thoughts while paying close attention to the concrete details of other people's reactions and emotions, Carolyn exposes both the inner world of a vulnerable, suffering, and searching self and the outer world of a grieving community of fellow sufferers coping as well as they can with tragic circumstances. The text she produces invites us to experience and reflect on how loss is written on and expressed by one's body, how it is lived through and coped with over time, and how cultural practices are used to restore a sense of order and continuity in the aftermath of tragedy.

As an academic monograph, Carolyn Ellis's text raises the question of what place narrative should occupy in social science inquiry. Should all social and educational research be driven by a search for general principles? Are the standard methodological practices of science useful when one wants to know what to do or how to act (Jackson, 1995)? To what sort of research can one turn for moral and political guidance (Rorty, 1982)? Is theory always to be preferred to story (Bochner, 2001)?

Richard Rorty (1989, 1991) strongly prefers narratives over theories: "The attempt to find laws of history or essences of cultures—to substitute theory for narrative as an aid to understanding ourselves, others, and the options which we present to each other— has been notoriously unfruitful" (1991, p. 66). He advises "that we should stay on the lookout . . . for the rise of new genres—genres which arise in reaction to, and as an alternative to, the attempt to *theorize*—about human affairs" (1991, p. 73.) Using novelists such as Dickens and Kundera as his model, Rorty (1991) advocates a social science that pays attention to the concrete details of human suffering. Compared to theorists, Rorty observes, what is important about storytellers is that they excel at details. In Rorty's ideal academic community, social science is continuous with literature, in part because the social sciences have a moral importance, whether they accept it or not, and also because, as Rorty (1982, p. 202) notes, "What we hope for from social scientists is that they will act as interpreters for those with whom we are not sure how to talk . . . the same thing we hope for from our poets and dramatists and novelists."

Autoethnography is a species of narrative inquiry that has blossomed in reaction to the excesses and limitations of theory-driven, empiricist social science. Whereas empiricist social science fuels an appetite for abstraction, facts, and control, narrative social science feeds a hunger for details, meanings, and peace of mind. In some circles, narrative has become a rallying point for those who believe strongly that the human sciences need to become more human. We are supposed to be studying people, trying to understand their lives, and narratives come closer to representing the contexts and preserving the integrity of those lives than do questionnaires and graphs. But it would be a mistake to conclude that the enthusiasm for narrative is simply the reflection of a scholarly change of heart. It also is an expression of the desire to produce work that is personally meaningful for the researcher. Richardson (1992a) describes her turn toward narrative as a longing for forms of expression that would turn sociology—her research field—into a non-alienating practice, where she wouldn't have to suppress her own subjectivity, where she could become more attuned to the subjectively felt experiences of others, where she would be free to reflect on the consequences of her work not only for others but also for herself, and where all parts of her self—emotional, spiritual, intellectual, and moral—could be voiced and integrated in her work. In short, narrative inquiry is a response to an existential crisis—a desire to do meaningful work and to lead meaningful lives. As Freeman (1998, p. 46) says, "We need to understand lives and indeed to *live* lives differently if we are to avoid further fragmentation, isolation, and disconnection from each other." While some narrative research may make traditional knowledge claims, most narratives function ontologically, practically, and existentially. Jackson (1995) advises a shift in how we construe the purposes of research, suggesting that we should be less concerned with the question of how we can know and more concerned with the question of how we should live. This is the moral of stories—its ethical domain. When it comes to communicating ethical consciousness, as Fasching and deChant (2001) advise, it is much more effective to tell a story than to give an abstract explanation.

Carolyn Ellis admits that her brother's death threatened the meaning of her life "like nothing before" (p. 728). Telling her story is a way of restoring meaning. She may not have been able to save Rex's life but she can save her own. She isn't seeking pity, nor is she portraying herself as pathetic, helpless, or downtrodden. Instead, she engages in an act of self-narration. She tries to make a life that is falling apart come together again, by picking up the pieces and molding them into a coherent story, shaping a view of the world from which she can envision a hopeful, promising future. For Carolyn this narrative challenge—to create meaning out of chaos—is a terrible and crucial struggle. The sense of unity in her life had been unceremoniously ruptured by Rex's sudden death. One decisive blow of fate erased any illusions Carolyn may have harbored of living a well-planned and orderly life. But it didn't erase the memory of Rex, of what he meant to her, of how frightened she felt to face her life without him in it—not to be able to hear his voice, to touch his breathing body, to share stories with him. Out of the incoherence and numbness of her painful loss, Carolyn struggles to create a story that will defend her against the prospect of a meaningless, fragmented, and isolated existence. At risk is the integrity and intelligibility of her selfhood, the story she uses to link birth to life to death as a continuous and sensible stream of experience. As a researcher, she understands that her experience per se is not the story but rather she must discover the story that is in her experience.

The story comes to a climax when Carolyn reveals a series of dreams she had about Rex more than a year after he died. The dreams appear to be about Rex, but they are just as much about Carolyn. They animate Carolyn's unconscious struggle to keep Rex alive. In the first dream, Carolyn and Rex are innocent children—curious, imaginative, playful. They live in the moment without fears, anxieties, or worries about the future. In the second dream, Carolyn and Rex have grown up. She knows he is going to die but keeps it a secret from him because "Rex hates to be out of control." Is she keeping what she knows from Rex or from herself? He won't have to deal with it if she keeps it secret. Nor will she. The dream suggests Carolyn wants to hide from the reality of Rex's death. She is no longer innocent. Now she must make a choice. Suppress the knowledge of Rex's death or admit it and deal with it. She is not ready to confront her loss. The third dream reveals the intricacies of denial. Carolyn is confused and uncertain. Did Rex die or didn't he? The unreality of his death reveals itself as if it were a dream. Though Rex appears to have survived, Carolyn still can't talk to him about what she knows or tell him that she thought he had died. Now it becomes evident that Rex and Carolyn are different parts of the same person. In the fourth dream, these parts begin to merge and integrate as Carolyn realizes that Rex is dead. She sees that it is not a question of how he will handle it, but how she will. After telling him he is dead, in her final dream, she has no need to dream about Rex again. She may never feel resolved about his death but she can go on with her life realizing that Rex lives on inside her. He stays alive in the stories she tells, the memories she clings to, and the emotions she feels when she thinks of him.

Carolyn refers to "There Are Survivors" as a story of sudden death. Certainly, the suddenness of Rex's death leaves a scar of sorrow that will never heal completely. For Carolyn's mother, it may never heal at all. But Carolyn's story is not only about loss and grief and sorrow. It's as much about life as it is about death. It's a story about memory and truth and connection. It's a story about recognizing what's important in life. It's a love story.

Meta-Autoethnography: Rereading Responses to "There Are Survivors"

Many people have responded to "There Are Survivors."[3] The two reactions featured here by Sherryl Kleinman, a friend and colleague, and Art Bochner, my romantic partner and coauthor, show two related, yet different ways to read this story. Both authors use a personal and analytic voice. Sherryl is more concerned with thinking about emotions and analyzing cultural difference, while Art concentrates on emotional identification and an analysis of the academy. Both authors imagine being in a situation similar to mine, and they invite readers to imagine the same. Sherryl's text asks readers to think categorically about their cultural identities; Art's text invites readers to feel with him—and stay in their feelings—as they imagine finding out about the death of a loved one.

Sherryl stays at some distance as she describes thoughts and feelings she might have had in my situation. She briefly compares her anticipated guilt to my lack of expressed guilt, attributing our differences to our varied upbringing—hers, lower-middle-class Jewish and mine, working-class, southern Protestant. Art comes close and personal, entering my experience, opening himself to feeling my feelings and showing his, as he responds vulnerably to the feelings the text creates. Sherryl's primary identity as writer is that of a feminist sociologist who is interested in analyzing cultural concepts, such as "the good daughter," "culture clash," and "integrity of self," and how culture informs lived experience. Her focus on my ambivalence toward conventions surrounding death in my working-class town and comparison of her experiences to mine provides the reader with sociological understanding of how culture informs experience.

Though Art uses this story as an exemplar upon which to contemplate the place narrative should occupy in social science inquiry, his primary identity is that of an interpretive scholar engaged in the details and emotions in my story. He emphasizes "feeling with" me as I reveal the inner world of a "vulnerable, suffering, and searching self" and the outer world of a grieving family and rural community coping with loss as well as they can through ritualized grieving practices. He describes being "swept into the experience of sudden loss," having all his senses pricked, and feeling overwhelming sorrow. The main truth he takes from my story is the truth of my experience, which he knows from feeling it in his gut. His role as my partner no doubt makes this experience more poignant for him. But Art advocates and practices this kind of reading for all good narrative autoethnography, not just for the words of authors one happens to know (Bochner, 2001). He leaves readers with a sense that stories in and of themselves can provide understanding.

Sherryl's response makes me contemplate further my estrangement from and connection to my family of origin and home community, my working-class identity, and cultural differences in feeling and expressing emotions. In the story I tell of losing and grieving for my brother, my ambivalence toward my community is muted, showing up only briefly in my resistance to community and family feeling rules, religious values, and death rituals. This is primarily a family story, as stories of death and grief often are, a story that reconnects me to my family and to my working-class roots where the "meaning inherent in concrete experience, stories, and dialogue was privileged over the theoretical and general" (Ellis, 1993, pp. 727–728).

Two years later, I published "The Other Side of the Fence" (1995d; see Chapter 2), and there I expressed more openly the ambivalence anticipated by Sherryl toward my home town and family. I wrote:

I experience the contradictory pulls of several worlds . . . the small town of my childhood, and the urban university community outside of Luray that I now call home. . . . The bond to Luray, stirred up from participating in this scene from my past, surprises me. I was sure I had left this connection behind. My feelings remind me that I am still a part of this community. (p. 149)

Later, I continue:

I wonder, where do I belong? Where are my loyalties and commitments? I glance across the fence at Bobby and I think, this community is racist; it violates one of my deepest held values. Then I turn toward my family and Rex's friends and I think, this community is family; these are some of the strongest ties I ever had. Fragmented, I am confused by my contradictory thoughts and feelings. (p. 159)

Art's response makes me cry when I read it. I cry because I reenter the experience through his words. I cry because I feel his compassion and empathy as a reader and loved one, his willingness to enter so fully into my experience though it is excruciatingly painful, and his understanding of my loss as well as my reasons for writing this story. From his reactions, I learn more about grief, my own emotional responses, writing evocative narratives, and the importance of reader response to our stories.

Sherryl's and Art's responses together connect my ethnographic attraction to understanding community with my autoethnographic pull to telling emotional stories. Both responses make me want to write more stories like this one.

Sherryl and Art hope that this kind of work changes social science. Sherryl shares my wish that bringing our selves into our sociological work and comparing our stories will help us write our way to survival and "breathe new life into sociology." Art shares my desire that emotional autoethnographic narratives that offer compassion and empathy in our responses to suffering will make human sciences more human and produce scholarship that helps us figure out how we should live. Though I fear that those in the traditional corridors of sociology are still gasping, I am heartened by how much progress interpretive social scientists have made toward producing humanizing work that makes a difference in people's lives.

During the fifteen years since I wrote this story, autoethnography has touched a nerve and writing from the heart has become more accepted as an approach to social science research (Pelias, 2004). For example, we now have an active autoethnography list serve with over three hundred members (autoethnography@yahoogroups.com); several book series that feature autoethnographic narratives[4]; a number of monographs written with heart and spirit about heart and spirit[5]; edited collections oriented toward

autoethnographic stories and arts-based research[6]; many journals and annuals that publish interpretive and autoethnographic work oriented toward making a difference[7]; and
a number of conferences that feature autoethnographic work.[8]

"There Are Survivors" was the first of my personal stories to be accepted by a journal. The publication of this story in *The Sociological Quarterly* and the positive responses
from readers spurred me on to finish *Final Negotiations* and to continue writing stories
about emotional experiences.

Meta-Autoethnography: Rereading Feelings—Catharsis or More Grief?

Readers' emotional responses to this story, including Art's, make me consider the impact
of Rex's death on my life now. Living, writing, and publishing this story about the loss of
my brother changed how I live and think. I came to appreciate more than I had the qualities of caring, love, vulnerability, and relational connection. For me, these characteristics
are part of the core of what makes us human, and I want to express them in my writing.
Writing this story has helped me survive the loss of my brother (and perhaps subsequent
losses) and understand the value of writing in overcoming trauma (Pennebaker, 1990).
In the process, I hope to have provided a story to which others might compare their
experiences of loss and grief as they try to figure out how to live.

None of these positive sentiments mean I am free from the pain of loss. Every time
I reread this story I shed tears, even now, more than twenty-five years after Rex's death.
Though the pain is not as intense as it was shortly after he died, the powerful way it
descends on my life still rattles me. When Rex died, the acute pain and shock took over
my life. That sense of being overwhelmed has been muted by the passing of time. But
in its place is a consistent gnawing hole of long-term grief that sometimes feels like
it is trying to ingest my very being. I don't feel grief all the time, nor is the sensation
always intense. But its presence reminds me often that I will lose others, that I likely will
become ill, and that I surely will die. Every time I experience a new loss, I feel that it also
contains renewed grief over losing Rex (see Rosenblatt, 1996, p. 50). Losing Rex was my
first significant loss—a loss that showed me I had no control over death, that made me
realize my own mortality since we were close in age, and that led to the loss of the innocence I experienced earlier in life when death appeared irrelevant to my life (Rosenblatt,
1996, p. 51). Perhaps this loss hits me so strongly because Rex's death was so sudden;
the majority of studies describe sudden loss as leading to more intense, distressing, and
prolonged grief than does anticipated loss.[9] It also was a loss of someone whose role in
my life would not be replaced, a loss of someone who knew me from childhood and, had
he lived, would have known me for most of my life.

Since I experience sadness and grief whenever I assign, reread, and discuss "There Are Survivors" in my classes, workshops, and lectures, I often wonder about the value of continual exposure to this story and the value of reading and writing loss narratives in general. Does my exposure to this story make my grief more frequent and deeply felt than otherwise might happen? Perhaps reentering the experience as I do every time I read this story does bring up those sharp signifiers of loss that generate the "gnawing hole" feeling (as other remembrances do as well). Does that mean it might be better not to expose myself time and again to this story? Might it be better to "just move on"?

Some of the feelings of loss I experience on revisiting this story are intentional on my part. When I reread this story, I seek to place myself in an emotional space of grief so that I might better talk about what happened; thus I expect to feel grief. Yet I also distance myself so that I might analyze from afar and not break down emotionally as I speak about the story; thus the feelings are controlled to an extent. The acute effects of relived grief are short term, halted by the responsibility of leading seminars and helping students comfortably discuss loss and grief—their own as well as mine—and by the need to continue on with the day's activities and demands once the class is over.

Frequent exposure to this story also brings its own rewards. Reading and remembering enhance the attachment I continue to have with my brother. As Arthur Frank (1991, p. 41) says: "To grieve well is to value what you have lost. When you value even the feeling of loss, you value life itself, and you begin to live again." By writing about my brother, I make him a part of my world again (see Ernaux, 1991, p. 31). Every time I read this story, I feel Rex's presence and remember how much he meant to me. In spite of my mother's protestations that you can't talk to the dead, I continue to have conversations with Rex in my mind and with my students and workshop colleagues about him. I appreciate the gift of stories: that Rex can be a topic of conversation and memory for me and that I can keep him present for myself and introduce to many people my relationship to him. Narrative then has a memorial function (Bochner, 2007). In this way, instead of "letting go," which is the conventional wisdom offered by most grief counseling, I can continue "holding on" (Hedtke & Winslade, 2004).

Rereading this story and having these feelings remind me to be compassionate and caring rather than critical and judgmental. My feelings of vulnerability make me more sensitive to others' vulnerabilities and our common plights. When people react to this story out of their own grief or empathy for mine, I feel part of a community of caring people. That belonging gives me comfort and makes me want to comfort others, to feel we are not alone in our despair. In the process, I feel human and alive.

Readers, including students, who respond to my writing say they appreciate the anticipatory socialization into feeling and coping with grief that my stories provide. Those who have experienced grief welcome the companionship and the opportunity to feel from an aesthetic distance about the experience. Comparing their grief to mine helps them feel less alone. Many express that what I write gives them permission to tell their stories. I believe that writing and reading stories such as these has the potential to help us all be more empathic.

But is empathy always positive and desirable? Maintaining distance, even denial, is sometimes a good coping mechanism, at least in the short term. For example, many undergraduate students who read my stories of loss, such as "There Are Survivors," are willing to stay with grief only so long. In my course "Communicating Grief and Loss," students enthusiastically and passionately read and discuss the assignments in the beginning of the semester; but near the end, they often slack off to a much greater extent than happens in other classes I teach. Some express that they have gotten the point of the class—that loss is painful, ubiquitous, and there is value in writing and talking about it—and say they'd rather celebrate life. "We don't have to think about this now," they say. While I tell them this course is a celebration of life, I know it is no contest for the fun of playing tennis, flirting with another student, or going to the pub or frat party. For that matter, the content of this course is no contest for the many daily responsibilities and pressures many of them have in their lives—unless they are suffering from loss of a loved one. Though their resistance is not the reaction I want, it probably helps them keep death and illness at bay—at least for now. As long as students recognize that life is finite and consider taking that fact into account as they figure out how to live their lives, then perhaps their resistance gives them a reprieve and allows them to live as well as they can in the moment. Because of my age and experience with loss, I no longer have the same luxury of forgetting and denying.

Sometimes when I read this story, I pretend I am reading someone else's story. Then I feel for Rex's siblings, who try to cope and often stifle their own grief to help their parents through theirs; for this family, who has suffered the ultimate interruption and whose lives will never be the same; for this little town, represented by the policeman who cries as the family drives by on their way to the funeral. I feel for Carolyn: the young woman whose world has fallen apart and whose world view has been disrupted, her optimism shredded by the reality of loss; the young woman who tries to be strong, hoping that somehow strength and control might ward off her grief and vulnerability. I wonder about the confusion she experiences when she can't connect with her mother, a person she needs to touch and love, and be loved back, to release her own grief.

Meta-Autoethnography: Rereading Family

But these are not just characters. This is not someone else's life. This is not a story I can read, empathize with, and then put down. These are people I love and care about, some I have since lost and grieve for; the young woman is me. The participants continue to be a part of my life, even those who have died. Though I do not have sensory relationships with their physical presence, I have relationships with them in my heart and mind. How these relationships evolved, the events in the twenty-five years since Rex's death, and others' responses to the story (such as Sherryl's and Art's), all impact how I reread and reinterpret the story.

I feel for my father, who is filled with hope that his son is still alive, the man who quietly yet openly grieves when he finds out his hope is for naught. He will die a few years later, partly, I always believed, from feeling defeated by Rex's death. When Rex died, my father not only lost a son, who was so much like him, he also lost the family construction business, which he had built from scratch and given to Rex a few years before my brother's death. When Rex died, my father lost his identity as a contractor and he literally lost a place to be and a reason for being because he couldn't continue to hang out at the office, run errands for my brother, and give advice about being a successful contractor. These were his passions.

I feel for my mother, who is in shock, and who knows her day-to-day world will never be the same. I cry when my mother says angrily to me, "It won't be okay. He's dead. He's not coming back," and, similar to Art's reaction in his essay, I cry more when she pleads to the sheriff, "Bring my boy home." She thinks her life is over, and almost convinces her family of this through her immediate reaction, as well as during the next few years as she lives a life shrouded in grief. I believe these feelings of loss stayed with her every day until she died twenty years later. Though on her deathbed she was reluctant to leave her three remaining children, she spoke often of her longing to finally be with Rex. I do not share those yearnings, though I often long for Rex to be here still with me.

After my brother's death, my parents and I clung to our attachment. We all wanted to see each other more often. Instead of coming home twice a year, which had become the norm, I came three or four times and often stayed longer than my typical three- or four-day visits. My visits, though, seemed a mixed blessing for all of us. More than anyone else in our family, I looked and acted like Rex. That and the immediacy of their feelings for me as their child, I believe, reminded my parents of their loss and brought on acute feelings of grief.

My visits reconnected me to my parents but also brought me to live viscerally in the scene of my loss. Rex's absence made his loss more present—for example, the absence in the empty chair he usually sat in at our family dinners, the absence of his name on his former construction office (now filled with strangers) we drove by to get to my parents' house—what McClowry et al. (1987) call "empty space." The loss of Rex also was made more present in the changes in family rituals—in the lack now of Christmas decorations adorning our home, of exchanging presents, of joking around and laughing together.

I craved and dreaded going home, just as my parents probably craved seeing me, yet dreaded the memories I evoked.

I remembered the last conversation Rex and I had about buying presents, much as my mother remembered the last conversation she had with him about leaving to come visit me. Though we all talked some about Rex, eventually what was there to say other than that we missed him? No one in my family could reminisce about Rex without incredible sadness. Sometimes I wondered if all of us felt guilty for being alive when he was dead—a survivor's guilt of a different order from the guilt Sherryl describes.

As I write from my position now, I am struck by how many characters in this story are dead—Rex, Gene, Gene's daughter Beth, Aunt Florence, and my father and mother—and how many other loved ones my friends and family have lost as well. I can't help but think about how many more losses I will experience before I die, if I am lucky enough not to die early. I am reminded again of the shortness of life and how I hope to live it. The truth of long-term grief, for me, is that the hole doesn't get filled over time; the gnawing doesn't stop; the pain doesn't cease completely. Losses accumulate and I know from experience that loss brings pain. But while the constant reminder the gnawing provides makes me weary, it also helps me figure out how I want to live today and consider how I might prepare myself for what is to come.

I have not lived—and do not want to live—inundated by death but I want to be aware of it. Staying aware of loss reminds me of the dialectic of vitality and mortality[10]; this consciousness helps me incorporate absence into my life and sensibilities and, at the same time, strive to live a vital life. As Shames and Barton (2004, p. 7), quoting the Talmud, recommend, I try "to live as though [I'll] live forever, yet be prepared to die tomorrow." When I keep death on my shoulder, my day-to-day world also is filled with happiness, satisfaction, passion, and engagement, in spite of (because of?) the losses I have experienced and the ones I know will be there again some day. Part of this good feeling for me comes from writing from the heart and rewriting myself and my intimate relationships.

Story Interlude: A Safe Landing (May 30, 2007)

As my partner Art and I fly into Reagan National Airport in D.C., I stare out the window at the lane after lane of rush-hour traffic that flashes just beneath the plane. As each lane flickers by, another wave of grief emerges. We are so low to the ground, the plane wobbles. I hold tighter to Art's hand. Even when we sit across the aisle from each other, we hold hands on all takeoffs and landings, a practice we started when we first met.

"We're really close to the road," I say. Art doesn't respond but he squeezes tighter. Tears form in my eyes. I take a deep breath, peering out the window, looking for "it."

Suddenly there it is—the water. I am transported back to January 13, 1982, the day Rex died on takeoff on his way to visit me. Right here in this spot. I shake the image out of my mind of a plane dropping quickly and Rex's head snapping forward, in spite of the seatbelt, against the back of the seat in front of him. I have trouble breathing. Just as the wheels touch down, the landing strip appears.

"The great Potomac," Art says ironically. The noise of landing as we try to hold ourselves back in our seats makes the fog I'm in more smothering.

Don't stay in this emotional space, I tell myself, and I work my way through the fog back into the present. I reach for my backpack under the seat in front of me. I think about how my mother always insisted I call her as soon as I arrived anywhere on a plane. Sometimes that seemed an encumbrance; often now I miss it. Sometimes nobody (other than Art) even knows where I am.

That evening, eating blue crab caught in the Chesapeake Bay, my voice catches as I say, "It was hard flying in here."

"I know. I could feel it from you," Art replies.

"It was intense, what I felt." Tears form and grief comes again. I wipe my eyes and sniffle, holding back sobs, and then quickly move to another space. "This crabcake is superb," I say. "There's nothing like lump crab meat."

"We should go to your fishing communities the next time we come to D.C.," Art says.

"That would be good, though I don't know many people there anymore," I say, thinking how time seems to pass so fast when you're older.

"But I'm excited about going home to Luray in a few days." I think about the seventieth surprise birthday party we are planning for my older brother, Arthur. My brother's wife and two sons, my sister and her husband, their daughter and son-in-law and new grandchild, all will be there. "This will be the first time we've all been together for a family gathering since Mom died. It's nice to be going home to celebrate rather than to mourn, and to know we can still be a family without my mother to gather round," I say, crunching down on a big bite of crabcake.

Meta-Autoethnography: Questioning the Story

Reviewers' critiques, such as Sherryl's, raise questions about how I wrote and interpreted what happened in "There Are Survivors." Sometimes now I ask myself to think outside the box, by which I mean outside the published story, which in so many ways has become the story—the story I remember and the one I tell. I ask myself to reinterpret what happened then from my perspective now, rather than relying solely on the published version of the events that took place, which is an interpretation from another point in time. This reframing is necessary to advance my own thinking and growth. My interpretation of the experience changes as my relationships and the world around me change. The story I wrote must be open to change as well.

After reading my story, Beth Harry (2005) asks why I do not concern myself more with cultural differences, a point that Sherryl makes as well. Harry wonders how group rituals negate the individual experience in my narrative. Critical theorist George Noblit (2005) asks why I don't deal more with the airline industry and its response, or with gender roles, family dynamics, and dimensions of power in emotions. For example, Noblit (2005) asserts that the men in my story seek to be in control; they show less emotion and have more power than the women. For him, the interesting exception is my father, who shows more emotion and seemingly has less power in the family and narrative than my mother. Whether Noblit is correct or not—after all, two cases (my brother Arthur and partner Gene) out of three do not make a pattern—his comments make me contemplate: did I model myself after my older brother, wanting to be strong like he was being? Did I think I would be a failure if I didn't control my emotions? Should I, as Lynda Stone (2005) suggests, have asserted myself more as a woman writer and celebrated the feminine?

These comments make me ask questions about family dynamics in my story. I wonder now why my father doesn't have a larger role in my narrative.[11] Though at the time I worried more about how my mother was handling Rex's death, ultimately the loss affected my father as much as, if not more than, the rest of us. Why didn't I seek out my father to share more of my emotions and take in more of his? Does this neglect reflect the lack of shared emotions in my family? Does the emphasis on my mother reflect the attention that typically was lavished on her when she was distressed? Does it reflect the value I and others in my working-class family placed on emotional control? Or were we really any more controlled than most other families? I recall now my mother's anger, quick and vicious, then followed by silence—a style I copied and one on which I have had to work. My sister responded by turning anger inward. Both my brothers inherited my father's propensity to hold in pain, expressing it when drinking alcohol.

Sometimes I reconsider things that happened in light of personal experiences and changing relationships. For example, though no critic has mentioned it, in recent readings, I have been perplexed by the audacity of the decision not to tell my sister Judi about Rex's death until the morning after he died. Was it so much that my brother and I wanted to save her from a night of agony, of waiting to get the verdict? Or were our actions selfish and thoughtless? My sister never said anything about our delay in giving her the news, even after she read my story about Rex. I wonder now how she felt about it, but I have decided not to revisit it with her unless she brings it up. I know I would have been angry, hurt, and morally outraged if this information had been kept from me. I can't imagine doing anything like that now to anyone, especially not to my sister. Of course, I am much closer to her now than I was then and much more likely to enter her pain willingly. I would want to be there to support her grief from the beginning, no matter how deep and needy it was, and I would need her there to support mine in the same way (as we did later when our mother died).

Meta-Autoethnography: Questioning the Portrayal of My Mother

I look back at the story now from a different relational position with my mother than I had at the time Rex died. As will become apparent in the next chapter, my mother and I developed an increasingly loving relationship prior to her death in 2002. Critics, students, and other readers also have asked questions about the way I portrayed my mother. For example, Nel Noddings (2005) asks if my mother could have been hurt by this account and Yvonna Lincoln (2005) asks how family members, including my mother, felt about having their grief appear in print. Similarly, Beth Harry (2005), who has lost a child of her own, points out my impatience with my mother and sees a history of mutual disagreement between us, at least in terms of religion.

Immediately after my brother's death, I felt my mother's standoffishness, which I attributed to her absorption with her own grief. I wondered at the time, How can her grief be more unbearable than my own? And I thought it odd of her to say it was. Grief should not be a contest or something to be compared, though it often is. Now I think my mother was probably right, given the depth of grief reported by those who lose children (Sanders, 1979/80; Rubin, 1996), and given the grief my mother displayed after Rex's death.

Rex was a large part of my mother's identity, daily life, and future plans. She had lunch with him every day, depended on him when she needed advice or assistance, and knew that Rex would care for her in the future. Their relationship was close and strong, and his death created a huge physical and emotional vacuum in her life. She was reminded of it and lived in it every single day. Since I lived in another state, I did not have the daily reminders my mother had, and the hole I experienced occupied a smaller part of my everyday life. I had a full life to return to at the university and with Gene that hadn't included Rex on a day-to-day basis for more than a dozen years. And, I had my future still in front of me, a future that didn't stop at Rex's death. Retired, my mother had primarily her soaps to occupy her mind and she often said she got lonely watching them by herself.

In retrospect, I think my mother's ability to let herself feel her grief perhaps contributed to her long life, unlike my father who tried so hard to "go on" (and without the alcohol of his earlier life to turn to) and then died of a heart attack five years after Rex died.

Of course, I can't know for sure why he died. His age of death, almost seventy-two, was near the median for men in this country and was perhaps a product of gender, genetics, and/or "living hard." But I do know that he seemed different after Rex died—depressed, sick, and fragile—and he never seemed to regain the degree of health he had prior to this loss.

I return now to Sherryl's focus on guilt. Did guilt play a part in how my family responded to death? Did its counterpart—blame—have a role? It's hard to talk about this without sounding like I'm blaming my mother for the rejection I felt from her. But such an interpretation would be mistaken. Given the close to "unconditional positive regard" with which we held each other by the time my mother died, casting blame now would serve no purpose. Instead, my exploration represents a desire to understand what was going on between my mother and me at the time of Rex's death, and perhaps in doing so, to understand aspects of grief, my own identity, and working-class families that still mystify me.

Did my mother, in some crevice of her mind, blame me for the accident? I don't mean that she thought I intentionally caused it. But did she ever think, If Carolyn hadn't left home, Rex wouldn't have been on his way to see her? Did she ever consider, Why did Carolyn have to get the cheapest ticket for him and not one on a major airline? I recall that she asked me about the price of the ticket. Did that mean anything or was she simply seeking information? I didn't blame myself and I don't recall feeling guilty about anything that occurred because I, like Sherryl, knew I didn't have the power to ward off plane crashes or cause them. Unlike Sherryl, I wasn't raised in a guilt culture, and I seemed not to have the personality or ethnicity that evoked guilt under those circumstances. I refused to imagine that anyone would blame me for something I had no control over and about which I felt so much pain. Perhaps I couldn't bear to imagine it.[12]

The first time I remember thinking about blame was during a recent discussion of this story in an undergraduate class on emotions. A student asks about my mother's reaction to me. As I answer her, suddenly a flash goes off in my head, and I hear myself say, "My mother couldn't grieve with me because she was mad at me. I think she blamed me for Rex's death. I've never understood this before, though perhaps I felt it then. But if true, her reaction to me is more understandable.

"I can see it in her first words to me after Rex died," I continue. "'It won't be okay . . . He's dead. He's not coming back.'" I close my eyes, remembering. Do I feel blame or displaced anger in her body's rigid response to my hug?

I become animated, and the students appear spellbound as I continue with my "discovery." "I was then and am now silenced by the truth of her response," I admit. "I was naive to think my words could ease her pain. 'It's going to be okay. We'll talk,' I told her.

I felt I had nothing but words to offer, and she rejected those. I felt such sadness that she couldn't reach out or open herself to me, which meant I couldn't open myself to her."

I am silent for a moment, thinking. "But another part of me might have been afraid she would open up and then what would I do? Could I handle it? Would I lose control myself? What would be expected of me? I couldn't stay in Luray and ease her pain. I had to go back to my life and my work.

"The truth is that I was a novice at grief. I'd never felt anything like this before. I had no idea how to expect to feel or what to do with these powerful feelings that washed over me. Certainly I was in no position to teach another person how to grieve. You can't impose your own style on anyone anyway, even if I had known then what my style was. I'm not sure I know even now."

As I write this now in 2008, I remember back, many years later, when my mother was bedridden. Once, when I was leaving after a visit with her, she sobbed and begged me not to go. She clutched at me, embraced me, pulling me to her body. I sobbed too as I cradled her and felt the warmth of our love and need for each other. It was the closest I ever felt to my mother and the most heartrending experience I ever had with her. She apologized later, and after that, we went back to our usual pattern of being loving but stoic when we parted. Remembering this now makes me cry. Would anything have been better if we had sobbed every time we parted? Or would it have made the agony of separation worse?

In class, my voice cracks and I am astonished at how much emotion I feel. From the sniffles that pour into the silence, I sense that the students are with me, so I continue. "Of course, I don't recall my mother opening herself up to other family members either, so her coldness might not have been just about me. I did see her take in condolences from others in the town, and sometimes I felt envious when they offered and she received their support, or when they cried with her. But they were coming to give her empathy and comfort, not asking that she share her grief with them as I was," I analyze, now getting some distance. "That might be different. She just didn't seem able to share it with her family at the time—not with me, my siblings, or my father—at least not where I could see. I didn't understand that, because when I could share my feelings with someone else who loved Rex as I did—like my father those few times—it helped me considerably."

Looking back at the story now, I recall that my mother did express her emotions. She literally screamed her sorrow at the funeral home in front of Rex's body. But even there, she didn't turn to the family she had left. Perhaps she was afraid to scream her raw grief at us. Maybe she feared she would rage and hurt us. Perhaps her "control" was to protect us, as much as herself. Instead she screamed toward Rex, while we hung onto her. Rex was the only person who could ease her pain. Or perhaps she knew that nothing could, and she simply cried out, perhaps to God. I didn't express, much less scream, my feelings then. But I have screamed them ever since in the prose I have written.

"It's interesting, though, that I don't recall breaking down with family either, except with my sister when we met in the airport in Atlanta to go home, and with my sister-in-law when I arrived home," I say to students, thinking out loud. "My brother stayed in control in public and didn't want to break down. Sometimes I wonder if my sister felt the same way toward me as I did toward my mother." Why is emotional control so important to me? And is the need for control, and its counterpart, the need to rebel against control, the reasons I study emotions in the first place?

"Though I have little memory now of family members comforting each other, other than at the funeral," I continue in class, "I remember tears and sadness and feeling that we were all in tremendous pain and somehow coping together." Perhaps comfort is the "job" of those outside the inner circle. How can you comfort when you yourself feel so bad, are so preoccupied and depressed, and need so much? Perhaps my mother intuitively knew that. Grief is tricky, especially for the inner circle of people experiencing it.[13] In some ways you may lose each other for a time as each person is so fully taken up with their relationship with the deceased (see Rosenblatt, 1996, p. 52).

Who was I to my mother? Though we did not have a bad relationship, we had relational problems, as Harry (2005) suspected. My mother accepted and supported my going away to college, then to graduate school, and then to Florida to take a job, but she was always unhappy about not having me in her day-to-day world. She also did not understand some of the changes that occurred on my way from a small-town girl to an educated "hippy" professor—for example, that I no longer went to church, used "bad" language occasionally, drank alcohol, and dated older men who did not fit her stereotype of an ideal mate for her daughter. She often felt I neglected her—that I did not visit her often enough or stay long enough. Once, for example, she returned my Christmas gifts, refusing to talk to me for three months, because I spent a few days of my Christmas vacation with a boyfriend instead of all of it with her. At least that was my version of events; I never asked for hers. I was just happy that she started talking to me again when I called home because I needed financial assistance for a medical condition. My mom always came through when any of us needed money.

Did I feel guilty for leaving my family to go away to college? Maybe I did, though I never questioned that I had to go. Perhaps it is not that guilt (and blame) are lacking in working-class southern culture; perhaps the difference from Jewish working-class culture is that for Southerners these emotions often are held in, working their way out in other destructive ways.

As I have written about my relationship with my mother,[14] I am more aware of my role in some of our relational problems and how difficult it must have been for my mother to see her daughter become someone she didn't recognize, living a life that she didn't understand (see Myerhoff, 1978). We didn't talk about any of this. Later, when we grew closer and could have talked about what happened, there no longer seemed any reason or need to do so.

My mother is dead now and I can't ask her if she blamed me for Rex's death. I wouldn't want to if I could because I don't need to know the answer, nor would I want to make her feel bad if that had been the case. Maybe my mother assigned no blame, or if she did, perhaps it was unconscious. If she did, most likely the feelings were something she couldn't control. If she did, perhaps it was a desperate attempt to avenge her pain. Perhaps she, as do many people, needed someone at whom to direct her anger, much like the Ilongot headhunters who expressed their after-death rage in headhunting rituals. One headhunter told Rosaldo (1989) that "rage, born of grief, impels him to kill his fellow human beings" in hopes that he can "throw away the anger of his bereavement" (p. 1). After the funeral, my mother expressed her grief and sadness but held most of her rage inside. Possibly she feared that if she released those ferocious feelings, she might lose me, the rest of her family, even herself.

I must stop speculating now because these feelings that my mother might or might not have felt don't much matter now to the memory of our relationship. What does matter?

I look back again at the text of the story. I hone in now on the gentle and caring moments my mom and I shared and the love and tenderness I felt for both parents at Rex's death, moments that perhaps are camouflaged by my focus on my mother's distancing posture. I see in the text—and remember—the concern I felt for how she and my father were doing; the time and effort I spent taking care of arrangements with my brother so that things would go smoothly and not present additional problems for my parents (which also gave my life purpose and helped me control my emotional pain); the grief I felt for my parents' loss and pain and for my own. I remember the tender moments my mother and I had every night when I kneeled by the couch she slept on and asked her questions about Rex leaving so that she could tell over and over her story of the last few minutes she spent with him. I needed to hear it and she needed to tell it. In those moments, I believe she did the best she could to recognize my grief and love for Rex as I did to recognize hers. I know now how difficult it is to get outside one's own feeling at the moment of grief and empathize with others' pain. I recall the care with which she and I made up a list of pallbearers, our decision to put my gold chain around Rex's neck. I remember all of us gently putting my mother to bed on the couch after Rex's burial, and my visits to her in the hospital before I left to go back to

Tampa. Remembering all this now as I write makes me ache and cry, yet reexperience the love and attachment, which is the way remembering grief has come to be. Granted, my mother and I didn't express our love verbally then—something I will discuss in the next chapter—but that didn't mean we didn't love each other.

Somehow in my former readings, these connecting points have been set aside. Reviewers also have failed to mention them, concentrating instead on my description of my mother as weak and self-centered (Noddings, 2005) and the mutual disagreement in our relationship (Harry, 2005). Did they not see the love and tenderness? Do such things naturally get overlooked in critical essays? Or did I underplay them in my initial telling? Perhaps the responses reveal as much, if not more, about the responders and their lives as it does about mine.

Perhaps I end with this interpretation because this revision is the way I want things to have been. Perhaps the reason doesn't matter, only the result.

I explore all this, not to find answers, but to rethink my story about the events surrounding my brother's death. As in the original story about my brother, I write these stories now to share the unity and wholeness of lived experience with others and to reinterpret my life (Parry 1991). As in the original story, I write to continue the process of constructing myself as "survivor" (Ellis, 1993, p. 728).

In revisiting this story and considering others' responses, I write to reflect on my experiences and my family then, to probe the buried assumptions in grief and emotional storytelling, and to understand emotional control and release in working-class families. In particular, I have tried to explain my relationship with my mother to myself and, in the process, I have come to feel better about anything that wasn't quite right between us in the past. Revising is therapeutic!

In the next chapter I turn to stories I wrote about my mother after Rex died, which explore the development of our relationship and the ethical issues that writing about her created. These stories show how our relationship developed from the tentative connection you see in the story of Rex's death in 1982 to the unconditionally loving bond we had when my mother died two decades later in 2002.

CHAPTER EIGHT

Rewriting and Re-Membering Mother

Personal Storytelling

"Any sorrow can be borne, if you can turn it into a story," I say to my undergraduate personal storytelling class, paraphrasing a quote of Isak Dinesen's (1992). I smile as the students sit quietly in their seats listening to my introduction. I know from experience that they will not be this quiet again the rest of the semester.

"'Let me tell you a story' is a phrase we often hear in our day-to-day interactions," I continue. "We tell stories so that others might know more about us, what has happened to us, and the things we care about. But stories are not only a way of telling about the events, people, and emotions in our lives. We also tell stories to fashion our identities. We tell stories as a way to relate to other human beings. We tell stories to find meaning in and to understand our individual and collective experience. Stories are the best way to understand human experience because, as Richardson [1990, p. 65] says, 'It is the way humans understand their own lives.'

"Our stories and our feelings about telling them are not solely individual or self-determined matters. The groups we are a part of and the culture and time we live in contribute to our sense of which stories are appropriate to remember and tell, as well as to our understanding of the way they should be told. By getting a handle on the collective stories we receive from our culture, families, and peers, we can understand better our own individual stories and how they are intertwined with others.

"As the world becomes increasingly diverse and more closely connected through media, mobility, economic interdependence, and the internet, the stories we are exposed to increase in number and kind. To understand others who are different from us, it becomes necessary to listen closely to their stories.

"Telling and retelling our stories can be transformative. By telling and writing, looking back, reinterpreting and retelling, we can sometimes reframe our lives in ways that are easier to bear. We can learn from thinking systematically about our experience and come to see our lives and our selves in new ways. At all times until death, we are in the middle of our stories, with new elements constantly being added. The end is not predetermined, and we can affect how our stories turn out by consciously reflecting on them and considering how others respond to them.

"Stories can be transformative for listeners and readers as well as for tellers and writers. As Arthur Frank [1995, pp. 17–18] points out, 'Storytelling is *for* the other, just as much as it is for oneself.' Telling a story is an attempt to 'change one's own life by affecting the lives of others.' In listening to a story, we open ourselves up not just to the possibility of sympathy and tolerance, but also 'to the possibility of radical self-transformation' [Arras, 1997, p. 74].

"In this class, you will try to write yourself as a survivor in a challenging story that you are living. You will work on the story, writing and rewriting, linking details of what happened to feelings about the events then, and what you felt then to what you feel now [Pennebaker, 1990; see also DeSalvo, 2000]. The more your writing succeeds as a narrative—detailed, organized, vivid, compelling—the more helpful it will be to you and the more it will engage others and evoke their stories.

"You should write and revise until you have insights about your life that point toward a positive future. Perhaps that means only reframing what has happened in the past or opening up questions about what you want in the future and how you can make that happen. Maybe you can't change your lives the way you want, but perhaps you can make yourselves survivors of the lives you were given.

"We also will read published personal narratives. For next week, read the two stories I wrote about my mother. The events in 'Maternal Connections' [1996] took place in 1993 when I was forty-three and my mother was seventy-nine. The events in 'With Mother/With Child: A True Story' [2001] happened in 1999 when I was forty-nine and my mother was eighty-five. As you read, think about the meaning the stories might hold for you, the listener, as well as for me, the teller. Think also about the cultural context in which I wrote them and how your experiences might be different from mine. I'll look forward to learning more about my own story and yours from your responses next week."

Looking overwhelmed and dazed after reading the long syllabus and hearing the numerous reading and writing assignments, the students grab their books and quickly leave class.

Maternal Connections[1]

With one hand, she holds tightly to the support bar along the wall of the bathroom. I take her other hand gently in mine, wash each finger, noting the smoothness of her skin, the beauty of her long, slender fingers. "My fingernails," she says, "they're dirty." Without speaking, I run my index nail, covered with a washcloth, under each of her nails, systematically snapping out the dirt as I go. It's a good sign that she cares. Until now, she hasn't been that concerned even about urinating in bed.

When I push hard on the soap dispenser, small globs of thick, pink liquid soap, smelling of perfumed bleach, drop onto the translucent washcloth. I load the white cloth with many squirts, hoping to wash away the lingering smell of feces, urine, perspiration, bile bags, plastic tubes, stale hair oils, and hospital odors.

She extends her arm and I slowly wash from wrist to shoulder, observing the intrusion of the spreading black bruises marking needle points. Her washed hand holds onto my wrist for support now as I unclasp her other hand from the railing. I repeat the process on that side.

"I'm going again," she says, sucking in slowly through open lips and closed teeth, eyebrows raised as though she is asking my permission and apologizing at the same time. I'm glad she is sitting on the toilet. It'll be less of a mess than before.

"That's okay," I respond, "maybe this will be the last time. Hopefully the laxative has run its course."

I hold her hand and touch her shoulder gently as she lets it all go. Then, "I'm sorry about last night," she says. "It seemed like it was every hour. You shouldn't have to do that."

"I didn't mind," I say, remembering my reflex gag reaction the first time her bowels exploded in the night. Only my determination that she not know how much the smell—that rotten, chemical odor—bothered me kept me from adding my regurgitation to the brown liquid I poured into the toilet on her behalf. "I'm glad I was here for you."

"Yeah, the nurses don't come right away," she says. "Even with you here, some ended up on the bed, didn't it?"

"Yes, but now we know better how to do it, get the bedpan under you sooner. It helps when you raise your hips."

"If anybody told me I'd have to be doing this . . ."

". . . you used to do it for me," I interrupt. We laugh like two good friends sharing a memory.

Being careful of the tubes and IVs, I unsnap and remove her soiled gown. She tries to help. I cover the front of her body with a towel, to protect her from cold. "It feels good when you wash my back," she says, and I continue rubbing. When she shivers, I run the washcloth under hot water. I wonder about washing the rest of her body.

Around front, I wash her belly, noting the faded scars of my younger brother's cesarean birth—and shudder at the reminder that he is now dead—and I look closely at the new scars of the gallbladder surgery. Her stomach is puffy, but almost flat now, not rounded as before. The extra skin hangs loosely. Then her legs. Although her skin is dry and flaky, I admire her thin, almost bony, yet still shapely, legs. Our bodies have the same form, I note. Long, slender, and graceful limbs, fatty layers on top of the hips and belly, and a short and thick waist.

I move to her breasts, still large and pendulous. Now they hang to her waist and, as her shoulders curve forward, they rest on her belly, like mine, only lower.

I take one tenderly in my hand, lift it gently from her belly to wash it, noting the rash underneath. "Would you like cream on that?"

"Oh, yes, it's real sore." She holds her breast while I rub in the cream.

Feeling no particular emotion, I observe from a distance. Her body is my body, my body in thirty-six years. So this is what it will look and be like. I see.

I hand her the soaped washcloth. "Can you wash your butt," I ask, "and between your legs?"

"I think so," she replies, taking the washcloth, holding onto the support bar to balance one side of herself a few inches above the seat. My pubic hair also will be thin and gray, I think, as I notice hers. Then I walk away, to give her the illusion of privacy.

"Are you ready to get back in bed now?" I ask.

"Yes, I'm worn out."

I extend both arms. The bile bag pinned to her gown threatens to become entangled in our embrace. "Put it around my neck," she cleverly suggests. "It'll be my necklace." I smile, appreciating her humor, which bonds us and makes it easier to refer to the bag. But what a breakdown in boundaries—her bile is on the outside of her body for everyone to see, more personally revealing than the butt that sticks out of the back of her gown!

I hold my arms out straight again. When she grabs on, she and I pull her to a standing position. When she winces in pain, I embrace her around her middle, steadying her for the long journey back to bed, eight feet away. The tubes extending from her chest and abdomen, the bile bag necklace—all are properly positioned. She shuffles her feet in baby steps, all the while holding onto my outstretched arms. She looks into my eyes as I walk backwards, to pick up my cues, when to move forward, when to turn. We are intimately connected. We are totally trusting.

Taking care of her feels natural, as though she is my child. The love and concern flowing between us feels like my mom and I are falling in love. The emotionality continues during the four days and nights I stay with her in the hospital. My life is devoted temporarily to her well-being. She knows it and is grateful. I am grateful for the experience. I do not mind that she is dependent on me. I am engrossed by our feeling, by the seemingly mundane but, for the moment, only questions that matter. Are you dizzy? In pain? Comfortable? Do you want to be pulled up in bed? Can't you eat one more bite? Do you need to pee? Have gas? Want water? Prefer to sleep now? As I help with these events, I do not question their meaning, as I so often do about most things in my life.

While my mom sleeps, I take my daily walk down the hall to peer at the newborn babies. On the other side of the glass partition, there are three—one boy covered in blue and two girls in pink. I wince at the institutional marking of gender roles and then shrug. I strain to read the identification cards, to have a story about each one: birthday, weight, length, parents' names—not much to go on.

A man stares intently at one of the girls. Knowing the answer, I ask anyway, "Are you the father?" He nods yes and beams. "She has jaundice," he says, "a mild case." I feel his bond to her even through the glass pane. I recognize the connection from the feelings I have for my mother. He leaves and another young man, in his early twenties, arrives. Ignoring the young son pulling on his pants leg for attention, this man stands off to the side, to peer through the glass into an inner room almost out of view. Out of the corner of my eye, I watch and imagine his story. His new baby must be in there, perhaps he is worried about it, like I am worried about my mother. If he could just get a glimpse, or better yet, do something, he would feel better.

I continue watching, fantasizing that one of the babies is mine, and try to generate what the feeling would be. What would it be like to take the baby home? To bond? The dependence? Experiencing unconditional love for my mother makes me, for the moment, crave to feel it toward and from a child as well. Do I just want someone who will wash me when I'm seventy-nine? What if something is wrong with the baby? What about my career? Travel plans? Yet how can I omit this meaning-giving experience from my life?

When I return, my mom is having her vitals read by a nurse who "usually works in the nursery," my mom announces. "How old is the oldest mother you have had?" I ask nonchalantly, hoping my question is not too transparent.

"Forty-two," the nurse answers.

I must look disappointed, because she adds quickly, "But I have only worked there for eighteen months, I'm sure there have been some older. Yes, I'm sure."

I'd be almost forty-four before my first child could be born, I think, turning back to my mother.

With Mother/With Child: A True Story[2]

"Mom, I'd like to read something to you, a story I wrote," I say tentatively, carrying my open laptop computer into the living room. "It's about the last time I visited and the routines you

went through getting ready for bed. It's about our relationship. Would you like to hear it?" My
voice quivers slightly, but I try to speak distinctly.

She turns toward me quickly, closely reading my lips, her own lips moving as she takes in
what I'm saying. "Okay," she says, clicking down the sound on her television. The lights from
the picture continue to flicker, calling attention as they intersect the sun setting behind the Blue
Ridge Mountains outside her front bay window. Sitting on the couch beside her La-Z-Boy chair,
I scroll through my files. I click on the one entitled "With Mother/With Child" and I begin to
read my story aloud.

* * *

"Guess it's time for bed," I say, looking at my watch.

Mom pulls the lever on the side of her coral La-Z-Boy chair, which lowers her feet and
raises her to an upright sitting position. She squints at her watch. "Yeah, I'm tired," she
says, taking her cues from the watch dial. It's ten o'clock, my mother's ritual bedtime.

I have been visiting my eight-five-year-old mother for the past week. She had been
scheduled for back surgery for a pinched nerve, and I had come to care for her. But the
surgery was canceled after she was prepped because the anesthesia caused her blood
pressure to fluctuate wildly. Now, surgery is out of the question. She and I have spent
several days working on routines to prepare her to live more comfortably and safely
with increasing back pain and decreasing mobility. In the evenings, we watch the nightly
women's movie on the Lifetime channel. Mom loves the melodramatic movies they air,
and I enjoy the communal experience of watching them with her.

Mom continues leaning toward me. From the look on her face—wide, concentrating eyes
and a look of reverence—it is clear she is engaged in the story I tell. This is the first time I
have read her a story I have written. I have not planned how to read it to her. I figure I'll
play it by ear. She has read a few stories I have written about others, but I purposely have
not given her "Maternal Connections" (Ellis, 1996a), a story I published about her. Although
the story depicted the positive relationship that evolved between us when I took care of her
after she had gallbladder surgery five years ago, I feared she would not like the references
I made to her bodily functions. How do I explain that these stories can be important for
others, for thinking about aging, caregiving, and mother-daughter relationships? I suppose
I should say just that. I've rehearsed the conversation we might have many times: I plan to
say, "People would not think about the story being about you, Mom, but rather about what
happens when parents are ill and their children become caregivers." I fantasize she will reply,
"But they'd know it was me. You say it's your mother. They'd know that I had diarrhea on
the bed." And she'd be right. Feeling unresolved about not showing her that story and being

committed to participants' right to know, I've been determined that I should inform her of other stories I write about her before I publish them.

I look ahead to the next paragraph:

I find these Lifetime movies predictable, simple, and sentimental, and I long for more complex plots. They are certainly better, however, than *Hollywood* and *Walker, Texas Ranger:* violent, action-packed adventure shows that my mom also loves. Mom encourages me to watch what I want, but when on the rare occasion I can find a movie I want to view on her limited cable TV, I can tell it doesn't interest her. Sometimes, she naps or looks off into space. Even when she is engaged, she takes in only the main plot. The subtleties and twists and turns, which I long for, escape her, partly because of her hearing problem, and partly because complexity is not entertaining to her. She likes a simple, linear story with an engaging plot and happy ending. A happy, tidy ending provides balance to the constant tension in her favorite afternoon soaps. From years of watching television with my mother, I understand that she is not attracted to thinking critically; instead, her ideal is to be passively [and mindlessly] entertained. Nothing wrong with that, I tell myself. When I'm not home, she often watches the same movie a second time, and occasionally she turns off the sound, even during the first viewing, she says.

I read only: I like these movies better than *Hollywood* and *Walker, Texas Ranger:* violent, action-packed adventure shows that my mom also loves. When I'm not home, she often watches the same movie a second time, and occasionally she turns off the sound, even during the first viewing, she says.

This is difficult. What would she have thought if I had read the entire paragraph? Who am I to say that my tastes are complex, hers simple? If I can't read this paragraph to her, maybe I should take it out of the final story. I compromise, making a note to omit "and mindlessly."

What do I know, anyway, about how she views these shows? Maybe there's more going on than I think. What about the role of vicarious emotional experience in her attraction to these programs? For someone like my mother, who spends enormous amounts of time alone, perhaps the adventure shows provide harmless thrills, and the melodramatic shows evoke vicarious emotional experiences, both of which get harder and harder to come by in real life. When these experiences do enter her life, usually they involve loss, something she's had plenty of. Perhaps these shows present not only an escape from the difficulties in her life, but a sense of friendship and sociability as well. They provide a way to try on the life of others, yet from a safe position because once they're over, she can forget the plot. Televised melodrama may become especially significant emotionally when one's network of significant others has diminished.³ Now, my mother's primary (almost only) contacts are her children: my brother and sister-in-law, who check on her daily, and her two daughters, who come home for celebrations and for crises like this one.

I don't mention these thoughts to my mother about why and what she watches; we never talk about any of it. I continue reading to her, a little nervous that I will make bad decisions about what to include, and hurt or upset her in the process.

"Yeah, I'm tired," my mom repeats, breaking into my reverie about the movies she watches. As she begins the task of getting up from her La-Z-Boy chair, she takes a deep breath and inches forward until she sits on the edge. Then, she pulls her walker toward her, places her left hand on the back bar, and pulls while she pushes on the arm of the chair with her right hand. She laughs when she falls back into the chair. "I'm like an old drunk," she says in her deep southern accent, with emphasis on *old*. I smile.

Sitting now in the same chair I write about, my mother laughs out loud as I read the last line about being like an old drunk. I appreciate her sense of humor. She enjoys laughing at herself.

Next time she tries to get up, I give her a hand under her arm and she comes out of the chair easily. Seeing the pressure she puts on the bar of the walker to help her rise, I worry that someday it might tilt on her. Later, I try to simulate pulling myself up with it and am amazed at the sturdiness and stability of the four-legged apparatus. For the next few days, I will follow her around, imitating what she does. I look for problem spots, trying to make life easier and safer for my mother, anticipating where she might fall or be injured.

Once she is on her feet, she pulls the walker toward her and grabs on with both hands. She bends over the walker as she moves, her back curved. I think of how straight her posture has always been. She walks quickly into the kitchen. "You're going to get a speeding ticket one of these days," I say, walking behind her.

She stops, turns; then smiling and nodding, she says, "Unhuh." It is the look and utterance I have come to know means she didn't hear me. Her look and sound appear vacuous, with little expression.

Before she starts moving again, I tap her on the shoulder, and when she is looking at my face, I repeat distinctly, "You're going to get a speeding ticket one of these days."

Her eyes concentrate on my lips, and she mouths the words as I say them. Her face breaks out into a huge smile, and she laughs a belly laugh. "And just who is gonna give it to me?" She loves to kibitz like this, and she obviously is pleased that she can move so fast and that I have noticed.

I watch my mother's expression as I read. She smiles and laughs out loud both times I mention the speeding ticket. I change the word kibitz to kid. I skip the mention of her curved back, concerned about how that will make her feel, and the word vacuous, assuming it will have no meaning for her. Or, am I worried that it might? I ask myself if I can claim that I revealed the story to her if I don't read everything.

Once in the kitchen, she bends over, both elbows propped on the counter, working just from her elbows to her hands to sort her pills. I suggest that she sit on the seat of her walker to make it easier, and she does. "Oh, I like this," she says. "It's so hard to stand." I'm delighted to have helped. When she can't quite reach her pills, I push them to the front of the counter, being careful to keep them in their proper order.

She picks up each bottle in turn, reads the label, removes a pill, and places it in one of two small plastic cups, sometimes changing her mind about the appropriate container. One cup is for pills she will take tonight, the other for pills for the morning when she will not feel well enough to stand and sort before she has her insulin shot, cereal, and Tylenol for pain. She tells me what each pill is for as she removes it from the bottle. Three pills are for blood pressure, one is a blood thinner, and one is for cholesterol. Then, there's her nightly Tylenol for arthritis, the only thing she can tolerate for pain. "The other pills the doctor gave me made me crazy in the head," she explains. I note she lays out four Tylenol, and I suggest she take only two. She hesitates, says okay, and puts two back in the bottle. Then, she adds her Centrum Silver multivitamin, vitamins C and E, and garlic. "Isn't this a mess of pills?" she says.

"Sure is," I reply. "You could open your own pharmacy."

She laughs another belly laugh. "Isn't that the truth?"

I watch how organized and methodical she is. Then, I look into the cups and ask her, "Why are there two blue pills in this one?"

"Oh, there's only supposed to be one," she says, quickly removing the intruding pill from the cup and authoritatively placing it back into the correct bottle. I watch her hand shake as she acts. I note she leaves each cap loose on the top of the bottle. Too difficult to get off, I imagine. I wonder whether she should have help with her pills. What if she's been taking them wrongly for some time?

"I guess you made a mistake because I was talking to you?" I say, more to convince myself than her.

"Probably," she replies, nonchalantly, busily concentrating on the task at hand.

"Let's leave the bottles near the front of the counter, so you can reach them from your walker without getting up," I suggest, and I am surprised when she agrees. Next morning, I find the pill bottles neatly placed once again in a row along the back. Mother is a creature of habit, and neatness is very important to her.

She reaches for the Advil. "Now don't take Advil," I advise, "because we have to do the stool test, and the doctor said no ibuprofen."

"Oh, yes, that's right. Sometimes I take an Advil with the Tylenol," she explains, quickly drawing back her hand.

"You can do that again after we do the tests," I say, "but even then why don't you wait and take the Advil during the day if the Tylenol wears off?"

Nodding in agreement, she seems to respect and want my opinion, and I am delighted that she seems to be holding her usual instantaneous "no" response at bay. I think she probably enjoys having someone with whom to work these things out. My brother, Arthur, and sister-in-law, Barbara, visit her every day, but nobody actually accompanies her through her day-to-day routines.

"Oh, and you're not supposed to take the vitamin C now either," I remind her, "because of the test."

"Oh, yes, that's right," she says, putting the large orange pill back into the bottle. There's so much for her to remember, I think. Thankfully, her mind is still sharp. Wanting to believe that she usually takes the correct pills, I chalk the mistakes up to recent changes in her routine.

"Does that sound right?" I ask my mom as I read. "Like the way it happened?" I want to connect with her, and I want her response, although I do not want to interrupt the continuity of the story too much.

"Oh, yes, it does," she says, nodding enthusiastically. Our short conversation provides time to think about my reading of the story. Gaining a little confidence now, I have read our conversation with lots of expression. She laughs at the mention of the mess of pills and opening her own pharmacy, and smiles in recognition when I say that she is a creature of habit. Still, I omit the sentence about her hand shaking. I am reluctant to mention these physical signs that perhaps she herself has not noticed: the curved back before and now the shaking hand. She is such a proud person. I don't want to make her feel worse about herself. Or, is it that I don't want to face up to the signs myself, or at least not while in interaction with her? Perhaps on some level, I prefer to pretend, or at least to maintain a balance between openness and pretense. That was true even in my failure to follow up on the possibility that she was making mistakes in taking her pills.

I think about how I changed stool test to test when I read. Will she think talking about her stool is too personal? Perhaps I think mentioning stool is too personal. Would I want others talking about my stool? That was the main problem I had with reading "Maternal Connections" to her: the description of the diarrhea. Can I ever explain to her why that detail was so important to the story? I recall how difficult it was to talk about Gene's stool in Final Negotiations *(1995a) and my own in "Speaking of Dying" (1995c). Maybe I'm the one hung up about bodily functions.*

"Want me to get you some water, to take the pills?" I ask.

"Okay," she says appreciatively. "You know I can take them without water."

"Well, no need to, here's the water." I hold out the glass.

"I can take them all at once," she exclaims, and before I can stop her, she tosses the whole handful of pills down her throat and follows with only a small sip of water.

"How do you do that?" I think how I sometimes gag on one pill.

"I don't know. I always have," she says, obviously proud of her accomplishment.

She stands and leans on the counter. "I need to stand a little bit. Otherwise I won't be able to get up."

"That's good," I respond. While she stands, I sit on her walker seat to explore how it works. The walker has two small wheels on both sides in the back and one slightly larger wheel on each side in the front. A wide bench seat connects the two sides about chair level. The seat opens to reveal a wire basket underneath for carrying items. When I sit down on the seat, the chair locks in place as my weight pushes the stationary legs, located between the pairs of wheels in the back, down to the ground. Raising up on the handle bars just slightly, I can take the weight off the legs, and then I can "walk" around by pushing with my feet. "Look, Mom, you can move yourself around while you're sitting down."

"I didn't know it would do that," she says, expressing her delight. She declines when I ask her if she wants to try.

"Too bad it isn't high enough to reach the stove. You could cook while sitting down."

My mother has had the walker only two months. Prior to that, she had a standard walker that had to be picked up and placed down with each step. When Arthur and I suggested a walker with wheels, Mom said she didn't need it. Finally, Barbara ordered one, saying, "We can take it back if you don't like it." Mom fell in love with the new walker immediately.

It's hard to know when to push things, I think. When are you doing "what's best," and when are you taking away control and decision making? Too often, it's both. Knowing the boundary is especially hard with my mother, whose first reaction to anything new or any change in routine is to say "no." I suspect this response is common among elderly people.

"Here, you take it," I say, offering the walker when I see she's having trouble standing.

She leans eagerly on the handlebars. "I guess I'm going to have to live with the pain," she says, a sad look on her face. "I may never get any better."

I sense that she is in the process of moving from thinking of a cure to trying to adjust to the continued presence of pain and deterioration in her life. She has been in severe pain now for almost a year, to the point of not being able to walk at times. Pain pills don't help, and surgery, which she has looked to as a cure, is too risky. How do I respond? I want to be honest with her and help her cope, but I don't want her to give up hope. "I don't know," I say, "maybe you'll get better. We'll try the Pain Clinic and see what they have to offer."

As I read this to her, I notice tears in her eye. I think again of how difficult it is to know what to say in these situations. I also think that bluntly acknowledging that she may never get better might be difficult for both of us. Our relationship, to some extent, is based on joy. I come home to make her feel better, and it usually works. Yet, perhaps feeling better might mean accepting the pain and living the best life she can in spite of it. Certainly, I don't want her to feel like she has to play down the pain or pretend to think she will get better just to make me feel good. Or do I? Do I want to acknowledge with her how bad her situation is? Could I stand it? How would I feel to admit that there is no hope for substantial improvement? How would she? I know there will come a time when she and I will have this conversation. But not yet. Not yet, I tell myself. Okay, then, when? How will I know when it's the right time? I think about how she has declined since the time period represented in this story.

She nods and starts moving toward the bathroom, suddenly making a detour through the living room. "I need my lotion," she explains, as she grabs a bottle of H_2O hand cream from the end table beside her La-Z-Boy chair and places it on the seat of the walker. I notice that the table is set up with items she needs: lotion, fingernail polish and polish remover, and emery boards; her pocketbook, Kleenex, and eyeglasses cleaner; a letter-size, quarter-inch-thick county phone book, a pencil, and a tablet. On the floor are two baskets: one is filled with catalogues and a weekly pamphlet offering a prayer for each day; a second contains a variety of lipsticks, mirrors, makeup, and other potions. Huge round buttons on her hearing-impaired phone display my brother's name and the name of a neighbor. When pushed, the third button rings directly into my brother's house, then the neighbor's house; if there still is no answer, it dials 911. I note the absence of my phone number. What benefit would it have? I live almost a thousand miles away. The portable emergency cord of the Medical Alert System lies beside the phone. "That doesn't do you much good laying there," I say.

"I don't want to wear that thing around my neck," she responds.

"But what if you fall?"

"I told you," she responds adamantly, "I ain't gonna fall." By the end of the sentence, her voice is again gentle.

"Well, you fell once," I remind softly. We speak like two good friends having a minor and unimportant disagreement. "If you won't put it around your neck, how about at least hangin' it on your bedpost in case you have problems during the night? You have your emergency phone here, so it doesn't do any good to keep the necklace on the same table."

She replies, "I don't have any trouble at night." We both hesitate. Then she picks up the necklace. I smile at her. She smiles back. We talk about the family pictures that fill each wall as I follow along behind her, first through the living room and then down the long hall. "I liked your hair like that," she says pointing to a high school picture. "Curled and teased so you had some height on top."

"Unhuh," I respond, and keep moving. I know she is saying politely that she doesn't like the straight, flat hairstyle I wear now.

I move rugs and furniture out of the way as we walk. The walker rolls smoothly over the thick carpet. "Daddy made these halls wide, so we could get wheelchairs down them," she explains.

"I know," I reply, having heard the story of my father's plans many times.

"I told him then, 'We won't need those.' But he insisted. Guess I *will* need a wheelchair someday," she says. I am happy with my father's foresight. I only wish the hall were shorter, I think, looking down to the far end, past her office, two large bathrooms, the living room, and yet another bedroom before her bedroom door comes into view at the far end.

"You ought to sleep in Daddy's room," I say. "Or Aunt Florence's room. It has its own bathroom." Although my father has been dead for thirteen years and my aunt for ten, we still refer to these rooms as their rooms. Because my family had moved into this house only fourteen years before, long after I had left home, I never had a designated room as I had in our previous home. Instead, after my father died, I always slept in his room when I came to visit.

"Oh, no, I couldn't do that. It wouldn't feel right," she says. I don't argue. For my mother, your bedroom is your bedroom.

She turns the corner and moves easily into the large bathroom. Even the doors are oversized, I note. She sits down on a chair placed immediately inside the door. She takes off her glasses and I help pull her white knit sweater over her head. "Want me to unhook your bra?" I ask.

"No, I can do it," she says.

When she has trouble unhooking it, I jump to help her, then remind myself to let her do the things she can. She keeps working until it is unfastened. "There," she says triumphantly.

"What about your girdle?" I ask. The brace, which we refer to as a girdle, had been given to her by her surgeon a few days before to help with the pain coming from her pinched nerve. I had little hope it would help, but she had begun wearing it right away and refused to take it off, as if it were a good luck charm.

"I'm going to sleep in it," she says. "It doesn't bother me."

"Mom, they said to wear it just when you were active. We can put it back on tomorrow morning."

"Okay," she says reluctantly. "I think I can get it back on anyway."

"Now watch how I do it," I instruct. I open the three Velcro pieces in the front. "Okay, now let's pull down your slacks and underpants a bit, so I can pull the girdle off." She bends slowly toward the front of the chair as I support her chest gently with one hand; with the other, I pull the girdle from around her back.

"It's like the corsets you used to wear," I say. "They came up to your bra and all the way down past your butt. Remember, I wore one to the prom, with a long-line bra." I think about how horrible they felt—I couldn't breathe—and rolls of fat always managed to find a place to sneak out. "That was thirty-one years ago," I muse.

"Makes me look big as a cow to have that thing on," she says, her southern accent turning cow into two syllables.

"No, it doesn't," I respond. "Actually it slims you down. Holds in your tummy."

She smiles. "Does it really?" She is obviously pleased by the thought.

I think then of how much care she takes of herself and how she still wants to look attractive. And she is attractive, I think, looking at her wrinkle-free face and alert, twinkling eyes.

"I'll get up when I hear you tomorrow morning and help you put your girdle on," I say, assuming the difficulty of putting it on is why she is hesitant to take it off.

"I can put it on myself," she says, slight irritation showing in her voice.

"Are you sure? You have to do the last part standing up, so you'll have to hold on to the walker," I instruct.

"Now I can weigh in the morning," she says, ignoring my caution. "I haven't been weighing because I had the girdle on. I like to weigh naked because you get a lower reading."

"Do you weigh every morning?" I ask, surprised.

"Oh, yes, except when the girdle was on. I like to know if I've gained weight. I try to keep my weight down, but it's not easy with the diabetes, because I have to eat to keep my sugar up."

"I know. You look good," I say, admiring her gracefully aging Rubenesque body, and smiling at the familiarity of her high-waisted and rounded figure, a carbon copy of my own body.

"I weigh 149 pounds," she says, proud that she is at the low end of her weight, which fluctuates from 149 to 155.

"What was your sugar this morning?" I ask, forgetting her ritual morning announcement.

Without hesitation, she says, "One hundred and three, so I took less insulin because I don't like it that low."

"Good, Mom, but don't be too quick to change your insulin. You don't want it to ping pong."

"I don't."

In the passages I just read, I note that I have attempted to rid the text of its personal nature. I call the foundation garment a brace, *not a* girdle; *I omit talk of her bra, changing to the generic* clothes. *Jockeying for control, I think about how I got my way (sort of, and for now) on the alert button, but she would not hear of changing her bedroom. I made sure to let her unfasten her bra, but I insisted that she take off the girdle. Even then, I realized that I had to work with her so that she could get the girdle on and off successfully, since I would not always be with her.*

I look at her lovingly. I think that she is an inspiration, an inspiration for how to do aging. Will I still have her spirit at eighty-five?

"You are something," I say. When she looks questioningly at me, I explain, "Your spirit. Your attitude. You are so positive."

"Well, I don't want to be out of sorts when people are trying to help me. That wouldn't be pleasant for them." She says this so simply, yet it is profound—and gendered.

As I read this, I think that I also feel loving because I feel loved and accepted by her as she allows me to be helpful. Caregiving and receiving can create such strong bonds. (Would the bonds be as strong if I had to take care of her all the time?) I wonder if I will be able to be in such good humor when my body fails me. On the other hand, I wonder, will I have a tendency to say "no" when people suggest changes? Given that I don't have children, to whom will I be saying no?

"Okay, you're going to have to stand up again," I say, "so we can get your underpants and slacks down." She stands up, steadying herself on the walker with one hand and holding to the arm of the chair with the other. Then I slide her blue elasticized polyester slacks and white full-cut nylon underwear down with both hands, being careful not to get too close to her private areas. She sits down, and I take off her white laced walking shoes and white turned-down crew socks, then slide her slacks and underpants over her feet. I notice the large, swollen purple bunions on the inside of each foot. From all those high heels, I think. *(I revise this paragraph as I read, eliminating mention of her underwear, private areas, and bunion.)*

She says, "Well you've seen your mommy's body now."

"It looks pretty good to me," I say, thinking that in some ways she looks more firm than I remember her. Her breasts are full and her arm and leg muscles look strong. Seeing me eye her breasts, she says, "My breasts are too big."

"They are not. They're no bigger than mine."

"Yes, they are," she insists.

"Want to measure?" I kid, approaching her with an imaginary measuring tape, and we laugh.

"You don't care, do you?" I ask.

"About what?"

"That I see your body."

"I guess not. We all have the same things."

"Want me to get naked so you feel better?" I joke. She laughs. "That's what you should tell the woman who is coming to help you bathe."

"What?"

"That she has to get naked too while she's in here with you." I think of the endorphins being released from her belly laugh.

"I *will* tell her," she jokes. "Now wouldn't that be something?" Then, "I don't like a stranger seeing me naked." Her voice now takes on a serious quality.

As I read these passages, I think that I have made good decisions about what to omit in my reading to her. She is such a proud person, a person who still weighs every day and cares that the brace makes her look heavy. She is concerned about being naked in front of others, although she seems to be easy about being unclothed around me. In this section, I do read about her breasts and her nakedness. They are mentioned jokingly, much like she'd mention them herself, and I talk about my own breasts and nakedness as well. In this context, the words seem more acceptable and less threatening. Perhaps I also am feeling more confident now that she is okay with my story. Still, I am relieved when she doesn't react negatively to my reading of these passages.

"Carolyn," she continues, in an unfamiliar pleading voice, "I don't need nobody here to help me take a bath. You saw how I can get in and out of the tub."

A few nights before, she took her bath while I watched her. She got undressed much like this evening. Then, she moved to a second chair strategically placed near the tub and rested for a minute while she filled the tub with water and bubble bath.

Holding onto the grab bar installed on the wall with one hand and the bar on the side of the tub with the other, she stepped into the tub with one leg, then the other, sat down on the side for a moment, then slowly let herself into the water by holding onto the tub bar with her left hand and the lower part of the grab bar on the wall with the right. After taking her bath, she draped her left leg over the side of the tub, reached for the bar on the wall with her right hand, and hoisted her body out as she pulled on the side tub bar with her left hand. She plopped into the towel-draped chair waiting just outside the tub. She had been so pleased with her accomplishment that night that she was sure I would then give in regarding a home health care person having to be with her when she bathed. I didn't, although I was amazed at her upper-body strength and ability to get herself in and out of the tub. Seeing her maneuver just made me more adamant that someone be there. "You could slip," I said.

A few days later, after I had returned to my home in Tampa, I called to find out how her bath had gone with her attendant. "Well, Sue kept peeking in to see if I needed her," she reported. "I told her I was fine. She wanted to know if I needed help getting out, but I told her no. Anyway she was here like you wanted. But I don't know why I have to pay her for just sittin' around."

"Mom, she is not supposed to be just sittin' around. She has to be in the bathroom when you get in and out of the tub. That's the point," I said sternly. "You should be holding her hand so you don't slip."

"I can't hold her hand," she explained, "because I need both hands to get in and out of the tub."

"That's true," I said, smiling at her logic in spite of the seriousness of the conversation, "but she shoulda been there ready to grab you if you slip. I ain't gonna give in on this one, Mom. You have to do this for us, for me and for Arthur and Barbara. Otherwise, we worry about you. The alternative is to start taking showers, but I know you don't like that." *(As I became increasingly worried and involved in what I am saying, I have slipped into the speech I used while growing up in Luray, my hometown in rural Virginia.)*

"I'm not gonna fall."

I am tempted to believe her, but I push on one more time. "But you did fall, Mom. And you didn't think you'd fall then. And you fell in the bathroom, the most dangerous room in the house."

"But I was already out of the tub then," she said defensively.

"Mom, nobody ever thinks they'll fall," I said softly.

"Okay," she agreed, responding to my softness. "But I don't need Sue to come three times a week like you planned. It's too much trouble. She eats with me and then I have to think about what I have for her to eat."

"Don't you enjoy the company?" I asked, realizing for the first time that having the assistant put an extra burden on my mother.

"I'd rather be by myself. It's a lot of money for her just sittin' around."

"If you only want to have her one time per week, we can try that," I said. "I want you to have some say in the decisions. So if you let her come in while you're bathing, then you can go to one time a week."

"Oh, goody," she said, sounding like a child who had gotten her way. I couldn't help but smile. Did my mother just manipulate me to get her way? I wonder. Where is the line between anticipating problems and taking away too much control?

As I read this, I think about the intricacy of the dance of independence-dependence. How difficult it is to help without controlling. How difficult it is to give up control of oneself; how complicated it is to take control of another. It is so tempting to take the easy way out, to believe that she is right, that she won't fall. But I fear feeling later, if she does fall, that we could have prevented it, that we should have taken more control. I fear she will fall, but for now I think she has to be part of the decision making, even at the risk of something bad happening. I do not want her to lose that wonderful independent spirit that still accompanies her dependence on others and adds to her personhood. Besides, I want to make her happy, and having control—with her children available to help—makes her happy.

Two weeks later she reports on the phone that she told Sue she didn't need her at all anymore.

I come back to the present and hand my mother her pajamas. "No, I want a clean pair of underwear first," she says.

She raises each leg as I slide on her underpants, then her pajamas, and pull them up to her knees. Before she stands up, I help her put on her pajama top, first one arm then the next. When I start to button her top, she says, "I can do that. You don't have to dress me."

I stand back. "You're right. Sorry." I realize how deeply I have gotten into taking care of her.

She buttons the top to her lightweight pastel green pajamas, and I wait until she has trouble with the top button before I offer again to help. "I know you can do it," I say, "but let me help while I'm here. I like to do it."

"Okay," she says gladly, now breathing hard.

She stands up and holds onto my shoulder while I pull up the bottoms of her pajamas. She buttons the side button on the elasticized waistband.

As I read, I am reminded that caregiving is an evolving process. There are no specific rules, and what is appropriate help in one situation, at one place and time, might not be appropriate in another. Success seems to demand improvisation yet a tolerance for routine.

"Okay, what else?" I ask.

"I have to wash my face, and put some cream on it."

"What about your teeth?"

"I should," she acknowledges, "but I don't always at night. It's hard to stand so long."

I pull the rug away from the sink counter and say, "Now you can pull your walker right up to the sink and sit down."

"This is better," she responds once she is situated on the walker and brushing her teeth. When she brushes for only a few seconds, I'm tempted to tell her she has to brush longer, but I don't. Instead, I think of how complicated her other bedtime routines are.

"Let's take all the rugs out of the bathroom," I suggest. "It'll be easier for you to get around." I am surprised when she agrees easily. *(When I return two months later, I am not*

surprised that the rugs are back in their normal places. Just like her pills and Sue, I think.) After
she brushes her teeth, I put cream on the purple blotches on her fair-skinned face. Finally,
she stands, says, "I'm done," and pushes the walker down the hall into her bedroom.

"Why do you leave your walker in the hall?" I ask, as she walks the final yard into the
bedroom without it.

"Because it won't fit through the bedroom door."

"I can fix that," I say. "All we have to do is move this stand partly blocking the
entryway."

"Oh, that's too heavy for you to lift."

"No, it isn't." I carefully lift the stand without disturbing the family pictures occupying every inch of shelf space. I move the picture stand about two inches back from the
door. "Now you can take your walker up to the side of your bed, where you can grab it
as soon as you get up, when you're feeling stiff in the morning."

"Oh, good," she says, a big smile breaking out on her face. "The pain is a lot worse
in the morning."

She sits on the side of the bed, her covers neatly pulled down ready for her to get
under them. "I don't make my bed anymore," she tells me. "Arthur told me not to. It's
too hard now." She slowly lies back on the pillow, while I lift the covers so she can easily
get her feet under. I smooth the covers along her side.

"Tuck in your baby," she says, and laughs.

I smile. "You are my baby," I say lovingly, noting how vulnerable she looks, and viscerally experiencing my love for her.

"Oh, I forgot my hairnet." She starts to get up.

"I'll get it," I offer.

When I bring the net to her, she says, "Don't want my curls to get messed up. My
weekly hair appointment isn't for a few more days."

Then, "Carolyn, I'm sorry, but I forgot to put Vaseline on my lips."

"Not to worry." I retrieve the Vaseline from the table beside her La-Z-Boy chair.

When I return, she says apologetically, "I also forgot to take my hearing aids out. Put
them on the dresser for me, will you?"

"You need a little table beside your bed," I say, as I search for a safe place for her
hearing aids, "to put things on. Then you could have duplicates of the things you need,
one beside your chair and one beside your bed. You wouldn't have to bring them in
every night. I'll put a table beside your bed tomorrow."

She nods. "Thanks, Carolyn," she says, "for everything." I lean down to kiss her
newly polished lips. She grabs me and holds me tight to her chest. "I really love you,"
she says.

As I read, I realize she spoke then with feeling deeper than I'd ever heard from her before. I enjoy reading the line to her with the same expression I remember she said the words to me.

"I really love you too, Mom."

I feel and express the intensity as I read. I recall that it was only a few years ago that my mom and I started saying "I love you" to each other. I had wanted to, but feared the words would make her uncomfortable. Fearing her discomfort made me uncomfortable, so at the end of every phone call, I'd say, "I miss you" instead. The first few times I tried out "I love you," I was disappointed when she replied, "Uh, huh." Once, my sister insisted my mom tell her she loved her, and my mom said, "I don't need to say it to feel it." Soon after that conversation, my mom said to me in a phone conversation, "I love all you kids." To that, I took a deep breath and replied, "And we love you, Mom." From there it was a short leap to "I love you." Once I said it, she echoed it, and we haven't seen each other or had a phone conversation since without both of us expressing our love. Why was it so problematic to say "I love you"? I say it to other people in my life all the time.

My mom smells like baby powder, clean, with a hint still of her morning perfume and underarm deodorant. I'm tempted to crawl into bed with her. *(Reading about this impulse makes me recall how much I enjoyed sleeping with my mom when I was little, a luxury usually reserved for when I was sick. Much to my father's dismay—he had to sleep on the couch during those times—I got "sick" a lot.)*

"Your baby's going to sleep now," she says.

"Good night, baby," I say softly and distinctly as I turn off the light and blow her a kiss.

* * *

I look up at my mom still leaning toward me, both elbows propped on the left arm of her La-Z-Boy. Tears form in my eyes. I feel deep love for her as I read this story, as I recall the feelings I had for her the night the story took place. She looks directly at me. Tears glisten in her eyes. I wait to see how she will respond. "That's really good," *she says after a moment.*

"Really?" *I ask.*

"Yes, I like it. Thank you so much for writing it."

I am surprised she is thanking me. "You don't mind my writing stories about you?"

"No, I appreciate it. It's really nice that you do. I really want to thank you."

"Thank you for letting me write the story," *I say.* "So nothing in the story bothers you? About your getting dressed? Or your body? Anything you want me to take out?"

"No, I don't care. You can write anything you want. Anything," *she says looking deep into my eyes.*

I smile, wondering what this means, but not asking. Is she thinking of the secrets she told me after my father died? Does she notice that I skipped over some of the prose? Is she trying to reassure me that this was unnecessary? "Mom, maybe next time I come home I'll bring the story I wrote about Rex's death. Would you be able to hear it? I know it's so hard for you."

"I think I could hear it now, though I might get tears in my eyes."

"We'd cry together," *I assure her.* "Oh, and I wrote another story about you that I've never shown you, about the time you were in the hospital for your gallbladder. I called it 'Maternal Connections.' Maybe I'll bring that home too."

"I'd like that. Is all that in that computer?" *she suddenly asks, pointing toward my laptop.*

"Yes, look." *I turn the computer screen toward her and scroll through the pages.*

I want her to comment on specifics in the story and talk about what she was thinking and feeling. I want to analyze the story with her, discuss back and forth the issues of control and independence, as I would with a colleague or in a class. I think of how multilayered and multi-voiced that would make my story and my understanding, perhaps deepen our relationship even further. This kind of discussion also might help her know me better. But it's five o'clock and time for supper. As in the stories Mom watches on television, she's got the main plot line. She likes it. That's good enough for her.

Coda

But is it good enough for me? I feel sad that I can't have more analytic conversations with my mother. The sadness dissipates quickly as I think about the caring relationship we've managed to develop in spite of our differences. I also think about how happy and proud my mother and I both were when I finally read "Maternal Connections" to her on my last visit home (and yes, I changed a few of the words).

As I write this, I wonder what my mother would say about the frame I've added now to my story about her. Would she think it unnecessary, even interfering with the plot? Would she know what a frame is or why it is here? Should I feel obligated to read this last version to her? Did I write this story for my mother?

Yes, I wrote it for my mother, but I also wrote it for myself and for others, who are involved in or interested in caregiving relationships and aging or who have concerns about methodological issues of writing about family members. I expect my conversations with these readers to provide the analytic exchanges I crave. What, then, are my obligations to readers? Should I raise issues about the metaphor of "burden" used extensively in the gerontology literature to describe caregiving? Will scholars be disappointed that I chose not to include references and a discussion of academic literature? Should I provide methodological justification for my story? Should I tell about the editorial changes I made and the reflections I added as I revised this text after reading the story to my mother? I fear if I try to add more layers, the plot of this story will become so multidimensional, turning around and around on itself, that it will be impossible to take in. I have learned from being with my mother that sometimes too much complexity can get in the way, even take the place, of what's important.[4]

I contemplate how taking into account my mother's imagined perspective affects the telling of this story and then consider how this role taking is similar to taking into account her perspective as we shared caregiving. I stop typing and put two copies of this paper in the mail, one addressed to Norman Denzin, the other to my mother.

One Month Later

Norman Denzin conditionally accepts this paper and, along with reviewers, is concerned that I have not yet resolved the larger ethical dilemma of writing about intimate others or the more particular issue of how much to tell about my mother. They ask, Is this story fictionalized? Did you really send the revised version to your mother? If so, what did she say? In response to these issues, I add the subtitle, "A True Story," and I write this section.

When my mother reads the revised version, she says, "I like it. It's nice." I wait. "Anything else?" "No, I just liked it." I wait again and then joke, "I'm making you famous." She laughs her wonderful belly laugh and suggests I give copies to other family members, which I do. Although that is all she says, her voice is proud, her laughter full of joy, and her few words make me feel our close connection.

In this context, I am delighted to publish this piece about my mother, although I know I am telling readers things that my mother might not have understood in her reading of the text.

My resolution in this particular case comes from, as one astute reviewer noted, the living through of the experience I write about as well as the feeling that comes with the telling of this particular story. My mother's and my own comfort in revealing our feelings in and about our relationship is reflected in our increasing verbal expressions of love in real life. As our feelings have grown in the context of caregiving, we have openly shared more of our selves—become almost naked—with each other, and this has enabled me to feel more confident in my decisions about what is appropriate to tell. You have to live the experience of doing research on other people, think it through, improvise, write and rewrite, anticipate and feel its consequences. In the best of situations, all of you feel better at the end, but questions always remain.

Perhaps my text and my answer to reviewers only muddles, rather than clarifies, the ethical issues surrounding what it means to ask and give permission to write about others. This muddle, however, feels closer to the truth of my experience than a contrived clarity based on prescribed rules would be. And for me, that's good enough for now.

Meta-Autoethnography in the Undergraduate Classroom: Listening and Responding to Personal Stories

"I assume all of you had a chance to read the two stories about my mother," I say during the next class period. Some students nod while others focus their eyes directly on the back of the person in front of them. "What was it like to read these stories?" I ask.

Joyce—an older student about my age—tentatively raises her hand. I nod. "We aren't used to knowing anything personal about our professors, or even thinking that you have personal lives." The other students chuckle, glad that she has said what they are thinking.

"I have to admit, it made me a little uncomfortable to read about you," offers Maria, a quiet young woman who blushes as she speaks.

"Most professors keep themselves removed from us," adds Tracy, full of enthusiasm as she speaks from the front row. "But then I decided it was pretty cool that you showed yourself as a real, vulnerable person, like you're asking us to be."

"It seems only fair," I say. "Would you want to share details of your lives with someone who doesn't share back?" The students shake their heads.

"Reading your story did make me feel better about writing about my life," says Maria.

"It helped me understand what it was you want from us," says Matt, his Tampa Bay Bucs baseball cap covering his eyes, as he peeks out from the last row of desks. "But I'm still not sure that I want to talk about personal things. Shouldn't they be kept secret?"

"We all have secrets," I say. "These are stories that we do not tell, or tell only to a select group of people. Why do we feel the need to protect them?"

"Because they are personal," says Tracy.

"But why do we consider them personal?" I probe, nodding in Tracy's direction.

"I think it's because we fear who we will become if others know them about us," Tracy responds. "We worry about what others will think of us."

"Good response. We worry that others will not like/respect/understand/agree with/ or want to associate with us, if they know our hidden stories. And what is the result of having these secrets?"

The students look at me blankly, so I answer my own question. "The result is that we often think of ourselves as 'bad' for having these stories, even in situations where we had no control over the plots we were born into or that were handed to us. In reaction, we may repress, censor, or choose to deny our memories and our desires. Unfortunately sometimes then our stories can run amok and impact us in all kinds of negative ways—sometimes much worse than if we had admitted to these stories and tried to work through them in the first place."

"But can't we lose control by telling them to others as well?" asks Matt. "I don't want to be that vulnerable."

"Maybe control is overrated and vulnerability is underrated," I muse. Then thinking better of that approach, I say, "Sure, which is why you want to make sure that the context in which you tell them is a safe one. And I'm not advocating that you should tell all," I hurry to add. "There are things that it might be best to keep to yourselves. Sometimes there might be danger associated in revealing something about your life and ethical issues involved in revealing the lives of others in your life, which you must take into account. Some deep-seated issues might be better left to a therapist's office, or talked about only to trusted friends. You have to decide what to reveal and what might make you feel too vulnerable and should be kept private.

"There are many 'secrets' we walk around with that perhaps don't need to be hidden. We think sharing them will make us feel vulnerable. Perhaps sharing them will make us feel less vulnerable, or maybe we'll find out that vulnerability is not necessarily a bad thing. Besides, sharing events in our lives opens the possibility that we will get feedback that might help us change our lives for the better. Perhaps we might learn from others in similar circumstances and offer them insights from our experiences.

"I also think we have to be careful not to concentrate too much on ourselves or get stuck in our stories. Ultimately we want to be able to be involved in the world we live in, care as much about others' stories as our own, and move on with our lives. In this class, I want to concentrate on experiences where writing and sharing stories can help us do that.

"We all have things we feel bad about. Sometimes we think we're the only ones who have done these things or had them happen to us. We idealize the lives we think others are leading and feel sad that our lives aren't like that. Then we feel like imposters because we present ourselves one way and feel another. But you know what? None of us has perfect lives; you don't and I don't. I think we can learn from each other and the silences we carry. It can be freeing to see that others have similar concerns to ours.

"Many of our hidden concerns have to do with loss, identity issues, complicated close relationships, and just plain getting by day-to-day—all of which I consider to be normal problems of everyday living. Of course, some are more problematic than others. I think there is value in working out these issues for ourselves, and with each other.

"Stories do not speak for themselves," I continue with my mini-lecture. "They have to be interpreted within the context and time they are told and within the history and life experience of the teller and hearer. We tell about our past and anticipate our future from the present [Parry, 1991]. Since our present situation changes constantly, so do our stories. The good news is that this means we have the possibility of actively constructing and altering our stories rather than accepting a culturally given plot line or a story we have constructed before that now has become difficult to live with or no longer what we want to live out.

"Telling our stories provides an avenue for changing what they mean to us. It's also important that we listen closely to the stories of others. In listening, we learn to think 'with' a story, which means to take on the story, live in it, and experience it affecting one's own life. It means, as Frank [1995, p. 23] says, 'to find in that [story] a certain truth of one's life.' In seeing our lives in the lives of others we open up new possibilities for living.

"Did you find yourself in 'Maternal Connections'?" I ask.

Matt's hand shoots up. "I didn't really see myself in your situation because my mom is still in her forties. Besides when she does get old, my sisters will be the ones taking care of her. I guess your story was interesting, but I was shocked that you described your mother's body in so much detail."

"The vivid detail was the power of it for me," says Tracy. "It's real. That's what bodies are like. It's like Professor Ellis was saying, Why do we feel we have to hide these details?"

"Matt, I'm wondering why you assume your sisters will take care of your mother?" Tim asks.

"I just always assumed that would be the way it was, that girls should take care of their mothers. I never questioned it," says Matt, looking slightly puzzled.

"Now, perhaps you will," Joyce says to Matt and gives Tim a thumbs-up. Then she turns to me, "I was taken with the love you felt for your mother in 'Maternal Connections.' You say you're 'falling in love' with her. That shocked me at first, but then I thought that it probably did feel that way, for you and for her."

"What way?" I ask.

"I guess ... ah ... unconditional ... new ... tender ... all-encompassing ..."

"It must be nice to have had a relationship like that with her," Maria muses.

"It was," I say, "but it wasn't always that way. Until the moment I describe in 'Maternal Connections,' my mom and I weren't emotionally close. I didn't think my mother understood me or could understand me and besides I didn't want to answer to her for my values or behavior, so I didn't share much about my life with her once

I was an adult. I think it's fair to say that I loved my mother, but I didn't always like her very much."

The back story piques the students' curiosity. "That shocks me. You seem so close in the story. How did you get from there to here?" asks Tracy, who has said she wants to write about the problematic relationship she has with her mother.

"Things began to change after my brother died," I say. "Family took on a new importance when I realized I could—and would—lose family members. Then my father died a few years later. At the funeral I remember looking at my relatives and my hometown with new eyes and a more open heart—grief does that sometimes. I realized on a deeper level that I was part of this town and family and they were part of me. Yes, there were things I didn't like about both, but becoming 'unlike' them no longer was a guiding principle for me as it had been when I first left home.

"We can come back to my personal story, but let's turn for a moment to the larger issues represented in the story. I want you to see that stories point toward cultural and social issues that transcend the personal and are important to all of us. What are some of these issues?"

"The most obvious one is caregiving of elderly parents," says Joyce.

"Say more."

"We have to face the issue of taking care of parents in a society where extended family don't always live in the same place anymore," Joyce adds.

"Good. What else?"

"We tend to think of caregiving as a burden, but you show it as an opportunity to develop a closer relationship with your mother," says Tim, who has clearly read closely.

"When I took care of my mother in 'Maternal Connections,' it was the first time my mom knew, really knew, that I would be there for her," I reply. "It was the first time I knew I'd be there for her, or ever considered how much she would one day need me. She knew I'd been there for Gene, my first husband, when he was ill and dying. It has always been a bone of contention with her that my boyfriends seemed to come before my family.

"Some day, most of you will have to decide whether and how to be there for your parents. How will you fit into their stories?"

"Your stories make me think about what it will be like when my mother gets old," Maria, who is an only child, says. "After I read them, I talked for the first time with my mother about whether she'd want to be in a nursing home. I told her she could come live with me."

"Think twice before you let that happen," Andrew, an older student, warns. "My mother just moved in with me. It's really changed my relationship with my wife," he admits. "We have no privacy. And I fight with my mother all the time." Andrew's comments bring forth a barrage of questions and comments from the students. I encourage him to write his story for the class, telling him it might help him with his situation. Each week after that the students ask him to update us on how this situation is working out.

"You say these stories, such as Andrew's, can be therapeutic for us to write. How do you feel these stories helped you?" Tim asks.

"Constructing these stories made me more cognizant of my complex feelings for my mother, how I wanted to feel about her, and how to express those feelings. Writing these stories made me more engaged in my mother's life and in our relationship, and they helped me figure out what to do for her and how to be with her, especially as she got older and needed me more. As a result, I saw some of the ways my mother must have viewed me: as a person who rejected her life and hid my own. I also came to see our problems in terms of issues broader than our particular relationship. It's hard to always see eye to eye during all the transitions that occur over time—she and I had a fifty-two-year relationship! We had to move from me being taken care of by my mother; to me leaving home and finding my way and both of us coping with our separation; to me appreciating my mother for who she was and my mother appreciating me for who I became; to me finding my way back home and my mother welcoming me back; to my mother aging and needing care and me being willing to provide care of her.

"In writing, I spent more time than I otherwise might have in figuring out how to cope with these complexities. I didn't always make the right decisions, even after writing. But the reflection in putting the story together helped me make good decisions more times than I would have otherwise. And, my mother responded to the changes in me with a few positive changes of her own. Of course, I think getting older helped both of us to see the other's position.

"As I wrote, I became more aware of my mother's independence, organization, strength, appreciative spirit, sense of humor, pride, confidence, discipline, inspirational acceptance of her own deterioration, practicality, and desire to not be a burden. Experiencing these positive characteristics moved me away from the deficit discourse [Gergen, 1997] I focused on as I rebelled in my youth: my parents were narrow-minded and provincial rather than sophisticated, worldly, and educated; they were conservative and stuck in a rut, rather than adventure seekers; they were old-fashioned rather than part of the sixties counterculture; all that, and yet they also were deviant in ways that were destructive—my father drank too much, my mother was not loving enough, they both had affairs.

"Looking back now," I say, somewhat surprised that I have revealed so much and so early in the class, "I still see those things, but I also see other, more positive aspects. My parents ran a successful business. Without an education, my father was a maverick at construction and both my parents got up and went to work five—often six—days a week. My parents lived frugally though they always made sure we children had what we needed. They made a life together and stayed together. There was laughter and love, though it might not have been as loud or as deep as I wanted at the time. They gave me freedom to be who I wanted to be and didn't complain too much about the ways I didn't become who they expected me to be. They supported me with their blessings through graduate school, applauded my successes, and gave me financial support the few times I needed it.

"This version of my life also is a true one," I say.

"How do you feel now?" Tim asks. "When you read and talk about these stories?"

"I miss my mother. I miss her body, her soft skin, her baby powder smell, her laughter, her caress, her generosity. I miss her smile when I came to visit, her sadness when I left. I miss having her to visit." My voice chokes up. "But all those things are in these stories and I can revisit them when I want—call up her smile, even smell her smell, remember events, and feel my love for her that continues to grow and change. The vivid prose in the story helps me to remember and reexperience the details and feelings I had during this time.

"Sometimes I feel that Mom is only a phone call away and that I can be 'with' her whenever I want. 'How's the weather there?' I hear her say. 'We've had a little rain. How about you?' I respond. 'We need rain. It's really dry here.' 'So what was your sugar today?' I ask, and she responds with a number and then we talk about how she's feeling."

"But that's an illusion," Joan, who has recently lost her mother, interrupts. "She's not a phone call away. She's not present with you."

"I know that, of course," I respond. "I know it every time I want to share something in my life with her. But so what if she's not a phone call away? She's only a story away. All I have to do is read one of these stories or walk to my keyboard and write another one, or tell it to you, and there she is . . . again.

"Listen to this," I say, and grab a book from my desk. "This author is describing how memory works in his maintaining a relationship with a loved one who died."

As we cherish memories, we return to freshen and deepen our understanding of those who died, attend to them again, bring them closer, embrace them in their absence, reconnect with some of the best in life, feel grateful, feel the warmth of our love for them, sense that they are grateful for our remembering, and feel the warmth of their love for us. [Attig, 2001, p. 48]

"The story—my memories—aren't just reminiscences about the past; they keep my mother in my life now," I say. "I 're-member' her in the sense of continuing to keep her as a significant peson in my life.[5] Sometimes I think we—including me—put too much emphasis on corporeal presence [Hedtke & Winslade, 2004]. Presence in our memory is a pretty powerful way to be with someone."

"Aren't you idealizing this relationship now?" asks Tim.

"Good point," Matt interrupts. "You said earlier that you didn't always appreciate your mother while she was alive. So what's up?"

"Of course I'm idealizing our relationship, but isn't some idealizing good? As Jules Henry [1971, p. 438] says, 'The secret of sanity is to exaggerate the good of the world.' My mother could be difficult, and we were very different," I admit as the students' laughter dies down. "There was a lot I needed from the outside world I didn't get at home. For example, it would have been really hard for me to have been her full-time caregiver the last year of her life, like my sister was," I acknowledge. "I would have gone a little batty watching soaps and the jewelry channel all day." The students laugh. "And the caregiving got extremely difficult at the end. A long weekend—four or five days—with her every six weeks was about right for me. I could be my best for that long, and so could she."

I ignore the hands in the air and continue, "Mostly I think, though, not about what I couldn't do, but about how I came to enjoy her company and even wanted to be like her in some ways. The good feelings and memories these stories provide are what come to mind when I read these stories now. My love is rekindled and I am reminded of how vital it is to love and be loved. I remember how important it is to voice our feelings and act so that we have few regrets.

"Okay, it's close to the end of class. We didn't get to the ethical issues raised in 'With Mother/With Child' about writing intimate stories about others in your life. But we'll pick that up a little later in the semester. Are there any more comments about 'Maternal Connections'?"

I wait, resisting the urge to fill up the silence. "Did you and your husband ever have children?" Tracy blurts out.

"No, we didn't," I answer. "Partly because we got together later in life. But our choice to not have children also reflects the cultural story I embraced growing up in the sixties and seventies. It was a story that ran counter to the canonical story handed down to me that said that women should want to get married and have children, above all else. The counter story I picked up in college and from being involved in the feminist movement emphasized how important a career was for women. I was adamant that I would resist the local cultural story that had me living in my hometown with no career and a baby on each arm."

"I didn't go to college then and I had the baby on each arm," says Joyce. "I'm only now trying to have a career. This was another way I related to 'Maternal Connections.' I read it as an historical piece about women, such as you and me, who grew up in the sixties and seventies and the tensions between having children and having a career."

"I'm glad you got us back to the cultural issues that permeate this personal story," I say. "Here we are, you and I, two old hippies, both women who grew up in the same period, and now our lives demonstrate the freedom and constraints of the choices that were available to us at an earlier time. You're finally ready to start a career and I'm thinking about retirement and wondering who will take care of me in my old age.

"This is a good place to end. See you next week."

CHAPTER NINE

Coconstructing and Reconstructing "The Constraints of Choice in Abortion"

Developing Interactive and Coconstructed Autoethnographic Methods

In addition to writing our own stories, autoethnographers coconstruct multivoiced narratives with friends, partners, and research participants. We weave our stories with those of others to show multiple interpretations and voices emergent in our lives, the coconstructed nature of memory, as well as the importance of relational contexts in the joint production of our stories (Davis & Ellis, 2008).

One interactive autoethnographic process consists of *reflexive interviewing* where the researcher conducts multiple one-on-one interviews, includes her story, and gives the research participant an opportunity to read and respond to transcripts from previous interviews. For example, Cris Davis (Davis & Salkin, 2005) interviewed her sister about sibling disability and included her own story with her sister's story about growing up in a family where one sibling had a physical impairment. A second variation is *interactive interviews* in which authors act as researchers and participants in a collaborative, small-group setting. For example, Lisa Tillmann-Healy, Christine Kiesinger, and I (Ellis, Kiesinger, & Tillmann-Healy, 1997) wrote about the meanings and embodiment of bulimia from group interviews with each other and reflections on each other's writings about women and food. A third variation is *coconstructed narrative* in which two people record and then share their stories on a topic, attempting to write a story that brings together their separate versions. For example, my partner Art Bochner and I wrote about terminating a pregnancy early in our relationship and coconstructed our separate texts into a script (Ellis & Bochner, 1992; Bochner & Ellis, 1992).[1]

Interactive forms of research also can be used in larger groups and communities, giving members the opportunity to reflect upon their practices and processes. For example, Cris Davis and I, along with other colleagues, studied women's discourse on aging in an *interactive focus group* where all five of us served as researchers and participants (Davis et. al, 2006; for other examples, see Davis, 2005; Vangelis, 2006). Similarly, Deb Walker (2005) and Elizabeth Curry (2005) worked as volunteers at a community abuse shelter and used interactive autoethnographic techniques to study staff and volunteers there. They participated fully in the community while community members participated fully in the research process. Community members read and responded to stories written about them, and their responses then helped the researchers better understand emergent meanings of interpersonal and group dynamics. Walker and Curry demonstrated the potential for interactive autoethnographic research methods to engage the community in research in a way that was multivocal, empowering, and enlightening.

In all these interactive contexts, the understandings, feelings, insights, and stories that emerged during interaction—what they learned together—were as important as the stories each brought to the group sessions. Additionally, engaging in a shared activity in a venue outside of structured interviews—for example, in a restaurant in the study of bulimia and in a hot tub in the study of aging and women's bodies—added to the understanding of the topic.

My exploration into reflexive, interactive autoethnography began with the narrative that my partner Art Bochner and I wrote about making a difficult decision when our relationship began. Writing and coconstructing this story presented us with a new autoethnographic approach that brought together the therapeutic aspects of autoethnography with the scholarly purpose of understanding relational dynamics. We encouraged other couples to study their relationships in the same way we had, and we also encouraged other researchers to serve as intermediaries, assisting such research to take place. Thus, we advocated studying relationships in a way that would more closely reflect how we live them interactively in everyday life. We wanted to show couples engaged in the details of daily living, coping and trying to make sense of the ambiguities and contradictions of being partnered. Our procedures were based on several premises about how relationships are practiced. We assumed, for example, that relationships between people are jointly authored, incomplete, and historically situated. Connections hinge on contingencies of conversation and negotiation that often produce unexpected outcomes. One of the actions we take in relationships is to assign significance and meaning to rather vague experiences and events in an attempt to bring order and make sense of events, ourselves, and our relationship. We do this by telling stories about what we've experienced. These stories are coconstructed continuously over time and, in that sense, unfinished. Each person's views and actions affect the other's, and the joint activity and mutual identification that result (or fail to develop) become part of the relationship.

Telling and Performing Personal Stories: The Constraints of Choice in Abortion[2]
By *Carolyn Ellis and Arthur P. Bochner*

> To see ourselves as others see us can be eye-opening. To see others as sharing a
> nature with ourselves is the merest decency. But it is from the far more difficult
> achievement of seeing ourselves amongst others, as a local example of the forms
> human life has locally taken, a case among cases, a world among worlds, that the
> largeness of mind, without which objectivity is self-congratulation and tolerance a
> sham, comes. (Geertz, 1983, p. 16)

The act of telling a personal story is a way of giving voice to experiences that are shrouded in secrecy. By finding words to express these experiences and share them with others, we "attempt to lift the interior facts of bodily sentience out of the inarticulate pre-language of 'cries and whispers' into the realm of shared objectification" (Scarry, 1985, p. 11). By making intricate details of one's life accessible to others in public discourse, personal narratives bridge the dominions of public and private life. Telling a personal story becomes a social process for making lived experience understandable and meaningful.

This story presents our personal account of the lived experience of abortion narrated in both the female and the male voices. The events depicted in the narrative were experienced as an epiphany. Denzin (1989) characterizes epiphanies as events in which individuals are so powerfully absorbed that they are left without an interpretive framework to make sense of their experience. During the time period in which these events took place, we were too engaged by what was happening to record our experiences. After the abortion, we found ourselves numb, self-protective, and unable to express our thoughts and feelings about the abortion. When we finally broke through our resistance, we realized how much the experience had affected us and how deeply we had ventured into our private and submerged registers of emotion.

Two months after the abortion, we independently reconstructed a chronology of the events that took place, including the emotional dimensions of our decision making, turning points, coping strategies, the symbolic environment of the clinic, and the abortion procedure as each of us experienced it (Bochner & Ellis, 1992). After completing our individual accounts, we read each other's versions and began to coconstruct a single story of what had happened. We took notes on our discussions and asked others with whom we had consulted during the decision making about the abortion to contribute to the narrative, thus producing a multivocal and dialogical mode of narration that attempted to capture the processual and emotional details of what happened.

We wrote our final story as a script, reflecting the way we lived this experience, as though we were in a play with part of us watching ourselves. Later, we performed this narrative at a professional social science conference, a step that became a vital part of our attempt to cope with and bring closure to this experience.

The text was written with the express purpose of being performed so that nuances of feeling, expression, and interpretation could be communicated more clearly (Becker et al., 1989; Bochner & Ellis, 1992; Paget, 1990). An audience that witnesses a perfor-mance of this text thus is subjected to much more than words: they see facial expres-sions, movements, and gestures; they hear the tones, intonations, and inflections of the actors' voices; and they can feel the passion of the performers. The audience is moved away from the universal and forced to deal with the concrete—particular people in particular places in face-to-face encounters (Conquergood, 1990).

The Story

Scene 1: The Pregnancy Test and the Test of Pregnancy

(Alice faces audience; Ted turns away)

ALICE: I experience it as a ritual, though I have never done it before. I think of the many women before me who have. Some, like me, assuming it will be negative, a false alarm. Some fearing, others hoping. I read the directions carefully, several times, and take deep breaths.

Why am I scared? Of course, I'm not pregnant. I'm thirty-nine and have never been pregnant. Ted's forty-four and has never had a partner who was pregnant. And, we were careful.

Cautiously, I urinate a few drops into the plastic container, then insert the stick that will reveal the verdict. In about ten seconds, the first dot begins to turn purple. No, that can't be right. I scan the directions, and, according to the picture, there are now two possibilities. Either I have done the test wrong and the next two dots will be white, or I am pregnant and the second dot will be white and the third will turn purple. Feeling my heart rate increase, I tell myself again that I can't be pregnant, but now my held breath and flash of warmth reveal I am no longer so sure. As I wait for the urine to saturate the third dot, I skim the directions again. My eyes focus on the 99 percent accuracy claim, then quickly move back to the third dot, already taking on a bare shade of pink, then pinker, and pinker, and now a tinge of purple. I compare it with the illustration. Again. "My god, I'm pregnant," I say out loud, softly, matter-of-factly, with no panic, only awe in my voice.

Rushing in are images of the trauma my body will go through. At the same time, mesmerized, my hands and eyes explore my abdomen. I now define the feeling I had thought was my period ready to begin as pregnancy. I want to locate *it* and am suddenly aware that there's something pushing out from inside. I have a baby inside me. My god, what a miracle. I experience *it* as company now, and then I interpret my response as feeling womanly.

Oh, my god, I'm pregnant. I'm going to have to get an abortion, and I hate doctors, pain, and agony.

Then that company feeling returns. I moan, and tears form in my eyes but don't fall. *(Ted turns toward audience, then toward Alice)*

Then Ted arrives and plays with the dogs before he looks at me. He knows I bought the test. Does he suspect that I am pregnant? "Well, what do you want to name it?" I ask, and immediately wonder if this is a good way to tell him. I feel none of the lightness that my words are supposed to convey ironically.

TED: "What? You are?"

ALICE: "Yes."

TED: "Pregnant?"

ALICE: "Yes."

TED: "Are you sure?"

ALICE: "The tests are 99 percent effective."

TED: "Oh, god. What are we going to do?"

(Alice turns away, Ted turns toward audience)

TED: I feel myself drifting away. Memories flash quickly through my mind. I recall conversations with former lovers in which I fantasized the birth of a "love child," created during a nearly perfect, mutually orgasmic sexual encounter and nurtured to birth by the compassion and tenderness characteristic of idealistic love. I particularly recall the brief moments during our passionate romance when Alice and I had played with the idea of having a child, more jokingly than seriously, but nevertheless opening possibilities that simultaneously were threatening and thrilling. I remember how easily and innocently we flirted with danger by finding reasons not to use a diaphragm. I conjured up sweet images of fathering that had been buried by the despairing experiences of three childless marriages in which the timing was never quite right or the love never quite sufficient. My head is spinning as I try to concentrate on the immediate circumstances, but my mind is crowded with memories and fantasies. Part of me wants to scream with joy; another part, to howl in agony.

Scene 2: Making the Decision

(Ted and Alice turn toward each other)

TED: When I ask Alice, "What are you going to do?" I think I already know the answer.

ALICE: "I don't know. I've called an abortion clinic, and I have a call in to my gynecologist. I'm only gathering information. But I guess I want to have an abortion."

(Alice turns away; Ted turns toward audience)

TED: I am surprised at how quickly she has acted to set an abortion in motion. Suddenly Alice has shifted from "what will we name it?" to "how can we find the right doctor to perform an abortion?" I feel an inner conflict about my own rights and obligations. As father of the fetus, don't I have any rights regarding whether to terminate the pregnancy? On the other hand, don't I have an obligation to defer to Alice's judgment? It's her body changing, not mine. It's in her womb that this life will nest, not mine. She's the one who will be sick in the mornings and who will have to labor in the last minutes or hours of her pregnancy to push a resistant source of energy into the world. I conclude without much hesitation that my obligations far outweigh my rights.

Moreover, I am not very sure about what I want. On the one hand, I'd like to rejoice in the splendor of this moment, knowing for the first time in my life that a woman I love is pregnant with our child.

But my desire to rejoice is counteracted by the obvious strain a pregnancy would place on our relationship, which is only a few months old. I am numbed by the feelings and thoughts rumbling inside me.

(Ted turns toward Alice; Alice turns toward Ted)

TED: "The decision will have to be yours. It's your body that will be in pain. You can count on my emotional and financial support. I'll support whatever you want to do."

(Alice turns toward audience)

ALICE: I am glad for his sensitivity and am suddenly relieved that we are in this together. But I am also afraid that he will want to have the baby. I don't have time for a baby. And, I've only known Ted for ten weeks. I'm just not sure. It would mean being connected through the baby forever.

(Alice turns toward Ted)

ALICE: "It's hard to imagine having the baby, but there's a real baby in there."

TED: "I know. Let me feel your stomach again. I want to share the experience with you. If you have an abortion I want to be in the room with you."

ALICE: "Oh, I would like that." I am appreciative, yet a little surprised that he would be willing to go through the ordeal.

(Ted turns toward audience)

TED: But she does not ask me to explain why I want this or how I feel about it.

(Ted turns toward Alice)

ALICE: I jump when the phone rings but wait to hear the voice of my doctor on the answering machine. "Hello," I say quickly so she doesn't hang up.

"I hear you have a positive home pregnancy test," Dr. Wilson says happily. "I hope this is an occasion of joy for you."

She is antiabortion, I think, and I am embarrassed when I say, "Well, as a matter of fact, it's not. I guess I want to have an abortion."

"Are you sure? Have you considered other options, such as adoption?" Why is she asking this? Does she disapprove of abortion? Or does she feel obligated as a doctor to ask these questions?

"Yes, I'm sure," I say, with confidence, then follow hesitantly with, "I guess I'm pregnant. Is a home pregnancy test accurate?"

"Yes, they are now. Do you feel pregnant?"

Surprised by her question, I reply, "Yes. Yes, I do," as I gently rub my abdomen.

Immediately I call the private doctor she recommends. "I'll make the appointment," I say to Ted. "We can always cancel it." He hesitantly nods. I am glad he doesn't stop me.

"Come in a week from today," the receptionist says. "We'll do a test to make sure you are at least six weeks pregnant. The cost is $350, which must be paid before the test. The whole amount. In cash. That's upfront. Then we'll schedule the abortion." When I hang up, the chaos of legal and illegal symbols, ideologies of right and sin, along with my fluctuating feelings of having a baby inside me and a thing that must be gotten rid of, all contribute to my confusion.

(Ted turns toward audience; Alice turns away)

TED: Alice and I lie on the sofa after the call and recollect when this child was conceived. We agree on the date, the place, and the position we were in when this predicament was created. It was a memorable Saturday afternoon when we had luxuriated in one of the freest and most passionate sexual encounters of our relationship. We walked around later that night under the spell of a halo cast by this loving and intense encounter as if we had been drugged by orgasmic release and stood apart from the rest of the crowded world. There was no way to know whether this was, indeed, the particular occasion on which we had conceived a child. But we seemed contented, perhaps even exalted, by romanticizing our conception this way. We never doubted the validity of the date we fixed for this event. Perhaps it provided an ironic balance to the tragic drama we were about to enact. At least we had experienced a transcendent moment together, however brief in duration and tragic in consequences, that could justify our having thrown caution to the wind.

Scene 3: Dealing with the Decision

(Ted turns away; Alice turns toward audience)

ALICE: The next day while I am working, Jeanie calls. She is one of many people I talk to about the abortion. I listen to my telling of the story over and over to work out how I am feeling and to provide opportunities for input from others. Since Jeanie is a sex educator and has had an abortion, I ask her questions. "Did it hurt?"

"No, it was like a pinch." I am relieved, then wonder if she is trying to make me feel better.

"I sort of like it," I say, "like that my body can do it, and the way it feels."

"I loved being pregnant."

"What do they actually do during the abortion?" I ask, realizing how little I know. Jeanie reads from one of her textbooks: "After the cervical opening is dilated, a thin plastic tube is inserted into the uterus and is connected to a suction pump. . . . Should I go on?"

"Yes," I say, although I feel faint.

"The uterine lining, along with fetal and placental tissue, is then suctioned out."

The imagery is overwhelming. That's a baby, my mind screams. And, that's my body. I lie down on the floor as Jeanie continues reading and I pass out.

(Pause, to indicate passage of time)

(Ted turns away; Alice turns toward audience)

ALICE: For the hundredth time, I think through the pros and cons of abortion. Abortion gets rid of the problem. I don't have to make major life decisions, everything continues on the same trajectory, my relationship with Ted is not artificially accelerated, I don't have to be pregnant for nine months. My work won't suffer. How would I meet all the obligations I have taken on? On the other hand, I have to go through the physical and emotional pain of abortion and cope with having killed a living being. It feels wrong, selfish. Why is this happening? Was it meant to be? I'm thirty-nine. Is this my last chance to have a baby? Perhaps I would find meaning being a mother that I could not know any other way. Ironically, I think of another advantage of having a baby—I wouldn't have to be department chair. Who would ask a pregnant woman/ new mother to be department chair?

But every time I work it through, it comes out to having an abortion. Still, that doesn't make me feel better. Perhaps I have forgotten something, not assigned the right weight to a factor. My decision makes me see myself in ways that make me uncomfortable. Am I a self-centered workaholic scared of commitment, willing to kill my baby to live the kind of independent, self-sufficient life to which I have grown accustomed?

Sometimes I fantasize that I am going to have a baby, not an abortion. Then I like the feeling of the pressure on my abdomen. I shake my head so that I don't get carried away with this thought. Then I grieve for the child that I will give up.

(Pause)

(Ted and Alice turn toward each other)

TED: "You don't have to do this."

ALICE: "What?"

TED: "Have this abortion. I'm with you all the way. I'll do whatever you want."

(Pause)

(Alice turns away; Ted turns toward the audience)

TED: "Alice is pregnant," I say to Diane, one of only two people I talk to about the pregnancy. I do not want to share my conflicts, be judged, questioned, or challenged. Nor do I want to be pitied or sympathized, but I feel obligated to tell Diane because she knows something is wrong. "I feel foolish about how careless we were. We're not teenagers, although we acted like we were." Then I am distracted by the crying infant and two other young children scooting around the table near us as we finish our lunch.

Diane nods her head in agreement, and later she writes, "I don't recall exactly how Ted told me, although I recall the message being delivered with nervousness in his voice and his eyes diverted from mine, looking beyond me. I do recall my thought (though I don't think I spoke it since it would sound too judgmental and would be better left unsaid): 'How stupid; there's no excuse.' However, Ted said it just as well, though couched differently: 'I know it's crazy, we know better, we're not teenagers,' to which I readily agreed."

(Pause)

(Ted turns away; Alice turns toward audience)

ALICE: I tell Joan about passing out. "No wonder," she says, "look at the imagery— tissue and blood being sucked out."

"And my pain," I add. "Being scared of the pain."

"I'll come over and do some visualization."

I don't know if I believe in visualization, but I agree since I seem to need another way of knowing now. Cognitive and emotional knowing confuse me and leave me in tears, and there is something going on that I can't understand.

In an incense-filled room, Joan and I sit quietly with closed eyes. I am deeply affected by the total context of the experience, more than by Joan's specific words. As soon as I hear her voice, I sob. Joan speaks quietly about my decision to abort the fetus. I feel sorry for myself and the decision I have made as I experience the fetus as part of my body. I am in touch with a deeper, perhaps spiritual world now, and suddenly I am aware for the first time of something else that is distressing me.

This is a spirit trying to get to earth. What if it's the spirit of my brother who died in an airplane crash in 1982? No, it can't be. How can we know? But what if it is? How can I kill it? How can I be so selfish?

I hear Joan talking about letting go of the fetus. "Embrace it and be with it, and then release it. It may not be time for this spirit to enter the earth. It will come back when the time is right."

I sob and melt into feeling. I am with my baby, experiencing loss, and saying good-bye. I forgive myself for the decision I have made.

Later Joan writes that she remembers "watching Alice soften her mind and body's resistance and struggle as she relaxed into the pure feelings of grief for an entity/organism that was physically indefinable, yet undeniably present to her. She went from conceptual linear mind into what I perceived as intuitive, right-brain 'knowing,' beyond reason."

Thankful to have experienced realities other than the cognitive realm in which so much of my life is lived, I am reminded also of the mythical construction of my own reality, where work and independence reign. I feel released now to continue with the abortion.

(Pause)

(Ted turns toward audience and then toward Alice; Alice faces audience)

TED: All of a sudden I see abortion everywhere. Passing a newspaper stand, the headlines shout: "A Chain of Tears: A Doctor and Abortion."

I take the paper home and read: "It is a five-minute medical procedure that has become a battle of extremes. . . ." The caption, "Abortion has been good to me," leads me to believe the article will be affirming and therapeutic, that it will further alleviate any lingering and unspoken doubts about the moral decision we have reached and any remaining fears about the severity of the medical procedure. I read aloud to Alice:

"A woman who is pregnant. A room beyond the protesters' reach. And a doctor.

"On this day, at a clinic in Houston, the doctor is Robert Crist. To the woman on the examining table, he is a stranger. Just as mysterious to her is the procedure she is about to undergo. But to Crist, who has been performing abortions since 1968, it is routine.

"'You're going to feel a pinch and a cramp,' he says, just before beginning. The woman, who is ten weeks pregnant, stares at the ceiling. The pinch, which is an injection of anesthesia, comes and goes. The cramp begins to swell.

"'OK, you're going to hear the machine.'

"Now the woman's eyes close. A low rumble fills the room as the suction machine comes on and the embryo is vacuumed from the uterus. The vacuuming lasts less than a minute.

"Then: 'All done.'"

Totally unprepared for what is to follow, I continue at the top of the next column. "And that's it. In all, four minutes have gone by. The woman opens her eyes and stares again at the ceiling as Crist examines what he has removed."

TED: I see the words on the page and hesitate to continue. A rush of emotion bursts through my cool facade as I stammer to get the words I am reading out. "He sees a hand. He sees a foot. He sees the tissue of the head."

(Alice turns away)

TED: Immediately, with no forewarning, my emotional shield is shattered. I am overcome with grief and sorrow. My pain is expressed in a loud and tormented groan. "Oh, god," I scream. The pain feels unbearable. Help me. Somebody, please help me, I think. I can't bear the horror. I can't hide from the images of hands, and feet, and a head. The grief is overwhelming. I have tried to bury the moral dimension of our tragic decision, to conceal it by echoing platitudes about choice and acting deferent to Alice's rights, as if I could escape any moral responsibility of my own. The burden of my denial is heavy. I now stand face-to-face with the terrifying reality of our decision. We are going to end a life before it can begin. These parts we call a body will never become a person. I have been walking around as if the pain were not there, as if I could pass through this experience without suffering any emotional loss or self-contempt. Now, without warning, I cannot control the pain of my loss, the fear of committing a diabolical act, the panic of losing control. I feel the tears streaming down my face.

(Alice turns toward Ted)

TED: Alice is crying too. We clutch each other tightly, but do not speak. I cannot express what I am feeling. Words fail me. The pain is unsharable. Now that I have felt the pain, I want it to go away. I am breathless and tired. My muscles ache. We go to sleep for several hours. When I awaken, my pain is under control. I cannot bring myself to finish the newspaper article.

(Ted turns away; Alice faces audience)

ALICE: The image of killing a baby with hands and feet breaks through the boundaries of my decision. And, while I know I am not going to change my mind, I'm tormented by what we are about to do. For the first time, I experience the depth of Ted's agony along with my own as I hold him close and feel the physical wholeness of our sobs take us over. Soon, my emotional agony and my fear that he will try to change my mind lead me to say,

(Alice and Ted turn toward each other)

"They're talking about ten-week abortions, not six-week ones."

TED: "Yeah, you're right."

(Pause)

(Ted turns toward audience; Alice turns away)

TED: Jeanie has been emotionally supportive of Alice and comes to visit prior to the preabortion procedure. When she sees me, we embrace. She hugs me affectionately, kissing me on the lips. She tells me, "I appreciate how supportive you are of Alice and how helpful you have been." She says this as if she had not expected me to be this way.

I have an ambivalent reaction to Jeanie's physical and verbal messages. Her affection is sympathetic and benevolent, what I would expect from a close friend. It feels genuine and I like it. At the same time, however, I feel some resentment. She has not asked me how I feel about the abortion; she does not sense that I am suffering a loss of my own, connected to but also independent from Alice's loss. I am not comforted by the realization that Jeanie's affection toward me is based entirely on my actions toward Alice.

Jeanie experiences this episode differently, as she writes later in a response to Alice: "I was at your house one day and Ted was there, and I gave him a big hug and said that I knew he needed support too, and he was very receptive. I was glad that he was being so there for you, and glad that he was also willing to 'let me in,' which helped strengthen my feelings of bondedness with the two of you as a couple."

(Pause)

(Alice turns toward audience; Ted turns away)

Alice: "What's wrong?" a female colleague asks the day of the preabortion procedure.

"I'm pregnant and going to have an abortion," I confide.

"I've had five," she responds.

"Holy shit," I say, irreverently. "You must be fertile." I think, but do not say, that she must not know much about birth control. From then on, I am amazed that almost every time I talk about my abortion, there is a woman present who talks about hers.

Scene 4: The Preabortion Procedure

(Alice turns away; Ted faces audience)

TED: The clinic is a large, attractive building, clean and polished. It gives no appearance of a place where dreams have been shattered. There are no marching protesters screaming bloody murder, no placards depicting abortionists as scumbags, no guards to protect the building from bombs or from vandalism by antiabortionists. This is a place where abortions are the exception, not the rule. I feel conspicuous among the other fifteen patients here. All are women. Pictures of babies and children line the walls and literature about childbirth and child care are on the tables. I feel hatred and disdain from the others in the room. They must know why I'm here.

I want to share this experience with Alice. I need to suffer some of the pain and humiliation of witnessing the consequences of our decision firsthand. Pro-choice is no longer a political ideal or theoretical abstraction. I cannot accept the notion that Alice's disclosure of her experience of the abortion to me will be the extent of my experience. I don't want a concept, an image, or a fantasy. I want to experience for myself what we are doing, what it feels like, and what it means. I already have a mental image of what is going to happen. Unless I am physically present, this experience will always remain disembodied.

(Alice turns toward Ted)

"Remember, I want to be with you," I say to Alice when she goes back for the blood test.

(Ted turns away; Alice faces audience)

ALICE: "Is this for a pregnancy termination?" the nurse asks.

"Yes," I respond. Um . . . *Pregnancy termination.* I like that phrase. It seems value neutral, while *abortion* seems so judgmental. From then on, I have that descriptor to use on insurance forms and for talking to other doctors and receptionists.

"We'll need $350 in cash," states the nurse.

"I know, they told me, several times. Do you get cash for your other procedures?"

"No, just this one."

"Is this because people are often in distress when they want an abortion and you're afraid they won't be able to pay?"

"It's just the way we've always done it."

"It feels strange," I say as I count out the money. The visions of illegality, coat hangers in back alleys, and sin loom large.

(Alice and Ted face audience)

TED: I have had to fight to be with Alice. Now I hold her arms as she lies back on the examining table. She spreads her legs, placing her feet in the stirrups. The doctor tells her that he is going to insert seaweed to dilate her cervix overnight. "You will feel a little pain, like a cramp, but it shouldn't last long," he says.

Suddenly, I am aware of the importance of the frame of this interactive encounter. I am holding the hand of the woman I love while another man—a stranger to me—prepares to enter her vagina. I will not stop him. Indeed, I am expected to thank him. How absurd. He's going to hurt her physically. We will not call it abusive. Indeed, we are paying him to do it. She's a patient, not a victim; he's a doctor, not an oppressor. This is medical, not sexual. We are pro-choice and this is the choice we have made. It's time to feel the terrifying constraints of our choice.

On the way home, we drive through a torrential rainstorm. The roads are flooded and the driving is hazardous. While I concentrate on driving, Alice vomits in the car.

Scene 5: The Abortion

(Alice and Ted face audience)

ALICE: "But we want him with me," I say to the nurse, repeating the same scene as the day before. When Ted insists, I am encouraged, and grab his hand defiantly as we walk to the room located in the very back of the building.

"You have to rest and be quiet. It's important," the nurse says, defeated.

ALICE: "We will. We won't talk," I respond. Finally, she shrugs her shoulders and says to Ted, "You'll have to leave when the doctor arrives."

Another nurse comes to give me a shot of Demerol. "Now you must rest. No talking," she instructs, and turns off the lights. Soft music plays.

Ted sits beside me and I hold his hand in my cupped hands near my pregnant belly.

TED: "I guess this is it. The end is near," and then we don't talk. I put my head down on the examining table near Alice's breast and close my eyes.

ALICE: "Yes, it's time to say good-bye."

TED: Tears well as I feel sadness overcome me. I feel momentarily like I am drowning and cannot breathe. I become weary and drift into a druglike slumber.

ALICE: It is a wonderful twenty minutes. Relaxed from the drugs, I am ready for what is about to happen. I let my mind wander and feel connected to Ted. This is not the time to be alone, for either of us.

TED: Suddenly, I am aroused from my slumber by the sound of other voices approaching. I open my eyes and see the lights above us come on. The medical procedure that will terminate this pregnancy is ready to begin. The doctor motions me to stand behind Alice, who places her hands above her head so I can reach and hold them. From above her, the position of her legs and arms looks unusually symmetrical.

ALICE: The doctor puts on his gloves, moves the light over to the table, and asks me if I am relaxed.

"Yes," I say. Ted moves behind me. We lock hands to wrists. When the doctor says nothing, I realize that he will let Ted stay. I hope Ted will be OK and that he won't be able to see the blood and tissue.

"I am removing the laminary now," the doctor says. My cervix feels strange, open for the first time ever. "I am numbing your cervix now," I hear the doctor say. "You'll feel a little pinch." I'm scared of the pain and hope this means there won't be any. I feel the pinch.

TED: The action speeds up rapidly. The assistant hands the doctor an instrument that I can't see but I assume is a pair of forceps. He reminds Alice that she is going to feel a pinch and perhaps a cramp. Alice is prepared for the worst. After yesterday, I think she expects it. From my angle, I cannot see what he is doing, but I know from Alice's reaction when he has reached inside her. She begins to moan and groan and move her upper body. He tells her to breathe. She squeezes my hand tighter as the intensity of her pain mounts, and her groans become progressively louder. The sounds in the room are chaotic and intense now. He tells her to hold on just a little longer. "It's almost over," he encourages.

TED: Suddenly I hear the rumble of the suction machine and I feel a vibration pass through Alice's body as the machine extracts the last remnants of the fetus. I see the blood and am repulsed by the horror of this crude technological achievement. I want to look away, but I can't. I am face-to-face with the terror of creation and destruction. Alice has a firm hold on my hands. I cannot turn away. She cannot escape the physical pain; I cannot feel it. I cannot evade the horror of what I see in front of me; she cannot witness it. My ears are ringing from the frenzied sound created by the simultaneous talking and screaming and rumbling that is engulfing the room. The action is fast and furious. Alice's ferocious cries submerge the sound of the machine. "Hold on, baby," I say. I clutch her hands as tight as I can. Her breathing intensifies, growing louder and louder. "Oh, god," she screams. "Oh, my god." Ironically, her cries and screams echo the sounds of orgasmic pleasure she released the afternoon this fetus was created.

ALICE: The suction machine is turned on. I tighten my grip on Ted's wrists, he tightens his. I feel excruciating pain. I moan and scream. Everything speeds up. The nurse yells, "Deep breaths. Deep breaths." I try to, but the screams get in the way. Ted's face is now right next to mine. I hear his voice, sense his encouragement. I don't know what Ted is saying, but I'm glad he's here. There is confusion. I hear the suctioning noise, and then they're pulling out my whole uterus. I bear down, my nails sink into Ted's wrists. Then I am in the pain, going round and round like in a tangled sheet. I feel *it* being sucked out of my vagina. My god I can't stand the pain. I hear gut-wrenching screams. Then the doctor's voice, "Five more seconds, just five more seconds, that's all." I am comforted and know that I can stand anything for five seconds. I feel I am with friends. The nurse continues yelling, "Breathe. Breathe." And I try as hard as I can to breathe as I imagine one should when having a baby. Ted is encouraging, gripping. Then I feel another cutting as the doctor does a D and C to make sure nothing was missed. The pain takes over my full consciousness.

TED: Then, abruptly, with no forewarning, the machine is turned off. Alice lies still, out of breath, quiet. The doctor's assistant whisks away the tray of remains covered by a bloody towel.

ALICE: Then quiet. The machine is turned off. "That's all," the doctor says. A nurse puts a pad between my legs and I have visions of blood gushing from my angry uterus. Ted's grip eases. I relax, but the leftover pain continues to reverberate through my body.

ALICE: This is going to be awful, I think. I am spent—emotionally, physically, spiritually. I moan and my body reflexes into the fetal position, just as the nurse says, "Bend your knees, it'll feel better." And it does. Now I need to protect myself from feeling and from these people who know. I feel sinful, unclean, totally done in, helpless. I have no dignity. Is it then, when the pain eases, or later, upon reflection, that I feel my womanhood has been jerked out of my body? And I have been raped— gang raped—at the same time for my sins. Held down by a person I love, raped by the doctor, who was encouraged by the nurse. Go get her, she deserves it, a just punishment for a baby killer.

The doctor comes back in. "I'm sorry we had to hurt you," he says tenderly, looking me in the eye.

I am thankful for the human contact, the kindness. "Thank you, thank you so much," I say, and I am thanking him as much for treating me like a human being as for having performed the abortion.

I am stripped at the moment of all my status, position, and prestige. I am a nobody, the word *sinner* comes to mind. Perhaps I have not cast off the demons of my Christian upbringing. Perhaps the right-to-life ideology has infiltrated my soul.

And then it is just Ted and me. "A wet cloth," I moan, "for my head." I am sweating, dopey. I feel I have no right to ask for anything. Ted hurries to get the cloth, seems glad to be able to do something for me. He still cares, even though I killed our baby. I am relieved. Then I realize through the fog that we did it together. But it was of my body, and I have internalized the sexism that makes me feel more responsible—and gives my right to decide more weight than Ted's.

Almost instantly, the physical pain disappears.

TED: There is silence again. It is quiet. The calm after the storm. The abortion is over; only the memory remains.

ALICE: When my body is hit by the sunshine, I feel free, released. It's over. My relief makes me feel I have done the right thing. I have no regrets, only guilt.[3] Thank god for pro-choice. Life can now return to normal. Normal?? What does this mean for my relationship with Ted? It's hard to imagine ever wanting to have sex again. But I can't wait to be cuddled in his arms and feel safe.

Epilogue

This project is an attempt to encourage social scientists to recover what Jackson (1989, p. 3) refers to as the "lost sense of the immediate, active, ambiguous 'plenum of existence' in which all ideas and intellectual constructions are grounded." Abortion is a subject so steeped in political ideology and moral indignation that its experiential side can be forgotten or neglected. What do real people feel during an abortion crisis? How do they experience the physical and emotional pain? What is their point of reference for knowing how to act? What is it like to live through an experience that potentially places you in a muddle of uncertainty, doubt, contradiction, and ambivalence? In the discourse on abortion, these questions are overshadowed by political and moral considerations, and the lived experiences of the women and men who face these choices play a minor role in pro-choice/pro-life debates (McDonnell, 1984).

As many as one third of all women of reproductive age have had an abortion (Henshaw, 1998). For these women, abortion is not an abstract possibility; it is a concrete reality. Every year, thousands of women face a situation in which they must make a tragic and difficult choice.[4] Confronted with rival and incommensurate claims upon them, these women find themselves immersed in a situation where choosing does not exonerate them from the authority of the claims they spurn. We know little about the details of the emotional and cognitive processes that are associated with living through this experience. The stories that are told are primarily about illegal abortions performed in back rooms or dark alleys, couched in generalities, and disclosed many years after they occurred (Bonavoglia, 1991; Messer & May, 1989). These confessional tales serve the useful purpose of redefining illegal abortion as a bad deed done *to* rather than *by* unfortunate women (Condit, 1990). But they do not allay the anxieties and conflicts associated with abortion. Indeed, the coexistence of numerous contradictory messages—pro-choice and pro-life rhetoric, symbols of illegality embedded within legal practices, political correctness, and moral servitude—only make the choices more confusing and paradoxical (Wasielewski, 1990; Zimmerman, 1977).

Recognizing that the literature rarely reflects the meanings and feelings embodied by the human side of abortion, we wanted to tell our story in a way that would avoid the risks of dissolving the lived experience in a solution of impersonal concepts and abstract theoretical schemes. We have tried to be faithful to our experience, but we understand that the order and wholeness we have brought to it through the narrative form is different than the disjointed and fragmented sense we had of it while it took place. Perhaps this is the way in which narrative constitutes an active and reflexive form of inquiry. Narratives express the values of the narrators, who also construct, formulate, and remake these values. A personal narrative, then, can be viewed as an "experience of the experience" intended to inquire about its possible meanings and values in a way that rides the active currents of lived experience without fixing them once and for all. Understanding is not embedded in the experience as much as it is achieved through an ongoing and continuous experiencing of the experience.

Performing the narrative extends the process of inquiry by introducing another form in which one experiences the experience. Turner (1986, p. 81) has argued that performing narratives and ethnographies is a mode of inquiry that operates reflexively to reveal ourselves to ourselves in two ways: "The actor may come to know himself better through acting or enactment; or one set of human beings may come to know themselves better through observing and/or participating in performances generated and presented by another human being." As narrators and performers of this story, we gained a perspective on our experience and a sense of what it meant that we did not have before. The responses of others to our performance strongly suggest that they have been moved to feel and think about themselves and others in new and important ways and to grasp and feel the ambivalence, confusion, and pain associated with experiences of abortion like ours.

As part of our life history, this story has significance and value for us, but it is also an act of self-presentation. Why should such an intensely personal story be transformed into an intersubjective or public one? It has not been our aim to draw attention to ourselves. Our decision to attach different names to the characters in our story is an attempt to focus on the experience instead of the particular persons in it. Many aspects of what occurred seemed unique initially, but we have become convinced by the stories others have shared with us that our narrative may be only a replaying of events experienced by many other people. As Abrahams (1986, p. 49) says, "Experiences happen to individuals and therefore sometimes are to be regarded as idiosyncratic; but these very same occurrences might, under other circumstances, be usefully regarded as typical." No doubt, other persons who have faced abortion have felt the sense of not knowing how to feel about or interpret what was happening to them. Others surely have been as bruised as we were by the contradictions and ambivalence associated with the constraints of choice. The absence of personal narratives to detail the emotional complexities and ambivalence often attributed generally to abortion (Francke, 1978; Petchesky, 1990; Wasielewski, 1990) may be only the result of people feeling forced to accept these blows of fate passively or being subjected to taboos against expressing these disturbing feelings openly. Because abortion may still be deemed immoral (Zimmerman, 1977), it can become nearly impossible to find the words to talk about what happened. Making public and vivid some of the intricate details of abortion may break the barriers that shield public awareness and prevent marginalized voices of both women and men from being heard (Black, 1982; Langellier, 1989).

"Lived experience," writes anthropologist Michael Jackson (1989, p. 2), "accommodates our shifting sense of ourselves as subjects and as objects, as acting upon and being acted upon by the world, of living with and without certainty, of belonging and being estranged." In the spirit of postmodern ethnography (Tyler, 1986), then, we offer this work as an experiment in formulating narrative as a mode of inquiry that should be judged not so much against the standards and practices of science as against the practical, emotional, and aesthetic demands of life (Jackson, 1989).

Meta-Autoethnography: Coconstructing Our Relationship in the Aftermath

In deciding to write about the abortion, we wanted to reveal ourselves to ourselves as we revealed ourselves to others. We wanted to understand our relationship and our feelings better and unify the past with a hopeful future, desiring to reframe this experience as one we might live with together (see Ellis, 2004, p. 77). The abortion threatened what we had together; coconstructing this story brought us back together. Things we could not speak, we could write. Things we could not hear, we could read. In coconstructing a version of the experience of the abortion we could live with and make sense of, we reconstructed our relationship. With the abortion, our feelings for each other had moved from the romantic glow of new love to the reality of making a difficult, collaborative, moral decision, the outcome of which challenged the all-encompassing experience of our love for each other and who we were together. Writing moved us to a more mature love that was as at home with understanding and compassion as it was with adventure and discovery.

Meta-Autoethnography: Living with Ambivalence

As I revisit this event in 2007, I hear Art typing in the office next to mine. We've been together now more than seventeen years and our relationship has matured to a deep love and lasting familial partnership. Though I have ambivalent feelings about the abortion, I have no ambivalent feelings about the relationship Art and I share. Perhaps the latter affects the former. Our rat terrier of four years, Buddha, lies at my feet, and Sunya, our aging twelve-year-old Australian shepherd, protectively guards the door. They look up every time I change positions, hoping that it is time for their evening walk. I think of the four dogs Art and I have lost in our seventeen-year relationship and the one I lost just before meeting Art. I have not been able to write about the deaths of our dogs, though I have tried. I found the reliving of their deaths too painful. Our dogs are like children to us. Some people have responded that this is "displaced love"—displaced from the children we never had; no matter their response, these are the feelings I experience. I guess you have to be a dog parent to understand how deep this love can be.

Not having read the story of our abortion for a long time, I make annotations of my reactions in the margins as I read. Several times I note the difficulty of reading this story and the nausea I feel when I skim the description of the abortion procedure. When I read the passages describing our emotional agony, especially Art's, tears form in my eyes and my gut retracts. Sometimes I note the justifications I used for the abortion—"they're talking about ten-week-old babies, not six-week ones." I write that the internalized sexism that made me feel more responsible than Art for the abortion also made me and others assume my feelings about the abortion should carry more weight than Art's. I think of how sure I was then of my decision, yet how I anticipated the ambivalence I might feel in the future. I question why some things—such as the visualization—didn't make me less rather than more sure of my decision. I feel immense love for Art as I read—for his struggles, for supporting me and being physically with me through this process. The love I have for him now makes me think that we would have enjoyed having a child together. Then I think about how much we have enjoyed our child-free lives, and I am nagged by the fear of forfeiting some of the memories from the life I have lived happily during the last two decades.

You become the story you write and publish. Nowhere for me is this more true than in this account of our decision to terminate our pregnancy. We became the couple who had an abortion and wrote about it. I have had mixed feelings about that image over the years, though I am glad we wrote the story because I think that it helped heal my relationship with Art and that it has helped others in similar positions tell their stories and know they are not alone.

Readers have responded positively and negatively to the moral content of the story, which of course was our intent. Nevertheless, it is still difficult to hear some of the accusations readers make, for example, that abortion is murder. I know some people feel this, but it doesn't dull the pain of seeing the condemnation in print, a pain that can be part of the cost of doing autoethnography deeply and honestly. I also have grown cautious in assigning this piece in my classes. I do not think it is fair to students (or to Art and me) to ask students to grapple with the morally complex parts of their professors' lives.

I have come to feel that this piece exists on the edge of the limits to the openness of autoethnography—at least for me.[5]

In 2003, I wrote the following about the last time I discussed this story in a class.

Story Interlude: Abortion Revisited[6]

My thoughts are heavy as I turn the corner to the dead-end street where Art and I live. I can't shake the intensity of my feelings, even when the dogs assault me with their kisses as soon as I'm through the door. Once I have undressed, put on my favorite nightshirt with a painted dog on front, and am seated at the table, Art asks, "What are you so deep in thought about?"

"We read the two abortion pieces tonight in my graduate class, and I was just thinking about it." I am glad he notices my moods.

"The abortion? Or the class?"

"Both. Um, smells good." He places the overflowing plate of steaming pasta with grilled chicken, broccoli, and red peppers in front of me and I dig in. "I'm starved. It's good we cook for each other on teaching nights."

"What were you thinking?" he asks after a few bites.

"Whether we should have written the abortion story or not."

"I'm surprised to hear you say that," Art replies. "Writing this piece was crucial for our relationship and for our autoethnographic project. It opened up the way we looked at method and each other."

"I know all that," I say, talking now with my mouth full, "but I'm uncomfortable thinking about people reading it. They can't help but see us as the couple who had an abortion. That's not how I want our relationship to be viewed. Especially since that's not the decision we would make now."

"I know," he says, quietly, "but we weren't living *now* then."

I nod in agreement. "Maybe we went too far with that piece. It's so intimate. And the moral issues—well, I don't even like to go there."

"You wrote intimately about moral issues in *Final Negotiations*, and they don't seem to bother you in the same way," Art asserts. "Why?"

"I'm really not all that concerned when people condemn the activities I revealed in *Final Negotiations*. Guess it's because I'm clearer about the practices I describe there—sex, drugs, and having a relationship with a professor. These activities were part of the culture then—a select culture perhaps, but a culture nevertheless. Some of what I participated in then seems pretty crazy now from our perspective of a committed couple in the world of AIDS at the turn of the century, doesn't it?"

"Yes, the same is true of my life," Art replies. "I'm just glad both of us made it through pretty much unscathed."

"Yes, fortunately. And we sure learned a lot."

"It's all part of who we are now."

"And probably part of why we get along so well," I laugh. "You know, I'd probably do it all over again. But the abortion, well that's a different story."

"Have you changed your political position on choice now?"

"Of course not. I can be pro-choice and still feel moral ambivalence about abortion, especially for myself. But living and writing the experience have forced me to confront how morally complex and painful the issues are. I think everyone should have the right to choose, but it would be difficult, if not impossible, for me to choose to have another one. Of course, given my age, that's not a decision I will be faced with again. Perhaps that makes it easier to take a moral position for myself, but I am committed to other women having the same choices I had. Anyway, all these feelings make it hard to talk about in classes."

"Then why do you assign this story? I quit using it because the content and the conservative politics it arouses overshadowed our purposes for the piece—to show that one's theory about what one would do if faced with this decision, and one's actual decision process in this situation, can be agonizingly complex and different . . ."

"And," I add, "we also wanted to create a space for emotionally evocative work and demonstrate a workable method."

"So, why don't you just use the methodological piece in class and forgo the story?" Art asks, putting down his fork and rubbing my shoulder.

"Because then it looks like I'm trying to hide the story. And the narrative is useful for making the method come alive. Still, I doubt I'll use it again."

Art nods. "Are you sorry we wrote it?"

"No, I'm not. I think people talk less about these things now than they once did, given the increasingly conservative politics of recent years. I think we need to talk. Many readers have had similar experiences and don't know how to think or talk about them. Our experience seems to help people reflect on the issue and their lives even when some of them end up condemning us for our actions. I see this kind of reflection as a pedagogical strength of autoethnography. The story offers a sense of companionship to those who have had to make difficult decisions about terminating pregnancies and feel they must suffer their shame in secrecy . . ."

"It might also offer companionship to people who decided not to terminate a pregnancy but now feel shame for considering it, or even some remorse for having children," Art interrupts.

"Good point. We can't assume that shame and remorse go in only one direction. Remorse for having children is probably harder to talk about than remorse for having an abortion," I respond.

Art nods. "I hope our story frees people to think and talk about complex moral decisions they've had to make in their lives in general."

"Me too. That has to be good. I just am not sure it should happen in our classes—yours and mine, I mean."

"I agree," says Art. "I think our being the authors of the piece constrains conversation in our presence. I don't like reading people's responses to it. You know, I sometimes wish I had pushed you harder during the experience to reconsider the abortion."

"It wouldn't have made a difference," I say, taking his hand in mine. "I was so involved in my career and I wasn't ready to have children, even though I was thirty-nine." I laugh. "I wasn't sure I wanted children. In fact, I didn't think then that I did. But even more importantly, our relationship had just begun. Who knew what was going to happen?"

"I knew," Art replies.

I lean over the table and hug him. "Well, I know now."

"I love our life together," he adds.

"Me too. Too bad I had a miscarriage the second time I was pregnant."

"Yes, I remember how happy we were when you were pregnant, before the miscarriage," says Art.

"Though we had plenty of opportunities to seek help in getting pregnant again, and we didn't follow through on them," I remind. "That should tell us something."

"I sort of wanted to," Art admits.

"So did I, but I was never without ambivalence, even when I was pregnant. Though the farther away the possibility got, the more it looked attractive to you, and to me too," I admit. "And when I was being most reluctant, you usually were most willing. I think I counterbalanced you—my holding out made it safer for you to let yourself want it more then."

"I guess it's easier to romanticize what you don't have and to romanticize it more the farther away you are," Art responds.

"Your ambivalence was clear too. You never even went so far as to have a sperm test after we stopped using birth control."

Art doesn't reply to my statement. I wonder if he perceives what I say as critical of him, but I decide not to push it. "Even now, I wouldn't exchange the life we live with any of our friends who have children," he says.

"I agree there," I say. "And we have all our Ph.D. children."

"And they're wonderful."

"And demanding," I chuckle.

"And we have our puppies," Art says, as Traf jumps into his lap and insists on attention.

So if we're so sure, why does the wondering continue to linger through the evening and reappear periodically? Is it because we still imagine a road not taken? Or is it the safety of a decision now made? After the abortion, why didn't we take more of a stand about having children? By not deciding, the decision was made for us. Yet, in essence we did decide. We decided that we were willing to accept either a child-free life or a child-filled one. Maybe this isn't about "deciding" at all; it's about life and sometimes life "just happens."

Living a child-free life for us means there are attachments we won't experience, but our own attachment may then be even more meaningful—one of the unintended and unforeseen consequences of this shaping decision. Living a child-free life also means we have more energy to devote to creative endeavors that contribute to a caring world. Our role may not be to produce, lavish attention and money on, and care for our own children—which, while it involves sacrifice, might also be viewed as symbolic of the narcissism and ego involvement of focusing our resources on reproducing ourselves (Freud, 1914/1984). Instead, our role is to work with and care for members of the next generation, no matter their genetic inheritance. This responsibility we take on gladly.

Meta-Autoethnography: Reflecting on Both Sides of Ambivalence in 2008

When Judy Tanur, a friend for more than thirty years, reads this section, she writes: "As I read this, I was struck by the differences between our memories of the time when you were trying to get pregnant. As I recall, you were trying very hard and quite invested in it. Or perhaps I either was or am projecting."

Reading her response makes me think about the daughter Judy lost to cancer a few years ago, and I wonder how much that affects her memory. I also recall that she is right, that for a time I *was* invested in getting pregnant. I think about taking and recording my temperature through several menstrual cycles, timing intercourse during ovulation, and taking several negative pregnancy tests. I also remember that one night Art and I were sure we had gotten pregnant. We were ecstatic, then disappointed when we found we had not. I remember going to a gynecologist at the age of forty-two or forty-three for a checkup and announcing to the doctor my attentions of getting pregnant. The doctor replied, "You had better hurry up." That is when she gave me a prescription for a sperm test for Art—"the easiest place to start," she said. I remember thinking and planning how Art and I would incorporate a baby into our busy lives and among our four dogs, and which room would be the nursery. And I remember again the joy I felt when I found out we were pregnant and the sadness when I miscarried a few days later.

At the same time, I also remember that the feelings of ambivalence rarely left for more than a few moments at a time. I remember that I cried passionately in the car with Art when we went to the gynecologist because what we were putting into action frightened me. I remember that Art never got his sperm tested. (When Art reads this text in 2008, he writes, "Given that you had gotten pregnant twice, the fertility of my sperm never seemed in question to me.") I remember that I never reminded him or talked to him about taking the test—the prescription lay in a pile with other "to do" things for many months. I remember that I never returned to the gynecologist for a follow-up. I remember chairing an oral dissertation defense while I was pregnant, feeling spacey and wondering if that was the way my head was going to be for the next nine months, facing both my possible decreased academic capacity and the excitement of a new adventure. (When Art reads this in 2008, he reminds me of the additional fear and uncertainty that came with being older parents. "Perhaps," he writes in the margins, "choosing what we could anticipate won out over the adventure of unknowing.")

Sometimes now I listen to myself tell the abortion story and I note that it comes out differently depending on how I perceive my audience. For example, if the person receiving the story is a mother, I emphasize my sadness, loss, and regret; if the listener is a childfree lesbian, I am likely to focus more on the choice and ambivalence in my decision. Both stories are true and my awareness of their coexistence leads me to finally embrace fully both sides of my ambivalence—the desiring along with the not-desiring I always have focused on in the past. This embrace comes now perhaps because sometimes I do think of how much I would like to have an adult son or daughter. No doubt, the desire comes because I do feel myself growing old in ways I have not felt before. My incorporation of both sides of ambivalence comes also from being able to question more fully the decisions I have made in the past—not to condemn myself or even to regret, but simply to acknowledge that is the case. Revision asks this of me and, in good conscience, I can try to do no less.

Meta-Autoethnography: The Politics of Abortion, Revisited, 2005–2007

My friend Marilyn and I are driving back from a Planned Parenthood meeting in 2005 in which Barbara Ehrenreich spoke about the conservative political backlash to abortion rights. What she has said keeps running round and round in my head: "Women who have had abortions have to speak out. We have to own up to and acknowledge our abortions. We need more women willing to say that having an abortion was not a problem, that they are not racked with guilt."[7]

"Marilyn," I say cautiously, after she has maneuvered onto the interstate. "Like Ehrenreich, I am willing to acknowledge my abortion, and even write about it. But I cannot say that I suffered no guilt. That would camouflage the moral complexities of abortion that are so important in coping with the truth of my experience."

"I had no guilt over mine," says Marilyn. "You know what happens when you admit guilt..."

"I know," I interrupt, "the guilt gets interpreted as justification to legislate women's bodies. I don't want that either. It was very important to me that I had the choice and important for women's rights as well. I don't want to go backwards in that arena. That is nonnegotiable."

*   *   *

I see our fears are justified, when I read two years later that anti-choice forces have begun to feature women's stories of how abortion ruined their lives as a justification for prohibiting abortions: the argument is that abortions not only harm the fetus, they harm women as well (Bazelon, 2007). Some pro-life advocates are replacing pictures of dead fetuses with the "voices of women who narrate their stories in raw detail and who claim they can move legislators to tears" (p. 43). At the Supreme Court ruling on April 18, 2007, that set limits on how abortions are performed, two thousand testimonials were submitted from women about how abortion had hurt them. Justice Anthony Kennedy cited the testimonials in his majority ruling banning "partial birth" abortions (Barry, 2007). No testimonials were provided by women who did not regret their decisions to have an abortion (which helps me see Ehrenreich's point more clearly—that we need to speak out about having had abortions).

The prevailing scientific research, however, claims that abortion "does not pose a psychological hazard for most women," that the evidence does not support an "abortion-trauma syndrome," and that the psychological risks of abortion "are no greater than the risks of carrying an unwanted pregnancy to term" (Bazelon, 2007, p. 44; see also Adler et al., 1990; Cohen, 2006).

The current emphasis on personal narratives in the political debate, while one-sided, has brought to the foreground that women often experience "a range of often contradictory emotions after having an abortion" and that being able to express those emotions "is a healthy part of the process toward emotional well-being" that perhaps has not been given the attention it deserves (Cohen, 2006, p. 11).[8]

Story Interlude: Having Children, June 2006

"Feel her stomach," my sister instructs, pointing to her daughter's pregnant stomach. "Feel the baby kick." I place my hand on my thirty-year-old niece's stomach and wait for the action, remembering how I touched my own stomach when I was pregnant. All I feel is hardness under tightly drawn skin.

"I told my daughter," my sister says, "that if she thinks she loves her animals, just wait until she has this baby. It will be a thousand times more intense, or more. There's nothing that compares to a mother's love." Or loss, I think, remembering my mother's words. I nod and don't say anything.

My niece's baby shower is the second shower I've been to in two weeks. My sister is totally caught up in the world of babies; she's crocheted a dozen blankets, bought more than twenty pink outfits, and babies is the topic of most of our conversations.

On the surface, I get caught up in the frenzy and gift ohing and ahing, though it comes from a place outside of the scene where I observe myself watching. I am intrigued by the all-encompassing nature of this act. I think about what it would be like to be in my niece's place. The joy of cuddling and loving fades away as teenage rebellion takes over the home movie playing behind my eyelids.

I can't help but wonder: are the feelings I have really so inferior to a mother's?

*   *   *

July 2006
From: Sheree Wood
Sent: Monday, July 17, 2006 11:19 AM
To: Carolyn Ellis; Art Bochner
Subject: Question for you

Hi Carolyn & Art,

For the last few months, as Susan's death drew closer and closer, and then in the months since she died, Nancy and I have been trying to decide who we should name as guardians for our children in the event of our premature death. You two have been named as the backup to Susan for quite some time, but it seemed a remote possibility that all three of us would die, thus, we did not worry too much about calling you into service. Now, of course, with Susan gone, the issue has come back in a big way for us and here is our dilemma: After going through all of our friends and family, and discussing each person's/couple's pros and cons for parenting our children, we have consistently arrived at the conclusion that you and Art, more than anyone else, embody what is important to us in considering guardianship of our children. In our minds, no other couple we know has a value system as close to ours, as do you two. You are not religious, but have a spiritual side. You are intellectual, but fun and engaged in life. You are passionate about what you do, but also understand the value of balance and living in the moment. We know you would love our kids and provide the emotional and psychological support they would need if we died. At any rate, we cannot imagine anyone else, aside from Susan, who could pick up parenting our children where we left off, in the event of our death.

Our primary concern in asking this of you is that we realize that it would be a tremendous sacrifice for you and would require you to so dramatically change your lives and give up the freedom you have now. It is so much to ask and we don't want you to feel pressured or compelled, in any way, to say yes.

We envisioned that Susan could have quit work (something she always wanted to do) and become a full-time parent. She would not have had to make the kinds of sacrifices you would have to make to parent our kids.

So, we are asking you whether you would consent to being our kids' guardians, with the understanding that you can say "No" and we will understand completely.

Love,

Sheree and Nancy

Immediately after reading this message, I walk downstairs and interrupt Art, who is reading. "Art," I say.

"What's wrong?" he asks, grabbing my arm, panic in his eyes as he sees the tears in mine. "Oh, no," he says, anticipating bad news before I can speak.

"No, it's okay, it's not bad, it's a happy sadness. Sheree and Nancy want us to be next-in-line guardians of their two girls."

He sighs in relief. He smiles. His eyes twinkle. I wait.

"Is that okay?" I desperately want him to say yes. I think he will.

"That's wonderful," he says, pulling me close to him, his eyes wet as well.

"You have no hesitation?" I ask.

"No," he says.

"Neither do I. None." I hug him tightly.

From: Carolyn S. Ellis
Sent: Monday, July 17, 2006 11:51 AM
To: Sheree Wood; Art Bochner
Cc: Faggianelli, Nancy J.
Subject: RE: Question for you

YES! Definitely yes! Absolutely no hesitation. We are thrilled, touched, and honored, and cried when we read your note. Being your daughters' guardians would not be a sacrifice for us, because it would enrich our lives. We too feel the same way about both of you! And we care about your girls already—they've always occupied a special place for us because we were their second-in-line guardians. We hope and pray to the earth that nothing tragic ever happens to the two of you—our world would diminish greatly if it did. But if it did, our love for the girls would grow and we'd devote ourselves to their well-being and raising them with the values that you two and we share. Thanks for being in our lives, Love, Carolyn and Art

July 23, 2006

The neighbor has her baby and we go to see it. It is adorable, with a full head of hair. I sit beside the mother and watch it, curled up on the mother's still-full belly, in the same position it no doubt occupied in the womb. The mother says, "We watch her, just watch her, for hours. Look at her long fingers, her hair, her little arms." She rubs each as she speaks.

"I could watch her for hours," I say, feeling it at that moment and thinking of the meaning a baby brings to your life.

Art and I return home to visit with our company, a thirty-something professor who has just separated from her husband. Lisa thinks of us as her second set of parents; we see her as one of our children and have asked her to be the trustee of our estate. We love her and feel deeply for her agony. The topic that occupies our evening—infidelity and relationships—seems far removed from watching a baby.

July 24, 2006

Art comes into my office to view the pictures of our newborn great-niece, which my sister has sent over the computer. It seems like babies are everywhere I turn. Grace is cute; her mother and father look so happy. Art emits a sigh over my shoulder. Though I don't know why he's sighing, and I don't ask, I interpret it as a sigh of loss. I also feel like sighing, but don't because I don't want to revisit those feelings. When he leaves, I let myself sigh for what will never be. The sigh is short-lived. I return to writing my book.

Sometime later, after receiving even more baby pictures of several more babies, Art says, "I'm tired of looking at baby pictures. Enough already. All people ever talk about are their children."

"And now their grandchildren," I say.

June 2007

Sheree and Nancy and their two children come to visit us in the mountains. Art and I take walks, catch salamanders, and gather flowers with the two girls (aged four and eight) and their two mothers. There is constant activity for the five or six hours we are together. The girls are beautiful, warm, loving, interesting, engaged in the world. They say they want to come spend the night and Art and I say, yes, of course. I enjoy them immensely. My heart feels more open than usual. I feel that being their next-in-line guardians gives us a special place in their lives. I am amazed at the constant supervision that Sheree and Nancy give them, how much energy it takes just to put on their shoes and get them in the car. As I assist them, I tell their two mothers that perhaps the Mormons have it right. Every family needs at least three mothers. They wholeheartedly agree. As I watch this family, I realize how strong a mother's love—and her communication skills and patience—must be.

Meta-Autoethnography: *Mnemosyne*

Kelly Clark/Keefe showed me her painting at the International Congress of Qualitative Inquiry in May 2007, where she had featured it in a presentation (Clark/Keefe, 2007). Mesmerized by the painting, I later inquired if I could use it for the cover of my book, which I did. I didn't know at the time that the painting was titled *Mnemosyne*, who is the goddess of memory and the mother of the muses.

After reading her presentation[9] and viewing the painting again, I write to her:

I love that the body is so central in your painting. It is in my work as well, though I talk in terms of emotions more than physical body. But how do you separate the two really? I can't. Emotions are felt in the body and processed in the head, which is also part of the body. I like that the figure is nude but yet not nude, in that you can't really see the body parts, none of the private ones anyway. You just know they are there. They are not hidden, yet they are not thrust at you. Hopefully that's true of my work as well. The painting invites the observer in. It is gentle (yet it also can turn in my head to something more sinister/turbulent, as memory can). I love the aqua head, startling a bit at first, but then it blends into the aqua memories flowing from/to it. At the same time, the body maintains some delineation. Is the body separate from our memories? The body is floating in/on a sea of memories. The different colors represent the different emotionalities of memory. Aqua is mild, the dark, blue-black is frightening a bit, the orange could be red and bad or go lighter orange and be gentle and happy. Her hands are grasping/reaching, either trying to hold onto memory or to the present world, or both. And/or trying to recall/pull toward. I love how the orange blends with the body, the aqua with the head, symbolizing for me "connections," the breaking of the binaries, what's now/what's memory. As I view the painting, I'm mesmerized by motherhood, a part of me feeling loss and a part of me wondering, can it really be that good/powerful? Would it have been for me? For a moment, I think this painting doesn't work because I'm not

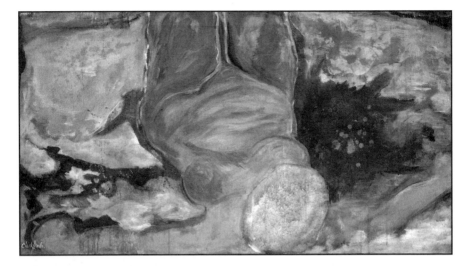

Mnemosyne *by Kelly Clark/Keefe (2007)*

a mother, but then I think about how much of a mother I am to my students, my dogs—and how much of that role I play in my life/work. I think also that autoethnography is about the feminine, the caring, the mothering. It is a feminist methodology.

Kelly writes back:

I'm still wallowing in wonder about your "dialogue" with my Mnemosyne painting. So much of what you write has caused me to think differently and go more deeply into certain reads of my expressive efforts. The painting was actually started within hours of having a miscarriage. I continued the work after becoming pregnant with Cassidy—stopped working on it after he was born—and reentered it when I began writing autoethnographically about simultaneously giving birth to a baby and an academic career. Like you, I read the work as a resistance to separation (between head and other parts of the body; between professional and personal; between easily discernable figure/form and abstract shape; between thoughts, emotion, physicality, etc.). Also, as you note, the memory work that the painting stems from is unsettled, evocative of more memory work, undone and turbulent.

That she evokes the sea for you is affirming (speaking as the artist ☺). This painting has always been about the power and peril of fluidity—in its physical form (miscarriage, pregnancy, birth, newborn care is ALL about fluids—reading fluids, responding to their various meanings). Your comment that the colors represent the different emotionalities of memory is beautifully stated and spot-on—I want very much for you to see the real painting! The head's color and prominence is intended to startle a bit. Perhaps of interest, Mnemosyne is depicted throughout history by painters as having long, flowing, auburn hair. Part of the Greek myth explains that it is Mnemosyne's hair that first attracts Zeus. It is her hair that seduces him, and draws him to want Mnemosyne. He sleeps with her nine nights, and she consequently gives birth to the nine muses. Interesting story—obviously written by a man ☺. Anyway, the feminist in me had no trouble deciding that my depiction of Mnemosyne would be that she's bald—better than bald ☺.

I couldn't agree more regarding your role as an academic mother—a term I and other close members of my doctoral cohort used to refer to the handful of incredibly supportive, nurturing, maternal women figures we had as faculty in our program. The Mnemosyne painting is indeed about motherhood—and about the full range of feminine subjectivity, especially as it relates to inquiry and meaning making through story, through discourse—through evocation of memory's work on the production of the present.

PART FOUR

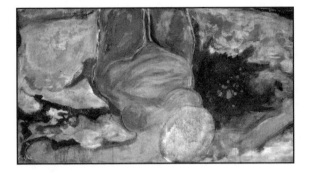

Doing Autoethnography as a Social Project

CHAPTER TEN

Breaking Our Silences/Speaking with Others

The navel tells the story of our first connection to another . . . The question we should be asking is not if our writing is as good as the best novelists and poets (though it may be beneficial for us to strive for that), but if we are sufficiently skilled with our literary craft to do what needs to be done in scholarly circles—to uncover and to make present what has not been written before. —Pelias, in Ellis et al., 2007

Autoethnography as a Social Project

The stories in Part 3 focused on interpersonal and family relationships. In telling about the loss of my brother, my mother's decline and death, and terminating a pregnancy, I sought to speak about the processes of attachment and loss in ways that would resonate with readers, speak to similar issues in their lives, and open up conversations about emotions of love, grief, and loss in romantic and family relationships. My goal in Part 4 is to more directly present autoethnography as a social project that helps us understand a larger relational, communal, and political world of which we are a part and that moves us to critical engagement, social action, and social change (see also Holman Jones, 2005). With its emphasis on self-understanding, examining lives one at a time, and encouraging voice person by person, autoethnography is a useful way—in addition to traditional social science analyses—to understand the world we live in; autoethnography is a constructive approach—in addition to changing laws or other macro-political structures—for changing and improving that world.

Expressing feelings vulnerably on the page invites others to express how they feel, comparing their experience to mine and to each other's. Good autoethnography works toward a communitas, where we might speak together of our experiences, find commonality of spirit, companionship in our sorrow, balm for our wounds, and solace in reaching out to those in need as well. As Coles (1989, p. 22) says, a good story is one that others can take in and use for themselves.

In Part 4, I write about situations that are difficult in a communicative sense—some might say they are "failed" cases. Sometimes we might know what to say, yet be silenced by our difficulties in speaking. Other times, we might not know what to say, our words silenced by tragedy and the "unspeakable." And, still others, we might say and do the wrong things because we are uncomfortable in interaction with others or not cognizant of norms in a particular setting. Difficulties in speaking, which may result in communication breakdowns, are represented in this chapter by two stories: the first, "I Hate My Voice," describes and analyzes speaking with a lisp, which leads to reflections on the category of minor bodily stigmas; the second, "Speaking of Dying," describes and analyzes my inability to speak intimately about dying with a friend who has AIDS, which leads me to reflect on the meaning of the world of the dying and the world of the living.

In Chapter 11, I tell of the personal and collective grief, the trauma and shattered illusions I experienced on September 11, 2001, and show one response to this tragedy—racially profiling a Muslim cab driver—which leads me to reflect on how Americans might live post–September 11th without resorting to discrimination. During this tragedy, I learn to keep memory alive by being fully "with" my mother who is bedridden and terminally ill and "with" Ground Zero, situations where finally there is nothing more to say and nothing more to see. In Chapter 12, I offer a story about a situation in which autoethnographic practices conflict with community expectations about how we should communicate, which leads to reflections on the difficulties of applying autoethnography in communities outside of academia.

Constructing these stories helped me work through and find meaning in these experiences. The stories also provide companionship, understanding, and a benchmark for others trying to process their experiences and feelings about communication difficulties and how we want to live and do research. Additionally, they serve to address critics' accusations that autoethnography is atheoretical and a turn inward away from social change and praxis, and that it offers little theoretically about the larger social world. I turn briefly to a summary of critiques of autoethnography before telling my stories.

Meta-Autoethnography: Considering Critics

Autoethnography is "dangerous."

"The self-questioning that autoethnography demands is extremely difficult," I tell a student in the class I describe in *The Ethnographic I* (Ellis, 2004). I continue:

> Often you confront things about yourself that are less than flattering. Believe me, honest autoethnographic exploration generates a lot of fears and self-doubts—and emotional pain. Just when you think you can't stand the pain anymore—that's when the real work

begins. Then there's the vulnerability of revealing yourself, not being able to take back what you've written or having any control over how readers interpret your story. It's hard not to feel that critics are judging your life as well as your work. (p. xvii)

Lately I've been thinking that autoethnography is equally as dangerous in terms of the response and judgments the work itself generates, regardless of the life it describes. In the last decade, autoethnography has been gaining ground and adherents at a fast pace. "We've never been healthier," says Ron Pelias (Ellis et al., 2007), and I agree. At the same time, critics have pounced on autoethnography, and the critiques come both from inside and outside of the community of autoethnographers.

I see critiques of autoethnography as falling into three categories. Though in reality critiques vary, overlap, and are joined more than these categories might indicate, these categories are heuristically useful.[1]

   1. **Autoethnography isn't sufficiently realist and it tries to be too aesthetic/literary:** *Social science critics* complain that autoethnographic "data" are suspect, not real data, and autoethnographers provide no systematic analysis. The work is described as atheoretical and as insufficiently tied to other ethnographic findings and contexts. The writing of autoethnography places too much emphasis on the literary, aesthetic, emotional, and therapeutic. Often, autoethnographers are accused of not doing legitimate social science, though some critics argue that the kind of reflexivity embraced by autoethnographers is already part and parcel of realist ethnography. Social science critics rail against the "auto" in autoethnography. The more critical say autoethnographers are navel-gazing, self-absorbed narcissists who don't fulfill their scholarly obligation to offer conclusions, analyze results, or theorize social and cultural contexts.

   2. **Autoethnography is too realist.** In opposition to the social science critics, *poststructuralists* complain that autoethnographers tend to be too realist. Some poststructuralists see those who write personal narrative as naive realists who assume they can reveal the secret self, when the self is unknowable. Poststructuralists want autoethnographers to problematize and destabilize the "real" self more, making it more performative. These critics join social scientists in their characterization of those who do this research as not dealing sufficiently with theory or analysis. Their solution, however, differs from that of social scientists: They don't want more and "better" data; they want writers to engage with more texts that will interrupt the linearity of the personal stories and turn them into more useful, unresolved, untidy, skeptical, and fragmented ones. These critics embrace the need for abstract, theoretical texts, such as those of French poststructuralists. The more critical reviewers question the therapeutic orientation of the work, the lack of critical engagement with and attention to the social construction of the self, and the ways in which autoethnography contributes to the "trauma culture" presented on television.

   3. **Autoethnography isn't sufficiently aesthetic:** *Literary/aesthetic critics* often begin by demeaning the quality of autoethnographic writing. Autoethnographers are not good

enough writers, they say, to carry off the aesthetic and literary goals of autoethnogra-phy. Instead, they are second-rate writers and poets concerned with being scientific and achieving legitimacy in the academy as social scientists. As long as autoethnographers have those kinds of concerns, the argument goes, they won't be able to write aestheti-cally, even if they have writing talent. Similar to poststructuralist critics, those critical of autoethnography's aesthetic merit label the work as naive realism. Autoethnographers need to connect with more texts, but the texts important to the aesthetic critics are lit-erary texts rather than the abstract theoretical texts advocated by poststructuralists or the ethnographic, data-driven texts advocated by more orthodox social scientists. The extreme among these critics view autoethnographers as literary poseurs who write transparent realism and care little, if at all, about the complexities and nuances of the literary imagination.

* * *

I'm not too bothered by these criticisms. To me, critiques from outside autoethnogra-phy offer a sign that scholars from other areas are paying attention, that they find some-thing of interest to push back against or something so irritating that they can't help but respond. These responses indicate that autoethnographers have gained enough of a fol-lowing that critics feel it is important to speak against rather than ignore what we do. I am hopeful that critiques from inside autoethnography signal a maturation of this ap-proach and that we are ready to expand our horizons. I trust and am hopeful that those formulating these critiques from inside ultimately have the goal of improving autoeth-nography.[2] If that is true, their critical responses should serve to make autoethnography more nuanced, evocative, and complex.

As has been the case in the past, sometimes I find something valuable in these reac-tions that helps me think more deeply and clearly about autoethnography. For example, the raison d'être of this book is to show selves as in motion and meaning as changing in the stories I tell, which responds to the poststructuralist criticism that autoethnog-raphers tend to present selves and texts as fixed (see Davies & Davies, 2007; Gannon, 2006). In this work, I have tried to show how I present myself and others at this moment, and again at that one, and then again here. I do not know who I and others will become to each other later, since we are all "becoming" and are not finalized (Bakhtin, 1984; Frank, 2005). The meaning of a story depends on the other stories it will generate. "One story *calls forth* another, both from the storyteller him or herself and from the listener/recipient of the story. The point of any present story is its potential for revision and redistribution in future stories" (Frank, 2005, p. 967).

Likewise, I have paid attention to critics, such as Tierney (2002), who claim that auto-ethnography is a "movement away from trying to understand the world of the 'other'"(p. 8), "a turn away from praxis" (p. 8), and "a veer(ing) inward away from engaged social criticism, critique, and civic renewal" (p. 12). From my perspective, good autoethnographies always have included the other, and they always have involved critical engagement, social problems, and social action (Ellis, 2002a).[3] Perhaps autoethnographers need to make our claims in that arena more explicit or put more emphasis on the value of stories and "turning inward" in social movements and social change.[4]

While some of these critiques are useful, turning my full attention to a defensive or attacking posture against all these criticisms does not serve my purposes for this work.[5] How much is to be gained by speaking to critiques that are contradictory and cancel out each other, that speak solely to what autoethnographers do *not* do rather than assessing what we do, or that seem to ask us to work from the same perspective as that of the critic? Given the number, variety, and contradictory nature of some of the critiques, I have a sense that we must be doing something right and that we should continue doing what we are doing.

In this book, I have chosen to speak to more melodious voices, those outside the lash of the critic's tongue, that clamor for my attention—the voices of those we study, our collaborators in community agencies, other scholars constructing ideas about autoethnography, those risking writing their stories for the first time, students and young professors who want to do autoethnography but face roadblocks erected by those who resist this approach, and, of course, those who seek out autoethnography to better understand themselves and the world they live in and who desire to change it for the better. I trust that those who critique autoethnography for the purpose of making it better will find a place in the stories I tell and see that their perspectives have been honored. I doubt those who have different scholarly philosophies and goals will be convinced of the value of my perspective, no matter the quality of my stories I tell or the arguments I make.

Similar to my reaction to the critics of introspection early in my career, I once again see value in following Art Bochner's (personal communication) advice to take it for granted that what you are doing is important and focus on showing what it is that our work can do. I continue to believe that the "attack and defend" style of communicating differences in perspectives on inquiry, while perhaps necessary and useful for some purposes, has rarely changed anyone's mind. I doubt it has opened anyone's heart (Ellis, 2002a). My purpose, as is Pelias's (2004), is to open hearts and minds, to continue the project of "mak[ing] heart and head go hand in hand" (Bochner, 1981, p. 70). I know no better way to do that than through autoethnographic stories.

"I Hate My Voice": Coming to Terms with Minor Bodily Stigmas[6]

"I hate my voice," the clerk says, spitting out the word "hate." As I leave the store, his words reverberate inside my body, enter my consciousness, and only now, many months later, find their way out onto these pages. I hate my voice too, but I never have said so to anyone.

The words uttered by this clerk have moved me to write about hating my voice as an example of "minor bodily stigmas," those small physical imperfections that make us fear we stand out and might be rejected. While often evident to others, minor bodily stigmas rarely are severe enough to become the focus of attention or to interrupt social interaction. Nonetheless, minor body stigmas often are "interiorized" to such a degree that they produce distress and anxiety regarding how others perceive and attribute meanings to them and how these characteristics influence self-presentation, social location, and subsequent action.

In this article, I move back and forth between theory and personal narrative to understand and convey the process of living with a minor bodily stigma. I try to show that the personal and the categorical go hand in hand in understanding the interactional experience of minor bodily stigmas (cf. Daly 1997). I begin with the story of the shopping excursion that initially raised these issues to my consciousness.

* * *

My partner Art abruptly makes a ninety-degree turn into a small Greenwich Village store. I follow him into a kaleidoscope of colored handbags propped in layers on every shelf, hanging side by side on walls, and dangling like mobiles from the ceiling. My hand affectionately pats the functional bag I have carried on my shoulder for more than a decade.

A small board of earrings off to the side immediately catches my eye. You see, I have a harmless earring fetish, aptly demonstrated by the numerous pairs occupying every inch of spare space in my bathroom—on corkboards, pegs, wicker shelves, even decorating the top of the toilet tank. For me, earrings signify frivolity and lightness in a life that often threatens to become overly serious. Earrings decorate and let me play with my surface identity, yet ironically do not violate my feminist consciousness that eschews other decorations such as makeup and high-heeled shoes.

Since a petite woman stands in front of the earring display, I reluctantly turn back to the pocketbooks. "These are nice," I say with mild enthusiasm to my partner Art, who closely examines the various styles.

"These are all hand-made, tanned, and designed. Real leather," the handsome, middle-aged, African American clerk says quietly in a melodic voice as he passes by and disappears into a back room. His graceful, flowing stride matches his soft, rhythmic voice.

Although the clerk's words remind me of the environmental incorrectness of leather, I place a bag on my shoulder. It contours snugly against the upper part of my hip, allowing my left hand to fall comfortably on top. As I fantasize owning this attractive purse, I search discreetly for the price tag unobtrusively attached to the bottom. When I see the price, I put the bag on the shelf and start for the door, almost colliding with Art, who is heading down the narrow aisle toward me. "How much?" he asks quietly, his hands placed momentarily on my shoulders to steady our near collision.

"Too much," I say without looking up, as I move around him and continue walking slowly toward the door.

"Everything is half price," the clerk says soothingly, as he reenters the store from the back room. He speaks as though he just remembered the sale and not because he saw my response to the price tag.

"Everything?" I ask.

"Yes, everything." My eyes open wide in delight, although I quickly narrow them to conceal that my earlier disinterest was connected to price.

Now I'm especially interested in examining the earrings. Since the same woman continues to monopolize the earring board, I think of approaching her from the side, excusing myself, and reaching in front of her to take an earring from the display. But, no, the awkward movement would violate shopping etiquette regarding space and turn taking. Besides, she places in her hands earrings from the two pairs that, from a distance, seem the best. I watch her as she holds the earrings in front of her lobes, tilting her head, first to the right, then the left, and back again, many times. Still grasping both earrings, she pushes her lush black hair behind her ears with the three available fingers on each hand, then brushes it quickly forward, showing no signs of making up her mind.

I drift slowly to the pocketbooks along the back wall, and Art follows. Picking up the bag I had admired, I hold the price tag so that it is visible to both of us. We calculate silently: $490 divided in half is $245. Art's raised eyebrows ask what I think. "Still too much," I convey by narrowing and moving my eyes quickly to the right and left, puckering my eyebrows and mouth slightly.

"It sure looks better than what you're carrying," Art responds, nodding toward my old pocketbook

"The bags are lovely," I say to the clerk, who approaches and describes the materials in the pocketbooks and their artistic construction. "They're all made by the owner. . . . He combines the colors. . . ." I hear only part of his well-practiced speech, though I am lulled by his voice.

Just then Art reaches up for a bag high on a shelf, a bag I haven't yet noticed, our different vistas no doubt affected by his extra seven inches of height. Slightly larger than what I am used to, the purse he pulls down is a beautiful tweed of light brown, dark brown, and almost black leather, overlaid with half circles that give it the texture of alligator skin. A vertical leather braid and long double shoulder straps communicate a casual yet elegant look.

"The one you're holding converts into a backpack," the clerk says, again piquing my interest. He shows me how to loop the straps through the snap on the bottom. I put the straps over my back, look into the mirror, then back at Art. I like my stylish, sophisticated, yet playful image, just the right suggestion of hippie, yet not enough to indicate that I am stuck in the sixties or trying to look younger than I am. "I think I have to have this," I say, ignoring my concern that it costs $290.

"Do it," Art says.

Now on a buying spree, I finally approach the woman still trying on earrings. To make my intrusion more appropriate, I say, "Those are nice on you. Both pairs." I speak to her neck and the side of her hair. The partial image of her face with different earrings held up to each ear reflects back at me from the mirror she looks into. She stands so that I see the earring closest to me, but her face is turned away to such a degree that I must awkwardly walk around her to see the other earring. When I do, she turns that side of her face away.

"They're a gift for a friend, not for me," she says, sounding apologetic.

Since her voice is friendly, I continue, "Still they're lovely on you. Let me see the other one again?" I ask. When she turns to face me, she quickly raises her elbow so that her hand and wrist turn in front of her face, all the while holding the two earrings to her ears. I admire the earring before she hurriedly buries her face back into the mirror.

I scan the small display of earrings. Just as I thought, she has the two pairs I like most. Feeling disingenuous now, I hope she doesn't buy both of them. From my partial view, I try to decide which pair I want, although choosing is difficult without seeing the earrings against my face and fine, light brown hair. The beige bone tubes linking a red ball at the top to an opaque white glass circle at the bottom are elegant but would demand I wear red, not one of my favorite colors. I am pulled to the pair with darker bone cylinders connecting a white ball to a pink glass circle, translucent enough to reflect the color of my clothing. Although not as dramatic, they have that funky, yet sophisticated look with which I identify—not so extreme that they will attract undue attention, yet they are sure to engender mild celebration, a second glance perhaps, or a few words of approval and admiration.

The woman continues to hold the earrings to her ears. I can tell from her intense, yet microscopic movements that she tries hard to imagine how they'd look on her friend. Perhaps she pretends to be her friend. "They're the two best," I say, to make her feel confident of her choices and to hurry her along.

"Oh, yes," she says still facing away from me and providing only a partial reflection in the mirror. Does she think that the face in the mirror is different from the face I would see if she turned around? "But they're not for me," she repeats.

"I don't know what your friend looks like, but they look wonderful on you," I say. She turns around for a moment, eyes open wide, looking straight at me for the first time, now not hiding, as if to ask, Do you mean it? I admire the Asian face in front of me, though I am surprised to see scars extending into her chin, around her mouth, and up both sides of her face. I nod, then smile at her. She turns back quickly, and I move away so as not to appear to rush her.

When the woman finally moves from the display, I'm happy to see she has left behind my favorite pair. I quickly take the bone earrings from the display and glance at the back. Half price, only $40; what a steal. As I carry my purchases to the counter, the bargain makes me feel better about the cost of the purse.

While the clerk wraps the earrings the woman chose, I show her the pair I am about to buy. When she smiles at me, I see her face is more scarred than I thought, the surgically repaired sides unmatched in size and shape. I wonder if she had enjoyed pretending her friend's face was her own as she looked in the mirror. Is that why the purchase took so long? I wonder if she ever buys a gift to decorate her face. Might she see her face differently after this experience? Maybe she'll keep the earrings for herself, be unwilling to let something go that looks so good on her.

"This is buffalo bone," the clerk says, turning now to my purchase and pointing toward the cylinders. "This white bead is over four hundred years old. It's from China. The bottom disk is clear quartz." His description reminds me that neither of my purchases is environmentally correct.

I begin to pull items out of my old pocketbook, packing them into my new one. Empty, my old bag tiredly sags into itself, readied for retirement. The clerk laughs out loud when I say, "I guess my husband was right. I did need a new purse." I think again that the clerk is attractive. In addition to his harmonious voice, he has a pleasant face, soft demeanor, and an open and inviting interactive style.

"Have you lived in the city long?" I ask, intrigued to know more about him.

"Oh, yes," he says and smiles, "for twenty-five years."

"I lived on Long Island for eight years," I reply, to draw a connection.

"Where?"

"Stony Brook."

"I grew up in Riverhead," he says.

"That's a long way from Manhattan," I respond, chuckling and emphasizing "long," as I think of the potato and cauliflower farmland of Riverhead, an area stuck between Stony Brook's radical intellectuals and East Hampton's rich and famous.

"Only about ninety miles," he says, not getting my double meaning.

"But culturally it's much farther than that," I explain.

"Oh, yes," he says, and smiles again. "My family still lives there."

I wonder what a black family did in Riverhead twenty-five years ago. Maybe they were farmers or migrant workers. I think that this man is similar to me—grew up in a small town, probably with parents who had little education, then moved away.

"Would you like a shopping bag for this one?" he asks, pointing to my old purse.

"Thanks, that would make it easier to carry."

I put the earrings I purchased into my new pocketbook and hand the old one to the clerk. Treating my old pocketbook with the same gentle reverence he would a new one, he smoothes out the wrinkles, wraps it gently with purple tissue paper, and inserts it carefully into a shopping bag.

I pick up the package and start toward the door. "Did you get the earrings?" he asks, at the same time I look back and say, "By the way, I love your voice."

"What?" he asks, frowning and somewhat befuddled.

"Yes," I respond, our conversation now out of sync. "Your voice. I love your voice."

"Oh, I *hate* my voice!" he says, blushing through his dark brown skin, his speech taking on a coarse edge.

"I'm sure others must tell you this all the time," I say. "Your voice, I mean. How nice it sounds."

He leans over the counter, rolls his eyes, and waves his hands in dismissal, as if my compliment is the most absurd thing he has ever heard. "I've always hated my voice," he continues loudly. "I won't even let it be taped. I can't stand hearing it. Oh, I'll speak into an answering machine, if I have to, but I don't even like to do that." The words fly fiercely from his mouth.

As he talks, the roughness of his words more and more camouflages the melodic qualities of the voice that attracted me so strongly. Concentrating on his face as he talks, I note that his front teeth are crooked. Suddenly I hear the sound, more apparent in the passionate voice he uses now than when he spoke calmly before. Later, when I re-create this scene in my mind, I will realize that the imperfection was always there, lingering in all his quiet talk. For now, though subconscious, a sense of identification starts to form.

"The earrings?"

"What?"

"Did you get them?"

"Oh . . . yes," I say, patting my new backpack, as a distinct image of putting them carefully inside comes into focus. Taking his repeated question as the end of the conversation, I follow Art through the doorway. "Well, now maybe you'll change your attitude about your voice," I say, unwilling to drop the conversation.

"No, maybe you'll change *your* attitude about my voice," he says in a surprisingly aggressive tone, as the door swings shut. I sense that his anger is not at me, but at himself, his voice, a lifetime of self-consciousness about how he talks, and how others hear his sounds. I am amazed at the vehemence and passion with which he uttered the last words to me, a stranger.

Out on the street, my emotions and desires collide as I hurry to catch up with Art who has walked a few steps ahead. I want to rush back into the store and continue to talk to the tall, good-looking, African American man with the crooked teeth and melodic voice, to the one who has a slight lateral lisp on the "s" sound that he tries to cover by speaking softly, to the one who hates his voice.

I understand how he feels. I want him to know that I hate my voice too, hate it every time I have to listen to it, every time I have to say a word that has an "s" sound. I'd tell him how much I hate repeating my office phone number—974-3626—even my last name. We'd laugh at how often I practiced before recording the message on my home answering machine and then how many times I recorded it before I was satisfied. "Hello. You have reached 989-0544 [better to say "oh," not zero]. Please [the "l" and "s" combination are a disaster] leave a message [double "s" in that one] at the sound [remember to place tongue in the "t" position] of the tone."

I'd tell him that I make my living with my voice and how, as a professor in a speech communication department, I fear I'm judged by my voice. I want to tell him how hard it is to speak in public without being aware of my voice; how I sometimes hear the slurred "s" sound as I talk, my self-consciousness at the moment making the slurring worse; how I rarely make short comments in a public forum because I know I am most nervous then about my lisp; how I refuse to watch myself on videotape because I don't want to be confronted with my voice. I can't stand to hear my voice either, I'd tell him with passion, perhaps a touch of anger and frustration, and not worry that, in that self-conscious, emotional state, my lisp would be more apparent, and I more aware of it.

At that moment, I realize that I have never admitted these feelings to anyone. I am ashamed of the strength of these feelings. I regret, yet am relieved, that the opportunity to have talked with the African American man about our mutual experience has passed.

As my emotions recede to a familiar and protected place, I say to Art, "I think I gave that man a very important gift. What I said to him, I mean. I know why he hates his voice."

We both say, "Because he has a lisp." I am surprised, and then I am not, that Art understands exactly what has happened in our interaction. So he heard the lisp, too. Just like he hears mine. Just like other people hear mine.

"I understand because of my own lisp," I continue, feeling self-conscious even with Art and realizing, as I speak, that the word "lisp," cruelly enough, is probably the most difficult word in the English language for someone with a lisp to say. Perhaps I should call it a slur. No, slur is the second hardest word to say. Problems with "s"? No wonder I never talk about it.

"Go back and talk with him about your lisp," Art suggests.

I don't admit how uncomfortable that would make me. Instead I say, "I'd like to, but that would take away the gift, to admit I heard his speech problem, I mean." I know how happy I would feel if someone admired my voice, seemingly without noticing my lisp. I smile as I remember once receiving a misdialed call and continuing to talk to the man who said I had a beautiful, sensuous voice; I was too delighted to wonder at the time if he was an obscene caller.

"What I don't understand is why you think you gave him a gift. He certainly didn't react as though he were receiving one."

"Did he think I was insincere, or making fun of him?" I wonder aloud. Then, "I don't believe how much I just paid for a pocketbook," I say, suddenly changing the subject. "If it had been marked $290 to start with, I doubt I would have bought it. Probably the man's melodic voice lulled me to buy," I laugh. "Or my unconscious identification with him. Or the magic of watching the woman try on her friend's face," I add.

When Art looks questioningly at me, I tell him about the woman buying the earrings. I am not surprised when he remembers her but says he never noticed her scarred face. She did a good job of hiding herself. I think about how the woman reacted as though I *had* given her a gift when I complimented her face. I wonder about the differences between her reactions and the clerk's. Do they relate to gender? Ethnicity? Severity of the stigma? To the constant visibility of her scar? Or are the reactions simply a reflection of individual differences? I wonder whether the clerk and customer recognized my speech problem. Do they identify with me as I now do with them?

"Look. There's another handbag store," Art points out, "on the next block."

"And another," I say soon afterward. "This morning I had no eye for attractive handbags, now I see them everywhere!"

"Like being exposed to a new word or concept," Art responds. "Suddenly you notice it's always been there and you become more aware of its existence. The phenomenon is much more salient."

"Sure is," I respond. Silently, I wonder whether lisps also work that way.

Categorizing Our Commonalities

Minor bodily stigmas may include "blemishes" potentially perceptible by sight (that is, impaired appearance such as buck teeth, harelips, moles, scars, acne, psoriasis, scales, baldness, red hair, curly hair, big breasts, flat breasts, tall or short stature, heavy or skinny bodies; missing or damaged body parts, such as chipped or crooked front teeth, missing or malformed digits on fingers or toes, scoliosis, or one leg shorter than another; or impeded bodily movement such as tics, shaking, limping, squinting, unbalanced eye tracking or crossing); by hearing (that is, minor speech problems, such as lisping and mild stuttering, or speech impaired by lack of hearing); by smell (that is, chronic halitosis, body odor, or putrid cysts); or by the presence of an aid or sign of impairment (that is, a toupee, hearing aid, thick glasses, brace, or cane). Whether a particular characteristic is treated as a minor bodily stigma depends on the context in which it occurs, its degree of perceived distance from some imagined or accepted norm, the bearer's self-perception, and others' reactions.

To be included as minor bodily stigmas, these characteristics should be involuntary and perceived by self and/or some others as undesirable. Sometimes people are born with minor bodily stigmas, such as birthmarks; other times these attributes, such as scars or baldness, are acquired through aging or accidents. The characteristics may be present always, as in the case of disfigurement, or their performance may vary according to interactional context, as in the case of stuttering. Although not necessarily detectable at all times, minor bodily stigmas are difficult to hide. Still, they rarely if ever serve as master statuses or stand in the way of everyday life. Since only on rare occasions (such as in plastic surgery) are holders able to rid themselves of stigmatized characteristics, *they must figure out ways to live with minor bodily stigmas*. Many develop concealing or coping mechanisms (e.g., Rochford, 1983), while some, paradoxically, turn a potential stigma into something valued, such as a tall woman becoming a basketball player or model. In either case, except in severe forms of a stigma (e.g., extreme stuttering [Carlisle, 1985] or hearing impairment [Perry, 1996]), the solution usually is an informal interactive effort rather than a formal collective one (such as the formation of support groups).

The category of minor bodily stigmas shares many characteristics with Goffman's broader concept of stigma. As Goffman noted, there is nothing crediting or discrediting in the attributes themselves. Rather stigmas occur in the context of relationships with others (Goffman, 1963, p. 3); to some extent, we all take on both normal and stigmatized roles (p. 138); and ambivalence is built into the way both the holder and beholder view the characteristic (p. 38). Goffman argued that the same features are involved whether a "major" or "picayune" differentness is at question (p. 130).

In light of their interactional particularities, however, minor bodily stigmas deserve more attention than the phrase "picayune differentness" indicates. For example, the more minor the stigmatized characteristic, the more ambiguous the interaction may be: others' reactions and the holder's self-definition regarding the attribute can be hidden easily. Normally, a minor bodily stigma does not interrupt communication—thus, few situations require the stigma to be either acknowledged or actively concealed to maintain interaction. The holder of a stigma may wonder whether others have noticed the blemish and, if they have, whether they consider it stigmatizing. Interactants may wonder if the holder is aware of its presence and, if so, how it is defined and coped with. The very "smallness" of the stigma may make interactants less, rather than more, willing to call attention to the characteristic. The ambiguity in whether, when, under what circumstances, and by whom these attributes are noticed and defined is integral to the complex interactional character of minor bodily stigmas, more so even than in situations involving more critical stigmas.

Minor bodily stigmas appear to have become more important markers of difference today than Goffman may have anticipated when he published *Stigma* in 1963. Americans seem preoccupied with minor physical blemishes (Valdez, 1997), as demonstrated by the consumer-driven development of plastic surgery (liposuction, aesthetic reconstruction, spider-vein removal, tummy tucks, and face-lifts), cosmetics, exercise clubs, weight reduction plans, psychotherapy, and the emphasis given to overcoming natural signs of aging and avoiding the negative consequences of being overweight or out of shape.

Though minor bodily stigmas have become a salient part of everyday life, we have little guidance about how to act, talk, or think regarding them. That we have some guidance from support groups, lawmakers, media, and social scientists for responding to other stigmatized characteristics (such as disability, sexual orientation, or race) may make us even more apprehensive about our actions toward those with minor bodily stigmas—we think we *should* know how to regard them but we don't.

This leaves interactants in a Batesonian double bind (Bateson, 1972; Bateson et al., 1956) in two ways. First, without rules for how to deal with the minor bodily stigmas of others, social interactants often are confused about how to respond appropriately. If I mention my stigma, will it be easier or more difficult to interact around it? If you mention my stigma, is that evidence that my "spoiled identity" is salient for you or that the blemish is so trivial that it can be spoken of offhandedly? If you don't mention it, is that evidence of its triviality or its unmentionability (Robert Drew, personal communication)? If you do mention it, will I see you as an insensitive and uncaring person? Is our silence meant to protect each other's identities and, as Goffman (1956) says about embarrassment, the interactional encounter as well?

Second, the holder of a minor bodily stigma must cope with a subjective double bind of feeling not only shame for having the stigma but metashame as well—feeling ashamed for feeling ashamed about a seemingly trivial blemish, a point that Goffman (1963, p. 130) mentions in passing. The blemish is so small that we shouldn't care; at the same time, it is so big that it prevents us from measuring up to the images of perfection we are encouraged to seek by mass media. Thus, bearers suffer a blemish in moral character that might impact their experiences as much, if not more than, the blemish in physical appearance.

Stories of stigma that I collected demonstrate the deep emotional pain, shame, and metashame connected to minor bodily stigmas. For example, a woman with an amputated fingertip said, "I feel almost embarrassed to call it a minor stigma. . . . It is such a tiny stigma, but wow, it rules my life." A woman who has an eye that doesn't track properly wrote, "If you ever want to see me lose my shit during an interaction, arrange to be present when someone asks why my eyes don't move like they should. . . . My heart seems to suddenly freeze rather painfully, before resuming its normal beat. My goddess, someone notices! I'm a freak, a fucking freak."

These stories indicate that these stigmatized characteristics, though minor, often are so problematic that bearers go to great lengths to pass as "normals." For example, the woman with an eye-tracking problem wrote: "The way I have usually dealt with my eye problem is to turn my head a little to the right, so that I am looking at people more out of my left eye." Another wrote about the missing tip of her finger: "I do everything I can to hide it (put my right hand in a fist so the finger is less noticeable, etc.)."

The severity and complexity of the felt experience of stigma has not been developed in social science literature and is more likely to be found in novels, popular literature, and short stories (e.g., Jezer, 1997; Updike, 1989). This lack of attention by social scientists may stem from the interactionist emphasis on the "beholder" rather than the "holder" of an experience such as a stigma. Research is almost always conducted from the perspective of distanced observers with privileged insight, such as in Goffman's *Stigma* (1963). As Ann Branaman (1997, p. lii) points out, "In *Stigma* [1963], Goffman defines personal identity in terms which require no corresponding subjective experience of the individual at all. What matters is not how the individual identifies him or herself but rather how he or she is identified by others."[7] Likewise, the emphasis in C. H. Cooley's (1902) looking-glass self is on how we tend to see ourselves as we imagine others see and judge us. What about the individual looking into the looking glass who often takes an active role in presenting a particular characterization of self to others (Branaman, 1997; Goffman, 1959)? Except for the case of a one-way mirror, the looking glass reflects two ways—others also tend to see us as they imagine we see and judge ourselves, and the self feeling that results from the looking-glass process in turn affects how others see and judge us.

With these conceptual ideas in mind, I next continue my exploration, begun in the opening narrative, of my own minor speech problem. In contrast to most interactionist work on stigmas, I concentrate on telling my story from the perspective of the involved, emotional, interacting subject who feels a moral as well as a physical stigma. In place of a static, categorical portrayal of stigma emphasizing strategies or patterns in brief encounters and others' rejection of the holder of a stigma, my goals are to intersect categorical understanding with concrete experiences of stigmas in day-to-day life (Scott, 1970) and to connect the complexity and variability of interaction around stigma (Anspach, 1979; Hahn, 1985; Thomas, 1982) in a public setting (Cahill & Eggleston, 1995, p. 682) with the intimate experience of dealing with stigma over time (Frank, 1988; Wright, 1983) in sustained relationships (Bogdan & Taylor, 1989). In contrast to work on speech disorders, research designed with the goal of *correcting* stigmas (but see Carlisle, 1985; Petrunik & Shearing, 1983; Rochford, 1983), my narrative concentrates on *living and coping with* stigmas and recognizing the commonality of vulnerability that our differences may mask (Perry, 1996, p. 259).

Breaking My Silence

I have been silent about my lisp, rarely volunteering feelings or thoughts. Unlike stigmas where distinct physical markers, such as wheelchairs, are evident (Cahill & Eggleston, 1995), few people have ever admitted noticing my lisp or initiated a conversation about it. In the few incidents I remember, the details stand out and remain vivid (cf. Richardson, 1996).

The most painful memory I recall regarding my speech involves the first time someone acknowledged my lisp. As a child, I never suspected I had a problem with speaking, and the public recognition shattered my self-image. The event occurred in third grade when my teacher refused to let me read aloud to the class, a favorite activity for which I always volunteered whenever the opportunity arose. In front of the class in response to my outstretched waving hand, the teacher said, "Carolyn, I'd rather you didn't read because your voice is so hard to understand." That day I hid behind the girl sitting in front of me and cried. I thought I read so beautifully, with so much expression, and I always knew all the words. Hard to understand? Wasn't I the best reader in the class? Embarrassed beyond words, I never again volunteered to read in class, nor did the teacher ask me.

Many years later, in Spanish class, a high school teacher said, "You have a natural Castilian Spanish." Smiling and nodding, she demonstrated the slurred "s" sound, holding it long with lots of slur and loose spit sounds for emphasis. Although she was trying to "normalize" my speech, I turned red, feeling put on the spot and uncomfortable that my speech needed normalizing. After that, I hated Spanish with its frequent "s" sounds and spoke it aloud only when the teacher demanded.

My next memory is of a drama teacher who refused to give me a part in the high school senior play, even a minor one, while all my friends had major roles. "Because of your voice," was all she would say. Frankly, I didn't want her to elaborate. I attended the play, all the while feeling left out and disconfirmed, an experience that stood out all the more because of the rarity of these feelings during high school. By then, it was hard to deny that others perceived my speech as a problem.

I have no memory of similar incidents during college and graduate school, although I remember being quiet in classes. But I believe I was more concerned then with learning to "speak clearly" in other ways that, at that point, seemed more important than my lisp and over which I could exert some control (cf. Richardson, 1996). I concentrated on learning unfamiliar words and pronouncing and using them correctly, interrupting politely and speaking assertively, and controlling my heavy southern and rural accent as much as I could. I wanted to have the voice of a professor, one that clearly articulated ideas and sounded intelligent even though it had a lisp attached.

Early in my first teaching job, a student from an undergraduate class I had taught told me that at first my lisp "drove her crazy," but that after a while she liked the class so much she "didn't notice it." Soon after that, a colleague said that it was a shame my parents never did anything about my speech. These comments motivated me to go to speech therapy.

At first I dreaded hearing my voice so accurately represented on the high-tech recording machines—no denying my lisp then—but I loved listening to myself toward the end of therapy, when I had "improved." The problem is that speech therapy "works" only when I remember to place my tongue for "s" sounds in the same way I place my tongue behind by front teeth to make "t" sounds. When I read aloud, I get into the rhythm of proper placement. But when I have to think on my feet—well, it's just too much to consider at one time, and the practice (though I drilled myself for hours a day for months) never became routine. Besides, focusing on the "t" sound and making it so often and unnaturally makes my jaw muscles ache.

I told my mother I was in speech therapy, to see what she would say, since no one in my family had ever mentioned my speech to me. "There's nothing wrong with the way you talk," she said. "Did you ever notice I spoke differently from others when I was a kid?" I asked, wanting to know when this problem started, longing to get to the "cause." "You didn't talk no different than anybody else," she said and changed the subject.

But not everyone agrees with my mother. Once a colleague mentioned my speech problem in a scholarly article. He described meeting me: "I was surprised by her accent. She had a slight lisp and a southern trailer park drawl" (Shelton, 1995, p. 83). Actually, I celebrated the chutzpah it took for this author to mention my lisp in a public forum. I thought he had thrown in "southern trailer park drawl" for literary effect—there wasn't much of the southern speech left; I wondered how much "lisp" was for effect as well. How stigmatizing could it be if a friend would say it in print?

I fantasized about people reading this passage. Would they wonder how it made me feel? Would they imagine how they'd feel if they were me? I didn't mind being noticed for difference as long as the difference wasn't too extreme—sort of similar to the effect I looked for in choosing my earrings. At the same time, I feared this passage might make people more aware of my lisp, similar to the effect of examining pocketbooks in the story that began this article.

The few times I've opened up conversation about my lisp with my partner Art, he has maintained, "I hardly ever notice it. Your speech—the slight lisp, if you want to call it that—is part of your total presentation, not a characteristic that stands out." While his response pleases me, sometimes I'd like more concrete details. I think of asking, "How does my lisp compare to the lisp of the clerk in the store?" But I don't. After reading an early draft of this article, Art asked if I wanted to talk about my lisp. Actually I didn't. That's the strange thing. Sometimes I think I really don't have a problem, and that my focusing on it, such as in writing this article, makes a big deal out of what is, or at least should be, a minor inconvenience. After all, I often go long periods—at least weeks—without thinking about my speech. I am proud of my ability to teach and give speeches, and I think of myself as an effective speaker. As far as I know, my lisp has never stood in the way of friendships or romantic attachments.

Other times, I know I suffer from my speech difficulty, and I define it is an impediment, not merely an inconvenience. Yet Art has trouble pronouncing his "l's" so that "roll" becomes "row, " "cool" become "cole," and neither of us think of his speech as impaired. So why do I think of my own as impeded? Is there something specific about the "s" sound that makes it more likely to be stigmatized? Certainly we have a commonly known label of "lisp" for this problem, while there is no such label for difficulties with other letters of the alphabet. I wonder if our evaluations would be the same if we spoke a language that had fewer "s" sounds (Rhonda Rubin, personal communication). Even so, what is there to say about my lisp that will help? I know too well that the most successful strategy is to forget about it, because the more self-conscious and anxious I am about doing well, the worse the lisp seems to be (cf. Carlisle, 1985). There doesn't seem to be much I can do one way or the other about the way I talk.

How I do and should feel about, experience, and cope with my minor stigma are not simple issues. Since I'm ambivalent regarding how to think about and whether to talk about my lisp and how others' responses will affect me, most of the time I have found Art's rather neutral reaction and the silence surrounding my stigma comforting. Given my hesitations and concerns then, how did I decide to write about something so uncomfortable to acknowledge and reveal?

My decision was influenced by the scene I describe in the opening narrative. Fortuitously, telling this story allowed me to confront my stigma first through other characters, thus giving me the distance (and courage) I needed to begin this exploration. Having such intense emotions and reflections after interacting in the store made me think more deeply and analytically about the meaning of stigma in my life. Seeing the similarity between the clerk and me revealed my lisp as a social problem, where before I had considered it solely as a personal idiosyncrasy. Encountering the woman with facial disfigurement presented the commonalities of lisps and scars and spurred me to seek other stories about how people deal with minor bodily stigmas in our culture.

The more I wrote about and theorized from my personal experience, the less inhibited I felt writing openly about this issue—there's no lisp in my writing. The writing process itself and imagining readers provided companionship and a chance to "try on" my stigma. Yet I still gave vague answers—"a shopping trip"—to those who asked what I was writing about, since I did not want to talk face to face with others, who could observe the lisp as we discussed it. I feared that level of reflexivity and awareness and the resulting self-consciousness (and increased lisping) would make me feel out of control. Given that I have written and spoken rather easily about many personal topics in my life—for example, death, intimate relationships, and bodies (Ellis, 1993, 1995a, 1996a)—my difficulties in revealing myself seemed extreme. The rough journey made me realize how much I experienced my lisp as a stigma and how horribly difficult it was to speak out.

In February 1997, six months after writing the introductory story to this article, I broke the secrecy surrounding this work by agreeing to be on a panel on stigmas for the National Communication Association conference. That task left me encouraged yet a bit unsettled—I was taking a big risk to talk openly about my voice problem to academics who often judge each other according to verbal performances. How, I wondered, would I be able to present this work at a conference? Should I try to control my lisping when I presented? Art had told me that the only time he noticed my voice was when I read papers at conventions. "I can tell you are working to control your voice then. I wish you'd just forget about it and read more naturally." I felt the remnants of my third-grade teacher saying she didn't like the way I read. Reading without a lisp was the only time I felt proud of my voice. How ironic! To Art, my attempts at speaking "correctly" sounded odder than when I spoke "incorrectly."

I had solicited the feedback, and I appreciated how hard it was to give. I wondered how this feedback would affect me. What if it had been more negative? How will others react to me after reading this article? When I present it, might it be the only public performance I've ever given in which I don't worry about my voice? Or might I worry even more now that I've made my lisp into an object to be noted, talked about, dissected, and commented on?

The last set of questions brings me finally to another awareness. People interacting with me will more likely be concerned with how I, an ethnographer of stigmas, perceive *their* blemishes than how I sound. I have to wonder then whether this article will help those who anxiously experience their minor stigmas. Have I bought into a category (stigma), and created a version (minor bodily stigmas), that might be better left ignored? Might my work serve to remind people of their "flaws" when they would be better left unacknowledged? As a result of this work, might others redefine a personal characteristic as a stigma? Will the awareness brought to life then tighten the double bind that we all are made to feel regarding how we negotiate our stigma? What seems to be called for is a way to reframe stigmatized experience, to unravel the knot that entangles us.

Breaking Through Our Categories

This article offers autoethnographic storytelling as an alternative to the common practices of concealing, underplaying, manipulating, or denying stigmatized differences, practices that allow the "world of normals" to go unchallenged (Branaman, 1997, p. lix). In telling my own story, I seek to understand minor bodily stigmas and to decenter the normal in terms of these differences in the same way others before me have decentered the normal relative to race and disability. I problematize these categories by consciously moving back and forth, in and out of them.

I have engaged in a number of discussions about minor bodily stigmas with people who have read this article or heard me present it. These readers have helped me understand that my lisp is minor, though this validation was not primarily what I sought. After all, I realized from the beginning that my stigma was minor, but that knowledge had not helped me cope. Instead, the minor quality of my lisp generated a larger moral problem of feeling ashamed of feeling ashamed of something so small.

The alliance with people who share these feelings has lessened the burden of undesired difference. Readers have drawn comparisons from their own lives, telling vivid stories and expressing strong feelings about their interiorized anxiety, shame, and dread. Many have said that reading about my lisp encouraged them to speak about their stigmas, often for the first time. Focused on our common experiences, our talk defused some of the feelings of shame and stigmatization that we shared.

Although the physical manifestation of my lisp has not changed in any appreciable way, I rarely feel shame or metashame about it now. Without shame, the physical part of my lisp just does not seem like a big deal, and perhaps it *is* less physically prominent without the accompanying emotional stress of feeling shame. Sometimes I am able to laugh with others now about the ways we have twisted ourselves into pretzels to conceal and cope with our stigmas. I seem to have stopped fantasizing about how much better my life would be without a lisp. I noticed my lisp the other day in class; what stood out for me was how long it had been since I last paid attention to it. After this exploration, I doubt my lisp will ever have the same hold over me again.

I do not claim, however, that I am now completely comfortable about my lisp. Two nights before I submitted this article for publication, I dreamed I was giving a speech and my lisp was so severe that no one in the audience could understand what I said. Then, before I actually presented a paper from this work at the National Communication Association meetings in November 1997, I practiced it aloud daily for three weeks, making sure that I could say "lisp" without stumbling. Immediately before the presentation, I worried that I had practiced so much that I wouldn't lisp at all. Would the audience then wonder why I had written about such a trivial topic? If I did lisp, after all this practice, would I feel shame? These events help me hesitate whenever I move toward romanticizing stigma or claiming "recovery."

Nevertheless, I have been able to reframe my lisp as part of my total identity. Now I even think of what I like about my voice—its expressiveness in tone and the face work that goes with it—and consider the ways in which my lisp may have contributed positively to who I have become (cf. Updike, 1989). Perhaps my lisp reminds me to think before I speak and to try to have something worthwhile to say before I do. Perhaps my lisp makes it difficult to talk like a professor, preventing me from lecturing at the drop of a question and rushing to fill every hole in conversation. Perhaps my lisp enhances my desire to speak clearly in other ways, such as in my writing. Perhaps my lisp makes me a better listener, reminding me to be more empathic and sensitive to others' differences, insecurities, and frailties. Perhaps my lisp allows others to approach me more easily because they see me as vulnerable. Perhaps my lisp helps me serve as a role model—if she can do it, so can I. And perhaps my lisp has given me the gifts that accompany hardheaded determination, making me work harder to succeed and overcome my limitations.

I doubt that I would have been able to move outside the category of minor bodily stigmas without first immersing myself in it. Categories too often limit us without our being aware of their influence; once we are aware, too often we assume there is no use in trying to break through them. Telling and analyzing my personal story not only helped generate and make visible the category of minor bodily stigma, it also provided a way through. The categorical story offered a name to my experiences where before there was only dread; the personal story connected real people with feelings to the labels, where before there were only tactics of concealment and denial. This research helped me understand the inextricable connections between categorical and personal knowledge.

The fear I had initially that concentrating on lisps or minor bodily stigmas in general might make me and others see them everywhere—as concentrating on pocketbooks in the first story made us see pocketbooks everywhere—held true. But in seeing stigma everywhere, I came to see it nowhere. Now I expect to encounter minor bodily stigmas, but in the way that I expect to see beards or brown hair or hear accents and dialects. Minor bodily stigmas have become part of the landscape of human variability and commonality.

In surrendering attachment to myself as minor bodily stigmatized, I am able now to take attention off my mouth and how I speak myself out there. I end then where I began, with my ears, eager to hear others' stories of minor bodily stigmas, so that we all might continue "coming to terms with" and, in the process, learning to cope better with our differences, however minor they may be.

Story Interlude: Minor Bodily Stigma Revisited

Several years after publishing "I Hate My Voice," I return to the pocketbook store in New York City and find the same clerk working there. After some hesitation, I tell him that I have written a story about an encounter I had in his store a few years before. "It was about my voice," I say, "and how much I hate it, and how I was reminded of that because you said you hated yours when I complimented you."

"Oh, I hate my voice," he repeats, looking surprised.

"Would you like to read my story?"

"I guess so," he says hesitantly. I ask for his mailing address, which he gives me, and I leave the store.

A few months later, I return to the store when I am again in New York City. The man remembers me this time. "Did you get my story?" I ask.

"Yes," he replies. "It was interesting."

Wanting more response, I ask, "What did you think of it?"

"I don't know," he says, shaking his head.

"What did your friends say about it?"

"Oh, I would never show that to them," he exclaims. "I would be too embarrassed."

"I understand," I say. "If I hadn't written it, I'd probably be embarrassed for anyone to read about my speech as well." I wonder if he feels similar to the way I felt when my teachers mentioned my lisp. He does not seem to take solace from our commonality as do most of the students in my classes who read this article and share their stories about minor bodily stigmas. But, unlike my students, he has not shared his story voluntarily, and he does not have the advantage of sitting in my classroom, contemplating the ubiquitous quality of minor bodily stigmas and getting desensitized to one's personal stigmas in the process.

Not knowing what else to say, I pretend to be looking at pocketbooks, and he begins to tell me about the merits of each one. This time I leave without a new purse.

I still love his voice.

Speaking of Dying[8]

After leaving the earring store in the Village in New York City, I take the subway to the Upper West Side to meet my friend Diane for breakfast. Afterwards, we walk together on the street where she lives. When she waves to a slightly bent-over man slowly walking toward us, I assume he must be someone she knows. The man is accompanied by a dog on a long leash. When the dog's tail starts to wag, it dawns on me that this gaunt, sickly person must be Diane's partner, Peter, whom I have arranged to meet for tea.

At breakfast, Diane had told me that Peter looked better now than when I saw him a year ago. "We try to keep him pretty," she said. "That's something we both agree on. He should look good, not like he's dying."

Their performance is not working. The person in front of me looks unmistakably like a man dying of AIDS. He seems fragile, and I sense from his difficult movements that he is in pain and has no energy.

"Maybe if we were 'really talking' about what's going on," Diane had explained, "then the appearance thing, well it might not matter. You see?"

I said yes, though I didn't immediately grasp what she meant. Not really talking? They talk of dying every day, she had said, sometimes even suicide. But I think I understand. The talk is surface, minute-to-minute detail—what did you eat, how do you feel, did you take your medicine, what do you need? Maybe, though, in the end, mundane details are all we have to talk about.

My face breaks into a smile I don't feel as Peter walks closer. I lean down and pet the forty-pound dog—a low-to-the-ground terrier and basset hound mix—that Diane had told me they chose from the pound to be a "companion" for Peter. My stance provides a chance to reconstruct my smile as one that looks more natural, and to blink away the surprise and fear in my eyes. Quickly, I rise to hug Peter before he notices my discomfort. I reach to kiss him, on the cheek, but with feeling, like I mean it. Peter's been through this ritual before. He swivels to kiss me on my right cheek as I kiss him on his. It's a little awkward. I'm used to people with AIDS politely holding their cheek steady for the obligatory kiss, to let you show you're not afraid of getting infected. His hug is quick, uninvolved, as he turns his attention immediately to the dog who is trying to jump up. Peter is providing an opening, I think, in case I need to retreat from him quickly.

Though the caress is one-way now, I continue embracing Peter, who stands rigid. I want my arms to say, "I'm not afraid. I care about you." I rub along his side with one hand; moving while touching seems more intimate than passive, stationary holding. I push myself to take AIDS in viscerally and emotionally. At the same time, I don't want to intrude on Peter's body. His bones protrude. There's almost no soft flesh. This is what I would expect a Holocaust survivor to feel like. The image finally makes my hand retract.

I'm aware that I don't say "how are you" in response to his "how are you." "I'm fine," I reply, as I kneel again to play with the dog. "Great dog," I say glancing up at Peter. "You're sweet," I say directly to the dog, who licks my face. Peter tells me the dog's name, but it doesn't register. Glad that the dog appropriately takes my attention, I also long to be his friend because he is now Peter's companion and I sense the job that lies ahead.

"Great dog."

Now I must get up. "Great to see you," I say to Peter, self-consciously aware that I've said "great" too many times.

"I'm going to exercise. The two of you will have a cup of tea," Diane directs. We look at her longingly and don't want her to leave. She is our translator, one who moves comfortably between the worlds of the living and the dying; she protects me from thinking about my own mortality, she lets Peter talk about his. She and I define ourselves as living; Peter views himself as dying. Yet, she and Peter exist in the world of the dying; I need to believe I exist in the living world.

* * *

Now I am alone with Peter in a small dingy, dirty restaurant. It's okay, I think. I know how to talk to people who are dying; how to get past the bullshit and talk about real things; how to listen, make it comfortable for them to say what's on their minds and in their hearts. My partner Gene and I talked about death and dying for years, even when he was near the end. I can do it now.

We order tea. "Herbal," we both say. When they bring us Lipton's caffeinated, I ask, "Okay?" and we shrug.

I don't look into his eyes. "So . . ." I say, pausing.

"So, everything is okay here, not great but okay." What an understatement, I think, unsure of how to respond.

* * *

Peter orders a bowl of soup. "I have no appetite," he says. "Food I used to love, I can't eat now."

"Gene was like that," I say, wanting to normalize the interaction, even though my point of comparison is a dead person.

"Really?" he asks, seeming glad for the company.

As I talk about Gene and food, I am more involved in watching myself than in what I'm saying. I feel dizzy, like I might faint. The experience reminds me of a feeling I had a few weeks ago in a veterinarian's office, when the vet let me watch a castration of a dog. I left the operating room when I felt faint. Still, I couldn't get the image of the dog having its balls "ripped off" out of my mind. I saw *my* dog lying there, then my male companion, then it was me. This is where we all end up, I had thought. The dizziness had followed me outside, then back to the waiting room, where I passed out in a chair, sinking to the floor.

This is where we all end up, I think again, just like Peter, who I hear saying something like, "I guess it could be worse. I have a friend who just went blind."

What does he mean, worse? How much worse can it be? He'll probably go blind too. He's dying. The doctor just informed him the other day, Diane had told me, that he had two years to go. "He won't make it that long," she predicted, "because he has already given up."

"He had AIDS?" I ask, saying the word *AIDS* quietly.

"What?"

"The guy who went blind?"

"Yes, he had AIDS," Peter replies in a normal tone.

The feeling of passing out won't let go of me. I'm nauseated. As my bowels react to the stress, gas pains warn me I need to get to a bathroom. Sweating, I clutch my cup of tea with both hands to steady myself. It's an effort to talk and hard to breathe. The restaurant swirls in a thick haze of smoke and dust.

You are in the corner of a dark, dingy restaurant, I remind myself. Think about the larger world. See, the smoke is heavy. The dirt is real. There are other people here. And a world outside the restaurant. I watch talking and laughing people walk by the window. I can do this. I've done it many times. Talked of death, dying. I know what to say. But I don't want to be here, seeing this. He's so young, younger than I, still in his thirties. He always was so energetic, so good looking.

He won't get better.

I hear myself continue to ask questions, and feel myself breathe deeply while Peter answers. He doesn't seem to notice. Too depressed, I think, to pay attention to my state. He just shrugs his shoulders as he talks, as if saying, "What can you do?"

I can't pass out. What will he think? He'll know then how sick he looks. That he's so bad that his friend can't be with him without collapsing. Who would take care of me if I fainted? Would New Yorkers who are so accustomed to ignoring lifeless street people? Could Peter? He has no strength—physical or emotional. I wouldn't be able to face him afterwards. How would I explain to him what happened? Or to Diane? Their world of pretend would come tumbling down (as would mine). All because I couldn't handle talking about dying. They'd know then, yes they'd know, that their beautiful performance hadn't worked.

* * *

Peter's eyes are sunken, surrounded by dark rims that change color, like photosensitive sunglasses, as they widen around his eyes. Black, then brown, gray, and almost yellowish-purple. His posture is rigid, except for his head that hangs down toward the chicken soup he listlessly raises toward his mouth.

I watch the yellow droplets of yellow fat drip from the oversized tablespoon. Imagining the taste of grease increases my nausea.

"I've had trouble with depression," Peter says.

"Makes sense to," I respond. "Illness *is* depressing." Our eyes lock. I purse my lips, breathe in slowly through my nose, acknowledging his condition now, looking for his response. In reaction to my bluntness, his head sags further and he looks more depressed.

Diane was right at breakfast, I finally admit to myself. The best thing that could happen for everyone would be an acute infection that would take him quickly.

"I'm not taking drugs," Peter says, apparently in answer to a question I've asked.

"At some point, you may want to," I say, feeling I am giving permission. "You've proven you can stay away from drugs. For over ten years, you've shown that."

"Yeah," he says, "I know," and seems appreciative of the permission as well as the acknowledgment of his accomplishment. His friends will not think he has given in now if he resorts to drugs, the enemy that contributed to the AIDS in the first place.

"Gene and I took LSD to deal with his illness," I say, just to fill in the silence. "It was a life saver." Peter's eyes open wide in response. Why did I say that? Peter can't take LSD, not in his condition. He's too sick. Facing the reality that LSD demands would do him in.

"Before Gene got so sick, I mean." What I want to say is, "way before he was as sick as you are now." I don't, because I don't want to talk about *how* sick Peter is now. I want to participate in denial; I want a sanitized conversation about dying, the kind I used to hate when people had them with Gene.

Deep breaths, deep breaths, I remind myself.

He won't get better.

"Really? I don't think I could take LSD," Peter says.

"But you did, didn't you? Before?"

"Sure. Then."

I fill up time asking questions, while I concentrate on not passing out. As the feeling washes over me in waves, I see death in front of me—Gene's, Peter's, then mine. I have entered Tolstoy's world of Ivan Ilych.

When the feeling comes, I examine the larger world around me to remind myself that I am *not of* this scene. I am only visiting. I will leave it. Go back to normal. The word *normal* mocks me. Ha, ha. No, this is *not* my life again. I am not taking care of a dying person. And, I am not dying.

It *will* be your life again, some day, Death speaks inside my head.

I long to escape outside to the New York City streets, to take in the dirtiness, the beggars, and the constant odors—the smell of sweating people and garbage bins that are never far away—and to again be in the sensuous world of the commonplace.

How the fuck does Peter stand this? How will I? There is no way for me to make him feel better, nothing to say, no way to make something good out of his condition. Just watch what you say, I remind myself. The LSD thing, just to fill up space, that was inappropriate to tell a former drug-addicted person close to death.

"My crazy doctor gave me . . . ," Peter hesitates, then, "speed." Disappointed, I had hoped it would be something much more pleasurable—Ecstasy maybe. "It helped with the fatigue," Peter admits.

"That's good, then."

"But at the end of four hours, I was tense, strung out."

"I never liked speed, the feeling," I offer, wanting to relate to him by pretending we're just two people comparing experiences.

"I only took it one week."

"Do many people with AIDS take drugs to feel better?"

"Not at my stage," Peter replies nonchalantly, as if his healthier condition is the most obvious thing in the world. "But when they're sicker."

I'm glad for his answer, because with it he has given me permission to—no, actually demanded—that I pretend he's not as sick as the rest.

* * *

I want this meeting to be over and, at the same time, I'm afraid it will end without any meaningful communication, and I'll never see him again. How long do I have to stay so that it is not obvious that I couldn't wait to leave? What's wrong with me? I used to be able to do this, talk about dying.

* * *

"I'm thinking of going to Australia," I continue, suddenly remembering that Peter grew up there.

"The land is beautiful. You should go."

"What about your parents?" I ask, since Peter's parents live in Australia.

"They can't deal with this," he says, waving his hands over his body. "They never could cope with stress."

"If you like scenery, you should go to the Southwest," I suggest, to change the subject.

His eyes light up. "Yes, I'd like that."

"So do it," I command.

"Yes, we should do things while we can." He says this as though it's a cliché, not a matter of life and death, but more like I might have said it casually to another friend.

"Gene and I went. You can do it all in a car. It's easy."

"Did you take little walks to close places?"

"Oh, yes," I say enthusiastically, instead of explaining that, much of the time, Gene was in a wheelchair. "But you can see everything by car." I do not want Peter to have to admit he can barely walk.

"I'd like that."

Now I feel better, like I am helping. "You need long-range things to look forward to," I say, "and to get you out of the day-to-day."

* * *

"I'm going to the bathroom," I say, finally feeling I can maneuver it, and sensing the necessity for doing so. In the bathroom, my insides explode, freeing me to breathe again and cope. I look questioningly into the mirror over the sink, trying to find a clue about why this meeting is so difficult. Is it me? Peter? Nothing penetrates my confusion. The cold water I splash on my face renews my confidence slightly.

When I return to Peter, I am relieved, then disappointed, that Diane has returned. Maybe I could have helped more, thought of other strategies to help deny dying. But what else is there?

"Go to the Southwest," I command to Diane. "Long-range planning. It'll help." I sound like a travel agent, who knows the experience of the trip won't be a good as the advertisement.

Meta-Autoethnography: A World Apart

I realize as I write this story that my encounter with Peter had been riddled with intersubjective failure. I did not want to take on Peter's consciousness as my own. To do so would be to return to the world I escaped from after Gene died. Moreover, I knew from personal experience that this is not a world that is openly accessible to visitors. If you want to visit, you better be prepared to stay. I think Peter knew this too. He was unprepared or unwilling to expose his inner world to me. Why should he? How could he? Is it ever really possible to overcome denial and connect the world of living to the world of dying?

Is this the way people used to react to Gene and me? Is this why some people didn't come around? I had no idea. When you're inside IT, it's hard to imagine there's a world outside IT. When you're outside IT, you can't fathom life on the inside, even when you've been there before and know you'll be there again.

In response to his wife's death, C. S. Lewis (1963, p. 13) wrote:

> An odd by-product of my loss is that I'm aware of being an embarrassment to every-one I meet. At work, at the club, in the street, I see people, as they approach me, trying to make up their minds whether they'll "say something about it" or not. I hate it if they do, and if they don't. Perhaps the bereaved ought to be isolated in special settlements like lepers.

"Speaking of Dying" presents the other side of the difficulties of communicating across boundaries of living and dying, between those residing in the temporarily well and the terminally ill community. Through trying to understand the communication difficulties, I seek an alternative to isolating the dying and bereaved and to discomforting the well and concerned; I seek to accomplish what Rorty (1982) says we should expect from social scientists—"[to] act as interpreters for those with whom we are not sure how to talk . . . the same thing we hope for from our poets and dramatists and novelists" (p. 202).

Meta-Autoethnography: Growing Older in 2008

As I grow older, I have become more accepting of bodily imperfections. Minor bodily stigmas, such as lisps, seem of little concern compared to issues of health, chronic pain, and illness. Friends and I still mention our imperfections and sometimes threaten to do something drastic, such as plastic surgery, but so far we rarely go through with our threats and usually the conversations return quickly to issues of health.

Unlike Gene's, Rex's, and Peter's deaths, which felt out of the ordinary, now illness and death seem more a part of the day-to-day plot line of my life. As I have gotten older, it is much more common for friends and family members to contract serious illnesses and for some of them to die. Without parents or relatives from our parents' generation, Art and I call ourselves orphans and understand that we are now members of the older generation. I try to incorporate that sensibility into my life as part of the natural order of things.

Sometimes now I wonder if, for people who have lived long lives, there *is* such a gap between those inside IT (the world of the dying) and those outside IT; between the times we're inside and the times we're outside. These worlds, which once seemed distinct and bounded, have started to merge for me. Maybe that's what happens when you age. The boundaries become more permeable. There's almost always someone in my world now who is terminally ill or dying, and death is never too far away. Just this week, for example, two professors at my university passed away. Death always has been ever-present, of course, but now I pay more attention, especially since those who are ill and dying often are around my age and sometimes younger. I find myself going to more funerals and memorial services now, supporting more bereaved and dying friends, comforting more sick relatives, and giving more consideration to their (and my) deteriorating and ill bodies. But I also think I have learned to enter and leave the world of the sick and dying more easily than I did before. I move more seamlessly now from those events back to my daily life, where there are deadlines to make, errands to run, and responsibilities to meet; where there are friends and family to spend time with, moments of joy to enter fully, and accomplishments, markers, and happy events to celebrate.

At the same time that I move more easily between the world of the living and the world of the ill and dying and know that my time in the world of the living is only temporary,[9] I also have learned to put up walls and protect myself more effectively. For example, I seek out more comedies and fewer tragedies on TV, and I carefully decide which memorial services to attend and how much to participate in or think about the illness and deaths of acquaintances and popular figures who are not close friends or relatives. Sometimes I even shy away from entering and writing about the details of dying and death.

But then I haven't experienced the loss of a close loved one in a while. Perhaps I have forgotten how much close personal loss throws life into total chaos and how little any kind of barrier or protector works when a loved one dies. Perhaps I do not have to think about that now—another way I protect myself from being overwhelmed about loss.[10]

Along with the changes that have come from my getting older, the larger context of the country in which we live feels different since the events of September 11, 2001. Our reality consists of a faltering economy, an incompetent government, a ravaged environment, constant threats of terrorism at home and to world peace abroad. Most of us—myself included—feel insecure and vulnerable in ways that we have not experienced before. I turn in the next chapter to how the events on that fateful day shattered my/our worldview.

CHAPTER ELEVEN

Learning to Be "With" in Personal and Collective Grief

For most Americans, September 11, 2001, is forever stamped into memory. I know it is for me. When the terrorist attacks began, I was on a plane traveling from Tampa to Dulles Airport to assist my elderly mother, who, unable to care for herself, was in a nursing home in Luray, Virginia. I planned to return home to Tampa as quickly as possible to support my husband Art, who was caring for his dying mother in a nursing home in Florida. As soon as the captain informed us about the terrorist attacks, the frames I took for granted regarding flying on a plane, even walking through an airport, no longer fit. Immediately I was forced to reframe this experience, at first for expedience, so that I might figure out what to do after our plane was forced to land in Charlotte, North Carolina. Later I had to make sense of this experience in order to reconstruct a personal life and social world in which I could live, a life and world that held the possibility of a meaningful future in spite of shattered illusions of comfort and safety. No matter where others were or what they were doing that day, I suspect this is a task they faced as well.

Here I tell one story of what it felt like to live through that day and its aftermath, concentrating on details of how I made sense of and negotiated my way through the confusing haze of the first twenty-four hours after the terrorist attacks. My story is a chaos narrative (Frank, 1995), but as with all chaos narratives, it is harnessed and ordered, pushing chaos into the background so that a linear coherent plot can unfold and be featured. I wrote this story soon after the events transpired. In the next several weeks, I wrote and rewrote, added to and deleted passages, framed and reframed what happened, what this story meant and what readers should take from it. Obsessed with finishing this story about this tragedy, I put all other work on hold. I couldn't stop writing, because the writing held out the possibility of making this experience meaningful.

I wrote this story to help myself and others work through this tragedy and our shattered illusions. Along with stories of those killed, injured, lost, displaced, and left grieving for loved ones, and those heroes who risked their lives, the everyday stories of the rest of us—those not directly involved yet devastated by what happened and feeling deeply the country's collective grief—also merited telling. I provided my story as an incentive for others to put their stories into words, compare their experiences to mine, and find companionship in their sorrow (Mairs, 1993). I spoke my story so that others might feel liberated to speak theirs without feeling guilty that some suffered more and therefore their story was not worth telling, their feelings unjustified.

I believed we each needed to find personal and collective meaning in the events that transpired and in the disrupted and chaotic lives left behind. On the other side of our grief, I hoped we then might be inspired to live better lives—lives based on loving and caring relationships, community, and reaching out to those in need throughout the world. I also hoped that this story would stimulate dialogue among social scientists and qualitative researchers about the meaning of the events of September 11th and the role they might play in understanding and helping people cope with such tragedies.[1]

Shattered Lives: Making Sense of September 11th and Its Aftermath[2]

A Serious Announcement

"Ladies and gentlemen, we're on schedule for our arrival at Dulles at 11:21," the captain says, immediately after our on-time takeoff at 9:10 a.m. "In fact, we'll have you at the gate early. The skies are clear and it should be a smooth flight."

I am almost finished reading *USA Today* when suddenly the three flight attendants march decidedly and briskly in step to the front of the plane, enter the cockpit, and close the door. My body goes on alert. I look out the window; the sky is clear. I glance around the cabin; people continue reading and snoozing. I cock my left ear; the engine sounds smooth and steady. I look at my watch; it reads around ten a.m. Keeping a watchful eye on the cockpit, I return to my newspaper. When the flight attendants emerge in a matter of minutes and begin collecting trash, I relax and tell myself they must have responded to the captain turning off the fasten seatbelt sign. Not totally convinced, I submerge myself in the columns of numbers in the stock report.

"May I have your attention please?" the captain says a few minutes later. "I have a very serious announcement to make." I am alerted by the grave tone of his voice as well as by the word *serious* he emphasizes. "It has nothing to do with the safety of the plane," he reassures quickly. I breathe a sigh of relief, yet my body tenses nervously and my breath catches as I am reminded of my brother's death in a commercial airplane crash in 1982 (Ellis, 1993).

From my fifth-row seat, I lean forward to hear what he is saying. Others do too. "Our plane is being diverted to Charlotte," he says into the quiet. Passengers groan in unison. Damn airlines, I think, my body relaxing into moral indignation. Seems like every time I fly now, there is a problem. "All planes in the air are being asked to land," the pilot continues. What? I return to alert. "There has been a terrorist attack. Ladies and gentlemen, I've been flying for twenty-five years and I've never experienced anything like this. We'll let you know more as soon as we are informed. I really don't know what will happen once we land."

Did I hear him right? I replay the captain's announcement in my mind. A terrorist attack? Where? How? What does that have to do with us? Why are we landing if our plane is okay? Is there something he's not telling us? What happens now? Is this how my brother felt when his plane went down almost twenty years ago? Oh, no, that was much worse. I imagine the nose of the plane diving at speeds faster than I've ever experienced. I grab onto the seat in front of me, then quickly shake the image of crashing planes from my head.

A few people talk quietly to their neighbors, but mostly we sit in stunned silence. Time slows; few thoughts spin in my mind. I long to go back to the comfort I felt prior to the announcement.

Soon the man seated in row three turns around and speaks over the back of his seat to the female passenger in front of me. Overhearing, the flight attendants gather around him. I stand and lean in, listening. He must have news. How did he get it? At that moment, I notice the in-flight phone in the back of the seat in front of me, and I know. Removing the receiver, I hold it in my right hand. "Two planes have flown into the World Trade Centers," the woman passes back. "They're collapsing." Then, "The Pentagon is on fire," she relays in the same tone she might say, "They're serving chicken." I wait for more. "That's all he knows," she says, turning around again.

Did I hear her right? This kind of thing doesn't happen in America. There must be some mistake. Could it all be a rumor? My breathing quickens. I look around to see if anyone knows more. The news the man conveys is passed across the aisle, then backward, row by row. Nothing more. I sit down, in shock, not believing. I put the newspaper, still clutched in my left hand, on the empty seat. It is eerily quiet. We all sit in anticipation.

Noting the phone in my hand, I pull out my AT&T calling card, read the directions on the phone, and quickly dial my husband Art's cell phone number. I hear a fast busy signal. Again, the same. "Everyone is calling," the attendant says as she walks by. "You may have trouble connecting. There are only three lines out. Keep trying. At least there are only twenty people on this flight."

I punch in Art's cell phone number. Again, and again. Always a quick busy signal. I dial continuously; from the ruffling sounds, I assume many others are doing the same. We are all trying to connect to loved ones. We need to hear their voices. They need to hear ours. Am I overreacting? What kind of attack? Who? Why?

What about my mom? I must get to her. She is returning home from the nursing home in which she's been rehabing for seven weeks. I'm flying to be with her, to help with her transition. She is depending on me. My brother died January 13, 1982, in the crash of Air Florida flight 90 on his way to visit me. Ever since, my mother worries when I fly. She will be worried this time, more than usual. Given her slight mental confusion from her pain medication, I hope she has forgotten I'm flying today. Not a chance. And she's probably seen the attack on TV. I remember what it felt like to watch on TV the rescue from the cold Potomac waters of the survivors of my brother's plane. The world was watching then too. I remember what it felt like not knowing if Rex was dead or alive. I dial my older brother's number. He must tell my mother I'm okay. Rapid beep, beep.

I retrieve my cell phone from my pocketbook and place it on my lap. "I'm not sure that will work up here," says the attendant as she walks by again.

"Oh, I just have it ready for when we land." When it registers that she did not forbid me to use it, I hold the phone in my hand, tempted to dial. I don't, because I don't want to risk interfering with the operation of the plane. Just holding it comforts me. It represents the possibility of making contact and finding out more about what is going on.

The attendants huddle in the front of the plane. One tries to make a call but gives up when the line is busy. Several passengers stand and talk quietly over their seats. "There's been at least one more crash near Camp David," a woman across the aisle relays to me, and I pass the news forward. When I turn around, the information already is winding its way to the back. I pray that what she says is incorrect; yet I can't ignore that we've had the tragedy verified now from several sources.

I continue calling on the in-flight phone and listening to the rapid busy signal. Surprisingly, I do not worry that there might be a terrorist on this place. Instead, it feels like we are all companions, in this together. What has happened? This can't be terrorism. There must be another explanation.

"We're approaching the Charlotte airport," the captain says about thirty minutes after his initial announcement. "There are a lot of planes behind us and some already have landed. I don't know how long it will take. When we get to the gate, we'll let you off, then move away quickly so the next plane can get in. I don't know what will happen then. Remember, ladies and gentlemen, everyone is in the same boat here, including the pilots and flight attendants. Ground services is just outside. Good luck."

Ground services. Yes, I must figure out what to do. I work to clear my alternately jumbled and numbed mind by talking to myself. Think clearly, Carolyn. The most likely occurrence is that you are going to be stranded for hours, even days, in the airport. But if I am stranded, at least I have my laptop. I can write about what's happening. You will be uncomfortable and may be unsafe. What are my options? I could get a motel room or a rental car. Everyone will want rental cars and motel rooms. There won't be enough to go around. I must think quickly. But shouldn't you be thinking of others as well? Everyone will need assistance. I justify my self-absorption by arguing that I am a woman traveling alone and I need to get to Virginia to care for my mother. Oh, how I wish Art were here.

An abstract image of burning buildings interferes with my planning. I concentrate on it but, try as I might, I cannot picture the Pentagon burning or the World Trade Centers collapsing. Maybe the damage has been exaggerated, like in a party game of "gossip." Perhaps only a part collapsed; maybe there's only a small fire.

I take a deep breath and get back to the task at hand, the only thing I might possibly influence. My personal safety may be at issue. I really need to rent a car, but there will be fewer cars available in Charlotte than rooms. And it's a long drive to my mom's, probably six hours or so. Is it a good idea to drive? Maybe my sister and her husband, who are driving up from Mississippi to help care for my mom, could swing over and get me. Or I could stop at my sister-in-law's in Asheville. That can't be too far. Or maybe I should try to get back home to Tampa. That idea tempts me—to be safe in my home with my husband and dogs. But Tampa is at least thirteen or more hours away. Besides, I must go help my mother and she will need to see that I am okay. Suddenly the desire to be with family—my husband and dogs or my mother and siblings—overrides all other feelings.

Perhaps I could ask someone to rent a car with me. After all, everyone on this plane is headed to the D.C. area, about ninety miles from where my mom lives. I don't want to drive alone. What if it's not safe on the roads? Okay, now you're overreacting. Stop. That won't help. If I drive with someone else, we could help each other and make decisions together. Yes, that feels like the way to handle this situation. Maybe the woman sitting alone in row four would want to join me.

Landing

"Please make sure your seatbelts are fastened, the seat backs in their upright position, and the tray tables stowed for landing." The familiar directions calm me. I obey and then brace my hands on the arms of the seat for landing, as though I don't trust the plane's safety. We land smoothly and quickly taxi to the terminal. Soon as the fasten seatbelt sign goes off, I head for the bathroom to save time later. I dial Art on my cell phone on the way. Rapid busy signal. Again and again. Oh, god, I have to get through to make sure he's okay and to tell him I'm okay. I continue to push redial while I urinate. As I exit the bathroom, I dial again. Suddenly, I hear "Hello" screamed into the phone. I do not know if I have connected on an outgoing or incoming call. Later, my telephone bill will show a call dialed from my number to Art's cell phone at 10:28, lasting for two minutes.

"Hello," I respond quickly and calmly. A flight attendant watches and listens.

"Carolyn, Carolyn," Art shouts into the phone, and I am reminded of the time I was sick and passed out on the bathroom floor, aroused by Art's frightened voice. "Oh, thank god. Are you all right?" His breath comes in quick gasps.

"I'm okay," I reassure. "I'm okay."

"Are you in Charlotte?"

"Yes, I am. We've just landed. They're opening the door now." How does he know I am in Charlotte? Later he will tell me he asked a travel agent to locate on her computer where my plane was landing.

"Where are you?" I ask, heading for the exit.

"Driving back from my mom's nursing home. Get out of the airport, Carolyn, now," he says forcefully, adding slightly to my fear. "There have been several attacks. There might be more. Get a car and get out."

"I will. I'm headed out . . . ," I begin, and the phone goes dead. So the situation is as bad as I feared. Worse even. I walk through the jetway toward the terminal, dialing Art again. Then my brother. Back and forth. But with no success.

People from our plane stand in small groups near our gate. Recognizing the middle-aged woman who sat in front of me, I join her and an older couple who sat across the aisle. When their open mannerisms invite me into the conversation, I say, "Why don't we get a car and drive to Virginia?" All three perk up, interested. Then the woman traveling alone says, "But we don't have our luggage."

"I don't think we'll get our luggage," I respond. "I heard a US Airways employee say as we entered the airport that our luggage was secured. I think that means we won't have access to it. Officials are probably worried about what's in it. Besides our plane has already moved away from the hangar."

"Don't we have to stay here to see when we'll be rescheduled later today?" asks the man.

"Maybe we shouldn't leave the gate," echoes his companion. "Until they tell us what to do. Let's all stay together."

I am tempted; then I look around. People sit quietly in small groups, with glazed, concerned looks on their faces. Some stand in lines, talking to staff, looking expectant, hoping, like my temporary companions, they will be told what to do. I take off walking, rapidly, glad I am in good physical condition. Get to the outside, away from the airport, I tell myself, echoing Art's advice. My brain works quickly, in problem-solving mode now, which calms my fears. Rent a car preferably; if not, at least a motel room.

I pass a group of people gathered round a loud big-screen TV in a bar in the middle of concessions. This scene provides a striking contrast to the slow motion and quiet calm in the gate areas. I stop to find out what is going on, to be part of a community, even another temporary one, and to participate in a "normal" activity. Then, resisting the impulse, I move away quickly.

I walk rapidly, dialing as I do, first my brother, then my husband. I finally get through to my brother's answering machine. "This is Carolyn. I'm okay," I say. "My plane has landed in Charlotte. I may get a car and drive home, if I can. I love you." That call registers on my cell phone bill at 10:30 for two minutes. Shortly after, my phone rings. Since it is in my hand, I answer quickly, but no one is on the other line. I suspect the call is from my husband. I long for conversation with him; he would help me make good decisions. I don't stop moving. Destination: the rental car area. I call my mother's number at the nursing home time and time again; as I expect, nobody answers since my mother is on a home visit with a nurse and my brother, to see if she can manage the transfer. I call my brother's secretary and ask her to find my brother and tell him I'm okay. That phone call registers at 10:44 for two minutes.

Making Connections

On the lower level of the terminal, activity and sound increase. These are people who have been here a while. For them, as for me, the news is sinking in. The lines in front of the Budget counter, the only rental car company in view, are long and at a standstill. A man complains loudly. "Let me see your manager. Surely you can release those cars. You must have reservations for people who aren't here, who won't be able to get here." One agent stands defiantly with her arms crossed; the other two look confused. I stop and ask a man in line, "Are there cars available?"

I know the answer before he speaks. "Not if you don't have a reservation."

I keep walking, heading toward two phones equipped for dialing two-digit codes to connect to local motels. Without hesitating, I dial the first number on the list. I am about to try something else when suddenly, "Day's Inn. May I help you?"

"Do you have a room?" I ask the male voice.

"Yes," he replies, "hold on a moment." In the thirty seconds I wait, I scan the list of hotels trying to decide whether to dial another. By then several people stand in line behind me. I hang up suddenly and press the code for Triangle Rent-A-Car. Busy, again. Busy. Again. Busy. Maybe I shouldn't have hung up on the Day's Inn. Maybe I should call a rental car agency on my cell phone. Reluctant to give up my position to look for a phone book, I continue dialing and look around to see if a vacant pay phone is nearby.

"Triangle Rent-A-Car. May I help you?" I hear suddenly.

"Yes, do you have any available cars?" I ask calmly. I want to shout, "I need a car. Please help me."

"Yes, yes, we do," the woman says.

"I'd like to rent one." I fish out my credit card, not believing my good fortune.

"We can't guarantee you what kind of car."

"It doesn't matter. I'll take anything." Do I sound too desperate? What if she decides not to rent it to me, instead holding out for someone she considers more important?

"I'll need to return it in Virginia," I say, suddenly thinking about the future, then fearing I have ruined my chances of getting this car by adding a wrinkle.

"Where in Virginia?"

"Near D.C., Arlington, Alexandria, Falls Church area, anywhere in Northern Virginia." I try to increase the possibility of giving a right answer. I do not want to ruin this deal. What if we get disconnected? I glance at the long line of people now behind me.

"Let's see. My only Virginia locations are Richmond, Hampton, and Virginia Beach."

"They are all a long way from where I'll be, at least 120 miles," I say, thinking out loud and calculating the distance. "That's okay, I'll take it anyway," I say quickly.

"There will be a $100 drop-off charge."

"No problem." I don't ask the cost of renting the car.

"What zone are you in?"

"Excuse me?"

"Zone. In the airport. What zone are you in?"

"Zone D," I say, locating the sign outside the entryway.

"Walk across the road to the area for pick-up," the woman instructs. "We'll have a van there for you in about five minutes."

"Thank you." I walk outside toward my spot, finally letting out the deep breath I've been holding, feeling as though I have escaped. I am grateful for my good luck in getting a car. Quickly though, I begin to worry that I should have made a contingency plan. What if the van fails to show up? What if the woman rents my car to someone who gets there first and offers a large amount of money? Why didn't I get a back-up hotel room? I look at my cell phone but it will take too long to get information and numbers to dial. A local news van is parked at the curb and a reporter is interviewing passengers. I pass them quickly, tightly holding onto my cell phone and laptop computer. It seems absurd that I also carry a package with a massager in it, a gift for my mom.

Outside, movement speeds up; the sounds seem deafening. Yet the looks on people's faces—glazed, worried, fearful, and unsure—signal something is amiss. Many people walk quickly, unencumbered by suitcases. Cell phones glued to their ears, they move toward the other rental car vans with familiar names like Budget and Hertz that crawl slowly through the crowded pick-up area. I think of getting into a van and asking the driver if they have any cars. What if people do that with Triangle and there are no cars when I get there? The agent didn't take my name or a credit-card number. How will I prove the car is mine? Just trust, I say to myself. I concentrate on watching for my pick-up. Five minutes later, a Triangle Rent-A-Car van magically appears. I flag it down as I walk toward it.

"Are you the only one?" the sixtyish African American driver asks me.

"I don't know," I say looking around. Then realizing he means in my party, "Yes, yes, I am by myself." No one else gets in the van.

I sit in the front seat and lean toward the driver, wanting human contact. "I have to get to my mother," I say.

"Where is she?"

"In Northern Virginia, near Interstate 81."

He gives me detailed directions to the interstate. I ask him what happened. He tells me what I know already.

When we arrive at the agency, I am the only person renting a car. "All we have is a Mustang," the agent apologizes.

"That's perfect." I smile for the first time since the captain's serious announcement.

I register for the car, paying little attention to what I sign. "It has a half tank of gas," the woman says. "Bring it back that way."

I nod. Another person gives me a map and goes over the directions. A third takes me to the car and points which way to turn. My husband calls as I am getting into the car. "Your sister and brother-in-law called," Art says. "They're willing to swing over from Alabama to pick you up if you can't get a rental car."

For a moment I am tempted by the thought of being with family. Then, "No, I have one. I'm getting into it now. I'm driving to Luray," I say. "I hope I'm making the right decision."

"I guess," Art says hesitantly. "I know how much it means to you to be with your mother."

"Yes, it does," I respond, "even more now. I wanted to talk the decision over with you. I guess I could have tried to get back to Tampa." I feel homesick as I say those words.

"I had hoped you would," Art says.

"It's such a long drive, more than double what it is to Luray."

"I know. I would have come to get you."

"Virginia is so much closer than Tampa."

"It's just that it's hard not to be with you now."

"For me too," I respond.

"Be careful," he says. "Don't take any chances. And keep in touch. Every hour."

"I will."

"I talked to my brother," he says.

"Oh, your brother," I respond, suddenly remembering his brother lives in Tribeca, about ten blocks from the World Trade Center. Only now do I start to think of the people I know in New York. "He was crying. He said he had to get his kids from school. He and his wife saw the tail of the plane sticking out of the building from the first crash, Carolyn. They watched the second hit from the sidewalk outside their loft."

"Oh, my. I'm just glad he's safe. How is your mother?" I ask, suddenly thinking of our main concern prior to the attack.

"The same," he says sadly. "She lies there and doesn't speak. Just follows me with her eyes. Those eyes, I feel she can see through me. After I let you off at the airport this morning, I stopped to get coffee and saw the report on TV right after the first World Trade Center was hit. Then I heard about the second attack on the radio while driving to the nursing home. I called my brother then. I didn't even think about you being in danger because all this occurred in New York. Then when I got to my mom's nursing home, I turned on the TV and the Pentagon had just been hit. When they mentioned one of the planes originated at Dulles, I thought, Oh, my god, something could happen to Carolyn."

"That must have been awful."

"It was. My cell phone wouldn't work so I grabbed the pay phone out of someone's hands. Then when I couldn't reach you, I got in the car and drove home to use the phone there and to see if you had left a message or in case you called."

"You must have been panicked."

"I was." He chokes up. "It seemed like planes were going down right and left. I don't know what I'd do if I lost you."

"You won't. You won't. I'm fine."

"But Carolyn . . ."

"Yes?"

"I fear our lives will never again be the same. It's all so horrible. People were jumping from the top floors of the building." The words hang ominously in the air. I try, and then resist, forming a picture of the scene he describes.

We hang up and I get into my sporty white Mustang. As I check the mirrors, the van driver comes by to ask me if I know the way. "God bless you," I say, nodding. I am surprised at the foreign words I utter, which come from the strong connection I feel to him and my gratefulness for his concern. I also assume an older Black man in the South will have faith in God.

Finally, I turn on the radio, eager to hear the news for myself. I place my cell phone on my lap and its extra battery on the passenger's seat. What good luck that I have an extra battery in my purse. I check to make sure I have pills for migraine headaches. I do. Okay, I can get by. I think briefly about what I don't have—my clothes, toiletries, coat, camera, and shoes. Things: the least of my worries.

Throughout the five-and-a-half-hour drive, my phone rings constantly, and I call Art every hour. My cell phone bill for that day registers forty-three connected calls, more than thirty of them during the drive. Each connection I make involves at least five attempts. Each time I talk only a short while, to save battery power and to adhere to Dan Rather's plea to allow emergency calls to get through. I call my brother and leave another message about what I am doing. I talk to my sister, who is on the road in Alabama. My husband's sister calls. Then my friend Marilyn. When I stop for gas, I call my mother at the nursing home. "I am so glad to hear your voice," she says weakly.

"I'm okay, Mom."

"Your brother said you were, but . . ." Her voice trails off.

"Were you worried, Mom?"

"Yes, until I heard your voice. I've already lost one child on an airplane. I couldn't survive losing another one."

"I'm okay, Mom. I love you. I'll be there in about three hours. It'll be so good to see you. You're going home, Mom. Just keep thinking about that."

"I will. I love you too, Carolyn."

Getting the News

The drive goes quickly. Hooked to the radio, I scan through the stations, comforted by the familiar voices of Tom Brokaw, Peter Jennings, and Dan Rather. When one fades, I search for another. The radio makes me feel less alone and more connected to what is happening. The news sustains me and makes me cringe at the same time. With the information I hear, I try again to visualize the World Trade towers collapsing but I can't. I both want and dread finally seeing the pictures, like passing an accident on the highway. As in personal loss and grief, I keep listening, hoping to hear a different story. Please, someone say this has all been a mistake; or, at the least, say the damage has been exaggerated. Instead the story keeps getting worse and worse; it's an unfolding horror movie. No World Trade Center. Burning Pentagon. Planes down. People running for their lives. Good-bye phone calls to loved ones. Wounded, charred, and dead bodies.

Then revenge talk. Suspected Muslims. Suicide missions. Afghanistan. Osama bin Laden. Taliban. I am embarrassed that I don't even know who Osama bin Laden and the Taliban are. I doubt I could point to Afghanistan on a map. I realize how isolationist I have been, we all have been. How innocent and complacent. I listen closely and try to understand what has happened. How? Why? And what for? We should find those who are guilty and blow 'um off the face of the earth. I don't know who "'um" is exactly, but the vague picture in my mind is of dark-skinned men with turbans, long robes, and beards. The feeling, complicated as it is by grief and loss, doesn't last long, but it is strong and interrupts briefly the void of hopelessness, fear, and vulnerability I begin to feel. Not until later will I think more about the complexities of racial profiling and dealing with an enemy who hides among innocent, impoverished, despairing people. I get some inkling of what a privileged life I have led and how little collective grief I have ever felt.

Reporters tell vivid stories about people helping each other. Firemen jogging up the stairs of the burning building as workers run down to escape. I feel proud. Sad. Angry. Nothing. Nothing. I can't feel, think . . . I shake my head. What must it be like to be engulfed in fire? To jump out a window of a burning building? So high up. Someone reaches out a hand. Another refuses to leave a disabled colleague. I sob and ache for family and friends with whom to share my grief. I long for feelings of anger and revenge to return, but they are stifled by grief and sadness. The only balm for my pain is the love I feel toward and from those I care about, an intensity of connection born of loss and vulnerability. At that moment, these feelings extend to everyone I know, and to all those suffering in this tragic event. I feel a part of America in a way I have not felt before. This has been done to "us." It is only later that I raise any questions at all about devout patriotism.

To cope, I turn my focus to my mother and to the details of getting her home from the nursing home. These thoughts give me a sense of purpose and possible future. Interspersed periodically are flashes of the mundane: lost luggage, how I'll get back to Tampa, how far to drive before I stop, whether to buy a Diet Coke or continue drinking the water I have with me.

Then existential thoughts overcome me. I am alone in this car driving from some place to some place. I'm going back to the town of my childhood; but not back to child-hood innocence. That dissolved when my brother Rex died. Returning home was never the same after that. My mother will not be able to soothe my pain; she can't handle her own. Nobody will be able to take care of my pain, nor the pain of all those who have lost loved ones. The feeling is unbearable. I push it away. How I long for innocence right now; not death and terror and destruction; not burning and collapsing buildings, terrorists, and threats; not a mother-in-law in a semiconscious state, a mother in chronic pain who can't walk. The terrorist attack too feels like another nail in the coffin of innocence. This time the crisis is not just personal, it is global. How can our lives be the same? Will Americans ever feel safe again? I cry softly and hold onto my cell phone.

When I stop for gas in rural Virginia, I call my brother Arthur to report my location. I want my family to know where I am. When I go inside to pay, I watch a salesman joke with a female clerk in a gentle, familiar way that makes it clear they know each other. People comment softly that the pumps won't take their credit cards. The clerk apologizes. No radios blare. Nobody mentions the tragic events unfolding as we buy our gas. How can they be going about their business as usual? How can I? Yet, I am comforted that we are. Maybe life can return to normal. Still I detect a solemn feeling, even here in the backwoods of Virginia. People seem to be especially gentle and courteous. A man motions for me to go in front of him to the counter and I hold a door for someone exiting the store. Or am I just watching more closely than usual?

The Nursing Home

I arrive at the nursing home shortly after five p.m. When I rush into room 126, Mom's eyes light up and she raises her outstretched hands to me. Without saying a word, I lean down over her La-Z-Boy and eagerly embrace her. We hold tightly, appreciating physical presence, smell, and touch. She smiles when I do a little "happy" dance in my crouched position; my upper body shimmies in her embrace and I prance in place.

"What happened?" she asks suddenly.

"You mean the attacks?" She nods yes, her eyes fearful. "Did you see them on TV?" I ask.

"A little, but then I cut it off. I couldn't stand to watch it."

"What did my brother tell you?"

"Not much," she answers. "Just that there had been a crash, that people were hurt, but that you were safe."

I kneel down in front of her and take both hands in mine. Feeling protective, I speak gently, watching her reaction. "Two planes crashed intentionally into two buildings in New York City and another into the Pentagon."

"The Pentagon?" she asks. "In Washington?"

I nod, then wait for her to go on. I suspect she is thinking about Rex's plane crashing into the Potomac River in Washington, D.C.

"Did many people die?"

"Yes."

"How many?"

"Several thousand," I say. "Though we don't know yet."

"Did they get the people who did it?"

"They died in the crash," I say. "They committed suicide."

"Why?" she asks.

"They hate America. Our prosperity and values. What we stand for," I say. Already I realize this is a simplistic explanation.

But it's enough now for her. She nods, her eyes are far away. This seems to be all she can take in. The crashes remind her of her loss of Rex. She changes the subject and we talk about what it has been like to be in the nursing home.

"I hate it," she says, grimacing. "I want to go home. I thought I'd be okay here, but I'm not."

"I know, Mom," I say. "It won't be long."

Soon her dinner comes and I help her cut up the tasteless, burned American cheese sandwich. "The food is awful," she says and eats little of the dishwater-looking vegetable soup.

Glad to have something else to focus on, I promise, "I'll bring you something good to eat tomorrow." I think about the McDonald's hamburgers and Arby's Roast Beef she loves.

"Carolyn, I have to pee."

I help her get into her wheelchair, fearful of hurting her. When she cries out in pain from the movement, I hold back my tears and construct a temporary roadblock around my heart to ease the task. After she's back in her chair, I long to turn on the TV; out of respect for my mother, I don't.

In the next few days I will walk down the hall of the nursing home to watch the two TVs constantly on in the public areas. I watch alone. Residents stare off into space or sleep in front of them. Staff are too busy to stop. Nobody says much about what happened other than to inquire how I was able to get to Luray. A physical therapist worries about her son who works in the Pentagon. Otherwise, there are bedpans to be emptied, butts to wash, pills to give, careful steps to take. When I am in the nursing home, I feel as if this world crisis is a dream, something that belongs to a different province of meaning. My husband later will tell me that he had the same experience in his mother's nursing home in Largo, Florida. Maybe there are advantages to being old and sick.

Facing Loss

The TV reports I watch the next two nights before going to bed, and the falling and burning World Trade Center I see in my mind when I awake, all remind me this is not a dream. Screaming, jumping, running people. Now I have vivid pictures to go along with my nightmares. Unidentifiable, lost, and irretrievable bodies. The detailed imagery created by the pictures and words I hear on TV arouses memories of how much my family hoped to find my brother's body in the freezing Potomac River. I picture his plane crashing into the water; the unbearable grief that followed, the vulnerability, nightmares and tears, and my mother screaming out to the undertaker who was going to D.C., "Bring my boy home!" The relief we felt when he did, though no one wanted to see him in his coffin. I had to see him, to be certain, absolutely certain, that it *was* Rex. I visualize his flattened nose and gashed forehead that no amount of cosmetic work could cover. . . .

I release the memory from my mind. This is not my brother this time. I feel ashamed for thinking of my own situation when so many are dead, so many are grieving. I experience discomfort for being relieved my loved ones did not die. Then I wonder, did anybody I know die? My mind goes blank. I can't take in the collective misery right now. I can't fathom a future: what will the world be like post–September 11th? What will my life be like? Hell, what will tomorrow and the next day bring? I begin to suspect that Art is right: our lives—personally and collectively—will never be the same.

On the third day, my sister and her husband arrive and we bring my mom home. On the ride there, we stop at an attorney's office for my mother to sign her house over to my sister, who will live with her. When the attorney's assistant brings the papers to the car, my mother goes into a catatonic state and cannot respond or hold the pen. We fear we will have to turn around and take her back to the nursing home. "Mama, Mama," I yell, and wave my hands in front of her face, but she seems not to hear. If the legal assistant wonders what we are trying to pull, she shows no sign. When we get home, we put my mom in her chair and raise her feet. She comes back to consciousness and doesn't realize she went anywhere. We don't tell her. I wonder later if she had a psychological reaction to signing over her home or to being reminded of her loss of Rex. Or was it her dropping blood pressure, as we thought at the time? Maybe it was just all too much, the way her life had changed. The way our lives had changed.

"My life will never be the same," she says to me the next day. "I am never going to get better. If I could just get up and walk by myself."

I don't deny her reality. "We'll make you as comfortable as we can."

"I know you will."

I choke back the tears. "At least you're home." She smiles. I wonder if we will be able to keep her here.

From that moment, my mom begins her disengagement from the world. She refuses to watch the destruction on TV. "It upsets me," she says. She refuses to watch any TV, even her soaps, which have always engaged her.

"It's as though the terrorist attacks haven't happened for her," my sister-in-law notes. "Or if they did, it was another time altogether, not now."

"She has her own troubles to worry about," I respond. I look at her frail body hunched over in a chair, and I feel my stomach clench.

Our family has become very loving and united. We are loving because we share a common fear for our mother's deteriorating body and for ourselves when we anticipate losing her. We are united because of the danger in the world that compels us to stick together and support each other.

We have an eighty-seventh birthday party for my mother, even though her birthday isn't for another week. The three children give her a watch, our first joint present in our adult lives. I am reminded of the joint presents my brother Rex and I used to buy her. The watch is an interesting metaphor—how much time does she have? Do we? We buy pizza and a sugarless birthday cake. She manages to sit at the table for dinner. I say the blessing for the first time in thirty years and choke on my tears.

When I prepare to go back to Tampa a week later, the tears I have pushed down while I took care of my mother finally pour out unencumbered. My sister and I hold each other and I am appreciative of our renewed closeness and grateful that she is staying with our mother. I love my family then as much as I ever have, if not more. As I pull out of the driveway, I feel a renewed sense of the power of love and caring, and I cry out of love and fear. Will I see my mom alive again? Will Art's mom still be alive when I get back to Tampa? Will I ever stop waking up out of a nightmare of fears that feature buckets of my mother's urine and her gaze of unrecognition along with collapsing, burning buildings and screaming people? Will we ever stop waking up to this international nightmare? Will we ever feel safe and secure again? Will our lives ever return to normal or will normal be redefined? As I drive out of town to Richmond, where I will catch a plane to Tampa, I turn on the radio and am mysteriously mesmerized again by "The Attack on America," thankful that for the moment the news will allow me to put on hold the grief I cannot bear when I think about my mother's deteriorating condition.

Story Interlude One: Take No Chances[3]

"Your bags are light. That's good." The dark-complected, clean-shaven, fortyish-looking man scurries around the Royal Cab to load my small soft-sided bag and laptop backpack. I nod in appreciation as I talk on my cell phone, which has become my lifeline during the last week. "I am at the rental car agency in Richmond now," I explain into the phone. "The taxi is here to take me to the airport. I must go."

"Take no chances," my husband Art implores, resisting my attempt to end the conversation.

"Don't worry. I'll be careful." I hang up and get into the backseat of the cab.

"I lost my suitcase," I reply once I am settled. "My mother gave me this small bag and a few of her clothes."

"It'll be easier to get on the plane," the man says, "faster without so many bags."

"Will they let me take my things on the plane?"

"I don't think so. That's what I heard on TV."

"I was on a plane Tuesday morning," I say. Noting the man's Middle Eastern appearance, I wait to see how he will respond.

"If you see a group of Muslim-looking men together, turn and head in the other direction," my husband, worried that I was flying home to Tampa alone, had instructed on the phone. "If they're getting on your flight, don't get on. Take no chances."

"I doubt I'll be the only person watching out for Muslim men," I had replied.

"I guess you're right," he acknowledged. "Just take no chances. Be a good ethnographer. Pay attention to your surroundings."

"I haven't been able to talk for three days," the dark-complected man says now, as he pulls into traffic. "I am so distressed. I can't sleep. Nothing."

"It's awful," I acknowledge, not knowing how to talk about the terrorist attacks in New York and Washington that occurred almost a week ago now.

The man continues talking, seeming to have a running dialogue in his head. "It's bad for me in three ways. I am Middle Eastern, I am a Jordanian, and I'm a Muslim. But I'm also an *American*," he says with emphasis.

The word *Muslim* makes me flinch slightly. Yes, I thought he was Muslim. He's brave to say so. Normally I would not have thought about his being Muslim, and we likely would have had a lively conversation about what his home country is like. I listen to his words. He speaks of bin Laden, Israel, Jordan, Palestine; their relations, wars, and conflicts. I listen, nod, and shake my head. My feelings are jumbled. I am slightly apprehensive. Numb still and fatalistic. Yet I have a strong desire to communicate with him. Unexplainably, I feel excited. He doesn't seem threatening or like my enemy. But probably some of the hijackers didn't either, I think. *Take no chances, my husband had said.* How does he feel, other than distressed? Do I dare ask him?

"I have two sons. They are in Jordan with my wife, who is English," he offers, speaking intensely, in a quick cadence with few pauses. "She's there because she needed help from my parents with the children. But my family is too far away now. They are scared for me. Every day my wife calls and the first thing she says is, 'Are you safe?' They were supposed to come here next month. Now they won't. Too dangerous." I think of how frightened Art and I were to be apart during the attack. We too call every day now, many times, encouraging each other to *take no chances.* I feel a kindred spirit with this man's wife.

"In Jordan, my wife wears a *hijab*, the traditional headcovering. She asked me how she should dress and I told her. She put on the veil and asked me how I liked it. 'It is beautiful,' I said. Everyone wears it there," he explains, sounding apologetic, "even those who visit. She chooses to wear it." I cannot imagine experiencing the world in and through a veil. I wonder if this veil covers his wife's face as well as her head and neck.

"My sons ask me what it means to be a Muslim. They hear on TV that the terrorists were Muslim men. They know I am a Muslim man. They ask for explanations. How do I explain?" His question sounds rhetorical.

"What do you say?" I ask, interrupting.

"What?" he asks, turning again to look at me. He pauses. "I tell them these men are not Muslims like I am. It is not the same. But that is not enough."

Quickly he asserts, "Good Muslims don't go to stripper bars." I wait for him to say that good Muslims don't kill people, but he doesn't.

"Muslims died in the World Trade Center," he does say, "along with all the others. I've visited the World Trade Center with my brother, who is a general in the Jordanian army. It could have been my family on those planes."

"Have other Americans acted badly toward you?" I ask.

"No, no they haven't. My American friends, they have called and reassured me. They are worried. So are my Muslim friends. We met last night, all Muslims, and we talked and we cried. A woman from a church came to speak to us. She cried and we all cried. I cry a lot. I wear dark glasses," he says, turning around and taking them off, "because I never know when I will cry." His eyes are red and sad, very sad. "Can you imagine us all crying together?"

"Yes, yes I can. I cry a lot too. Your story makes me cry now," I say.

He turns again, looks at my wet eyes, and then continues talking. "I'm forty. I came to America because I wanted prosperity and security. I wanted to be safe."

"Like the rest of us," I say.

"To be safe, that is most important. The Americans, they argue over who should be president. But it doesn't matter if it is Bush or Gore, just that there should be someone and we should be safe.

"I watch the news a lot. I've lived with the idea of bin Laden for years," he continues. "I don't know how much Middle Eastern history you know, but . . ." Without waiting for an answer, the man launches into the history of Jordan-Israel relationships. I have trouble following, until, "My friends in Jordan, they hate Jews," he says. I cringe, thinking of my dark-complected Jewish husband and my own identification with Judaism. My husband had said that Jews in Israel were worried they would be blamed for this. Might there be violence against Jews here? Could my own bearded husband be mistaken for a Middle Eastern man?

Wondering the same, a few days later my husband will suggest shaving the beard he has had for more than a decade. I run my fingers lovingly through his soft salt-and-pepper facial hair and think that might be for the best. Take no chances.

"I lived with Jews in England," the man says, and I relax a bit. "I got along with them fine. If you treat them right, they'll treat you right. I dated a Jewish woman for three years. We would have married, but she said the children must be raised Jewish. I couldn't do that so we broke up."

"My husband is Jewish," I reveal hesitantly. He acknowledges what I say with a nod and continues talking about Middle Eastern history. I examine his demeanor, how he speaks, the emotion in his words, and wonder what living in America will be like for him now. I look closely. Did the terrorists look and act like him? What if he's a fake? What if he really hates all Americans? What if he means me harm? I shake my head. Don't let yourself even think that, I reprimand. What kind of world would it be if we let ourselves think like that? His pain seems authentic. Trust your feelings, I tell myself.

Take no chances, my husband had said.

"I love America," he suddenly says. "I'm loyal to this country."

"Are you worried about prejudice?" I ask.

"No, I'm not. When people yell slurs at me, I pretend I don't hear. I don't get upset."

"That's probably the best way to react," I say. What must it feel like to have experienced this as a tragedy and now to feel blamed for it? What about Muslims who lost loved ones? Is the feeling similar, on another level, to being considered a suspect by the police after your child is murdered?

I think of how African Americans often have had to pretend to ignore prejudice. Now American Blacks and Whites are on the same side of this crisis. No worry this week about young Black men and crime. No headlines or op-ed articles about "fixing" Black-White relations. The category "us" suddenly has gotten bigger and more diverse, but the line between this "us" and "them" feels ominous and sinister. Will Muslims take the place of African Americans in our class system? "They're not yelling at you, you know," I say in defense of "us" and to make him feel better. "They're yelling at a symbol." Does that make him feel better or worse?

"I know that. And I won't respond unless someone tries to do me harm, then I'll defend myself. But that's all.

"I love this country," he says again. "I pay my taxes because I am proud to be an American. I always make sure I pay them to the penny because, well, because I'm a stranger and that means they might look more closely at me and I never want them asking me for more."

"Do you understand the terrorists?" I ask.

"I understand them all right. They want everyone to look like them, to think like them, to act like them. And if you don't, they want to kill you. There are extremist groups in the United States too, you know."

"Certainly," I agree, a picture of White survivalists forming in my mind.

Blow 'um off the face of the earth, I hear in my head. *Take no chances.* We arrive at the airport three hours before my flight. The driver hurries around to open the door. "This is good, very light," he says, taking my small bag. "Now people won't rush to the airport at the last minute. This has been a wake-up call."

"Yes," I say, as he offers a hand. I check the meter and pay him: $29 for the fare and $3 for a tip.

When he reaches in his pocket for change, I put my hand on his arm, "No, it's for you." I wish then I had given him more.

"Thank you. I never forget tips that Americans give me."

"Good luck to you," I reply. "Let's hope for better times ahead." Sometimes clichés are the best we can do.

I face him and look directly into his eyes and he into mine. I push my laptop backpack that hangs off one shoulder toward my back. Without thinking, I put my arms around his neck. He gently places his hands around my waist, my head falls on his shoulder, his head bows over mine. We hold onto each other for several moments and we cry.

Take chances, I think as I pick up my suitcase and head into the airport.

Meta-Autoethnography: Framing and Sense Making in the Aftermath[4]

The tragic events on September 11, 2001, disrupted our lives and the frames we usually have for making sense of our experience. Bateson (1972) uses the concrete image of a picture frame to conceptualize what it means to frame our experiences. The frame directs us to focus on "what is within without attending to what is outside" (p. 187). Expanding on Bateson's use of framing, Erving Goffman (1974, p. 21) employs the term "frame analysis" to refer to the organization of experience. He suggests that people interpret what is going on around them by applying "primary frameworks," those frameworks whose validity is taken as given and whose usefulness as a frame does not depend on prior interpretation. Primary frameworks render "what would otherwise be a meaningless aspect of the scene into something that is meaningful." Karl Weick (1995) views framing as one plausible event in the act of sense making, which he defines as the attempt to structure the unknown (see also Waterman, 1990, p. 41) by placing stimuli into a frame of reference. To understand sense making, according to Louis (1980) and to Weick (1995), is to understand how people cope with interruption, a signal that something important has just occurred in the environment. Interruption to a seemingly continuous flow of experience typically induces an emotional experience, an arousal to which attention must be paid in order to figure out what to do (Weick, 1995, p. 45; see also Berscheid, 1983; Hochschild, 1983; Mandler, 1984).

As I reviewed my story after September 11th, I examined how I came to frame and make sense of the events as I did. On the plane, I quickly made the assumption that the announcement indicated this was *not* business as usual; yet I lacked a frame of precisely what was going on. This unfolding drama did not fit into my life story, or "life scheme," as Thompson and Janigian (1988) refer to the cognitive representation of self and worldview we construct to provide order and meaning to our lives. I was reluctant to believe that terrorism really had struck because it did not fit within my experience of life in America. Terrorism does not happen here. Moreover, terrorism seemed too horrible and terrifying to be real. Thus I questioned whether the information I had gotten was exaggerated, even wrong, and I kept waiting for an accounting of events that would fit coherently into my sense-making frames and answer the question: What story am I living in now?

The usual taken-for-granted activities of daily life no longer worked for me. We are accustomed in America to flying from one location to another. If an airline is unable to get you to your destination, normally airline staff take responsibility for providing alternatives, albeit not always convenient ones. This was not the case when I found myself alone in the Charlotte airport with no luggage and no information for how to get to my destination. At that point, it became imperative for me to quickly change my self story and the definition of the situation to one where I had to (and could) take charge of my own destiny. Taking charge also meant coming to grips with the idea that something horrible—terrorism—indeed had happened. Until that point, terrorism didn't have a definite meaning for me or more generally for Americans.

Once accepting the general framework of terrorism, how I perceived what had happened was influenced by other frames salient in my life at the time: first, my location during the event and, second, personal experiences of loss, both current and past. Examining these factors helped me to organize this chaotic experience in some intelligible way and better understand my response to the tragedy. Hopefully, my examination will encourage readers to think about what factors influenced their framing of these events.

Where people were located during the attacks impacted how events affected us. Friends in New York City and newspaper accounts (Archibald, 2001; Elias, 2001; Goode, 2001) said they and other New Yorkers experience this tragedy at a level we cannot begin to fathom, their senses pricked by the persisting smells, sights, inconveniences, and fear of further attacks. I know this drama only from TV and in my dreams, where I'm frequently wandering around lost on the streets of New York, as though the city is familiar yet not the same as I remember it. I am glad I am not living in or close to the scene of the crime, where "looming vulnerability," a sense that threatening events are "gathering momentum and moving to a crescendo," is even more palpable than in the rest of America (Riskind, 1999, p. 25).

Nevertheless, flying on a plane during the attacks made me feel as though I *were* a participant in the terrorist attacks. Part of this feeling came simply from the obvious commonality of being in the air that I shared with some of the direct victims of the attacks. The plane as a context offered a "finite province of meaning" (Berger & Luckmann, 1967), a frame I could not escape for a time—a trap and a barrier to finding out what was going on in the rest of the world. When I did find out, it was easy to think "that could have been me" and to identify with those who died in the crashing planes. That I was away from home and family, alone with strangers, added to the intensity of this experience. I was scared viscerally for my life that day and my partner Art momentarily felt immersed in a feeling of impending doom. At his dying mother's side when he saw the report of the crash at the Pentagon, he panicked when he realized I was in the air on my way to Dulles Airport and feared that I might die (Bochner, 2002). We both felt intimately involved in this experience; it was close to home, not "out there" happening to someone else.

Crashing airplanes, death, and grief were all too familiar to me on a personal level. From my brother's death in an airplane, I knew intimately the grief that family members felt. This intimate knowledge added to the vulnerability I felt upon hearing the serious

announcement on the airplane. Thus while I initially resisted the explanation of terrorism, it was not out of the realm of possibility that something horrible had happened
with airplanes. As vivid recollections of my brother's death flashed in my mind, I felt
compelled to act quickly to avert disaster.

In the aftermath of September 11th, I immersed myself in the personal stories of
victims and families, told and retold on TV, in magazines and newspapers. I felt deeply
for the agony of friends and family left behind. As I identified with their experience,
old questions resurfaced: How did my brother die? What did it feel like to be in a diving
plane? Did he die in pain? Was he aware he was dying? Was he frightened? I recalled how
much my family desired the return of my brother's body, though we didn't understand
why it had so much meaning for us. I recalled the hope we had that maybe he was one of
the survivors, the agony of waiting expectantly for good news, yet fearing the arrival of any
news at all. I reexperienced what it felt like to replay and replay what *might* have happened
instead of what *did* happen, waiting for a happy ending to emerge. And then, finally, to
cry because my life was forever diminished when that last shred of hope fell finally to the
floor. Every day still, I feel a permanent hole in my life and mourn the loss of my brother.

Along with these memories, my mother's and mother-in-law's deteriorating health
provided a powerful current context from which to view these events. To some extent,
at least initially, I used my personal crises to provide refuge from the larger world crisis. These crises distracted me with something else equally important, at least in my
personal world. My mother's illness particularly, along with Art's mother's impending
death, gave me other places to focus and, in comparison, seemed almost "normal": our
mothers are old; old people get sick and die. That's a difficult but not unexpected part
of life. By the end of the story, the world crisis—collective sorrow—seemed to provide
relief from thinking of the plight of my mother and mother-in-law. At the same time, all
of this together—both the world out there and the world in here, in chaos—placed a
burden on living and meaning that seemed nearly unbearable. This heavy load halted
any sense of continuity and control I thought I had. I tried to regain flow and order by
focusing on only one tragedy at a time. Becker (1998) says we try to capture continuity
in ordinary routines of daily life; I did this in caring for my mother though the care I was
giving her was by no means ordinary to me. I focused on the immediate, something
over which perhaps I could exert control. This focus helped me both to make my way to
Virginia and then to lose myself in the details of caring for my mother.

Two weeks after the terrorist attacks, Art's mother died and my mother became
completely bedridden. My world had never been turned upside down like this. Times
of deep personal loss had felt more focused and contained since I had still perceived
the world outside as ordered. On this occasion, I felt wrapped in the pain of the universe, one of many who were suffering and sharing collective grief. The wellspring of
emotions associated with unpredictability, fear, fragility, and looming vulnerability was
intensely a part of my daily life. My body and spirit cried out to get away from these

feelings—the feelings themselves scared me. Unharnessed, I feared they might ruin the life I had known. My initial impulse was to control or deny them so that my life might be shielded from disruption.

I tried not to succumb to what Lifton (1988) calls "psychic numbing," the diminished capacity or inclination to feel. I feared if I gave in to this feeling (or more aptly, the lack of feeling), I might find myself stuck in denial. While potentially adaptive in the short term, in the long term denial might lead to failure to integrate the experience of terrorism into my life scheme (Janoff-Bulman & Timko, 1987). I feared psychic numbing might deter the self- and other-soothing feelings in which I had been immersed since the attacks (Janoff-Bulman, 1992). I feared that psychic numbing might extend to other instances of collective and even personal suffering (Lifton, 1988). I feared giving in to numbing would pull me into silence.

I feared this numbing silence most—silent feelings, silent thoughts, silence in the night, silence of the moment before the bombs strike, silence of the acceptance afterwards of innocent lives lost, the silence of Art's mother who stopped speaking three weeks before death, the silence of my mother who refused to watch TV or talk about what happened.

Meta-Autoethnography: After Words—Feelings in the Aftermath[5]

In writing this story of September 11th, I sought solace and meaning in my attempts to make sense of and understand this crisis more deeply. It's not that I think personal understanding resolves emotional pain and collective trauma or that I can control what happens through understanding; but I do believe that engaging in the process of constructing deeper levels of ourselves and our community through autoethnographic writing can initiate the beginning of personal recovery and collective understanding. Storying one's experience offers the possibility of turning something chaotic into something intelligible and meaningful. Reexperiencing and reanalyzing events in our lives can help us transform our life schemes to incorporate the events that happen to us, as well as to transform the meaning the events hold for me (Thompson & Janigian, 1988).[6] As such, personal narrative offers a way to understand and begin healing ourselves and our nation.

As I wrote and relived, I pushed toward experiencing feelings as fully and as deeply as is necessary to write about them. I wanted to understand as much as I could about the personal and collective agony brought on by terrorism. When I felt deeply, I recognized that what was there was not all agony. Existing in juxtaposition to agony, enhanced by fear and vulnerability, was a sense of collective belonging. This belonging called me to care and love so deeply it hurt, to express it to those close to me, to reach out to help those in need no matter where they call home, to rethink who we are as Americans and who I am and want to be as an American citizen. If I closed down to intense painful arousal, I feared these intense positive feelings also might be squelched, and opportunities for positive social action might be lost.

The shifting feeling—from agony to belonging and caring—was intense and disconcerting, yet enlivening. Art and I held tightly to each other, humbled by looming vulnerability and the fear of losing each other. My family members were in touch frequently, and we expressed our feelings freely. I spent more quality time with friends. And, I also seemed to be taking time to talk—really talk—to the mailman, the carpenter, the person behind the counter in the grocery store, the van driver at Triangle Rent-A-Car, and the Muslim cabdriver I met on my way back to Tampa after the attacks.

Even while I tried to embrace the disruption brought on by the terrorist attacks, I also sought to get past it. I looked for narrative continuity and coherence, a way to connect to my past and link to a meaningful future where safety and collective hope would again figure prominently in our day-to-day lives (Crites, 1971). Ironically, the constant presence of the war on TV provided a sense of continuity to our lives much like a soap opera. We sought meaning in what happened today and added it to what we knew yesterday. Sometimes I had to remind myself that this was real life. Other times the TV plot became my life, and I had to work to think about something else and resist the canonical tellings on TV. Then I sought out the mundane pleasures of taking a walk, exercising, watching a movie, going shopping, or playing ball with my dogs—anything to normalize the life I lived.

My feelings of vulnerability have led to a new awareness of the despair felt by those in Eastern and Middle Eastern countries who live in fear (and poverty) every day of their lives. It has made me reassess what I take for granted and what I think my country takes for granted regarding its position relative to other countries. I have had to rethink the politics of revenge bombing; reassess discrimination and vow not to let it come into my life, even if it means taking chances in living; remember how fortunate I am to live in a country that values human dignity, freedom of speech and movement; and respect and appreciate those who serve our country.

As feelings pour through me, I wonder how they were similar to and different from those of readers and how they compared to the experiences of those in other countries who have felt vulnerable and frightened all their lives. I am astounded that I have never asked this question quite this way before. When I think this way, I see that, as Australian Karen Scott-Hoy (2002) reminded,

> Perhaps the world is not really such a different place, it has just become a less secure place for me, my family, and friends in the Western world. Perhaps I am just beginning to understand, to feel, to experience what millions of others in this world live with, and through everyday. Could it be that the world in which I felt so secure and safe was always an illusion? (pp. 273–275)

It is not just the illusion of a safe world that has been shattered by the attacks but the illusions that many Americans hold at the very core of our inner world as well: that the world in which we live is a meaningful and benevolent place where events that occur make sense and where people are basically good and kind (Janoff-Bulman & Frantz, 1996). Once these illusions are shattered it is hard to ever get them back fully; perhaps it should not be our goal to do so. Instead what we might get back is life that takes on new meaning when we come to understand and acknowledge the reality of terror, violence, and discrimination and the inevitable shortcomings of human existence (Janoff-Bulman & Frantz, 1996, p. 47). This vision will be hopeful rather than cynical. By opening myself to these thoughts and feelings, I feel transformed in a positive way. I face the terror in hopes that it will help me do my part in preventing this history from repeating itself, as Lifton (1986) points out about Nazi Germany and Hiroshima (Lifton, 1967). I face the terror in hopes that it will help me (and others) live more giving and rewarding lives. At the very least, I face the terror to find ways to talk about vulnerability in an unpredictable and dangerous world.

Story Interlude Two: Remembering: Ground Zero, New York City[7]

January 13, 2002. I fly to New York City to visit Ground Zero and see some friends, after which I will fly to Dulles Airport to visit my mother. Flying into Newark, I press my nose against the window, and strain, along with everyone else, to see. From the images on television, I know to look for a gaping hole, a crater. Though none is visible, still I peer. Then, I see something, or at least I see something not there. The skyscrapers are noticeably less crowded on the southern tip of Manhattan. I look as long as I can, twisting my head and neck when the plane changes direction. What there is to see is only what is absent.

The next day my friend Larry Russell and I go to the Empire State Building and strain again to see, along with the large group of people gathered eighty-six stories high on the south side promenade of the observatory. We try to find the spot where the Twin Towers used to be. "It's there. See the large flag on the tall building," says a man, pointing. Larry nods, but I cannot see the flag. All I can make out is what is not there: no Twin Towers loom above the buildings in the distance. Nothing. Zero. Ground Zero.

When I return to my hotel, I call my mother, because it is January 13, 2002, the twentieth anniversary of my brother's death. We talk about missing Rex and how swiftly the time has passed. Then we express our excitement at getting to see each other in two days.

The following day, another friend, Doug McAdam, and I make our way to the South Street Seaport booth to get tickets that will let us onto the newly constructed public viewing platform at Ground Zero. Our tickets admit us to Ground Zero at the next available time, 9:30 the following morning. We head over to the corner of Fulton and Church that evening anyway, since I will leave New York early the next day.

Approaching the corner, we first see St. Paul's Chapel, which miraculously still stands on the corner of Ground Zero, serving as a mission for relief workers. We are mesmerized by bright spotlights that shine down on the red, white, and blue canvases that cover the fence in front of St. Paul's Chapel and extend down the street. Banners and posters hang from the canvases, but it is the handwritten notes to which we are drawn. Written to relatives lost at Ground Zero, the messages express suffering, love, spirituality, and patriotism: "We miss you and vow to keep you alive in our hearts, your loving family." "God bless New York." "We love America." Tributes and letters of support are signed from people all over America and from other countries as well: "Keeping you in our hearts and prayers." "We could forgive but never forget." "We'll always love New York." I want to write something. I am a writer after all. I long to be part of this history in a visceral way. I don't write anything; I am wordless.

Doug stands for a long time in front of one letter. I stand back, perceiving his desire for privacy, then I approach and read beside him. In a childlike uphill script, the letter is written from a daughter to her missing father. "Dear Dad, This is your daughter writing . . ." I am surprised, and then I am not, when I hear sobs coming deep from within Doug's chest. I place my hands on his back and stand quietly. "I'm thinking how she must have felt to write that and what it would be like for my own ten-year-old daughter to compose such a letter," he says. Maybe I'd be more emotional if I had a child of my own, I think. Then I am reminded of my relationship with my bedridden mother and I feel something deep, but formless and unnamed, inhibited by the bright lights and color and hubbub of all the people, though they walk slowly and speak quietly. It feels as if fireworks could go off any minute.

The firemen's hard hats, police caps, and stuffed animals placed in front of the memorial canvases return me to the suffering I am witnessing and the pain I'm holding back. The layers of flowers, wreaths, burning candles, and incense make me feel I am in a sacred shrine. I think maybe I should pray, but I don't.

How much of these feelings do I bring with me from the images and messages I have gotten from the media? How much do I feel what I think I am supposed to feel? How much comes from the experience I am having here? My mixed feelings remind me of how I felt as a tourist hiking up the sacred rock of the Aborigines, Uluru, in Australia.

"I must see Ground Zero," I say to Doug, who holds up our useless tickets and shrugs. Doug stands back while I approach a group of policemen in front of a barricade. Because of September 11th, I feel more comfortable initiating contact. They are not just men and women in uniforms; they are real people who tried to save lives and lost friends and family. I tell them my dilemma and one man gives me tips on how to make sure we get to the viewing platform this evening. "Stand over here," he motions to the side, "and ask someone leaving the platform for their ticket. Or just get in line and they'll probably let you in since you have a ticket." I thank him. It feels okay that he told me what he did—I suspect he wants everyone who comes to be able to witness

Ground Zero. But it would feel like "cheating" to get a ticket already used by someone else, I decide quickly. I can't cheat in this sacred space. Instead, I ask the person in charge of admitting people if we can get in. "Go to the end of the line," he directs. "The only thing I'd ask is that if people come with tickets for an earlier time that you let them in front of you." I nod, and we walk to the back of the fifty people already waiting.

The line moves quickly and we continue reading the messages on the canvases as we move ahead. I feel part of a community, a community that extends beyond this line, a community of people who hurt and care. At the entrance to St. Paul's Chapel, I ready my camera to take a picture. A relief worker, identifiable by his hard hat, fatigues, goggles, and bright reflective vest, politely asks those of us with cameras not to take pictures of workers entering the chapel. He points to the sign that reads "No photographs at this point." "Respect the privacy of the workers," he says softly. "You can take pictures once you pass the entryway." Since I had snapped a photograph as he began speaking, I apologize profusely. Feeling I have violated a moral code, I hold my camera out toward him, willing to hand over my film if he asks. He nods and smiles at me, then reassures softly, "It's okay." I have the sensation of being a gawking tourist, made more manifest by the camera and ticket I hold in my hands. Why was it so important that I come? Is it okay to want to be here doing this?

"I'm glad there is no commercialism here," Doug says, as we note the absence of anyone selling trinkets to place on the canvas or products symbolizing September 11th.

"People seem so gentle, so sensitive," I say. This is not the New York we're used to, Doug and I agree. Nor the way I usually act in New York, I think, making eye contact with and approaching strangers.

As the sun sets behind Ground Zero, Doug and I take our turn marching solemnly side by side to the wooden platform. The feeling I get is how I've felt in the past approaching a casket of a dead friend or relative—suspended, apprehensive, curious, fearful, holding my breath, waiting for the ax to fall. When I finally look over the edge of the platform, I feel slightly disappointed that what I see looks like a huge excavation site. I look for signs of the disaster—fire, smoke, stretchers with remains, I don't know what else. Other than cranes, tractors, dump trucks, dirt, and what one would expect to see on any excavation site, all I can find is one large pile of scrap metal in the corner, a large hole in the middle of the site, and some bricks missing from the surrounding buildings. What I see is that there is nothing to see. Being here at Ground Zero, I realize, is not about seeing but about feeling and remembering.

In that context, I am disturbed when a man takes a picture of his girlfriend with the site as background. The amateur photographer makes sure his subject is in just the right spot; she pats her hair and adjusts her skirt, to make sure she looks her best. She smiles her practiced picture-taking smile. "What are they thinking?" I ask Doug, who is untroubled by the action. Then I snap my pictures. Is it okay as long as no human subject is featured? What if the destruction is many miles behind the human subject, invisible, such as in the pictures I took of Larry at the Empire State Building? Where is the boundary line? Finally the policeman directing the flow of visitors tells us to move to the side, where we can still see Ground Zero but will make room for others to enter the main viewing area. We are allowed to stay there as long as we want. When we finally leave, I hold tightly to Doug's hand, seeking closeness and refuge.

Waiting in line at Newark Airport for security check the next day, my thoughts are given over to my mother. What must it feel like to lie in bed with no possibility of ever walking again? What will it be like to see her? Will the disaster traces be more apparent in her body than at Ground Zero, the looming vulnerability more palpable?

No, I answer my own question as I stand in line to enter the plane. Because being with my mother now, just as being at Ground Zero, is not about "seeing" her. It is about the feelings and memories she and I share and it is about how I want to remember our time together after she's gone. Caring for my mother's body, loving and being loved by her, has become a sacred experience. September 11th has helped me be "with" her rather than being overcome with the pain of her anticipated absence. At least for now. But in recognizing my more settled and less vulnerable posture with my mother, I become aware of the risk that I'll forget what brought me to this place and these feelings.

As I find my seat on the plane and prepare for takeoff, my thoughts, as always, focus briefly on my brother's plane crashing on takeoff. The emotional power of that memory is less intense now than before when I used to live within the emotions of that event. Similarly, as time passes and life goes back to some version of "normal," the emotional grip of the terrorist attacks seems to be slipping further and further away. While we cannot continue living "in" the feelings generated that day, I believe we must continue being "with" September 11th. If we defend ourselves too strongly against the feelings generated by the attacks—the shock, grief, anger, and sorrow—then we stand to lose whatever lessons September 11th had to teach us: our inspiration to live better lives and make better connections to those in the rest of the world. We have to keep seeing linkages between how we live every day and what happened on September 11th, I remind myself. The question is, How do we continue being with these events, keeping alive their power to positively impact our lives? That's why I came to Ground Zero; that's why I must take care of my mother; that's why I have to tell these stories—to keep memory alive and make sure I don't forget.

"Ladies and gentlemen, we're on schedule for an on-time arrival at Dulles Airport," the captain interrupts the theoretical discussion in my head. "The skies are clear and it should be a smooth flight. But remember what we learned from September 11th. We are all responsible for safety and security. So introduce yourself to your neighbor. And if you see anything suspicious, please report it immediately to one of the flight attendants. Have an enjoyable flight and thank you for flying Continental."

Story Interlude Three: Remembering Lessons, December 2007

My mom died on September 9, 2002.[8] My sister and brother-in-law took care of her in her home during the last year of her life, I visited every six weeks and relieved my sister, and my brother and sister-in-law pitched in when needed. For days before her death, Mom had dreams, fantasies, hallucinations, and premonitions of the trip she was about to take. When she asked us to go with her, we told her we couldn't, but that we were sure Rex, Daddy, and Florence would be there waiting for her. That thought calmed her, since she had recurring visions of being with them already.

Our whole family was at her bedside when Mom died. The love and respect all around was palpable. I miss my mom enormously, but most of the time when I think of her— which is often—I feel warm and happy. My siblings and I continue to stay in touch, visit, and support each other. We remember the lessons our mom taught us.

But does our country remember the lessons it learned from September 11th? As I read and edit the story above, I feel sad and increased anger at our country's leaders, who started the revenge war in Iraq and led us away from the feelings of unity and mutual support that surrounded us in the aftermath of the terrorist attacks. Sometimes now I long for that time immediately after September 11th. Certainly I do not want to relive the destruction of that time, but I never want to stop taking chances or forget what it felt like when so many of us joined together as a caring and hopeful country after September 11, 2001. How could we forget the lessons that September 11th taught us? How could we lose hope, accepting our government's frame and narrative of the meaning of 9/11?

Meta-Autoethnography: Recovering Hope with Barack Obama[9]

I will end this war in Iraq. I will bring our troops home, but I will also end the mindset that got us into war. We have been engulfed by a politics of fear for too long, where 9/11 is used as a way to scare up votes instead of a way to bring us together around a common purpose to defeat a common enemy. . . . I've seen how the country's judgment has been clouded by fear and division, how we've been made to be afraid of each other, afraid of immigrants, afraid of gays, afraid of people who don't look like us. . . . I know how hard change is. But I also know this: that nothing worthwhile in this country has ever happened except somebody, somewhere was willing to hope. . . . That's what hope is: imagining and fighting for, working for what did not seem possible before. . . . This is our moment. This is our time. And you and I together, we will transform this country and we will transform this world.

Art and I listen to Senator Obama, tears rolling down our cheeks. We grasp hands and hammer out together, along with the crowd, "Yes, we can." We vow then to work to transform our country and our community. The audacity of hope (Obama, 2006).

CHAPTER TWELVE

Connecting Autoethnographic Performance
with Community Practice

Between 2000 and 2005, several graduate students and I worked collaboratively with CASA (Community Action Stops Abuse), a domestic abuse shelter. We wanted to do research that would be helpful to the organization and to our community in general. At CASA's request, Elizabeth Curry (2005) studied staff members and Deb Walker (2005) studied volunteers. In 2002, Elizabeth and Deb designed and published a booklet of stories they wrote about CASA (Curry & Walker, 2002). These were given to CASA to distribute among clients, workers, donors, and other social service agencies.

Once the research project was established, Penny Phillips, another graduate student, offered to give a performance about her own abuse that she had originally presented in a communication class at University of South Florida. Thinking this was a good way to show CASA staff members the kind of autoethnographic performance work done in the communication department at the university, I encouraged her to do so.[1] In the aftermath of September 11, 2001, I felt committed to showing how personal narrative and performance could be healing for communities.

In this chapter, I tell the story of taking Penny's autoethnographic performance to the community of CASA. The story demonstrates a situation where research objectives and community goals are not the same and, indeed, may be incompatible. Failing to understand the work the other is trying to do, researchers and community members speak past each other. It is only in listening and responding to each other that untangling of their positions takes place and appreciation begins.

This story is part of *The Ethnographic I*, which I published in 2004 as a methodological novel about doing autoethnography. Written in third person, this story differs from other stories of mine in that here I make myself an omniscient narrator. The different perspectives I offer come from transcripts of the researchers' discussions of what happened and transcripts of conversations the advocates at CASA had about the performance with graduate student researchers. I also include the written responses of the director of CASA to several versions of my story.

Speaking Against Domestic Abuse[2]

Carolyn turns the corner, looking again at the written directions. Ah, yes, here it is, she says to herself as she pulls into the residential facility of CASA for the first time. She has come to watch Penny's performance, which will be presented for CASA staff members. Though she has not thought much about this event and has not seen Penny for several months, she is excited to find out how CASA staff will respond. Following the confidential directions she was given, she rings the bell, identifies herself, and is buzzed through the door. Entering a large, cozy home, she is shown to the living room by a staff member. Comfortable, sagging couches line the outer perimeter.

"Penny," Carolyn greets with a hug, "how are you?"

Penny looks very thin and moves nervously, which Carolyn attributes to anxiety about the presentation. "I'm okay. My divorce was final yesterday. I can't believe I've now been divorced three times," she says.

Although Carolyn has known that Penny was having trouble in her marriage, the sudden announcement surprises her. What timing. Her body tensing, Carolyn admonishes herself for not checking in with Penny before today. Will Penny be okay doing this performance? Should Penny be engaged in something so emotional now?

"Are you okay?" Carolyn asks, placing her hand on Penny's shoulder to comfort and slow her down. "Are you sure you want to go through with this performance?"

"Yes, I'm fine," Penny responds, appreciating Carolyn's concern, though she feels it unwarranted. "I'm in a new relationship. And I've been looking forward to this presentation for a long time. It's very meaningful to me. I hope to do more presentations like these."

About a dozen staff members arrive from various locations around the house. Elizabeth is dismayed when she notices the advocates sitting on one side and the academics, including Deb and herself, sitting on the other. Not liking to speak in public, Deb's voice shakes as she introduces Penny. The advocates, who have not seen Deb be nervous, are immediately on alert, and wonder if the nervousness comes from the presence of Deb's professor. When Penny begins, Elizabeth wishes there had been more time for introductions; so does Carolyn. Carolyn feels a little awkward that they haven't had time to chat and get to know each other a bit. Later, they all will wish that they had spent more time informing advocates about the goals of the performance.

Elizabeth and Deb are seeing Penny's performance for the first time. Since they have worked at CASA for several months, they pay close attention to the advocates. Happily, they note that some of the women sit forward in their chairs, seemingly engaged by what Penny is saying. They see nods and hear grunts of recognition as Penny vividly describes her interaction with her former husband. Periodically, they interpret concern and confusion on the faces of the advocates. Deb and Elizabeth sense that some of the concern is triggered when Penny unknowingly pushes some of their "hot buttons." For example, Penny says that she and her abusive husband were like oil and water, which Deb and Elizabeth fear might sound as if she blames herself for the violence. As researchers, they're aware of Penny's academic purposes of uncovering and analyzing the complex intricacies of her relationship with her abusing husband; but they also identify with the advocates' belief that women are not to blame for domestic abuse. To some extent, Deb and Elizabeth have "gone native."

Though Carolyn senses tension and discomfort in the room, she feels the performance is going well. She rationalizes that these are normal reactions to a dramatic presentation about abuse. Besides, she is more focused on Penny than on the advocates because she wants to reassure herself that Penny is okay emotionally. Though a little rusty performatively, Penny seems fine.

The CASA advocates *are* feeling contradictory feelings. After all, they have been pulled away from their busy, understaffed work lives for this performance and given little explanation of what they have come to see. They are told that a person from the university will share her research. What they experience is Penny telling her personal story of domestic abuse. How is this research? For them, research involves experts who have interviewed or surveyed domestic abuse survivors and now have answers. Research involves analyzing materials, such as books or videos, and delving into the Internet or the library.

Is it research, questions Marti to herself in the middle of the performance, to just tell what's happened to you? What is the goal of this presentation anyway? To present research or to tell a personal story? Could Penny be doing this for a grade? After all, she is a student.

Frankly, thinks Donna, if I'd wanted to hear this, I could have stayed in my office and spent time with a resident who needed an ear.

How does this differ from training, where we listen to advocates' stories? wonders Jackie.

What makes Penny an authority who can speak this way about abuse? muses Kathy. Being a victim does not make someone an authority. I meet people in volunteer training all the time who think that because they're victims, they can fix everybody else.

Is this going to be presented to the public at large? questions Casey to herself.

Is this supposed to be entertainment? wonders Connie. If so, it's not the kind of entertainment I want to go to. We live this every day. It's almost as if Penny is giving us a theatrical performance more than a heartfelt one. Is she trying to work through her pain in a theatrical way? If so, I wish she had explained that.

Geez, I have work to do, Lani sighs, looking at her watch. She can't stop thinking about the intern she left alone to answer the phones while the rest of the staff is in this meeting.

Marti glances at Kathy, who reflects back the same confusion and contradiction she feels. Penny is a researcher, though apparently not a very good one. But Penny also is a victim, and when they think of her in that capacity, their hearts go out to her. How are they supposed to respond? Marti and Kathy sit quietly during the performance, yet try to demonstrate with body language their support and concern. The other advocates follow their lead.

Until, suddenly, Penny yells "Bitch, fucking bitch" to demonstrate how Don talked to her during an abusive episode. This makes all the advocates tense. They glance at each other, then at the door. What if residents hear her? What if one of the children walks in? What if the children are frightened by the cursing? CASA is supposed to be a safe space; abusive language is not allowed here.

Worries of this kind do not enter Carolyn's mind since she is unfamiliar with the norms and rules at CASA. Even Deb and Elizabeth don't pick up this violation, since no one thought it necessary to tell them that no loud, violent cursing is permitted at CASA. The academics are used to theatrical performances that use intense language to make a point.

Carolyn thinks that through vulnerably and dramatically telling her story, Penny is successfully bringing the audience into her experience, which is what autoethnographic performance is supposed to do. She wonders what stories this presentation will evoke from workers.

Penny finishes and the audience claps. She asks for questions. Hesitantly at first, advocates ask questions that have been on their minds during the performance. How does autoethnographic performance differ from training? What is the purpose of this presentation? How is this presentation a product of research? How does this differ from a resident telling her story?

Fascinated that they question the research value of this presentation in some of the same ways a mainstream academic audience would, Carolyn turns toward each speaker and takes it all in. Given the advocates' penchant for stories, she had thought they might share their experiences or talk about how Penny's experience dovetails—or doesn't—with the stories they hear from women or their own stories. That she was so wrong intrigues her more. She realizes that until now, CASA workers have been exposed only to traditional research. While social science research troubles them, they still operate from that definition of how research should be conducted. It's no wonder that they expected a traditional research presentation and that they have trouble seeing the research value of one researcher telling her personal story. Carolyn wishes now she had been more involved in organizing this event. Maybe she should have done the introduction and led the question and answer period. But then, given how naive she was about how CASA staff would react, would it have made any difference? Probably not.

To turn the conversation more toward content issues, Carolyn asks Penny to talk about how her research led her to look at relational dynamics. She knows this might be a hot button for the advocates, but she thinks that this is the value of the research they are doing together—to complexify how relationships are characterized so as to better understand how abuse happens. She wants to get all viewpoints on the table so they can learn from each other. Being a novice in researching abuse, she does not realize just how much even her question violates CASA's policies for helping women cope with abuse.

"I was hoping you wouldn't ask that," Penny says, aware now of how advocates will view her answer. Taking a deep breath, she continues hesitantly, "When I began this research, I saw myself as pure victim with no agency and Don as the evil victimizer. After examining our dynamics, I understood that I had a role in what happened. Now I am not blaming the victim here," she hurries to explain. "What Don did was wrong. But sometimes I contributed to setting up the situation. I knew when I was doing things that might lead to an abusive episode. Looking at our relationship this way helped me see I had agency. Just like writing this paper and doing this performance gives me agency.

"Don wasn't abusive with his second wife," she says. "She was a friend of mine, though we had contrasting personalities. She was laid-back. The relational dynamics with Don and me were different from theirs. Don and I were like oil and water."

That's the second time Penny used that phrase. Now the advocates are on alert. Something's not right. Telling her own story is one thing. But now some of what she's saying is dangerous for Penny—it's clear to them she's still tied to her abuser even twenty-five years later, and she thinks she's to blame for the abuse. CASA workers feel there's absolutely no justification for abuse. That's what they spend their time doing—convincing women they do not deserve to be abused. The advocates forget their questions about research and go into helping mode. That's what they're trained to do, and that seems to be what the situation in front of them calls for.

Carolyn listens intently. It's a matter of not understanding each other, she tells herself. The academic partners in this project will have to work harder to understand the CASA staff and to communicate their goals to the advocates. The two groups appear to come across to each other as simplistic: CASA sees academics as blaming the victim; academics see CASA workers as telling a nonrelational story of evil abuser controlling weak, pure woman.

To the advocates, Dr. Ellis seems more concerned about relational dynamics than about Penny's well-being. They can see it in her facial expression as she talks and in her body language as she nods toward Penny, encouraging her to continue. Can't she see that Penny is still suffering? That she blames herself? That she is not yet over the abuse?

"Don and I thought of writing this together," Penny says, unaware of the degree to which the advocates are concerned about her. "But, in the end, he decided not to participate."

That's no surprise, thinks Marti, making eye contact with Kathy.

She's not over him yet, several others think, glancing at each other.

"You still have feelings for him, don't you?" asks Donna, designating herself as spokesperson.

"Yes, I might even still love him," Penny admits.

"Would you go back to him?" Donna pushes.

"I don't know," says Penny. "But whether I did or not, I think it's important for me to forgive him for what happened. That's part of why I wrote the story."

"This is not about forgiving his actions," says Kathy. "His actions are unforgivable. You might forgive him as God's child, if you will. But it's unforgivable for somebody to hit you. It's more important for you to forgive yourself for having made the mistake of being with him." Kathy wishes she had said "for *thinking* you had made the mistake," but it's too late to rephrase.

"I've forgiven him for what happened," Penny says, determined to hold onto her story.

What the advocates hear is also dangerous for those who might hear Penny speak with authority. They recall that she wants to present her story to other groups. Yet, the story she tells violates what they do at CASA. Women come to them already feeling they are to blame for their abuse. They come thinking that if they give their abuser another chance, he will change. The advocates have to work through these issues with abused women. They tell them: You only have the power to change yourself. You do not deserve to be abused. You did not cause the abuse. Here are some options for you if you decide you want or need to live without the violence. You have choices even though they do not seem to be attractive at the moment.

"If women who were victims heard and identified with your story, they might feel guilty and take blame for the violence. Or they might return to a dangerous scene," says Kathy. "They might think, Oh, yes, I talked back and then he hit me. Or, If I had just shut up he wouldn't have hit me. Or, I hit him back. The truth is that nobody deserves to be hit no matter what they did."

"But I hit Don, too," says Penny.

"Everybody should be allowed to defend themselves," says Marti.

"Sometimes I hit first," Penny counters. "The relational aspects were important. He wasn't abusive with his second wife," she repeats.

Unknowingly, Penny has dropped several bombs on the advocates. They are taught to listen for statements, such as: I really love him. . . . I hit back. . . . He's not abusive with everyone.

"How do you know he wasn't abusive with his second wife?" asks Marti. "Did you talk to her about it? Did you tell her about your abuse?"

"No I didn't." Penny wonders why the advocates are putting her on the defensive like this. "But I know Don has changed," she continues. "We write letters now, and he tells me how much he misses and loved his second wife. He even sent me a letter she wrote to him before she died. In it, she expressed how much she loved him and what a good marriage they had." Penny feels she has made her point well.

"The letters he's writing you are part of the control and abuse," accuses Kathy. "Sending those letters is the most abusive thing he could do."

Surprised at the response, Penny retorts, "You're acting like my counselors now. I don't need counseling. I've had counseling. This all happened twenty-five years ago. You're responding as though it's happening now."

"We're concerned about you," says Marti. Kathy nods in agreement.

"But you're discounting my story and my feelings," says Penny. "This is my story. This is the way I experienced it."

"We're not discounting your story," says Kathy. "We know your story. We listen to stories every day. We know everybody has a different story, but we've heard yours many times before."

"It feels like you're discounting my story, saying it couldn't be the way I'm telling it because it doesn't match the story you expect or want to hear," Penny says angrily. Her accusation makes several of the advocates feel more defensive. Listening to stories is what they do for a living. They feel their professionalism and their values are being challenged.

"We're not challenging your story," says Marti. "We're challenging how you interpret it."

Carolyn wonders where a story stops and interpretation begins since all stories involve layers of interpretation. She also thinks about how interpretation is contingent on the interpreter's worldview. She doesn't say anything.

The advocates think that if Penny were just a researcher, she wouldn't be feeling this so deeply and being so defensive. She also is a victim, they remind themselves. They want to convey to Penny that they're with her, that they believe her, that she is not at fault for what happened to her. They want to protect and help, yet they realize they've upset Penny and that they're not giving her what she came to get. They can't. They wish they were speaking to her one-on-one. The exchanges they're having are not appropriate for a group context.

Penny seems alternately close to tears and on the verge of anger.

Elizabeth and Deb wish Penny would tone down and finish quickly. Then they feel guilty for having those feelings.

Carolyn is concerned now about Penny, but she doesn't know what to do. Things seem to have spiraled out of control. She wants to rescue Penny, but she doesn't know how or even if it is her place to rescue. She agrees with Penny that the advocates are discounting her story. Penny doesn't seem to be telling the "right" story. Did I push too hard? Carolyn wonders. Maybe I shouldn't have brought up the relational issue. But relational dynamics make up the crux of Penny's interpretation of the meanings she has grasped from her interpersonal courses and through writing as inquiry.

Maybe Penny's autoethnographic performance worked too well, Carolyn thinks. Just look at what Penny's story evoked in the advocates. They are so convinced she is the person she presents in the performance that they go into their helping roles on the spot. They believe her performance, though not her interpretation of it.

Could the advocates be right about Penny? Might she, Carolyn, be wrong? Perhaps Penny hasn't coped with what happened yet. What if she didn't become a survivor through writing personal narrative? Worse, what if writing the story has made her less able to cope?[3] Have I been so committed to the good autoethnography can do that I couldn't see what was happening? She considers these thoughts, then dismisses them. She's seen the positive benefits for Penny in writing her story—the increased self-confidence, introspection, and understanding of relational dynamics, domestic violence, and herself. Still, Penny is vulnerable now, given her divorce. What if doing this presentation, being in this situation, is dangerous for her? What if she is in no emotional state to be going through this kind of questioning, given her divorce? Oh my god, what if I've done her harm by not being watchful or caring enough?

The scheduled twenty-minute session continues for ninety minutes, before it is halted so the advocates can return to work. Immediately after the session is over, several advocates rush to talk to Penny, to assure her of their concern. Though upset, Penny likes the attention and their empathy.

Elizabeth hands out colored glass hearts she has wrapped for everyone, and says they represent the respect we all feel for the advocates' heartfelt work and the heartfelt relationships we hope to develop in this project. Pleased to be given a gift, the advocates immediately exchange them so that each person gets her desired color.

Carolyn approaches Marti, who was very outspoken, and thanks her for her participation. She tries to assure her that these kinds of discussions are difficult. She says, "Personal narrative evokes lots of contradictory emotions and perspectives. It helps to get differences out on the table."

Marti wonders why Dr. Ellis is thanking her for something she feels so awful about. She wonders if Dr. Ellis hasn't set up Penny. What does she mean—this is the way it's supposed to happen? We're all supposed to feel this bad, and Penny is supposed to be so vulnerable?

The advocates ask Elizabeth to come smoke a cigarette with them on the patio, their code for "we need to process." Feeling protective of the advocates, Elizabeth is glad for the invitation. They voice their concerns, and Elizabeth tries to respond. She feels like the interpreter between two worlds. She explains that Dr. Ellis really likes for people to open up edgy controversial issues and say what's on their minds and in their hearts. She is glad when the advocates connect that to the importance of their own learning to assert themselves. She tries to explain the purpose of Penny's performance. She wants to talk to everyone at once. She wants them to see what she sees: Because of time constraints, they had to stop the discussion before it was finished and all of this needs to be processed further.

Deb feels very confused and hurries around to talk to everyone. She wants to do damage control, to make sure the advocates aren't offended, that Penny isn't uncomfortable, that Carolyn is approving. She regrets that she didn't do more preparation with the CASA staff and she wishes she had said more in the introduction about what this project was about. There never seems to be enough time.

Deb, Elizabeth, Penny, and Carolyn postpone leaving. When advocates show them around the house, they stop in the hallway to talk, then on the stairs, then on the walkway to their cars. They all see what Elizabeth sees—that time ran out before they could process sufficiently what had happened.

Penny leaves, worried she has upset the advocates or ruined Carolyn's opportunity to do research at CASA. She feels her story has been invalidated. She wonders how she could have entered the room feeling strong and together, in spite of her divorce, and now leave feeling as if the advocates saw her as weak and vulnerable. Maybe she'd better rethink her desire to do more presentations. She also feels concern and caring from the advocates. And she feels strangely exhilarated. How will this experience affect the story she constructs for herself about her past, for now, and in the future?

Carolyn leaves feeling confused about why the presentation hadn't gone better. She, too, feels strangely exhilarated about what she might learn from this experience. She always likes it when other people's worlds open up to her. She vows to devote more time to this project and to keep in touch with Penny to make sure she is okay. She trusts Penny has the defenses necessary to protect herself.

After this experience, the advocates call each other. They meet as a group and talk about what happened. Elizabeth meets with them, and they process what they are feeling. The executive director meets with them for a debriefing. Elizabeth and one of the advocates calls Penny. Carolyn meets with Elizabeth, Deb, Penny, Donileen Loseke, who is another researcher, and Linda Osmundson—the executive director—to talk about the reactions to Penny's performance. Carolyn and Penny e-mail and talk. Deb and Elizabeth have lively discussions. Sometime later, Carolyn speaks informally with two of the advocates about how they felt at Penny's performance. The volunteer coordinator uses the session as a training session on victim blaming. "In telling her own story, one of the advocates at Penny's session acknowledged that she had a part in her own abuse," the volunteer coordinator says. "Now she might have been trying to identify with Penny and make her feel better. But it doesn't matter. We don't do that when we advocate—tell our stories to them as a way of relating to them, especially when our stories sound like we're blaming the victim. If an advocate sees herself as having a part in her own abuse, then she might also see a victim as having a part in her domestic violence. That's not what we teach."

Later Carolyn tries to unravel what has gone on. To do so, she recalls the story she has lived through and the emotions that were stirred; she tries to be open to questioning her premises about what happened; she listens to her colleague Donileen Loseke, who had studied battered women; and she goes back to the literature on gender and domestic abuse. Doni argues that CASA workers present a "formula" story of abuse.[4] This story includes the pure female victim who is not responsible for the abuse, and the evil abusive man who creates a dangerous violent situation in his attempt to control the battered woman. These are set identities with few, if any, relational considerations. Many abused women embrace the formula story CASA offers them. The popularity of this story encourages the public to treat domestic abuse against women seriously and to contribute financially and socially to the "creation of shelters, special counseling techniques, and special laws and court procedures" (Loseke, 2001, p. 121). Since it encourages women to leave dangerous relationships, it saves countless lives (Riessman, 1990). This formula works for the women most in need, and it helps women to heal and reconstruct their lives.

But this formula story sometimes conflicts with the messiness of lived experience of day-to-day troubles (Loseke, 2001, p. 110). Few abusers are pure evil; situations are sometimes ambiguous; battered women are not always or solely victims, nor do they always want to be portrayed as weak, passive, and out of control (Lempert, 1996). Sometimes leaving an abusive partner feels impossible because of economic, family, or personal circumstances. Perhaps we need new social narratives for relationships, narratives that challenge both the Prince Charming story and the dark diabolic one, the two relationship narratives available for women (Wood, 2001).

Carolyn wonders, what happens on a long-term basis to women who have repudiated their partners as evil? Do they ever get back together? Should they? And if they do, can they ever combat the notion of evil that led them to leave in the first place? What about children who get caught in the relational wars?

What happens to women who do not accept the formula story? Are there advantages to considering different kinds of relational stories, as Carolyn had hoped? Might more women be reached if the messiness of their relationship is acknowledged? Might there be interpretations, other than blaming the victim, for statements women make about loving the abuser, participating in mutual violence, or recognizing aspects of themselves and the relationships that are conducive to abuse? Might there be something beneficial in thinking about how abuse occurs and the agency of both partners?[5] About abuse as a relational pattern that requires both partners to play their parts? Or will opening up the categories simply lead to more confusion and fewer women being helped? Carolyn doesn't know.

She does know that the advocates have a point when they say that the canonical story they hear in CASA already is a relational one. The primary gender story culturally available to women normalizes superiority, aggression, and dominance of men, and casts women as dependent, deferent, forgiving, and loyal to their men, needing men to complete their lives (Wood, 2001, p. 243; Goldner et al., 1990). Most people outside shelters—those abused, the abusers, and the public—already believe the relational dynamics story—that the victim plays a part, that she in some way caused the abuse, that she is at least partially to blame because she did not live out her "proper" relational role (Wood, 2001, p. 244). So the public responds: If the relationship is so bad, why didn't she leave? If her male partner is so evil, how can she love him? Why did she go back? Why didn't she . . . ? CASA feels it is ultra-important to get across to women and to the public that these women did not do anything to deserve abuse. No one deserves to be beaten. Women's lives depend on this message.

"Does the simple formula story threaten to become ingrained in the workers as *the* story?" Carolyn asks. She thinks it does. It's the one they hear most often. But, she argues to herself, stories told by victims in shelters are unwittingly scripted through questions asked, rephrasing of stories, ignoring and dramatizing of particular aspects (Loseke, 2001). No wonder workers think this is *the* story. What would happen if this formula story and its counterpart—the canonical romance narrative—both lost their hold, making way for other stories that take into account the messiness of relational life as lived?

Meta-Autoethnography: CASA Speaks Back[6]

"It's not as if the advocates don't understand the complexities and nuances," Linda, the executive director of CASA, responds, after reading this story. "They probably understand them better than academics do. After all, they hear these stories all day and many have lived through these experiences themselves. We live with the women in the shelter and are quite aware they are not without fault. We simply believe that no matter their faults, they do not deserve to live in terror and violence. When women come to us, we reinforce how much strength and courage they have demonstrated by surviving and by coming to stay with us. We know some women continue to love the abuser, and we acknowledge and support these feelings in all of us. The reality is complex. We deal with that daily as we work with these women.

"We try very hard not to talk about the abuser as 'evil' because we know there is a good chance that a woman will go back to him. We have to give her a way to save face and leave the door open to her coming back to us. In my opinion, once trust is broken by the violence, even if they get back together, the relationship will rarely, if ever, be healthy or satisfying for her. She may never really trust him again.

"We think a lot about how abuse occurs. For many women, it is predictable and we can help them with safety planning. While occasionally there is mutual violence, women nearly always get the worst of it. We see this as a systematic pattern of control. We do not see this as a play with parts. One partner is in control, while the other, who is trying to survive, has little control.

"We use the formula story when we are presenting in sound bites, when talking to a reporter, or giving a fifteen-minute presentation to the Elks Club where they want a simple message," says Linda. "Advocates get only a few minutes in court with victims, so the story they tell also better be a simple one that achieves its purpose—to save the woman and get support for shelters that can rescue women."

Carolyn is convinced the CASA formula story is useful, humane, and therapeutic. How then, she wonders, do we put together an academic perspective that thrives on complexity with a practical approach that requires a direct, understandable message that gets the job done?

Maybe complexity isn't always the best approach, Carolyn thinks. There are times when autoethnographic inquiry may not be institutionally productive. With trepidation, she questions a premise she holds dear. She wonders if CASA workers can or will question theirs. Given the lives at stake, she is not even sure she would advocate they should raise questions. Not without doing much more fieldwork.

Linda responds that they question their theories all the time. After reading the revised version of this chapter, she replies, "I think it is fascinating. Your account elicits much more now." She gives the story to a few of her workers and sends a response from one of them back to Carolyn:

> I think it really is on target. The reaction was as interesting as the performance. I have been thinking for some time now about our "rubber stamp" approach and think so much more is needed. I also think this plays a part in the morale of shelter staff and their burn-out, and low effectiveness. . . . The movement itself is locked into a prescribed mind-set . . . one developed that funders will understand.

With this response, Carolyn feels she, as an academic, and they, as practitioners, now can talk *with* rather than *at* each other. There is much to learn.

Meta-Autoethnography: What About Penny?

How has this experience affected Penny? Did this performance to this audience set Penny back or open up new insights? Was autoethnographic inquiry productive and healing for her? Is it always beneficial to open up conversations with autoethnographic performance?

When she asks Penny these questions, Penny responds, "CASA made me question what I had believed about my situation. I did get a little crazy after my husband left, and I started thinking that maybe Don and I could get back together. That's why the advocates' response got to me.

"I also started thinking about whether my story might be hurtful to someone. I'd never considered that. When I described my part in the abuse, I saw myself as taking agency. I wasn't going to take what Don dished out anymore. But I can see how my story might lead to other women blaming themselves. I don't have all this resolved."

"It may be unresolvable," Carolyn says. "Though certainly we want our autoethnographies to help, not hurt people."

"Autoethnography has helped me," Penny says. "I worked through many emotions and questions I had about Don. But I did become very self-centered and so absorbed in my research that I'm not sure I was always sensitive to other people in my life."

"Like when?"

"I never thought about the ramifications of getting in touch with my ex-husband, for example, what it might do to him. Nor did I see the pain my husband was going through at the time, his downward spiral."

"Do you think he left because of your research?"

"Oh, no. There were other issues. He didn't pay that much attention to my research really."

"Are you sorry you got involved in autoethnography?"

"Oh, no. I wouldn't have given up my experience in autoethnography for anything. I mean for anything."

With this response, Carolyn is somewhat reassured. But she vows to redouble her efforts to consider the ramifications of autoethnography for all those involved. Are there people who shouldn't do autoethnography? And, what does it mean to do auto-ethnography ethically?

PART FIVE

Reconsidering Writing Practices, Relational Ethics, and Rural Communities

CHAPTER THIRTEEN

Writing Revision and Researching Ethically

Writing Revision

In this book, I have presented previously published stories and then reexamined and re-visioned them in meta-autoethnographies that connect the stories to my life now. I have cut and excerpted some of the original accounts and made minor revisions for the purpose of writing more clearly and succinctly. But I have sought to maintain the original meanings as well as the ways I thought and the style in which I wrote at the time I published each story. For example, in the chapter "Renegotiating *Final Negotiations*," I kept the word "subjects" when referring to those in my research study, where now I would substitute "participants." In "Talking Across Fences," I kept the discussion that shows my "othering" my Black boyfriend as exotic, though I add a note that acknowledges that I am aware of my practice.

Meta-autoethnographies consist primarily of current reflections, narrative vignettes, story interludes, and analyses in numerous forms: dialogue with friends and family; reactions from critics, reconsiderations of my positions, and talking back to critics; responses from participants and dialogues with them about the stories; scenic short stories; portrayals of classrooms, where students react to my stories and tell stories of their own; internal dialogues that I have with my own thoughts; e-mail exchanges; plays and scripts; artistic works; narrative essays; and analytic essays.

Each meta-autoethnography reflects back on the original representation and updates an interpretation and/or story. These meta-autoethnographies sometimes alter the way I framed the original story, ask questions I didn't ask then, consider others' responses to the original story, and include vignettes of related experiences that have happened since I experienced and wrote the story, all contributing to how I view and interpret the story now. My goal is to turn my stories, snapshots of a particular time in my life, into videos or "texts in motion" (Davies & Davies, 2007), where I tack back and forth between "now" and "then."

The overall plot in this book, which holds these original and updated scenes in place for the moment, is a two-fold story about my life and work. The first plot concentrates on the living of life. This storyline starts with my childhood in a small town and focuses first on family loss and then on communication breakdowns. In the concluding chapter that follows this one, I will end with a description of spending summers now in a small moun-tain community in which Art and I have built a second home, thus circling back to life in a small, rural community. The second plot describes my education and work career. I move from a small town to college and then graduate school, my work shifting from sociologi-cal and ethnographic studies of isolated rural communities to autoethnographic writing about personal and collective loss and communication. In the concluding chapter, I will end with an ethnography of a rural community and focus on ethical and value conflicts, thus circling back to issues in doing ethnographies of intimate and familiar others. These two plots twist and turn, join and fold back on one another like a Möbius strip until they ultimately become inseparable parts of the life I live and the work I do.

Most of the primary stories in this book are previously published stories and analyses. But Chapters 1 ("Goin' to the Store, Sittin' on the Street, and Runnin' the Roads") and 14 ("Returning Home and Revisioning My Story") are new, unpublished stories that I composed specifically for this book. In these two bookends, the meta-autoethnographies discuss the writing and revision of the stories in process. In Chapter 1, for example, I detail how I moved from writing about episodes of trauma to writing about the more mundane aspects of daily life; in Chapter 14, I showcase the process of thinking through the ethical issues of writing about familiar others.

In most of the chapters, I seek to take readers into the immediacy of particular scenes, dramatic action, vivid conversations, and forward-moving plots, which is my usual way of writing. Only two chapters diverge substantially from this style: in Chapter 1 I call on my sense memory to write about my childhood, and I try to bring forth the pace and rhythm of my everyday world in a tale that is often ethereal, general, and slow moving, rather than episodic, particular, and dramatic; Chapter 5, "Renegotiating *Final Nego-tiations*," features a more traditionally written scholarly essay that argues theoretically rather than shows narratively the place of introspection in research.

With the exception of "Maternal Connections" (pp. 166–169) which is a standalone narrative, the previously published stories also include traditional social and theoretical analysis, though they differ as to the degree and depth of analysis. At one end of the con-tinuum, "I Hate My Voice" (pp. 233–249) features conceptual development and views conceptual understanding on the same plane as narrative understanding; at the other end of the continuum, "Speaking of Dying" (pp. 250–256) includes only a short com-mentary without reference to other scholarly works.

Three of the original stories are multivoiced and experimental in form: "Telling and Performing Personal Stories" (pp. 197–212) is a two-person, two-voiced script; "With Mother/With Child" (pp. 169–187) is a multivoiced story where I—the author and a main character—speak and reflect from two points in time; a third, "Speaking Against Domestic Abuse" (pp. 288–297), is an omniscient narrative, written from transcripts and notes of meetings where this event was discussed. These narrative elements also appear briefly in sections in other chapters; for example, "Moving Together" (pp. 111–113) is a script and "Meta-Autoethnography: Thinking Ethically" (pp. 340–350) is a two-voiced discussion, where I am represented as two voices arguing with each other about doing ethical research. Additionally, I include in "Meta-Autoethnography: Mnemosyne" (pp. 224–226) an exchange with the artist about her painting that is used on the cover of this book.

Meta-autoethnographic reflections that complexify or raise questions about events and issues in the original or follow-up stories or analyses often occur as short vignettes or story interludes. For example, in "Talking Across Fences: Race Matters" (Chapter 2) I bring readers into a story about race relations in my Tampa neighborhood in 2007 to reopen racial matters that seemingly have been put to rest in the original story. In "Renegotiating *Final Negotiations*" (Chapter 5) I bring readers into the aftermath of a conference presentation in which my reaction raises questions about the long-term resolution of my grief over losing my partner Gene. Sometimes I include portions of other published stories as "story interludes" because they add to the complexity of understanding. For example, "Take No Chances" (pp. 273–277), the story about a Muslim cab driver, reflects on racial profiling in my experiences of September 11, 2001.

Meta-autoethnographic reflections often allow me to question my previous analyses. For example, in "Rereading 'There Are Survivors'" (Chapter 7) I query my perceptions of my mother at Rex's death. In "Breaking Our Silences/Speaking with Others" (Chapter 10) I reflect on my argument about the impermeability of the boundaries between the world of the living and the world of the dying, worlds between which I seem to move more often and more easily now that I am older.

Often meta-autoethnographic reflections occur as introspective pieces about how I feel and think now many years after having written the original stories. For example, in the four chapters in Part 3, "Surviving and Communicating Family Loss," I analyze my feelings about long-term loss as I reflect on losing my brother twenty-five years before. Likewise, I revisit my relationship with my mother, and this introspective discussion leads to the stories that follow, which reveal the deep and positive relationship she and I developed later in life.

I use different locales and forms for responding meta-autoethnographically. Often I have dialogues at home with Art, such as the conversation about having children, or with other friends, such as the discussion I have in a car with my friend Marilyn about the politics of abortion. Calling to mind the graduate class context in which *The Ethnographic I* was staged, several scenes take place in an undergraduate classroom, for example, the discussion with students of the stories about my mother. Occasionally, I return to the scene of the original story and have follow-up discussions there, such as with the clerk in the New York store, where I first encountered the idea of minor bodily stigma. Sometimes a scene occurs in unexpected places, such as the recent conference panel where I talked about my long-term grief from losing Gene, and in an airplane landing in D.C. where I found myself reenacting my brother's death.

Meta-autoethnographic insight sometimes come from e-mail exchanges, for example, the discussion I have with a friend about Art and me becoming guardians of her two children if she and her partner died. Understanding develops in dreams, for example, in the dream about being in the shower that began this book, those I had after Rex died, the one I had about race, and the dream about memory that will end this book. Even Barack Obama's speech on recovering hope provides insight and inspiration.

Some meta-autoethnographies are well-developed and continuous stories, such as my long-term introspection about Rex's death. Others are short, less well-connected fragments, such as the episodic portrayal of my thoughts on abortion. These forms reflect the experience: my feelings about abortion fluctuate wildly, depending on episodic turns in my life; my grief over losing Rex tends to be more constant and continuous and I immerse myself in exploring deeply and thoroughly how I (and others) feel and cope on a long-term basis. In some chapters, meta-autoethnographic analyses compose a small part of the story, often because analysis has played a central role in the original chapter. In others, such as the chapters on family loss, meta-autoethnographic responses take center stage, reflecting my life and work commitments at this point in my writing.

In addition to my stories, introspections, and analyses, others' responses to my work also carry the previously published stories forward. These responses may come from published reactions to particular stories I have written, such as the reprinted articles by Art Bochner and Sherryl Kleinman in "Rereading 'There Are Survivors'" (Chapter 7); they may be shorter published critiques to autoethnography in general, such as those mentioned in "Doing Autoethnography as a Social Project" (Part 4). Sometimes these responses are informal, such as the reactions from my undergraduate students in "Re-Membering Mother" (Chapter 8). Occasionally I ask for responses from people who were characters in my original stories, such as the letter from Grady, who reads my story about the relationship he and I had as teenagers forty years prior, or the written response from the director of CASA, a community agency dealing with abuse.

I have shared my writing with many of the characters in my stories and I have given them a chance to speak back: for example, with Sheree and Nancy, the parents of the two children for whom Art and I have volunteered to be guardians; my friend Marilyn, who reveals her own abortion in our discussion of a Planned Parenthood meeting; Art, my partner, who is implicated in many of the stories I write; my mother; and numerous students and colleagues. But where do I stop? Should I return now to every living character in any story I have told no matter when I told it or what has happened since? What is the ethical position to take?

Researching Ethically

From the beginning story about my childhood to *Fisher Folk* and through *Final Negotiations*; to the stories about my brother, my mother, and the pregnancy termination; to communication breakdowns with my dying friend, in minor bodily stigma, September 11th, and, finally, the story of CASA, I have had to think about the ethics of writing about other people's lives, my own experiences, and the communities in which I've worked and lived. If autoethnographic stories are to be an effective practice for learning and teaching about the intimacies of social relationships and family life and for effecting social understanding and change, we as researchers must act in ethical ways and tell our stories in an ethical manner. In writing this book, I have had to reconsider and re-vision again and again how I do research and writing and how I instruct others to do and write autoethnography.

"I Just Want to Tell *My* Story": Mentoring Students About Relational Ethics in Writing About Intimate Others[1]

"I just want to tell *my* story about taking care of Mom and Dad during their last days. Why do I have to get consent from others to do that?" a new student, Jackie,[2] asks, near tears. "My parents are dead, so they can't respond. My siblings can tell their own stories, if they want. We hardly talk about what happened. They're mad at me for taking control and I'm mad at them for not helping enough."

"When you write your story," I say, "by definition you also will be writing others' stories, including those of your siblings.

"You didn't act in isolation. One of the main tensions you experienced as your parents were dying was your disagreement with your sister over whether or not to consent to certain medical procedures. It's not possible to leave others out of the story. When we write autoethnographically about our lives, by definition we also write about intimate others with whom we are in relationships. Don't we have responsibilities toward them?"

"How do I decide to whom I have responsibilities and what all they entail?" the student inquires. "And what if those I ask don't like the way I've written the story? Does that mean I can't publish it? That doesn't seem fair. What should I do?"

This vignette brings to the forefront some of the ethical issues that arise when we include our lives in our research and writing. Most of these issues are not acknowledged by institutional review boards (IRBs), which ground their guidelines on the premise that research is being done on strangers with whom we have no prior relationships and plan no future interaction. This is not the case in autoethnography—where we include others who already are in our lives—and usually not the case in ethnography—where we often have prior connections with participants or develop relationships with them in the course of our research. In these instances, the question of how to honor and respect our relationships with intimate others while being faithful to what we perceive to be the truth of our story is a difficult ethical issue with which researchers must grapple.

These ethical issues are complex and no simple mandate or universal principle applies to all cases. Authors' stories about how they decided what was ethical to write about others demonstrate that many researchers thoughtfully consider their options when confronted with issues of relational ethics (see, for example, Adams, 2006; Carter, 2002; Ellingson, 2005; Ellis, 1995b, 2001, 2004, 2007; Ellis et al., 2007; Etherington, 2005, 2007; Foster, 2007; Goodall, 2006; Jago, 2002; Kiesinger, 2002; Marzano, 2007; Medford, 2006; Perry, 2001; Poulos, 2008a; Rambo, 2005; Richardson, 2007; Smith-Sullivan, 2008). Responses to these concerns include: not publishing the story, delaying publication until after the death of a person, publishing under a pseudonym, fictionalizing the story, using pseudonyms or no names for participants, deciding to publish without seeking approval from participants, seeking approval after the fact, working out with participants the story to be told and sometimes omitting or changing identifying details and problematic passages, adding multiple voices and interpretations, and seeking and successfully obtaining consent from those involved.

The ethical decisions are difficult and the choices many. Yet, similar to the speaker in my opening vignette, students who write personal narrative want to know, "How do I decide? What should I do?" In this section, I seek to address these questions by examining the discussions I have with students in mentoring sessions and classes when we talk about researching and writing about intimate others.

Relational Ethics

Relational ethics requires us as researchers to act from our hearts and minds, to acknowledge our interpersonal bonds to others, and to initiate and maintain conversations (Bergum, 1998; Slattery & Rapp, 2003). The concept of relational ethics is closely related to an ethics of care (Gilligan, 1982; Noddings, 1984), communication ethics (Arnett, 2002), feminist and feminist communitarian ethics (see Christians, 2000; Denzin, 1997, 2003; Dougherty & Atkinson, 2006; Olesen, 2000; Punch, 1994).

Slattery and Rapp (2003), after Martin Buber, describe relational ethics as doing what is necessary to be "true to one's character and responsible for one's actions and their consequences on others" (p. 55). Relational ethics recognizes and values mutual respect, dignity, and connectedness between researcher and researched, and between researchers and the communities in which they live and work (Lincoln, 1995, p. 287; see also Brooks, 2006; Reason, 1993; Tierney, 1993). Central to relational ethics is the question "What should I do now?" rather than the statement "This is what you should do now" (Bergum, 1998).

Relational ethics draws attention to how our relationships with our research participants can change over time. If our participants become our friends, what are our ethical responsibilities toward them? What are our ethical responsibilities toward intimate others who are implicated in the stories we write about ourselves? How can we act in a humane, nonexploitative way while being mindful of our role as researchers? (Guillemin & Gillam, 2004, p. 264).

Howard Brody (1987) contrasts relational ethics to decisional ethics in patient care. Ethical decision making in an intensive care unit, he says, falls under the purview of decisional ethics, since it occurs between people without a prior history, who must carry out "discrete and generally predictable actions" over a limited time, and who most likely will have no future interactions. In contrast, in a primary care physician's office, the parties involved plan to engage in a long-term relationship, their future actions and relationship are somewhat vague, and the maintenance of that relationship might be more important than particular behaviors (Brody, 1987, p. 172). Thus, in the decisional situation, the question addressed is likely to be: "Should I disclose this particular piece of information to this patient at this time?" The relational situation produces a series of relational questions, such as: "What can I assume this patient already knows, judging from past discussions? On the basis of those same past discussions, what can I assume he wants to know? What should I say now? How will I judge how what I have said has affected the patient? What will be my next opportunity to add to or modify what I will say, in light of that reaction?" (pp. 172–173)

A similar set of issues emerges in research situations when our participants are people we already know or people with whom we develop close relationships. What can I assume is appropriate for me to tell about my relationship with a participant in my study and/or a person in my story? How will this person feel about what I have said? Must I get this person's consent to write my story? What if this person doesn't like or agree with the way I portray what happened? Given our relationship, what are my responsibilities to my participants? How will what I write affect our relationship? Our success as researchers often depends on how deeply we think about and how well we address these questions.

Even after many years of field research, autoethnographic writing, teaching, and directing student research, these kinds of ethical questions continue to swirl around me like a sandstorm. Just when I think I have a handle on a guiding principle about research with intimate others, a student presents a new project and my understanding unfurls into the intricacies, yes-ands, uniqueness, and ethical quandaries of the particular case under question. Each choice has consequences, but choose we must. What, then, do I tell students to help them move on and avoid sinking into the quicksand of indecision?

What Do I Tell My Students?

First, I tell students that my experiences writing ethnography and autoethnography have taught me that I have to live the experience of doing research with intimate others, think it through, improvise, write and rewrite, anticipate and feel its consequences. There is no one set of rules to follow. As Arthur Frank (2004) says,

> We do not act on principles that hold for all times. We act as best we can at a particular time, guided by certain stories that speak to that time, and other people's dialogical affirmation that we have chosen the right stories. . . . The best any of us can do is to tell one another our stories of how we have made choices and set priorities. By

remaining open to other people's responses to our moral maturity and emotional honesty . . . we engage in the unfinalized dialogue of seeking the good. [pp. 191–192]

I tell my students to seek the good.

I tell them that "[t]he wisest know that the best they can do . . . is not good enough. The not so wise, in their accustomed manner, choose to believe there is no problem and that they have solved it" (Malcolm, 1990, p. 162). I tell them to be wise and self-critical but not cynical.

I tell them to pay attention to IRB guidelines, then warn that their ethical work is not done with the granting of IRB approval. I tell them no matter how strictly they follow procedural guidelines, relational situations will come up in the field and in interviews that will make their heads spin and their hearts ache. I tell them they should make ethical decisions in research the way they make them in their personal lives. Then I caution them to question more and engage in more role taking than they normally do because of the authorial and privileged role that being a researcher gives them.

I tell them to ask questions and talk about their research with others, constantly reflecting critically on ethical practices at every step (Guillemin & Gillam, 2004; see also, Canella & Lincoln, 2004; Ellingson, 2009; Mason, 1996). I tell them relationships may change in the course of research—that they may become friends with those in their studies—and to be aware that ethical considerations may change as well. Ethnographic and autoethnographic research is emergent.

I tell them that often relationships grow deeper over time, but sometimes they don't; and even when they do get consent from those in their study, they should be prepared for new complexities along the way. I tell them to practice "process consent," checking at each stage to make sure participants still want to be part of their projects (Etherington, 2005; Grafanaki, 1996). I tell them that people change their minds, back out, don't want to talk to you or participate in your studies anymore. I tell them that sometimes along the way their research projects will change in character and that what they have told participants may no longer apply.

"Then what?" they ask.

"Then you have to make sure your participants still want to be in your research," I say.

"But what if they don't? What happens then?"

"You need to have back-up plans," I tell them. "If you can't make what you're doing make sense to those in your studies, maybe you ought to reconsider what you're doing." The students doodle on the blank pages in front of them. This is all too complicated.

"Perhaps including multiple voices and multiple interpretations in your studies will help," I tell them, offering a ray of hope.

My strategy works; their faces brighten. Then I caution them not to ask too much of participants who may get little out of being part of their study.

I tell them to think of the greater good of their research—does it justify the potential risk to others? Then I warn that they should be cautious that their definition of "greater good" isn't one created exclusively for *their* own good.

I tell them to think about ethical considerations before writing, but not to censor anything in the first draft in order to get the story as nuanced and truthful as possible. "Write for yourself," I say. Then, I warn, "Later, you must deal with the ethics of what to tell. Don't worry. We'll figure out how to write ethically. There are strategies to try. You might omit things, use pseudonyms or composite characters, alter the plot or scene, position your story within the stories of others, occasionally decide to write fiction."

I tell my students they should inform people they write about and get their consent. "People in our lives deserve their privacy," I say. "Because of their relationships to us, they often are identifiable in our stories."

"My brother abused me," says one student. "I wouldn't be comfortable asking for his consent. But I still want to write this story."

"Isn't your brother's side of the story relevant?"

"I'm sure it is, but not for my purposes," she says. "I need to write this story for me so that I can move on in my life, not work out with him what happened. That's another project."

Situations like these make me modify what I think. I don't think a focus on consent should stand in the way of a student doing a project that might help her heal and get on with life. I tell her we'll consider how to handle the ethics later, if she should decide to publish this story.

I tell them that, whenever possible, they should take their work back to participants. "Write as if your participants will be in your audience," I say. "Don't hide behind our esoteric journals, thinking, 'Oh, they'll never see it there'" (Medford, 2006). I tell them how a former professor took my book about the Fisher Folk into the community and read passages I wrote about how the people smelled like fish, had promiscuous sex, and couldn't read (Ellis, 1986). "Because many were illiterate, I had thought they would never see what I had written," I admit.

Then I tell the students that a similar thing occurred when I wrote about racism in my hometown (Ellis, 1995c). "What happened?" they ask.

I tell them how a colleague in Tampa, an African American woman, moved to my hometown, a thousand miles away, and shared the story I had written with the parents of my best friend from high school. "I never thought anybody there would find out about the story."

"Oh my," their raised eyebrows and tense postures convey. "Don't you know publications are public? Why would you ever think that way?"

Why indeed? I contemplate, hoping that my mistakes prod students to think more deeply about their research. "It's not that in hindsight I wouldn't have said any of these things or written these pieces," I tell them, "but I would have looked deeper and considered more fully what needed to be said, who needed to hear it, who might want to speak back, how I was implicated, and how best to explain others' lives given the cultural context in which the events occurred" (Ellis, 1995b).

These experiences guide my response to a student studying mental health teams that care for at-risk children and their parents (Davis, 2005). Cris writes in an e-mail, "I plan to publish my dissertation, and while I can pretty well presume that the mother won't be reading academic texts, what if she does? I offered to everyone on the team that they could read it, and she was the only one who didn't express an interest. What if she had? Should I have given her an edited version? How ethical is that? When I interviewed her, I never let on that I thought she and her home were 'dirty,' so how surprised would she be to find out what I really thought? Should I have been more candid? Would that have been more or less ethical?" (Christine Davis, personal e-mail correspondence).

To Cris, I respond, "People never get over being called dirty. Rewrite the offending passages—try to show the dust and clutter without saying *they*'re dirty. Concentrate on what in your life makes you so bothered by her living conditions and leads you to construct her as dirty. That will take away a little of the sting if she ever reads your dissertation. Assume everyone in your story *will* read it."

"We have to take responsibility for our own perceptions," I tell students, when I relay this experience.

"What does it mean to inform anyway?" I suddenly ask. The students stare at me blankly, as though the answer is obvious. Before they can respond, I tell them about omitting some of the passages that I thought might be hurtful when I read a story to my mother that I had written about her. They say nothing, but their eyes are wide with surprise. "Haven't you learned anything?" the expressions of some of the more critical students seem to ask.

"What was more important?" I ask. "That I could tell my colleagues I read every word to my mother, or that I protect the loving relationship she and I had and try to ensure my words caused her no pain?" When I put it that way, an entirely different answer seems obvious. They nod in understanding.

"What if those we write about give us their consent but don't fully comprehend what it means to be written about?" I ask then. "Though my mother gave me consent to publish the story I had written about her and I let her read the text before I published it, I'm not certain that she understood everything in the story, especially the details that indicated she was working class with little education."

"So was it right to publish this story then?" one asks.

I tell them, "With each story I read her, each caregiving experience we had, my relationship with my mother grew deeper, more open, and more caring. As our feelings grew in the context of caregiving, we openly shared more of our selves with each other and this enabled me to feel more confident in my decisions about what was appropriate to tell. In this context, it felt right to reveal our life together even though my mother was not aware of every word I wrote nor every nuance in what it meant to be a main character in my tale" (see Ellis, 2001, p. 615). The students smile.

(At this moment, my decisive declarative sentences signal me to question if I'm really so sure. I resist the impulse to raise further questions out loud. It feels good to have a resolution and to feel I did the right thing.)

"What if those we write about give us their consent, but then are uncomfortable with what we write?" Robin asks, complexifying ethical considerations even further. Robin is writing her dissertation, *Southern Black Women: Their Lived Realities* (Boylorn, 2008), about her hometown, a small Black and rural community in North Carolina, and the everyday lives of women there, including family members. In the middle of writing her first draft, she sends me an e-mail about how she feels unable to write: "Something has paralyzed me. Is it fear? This story scares me at the same time that it excites me. I am not afraid of the story, but rather I am afraid about how the story will impact the participants, my family. I plan to share drafts with them, but what if they are hurt? Will they tell me? I read the first lines of the story to my mother over the phone and she listened, quietly. When an extended pause marked the end, I asked for her reaction. 'Well . . . that was how it was,' was all she said. I didn't know if that was a positive or negative reaction, but it paralyzed me."

"Another time my mother said that my writing made her 'look so bad,'" Robin tells me when we discuss this in my office.

I tell Robin, "No wonder you are paralyzed."

Robin tells me she wants to show her grandmother, another primary character in her text, what she is writing. I tell her that it might be too early in the process. "Wait until you have edited and revised, and are sure that this is material you want to include and the way you want to tell it."

"But I don't want to organize the whole manuscript around these scenes and then find out that my grandmother is hurt by them and doesn't want them included."

I tell her that I see her point. Robin and I have numerous meetings about these issues. I tell her that I think that for now she has to write her stories before we can figure it out. "Anything can be changed; the story can be re-plotted later."

"But wait a minute," a student objects, upon hearing what we have decided. "That's a lot of work to throw down the drain. What about your mother? Can't you just ask her?"

"I did," Robin says, "and she said I overreacted to what she said. That I should write whatever I need to write."

"Then it's okay," the students say.

"She wants her daughter to get her Ph.D.," I say. "That's what matters most to Robin's mother. Given that, perhaps she feels she has little choice about approving what Robin writes."

"I think you're trying too hard to psychoanalyze Robin's mother," a student accuses. "You can't know what she really thinks. People don't always say what they really feel. We can't be responsible for that. She approved it. That's all that matters."

"Is it?" I ask. "We try to make sure that strangers can refuse to be in our studies. Isn't that important for our loved ones as well?"

"Much more important," says Robin. "But if they feel obligations to us, if they feel they have to do these things so that we can succeed, then how should we respond? It's especially difficult if they don't tell you they're feeling that way. I've tried to convey my project to my family as honestly as I can. But it's not in my best interest to try to convince them not to give consent. I will struggle with this dilemma until this project is done, and likely years after it is published" (Robin Boylorn, personal e-mail correspondence).

"Even if we assume that Robin's mother approves, doesn't Robin owe something to the larger community of southern Black women?" I ask the students. "Shouldn't she think about whether what she says might reify negative stereotypes and hurt the very people she's trying to give voice? Shouldn't relational ethics be informed by a social justice agenda?" (Buzzanell, 2004; Dougherty & Atkinson, 2006).

"It depends on who we write for and for what purpose," a student responds. The rest sit quietly.

Situations like these make me modify what I say. Now I tell students that taking our projects back to those we write about is a complex undertaking and has to be handled with care. The student who tells the story about being abused by her brother writes a publishable paper at the end of the semester, but she feels that publishing this story will cause unraveling of a family system that is, after many long years, finally intact. (A few years later, she and her brother will become even closer and he will offer financial assistance so that she has more free time to pursue her Ph.D. I am glad now she never showed him what she wrote or published it.)

"If you decide not to inform, get consent, or take your work back to those you write about and you want to publish it, you should be able to defend your reasons for not seeking responses of those in your study." I tell them that sometimes giving our work to participants could damage the very people and relationships we're intent on helping (see also, Kiesinger, 2002). In rare cases taking projects back to those we write about might even be irresponsible. Sometimes getting consent and informing intimate others would put students in harm's way, such as from an abusive partner or parent (Carter, 2002; Geist & Miller, 1998; Rambo, 2005).

"Then shouldn't we wait to write about people until after they die? Then they won't see it or be hurt. And then they can't hurt us," says one student.

I tell them that writing about people who have died will not solve their ethical dilemmas about what to tell and sometimes the dilemmas will become more poignant. I tell them that dead people can't give them permission, approve what they say, or offer their accounts, that they will feel a tension between their implicit trust provisions (Freadman, 2004, p. 143) with those who have died and telling what is necessary for their own healing, construction of self, and offers of comfort to readers. "Besides, others in your life will still care and you'll have to deal with them," I warn.

They ask how I feel about having written about both the good and bad times in my relationship with my former partner Gene. I tell them that in writing *Final Negotiations* (Ellis, 1995a) I tried to balance my portrayal of Gene between what I needed to tell for my own healing and growth and my attachment to the narratively truthful account I felt I owed my readers (see Ellis, 2007a,b).

"But wasn't that really your story to tell?" a student asks, growing tired of the ethical complexities. "We just want to write our own stories," she tells me, defiantly, speaking now for the class. I repeat that self-revelations always involve revelations about others (Freadman, 2004, p. 128). I tell the students they don't own their stories. That their story is also other people's stories. I tell them they don't have an inalienable right to tell the stories of others. Intimate, identifiable others deserve at least as much consideration as strangers and probably more. "Doing research with them will confront you with the most complicated ethical issues of your research lives."

This issue hits home when I write about my own childhood, a topic that I have not written about before. The vivid and detailed experiences that come to mind involve family secrets. I write them and then put the pages in a drawer. At the end of a year, I get them out, read and work on them some more, and then decide not to publish them. I question whether they represent my childhood, whether this is the picture I want others to have of my family, whether it is right to freeze my parents in this frame when their lives and my relationship with them were always in motion, whether I need to tell these stories, whether these events compose the story I want to remember. Then I ask myself: "On the one hand, do I owe it to myself to tell this story so that I might learn as much about my life as possible? Do I owe it to students who I have encouraged to write what is hard for them? Do I owe it to the advancement of autoethnography itself? On the other hand, hasn't the writing itself—without publication—done its work?"

"Won't sharing with others do more, for you and certainly for readers?" the first hand argues back. "You've said as much in other publications, such as about your and Art's performance of abortion (1992). How can you ask others to write these stories if you don't?"

Instead of publishing these stories, I write stories about my everyday life as a child. I tell myself that these vignettes better represent my experiences growing up though they are not nearly as dramatic and engaging as the other stories I wrote. Focusing on these experiences helps me remember and frame my childhood as happy and contented, rather than traumatic. Sometimes I think we can let go of the trauma without writing about it, by just going on and getting caught up in living.[3] In this way, now, I write myself as a survivor. It is a different approach from the way I have announced and written through my trauma in the past. I am happy with the result—at least for now.[4] I do not know if it is the best thing to have done, but it is ethically safe, which feels important. I write an article about why I do not publish the traumatic stories. At the end, I claim the right to change my mind about this at a later time (Ellis, 2006).

"Sometimes we might need to write but not publish the stories of our lives," I tell my students, who then want to know how they will ever get academic positions if they don't have publications.

"And how will we know," they ask, "when to publish and when to hold back?"

I tell my students I have no magical formulas, but I do know they have to live in the world of those they write about, just as I have to live in the world of my siblings who might be upset about my revealing family secrets. I tell my students they have to live in the world of those they write for and to. I tell them they must be careful how they present themselves. "If you write about eating disorders, then also write about other less sensational topics," I tell students seeking academic positions. "If you write autoethnography, also write something more traditional. Make good decisions for yourself. Keep your options open."

I suggest to Barbara, a former student, that she might not want to write about her depression and suicide attempt while taking sick leave and trying to earn tenure. She does, saying that she has to write herself out of her depression (Jago, 2002). She gets a teaching award the next year, publishes more autoethnography, and earns tenure.

(Maybe I'm too cautious sometimes. But I feel I owe it to my students to be cautious for them; at the same time, I try to take on the risks myself. I understand the damage that can be done to young careers when those in positions of power deride or fear autoethnography. I want to protect students until they are settled in careers; then I hope they will share the risks for those following behind them.)

I tell students that our studies should lead to positive change and make the world a better place. "Strive to leave the communities, participants, and yourselves better off at the end of the research than they were at the beginning," I say. "In the best of all worlds, all of those involved in our studies will feel better. But sometimes they won't; you won't." I tell them that most important to me is that they not negatively affect their lives and relationships, hurt themselves, or hurt others in their world. I tell them to hold relational concerns as high as research. "When possible, research from an ethic of care. That's the best we can do."

"But what about those who kept secrets from me, who hurt me?" they ask, and I reply, "Write to understand how they put their worlds together, how you can be a survivor of the world they thrust upon you. How you can find meaning in the chaos." Sometimes I say, "I don't know."

Lately I've been wondering—but haven't dared say so—whether autoethnographers consider others too much as we write. Perhaps sometimes there might be value in throwing a temper tantrum and "writing mean" (Hoagland, 2003, p. 13)[5] at least during initial story drafts when we are trying to re-create ourselves as "survivors" of whatever happened to us. As autoethnographic writers, we tend to cleanse our stories. We want to be likable, sympathetic, and fair-minded narrators. But some topics—racism, sexism, violence, incest, homophobia, abuse—are not nice topics and writing mean might reveal important truths that help us find meaning in our experience. As Anne Lamott says, "If my family didn't want me to write about them, they should've behaved better"

(Douglas Flemons, personal communication). I have come to believe that the well-being of the researcher is not always less important than the well-being of the other, especially others who have behaved badly.

I worry that students will dredge up situations through writing that are too difficult for them to handle. I warn that they are not therapists so they should seek assistance from professionals and mentors when they have problems. I tell them I am not a therapist, but that I will be there for them. (Sometimes I fear I—or worse, autoethnography—will be blamed if their lives go awry.) I seek to make my relationship with my students similar to what I want their relationship to be with those they study—one of raising difficult questions and then offering care and support when answers come from deep within. I tell them we will take each project on a case-by-case basis, and I promise to be available to discuss conflicts each step of the way. I tell them that every case has to be considered "in context and with respect to the rights, wishes, and feelings of those involved" (Freadman, 2004, p. 124).

I tell them that not only are there ethical questions about doing autoethnography, but that autoethnography itself is an ethical practice. In life, we often have to make choices in difficult, ambiguous, and uncertain circumstances. At these times, we feel the tug of obligation and responsibility. That's what we end up writing about. Autoethnographies show people in the process of figuring out what to do, how to live, and what their struggles mean (Bochner & Ellis, 2006, p. 111).

I tell them that there is a caregiving function to autoethnography (Bochner & Ellis, 2006). Listening to and engaging in others' stories is a gift and sometimes the best thing we can do for those in distress (see Greenspan, 1998). Telling our stories is a gift; our stories potentially offer readers companionship when they desperately need it (Mairs, 1993). Writing difficult stories is a gift to ourselves, a reflexive attempt to construct meaning in our lives and heal or grow from our pain.

I tell them I believe that most people want to do the right thing, the sensible thing. As human beings, we long to live meaningful lives that seek the good. As friends, we long to have trusting relationships that care for others. As researchers, we long to do ethical research that makes a difference. To come close to these goals, we constantly have to consider which questions to ask, which secrets to keep, and which truths are worth telling.

That's what I tell them. Then I listen carefully to what they say back about their ongoing experiences, feelings, and thoughts. Working from specific cases to guiding principles and then back again, over and over—that's the process we use for deciding what we should do.

What Do I Tell Myself? An Accidental Ethnography[6]

As I look back over this book and the stories I tell, I continue to be intrigued by the ethical issues in ethnographic and autoethnographic writing and research. The next chapter tells an ethnographic story about the small rural community in which Art and I have built a summer home. I have written and rewritten this chapter now for two years, continually feeling that I have painted myself into a corner and am unable to get out. But now the paint has dried and I have to decide which route I'm taking out.

This chapter wasn't supposed to be so important; it wasn't supposed to be an ethnography—just a few vignettes about small-town life now that would connect me back to the community and values of my youth and complete the narrative circle. This story wasn't supposed to be about "them"; instead it was supposed to focus on me in the context of this community. But in the writing process, this chapter became so much more than I had envisioned. It became a return to my hometown community in ways I had not foreseen happening, a return in which I experienced in surround sound at top volume tensions similar to those I had experienced in Luray. These included coping with value conflicts inherent in my love for my loving and caring family and community in which the injustices of racism, homophobia, and sexism were prevalent.

This story became an accidental ethnography, a return to my study of Fishneck, where I had experienced ethical conflicts about the story I had written and the way I had gone about it. Unlike the story about Fishneck, this time I would reflect, revise, and question my actions before publishing my story. Unlike the story about Fishneck, this time I fully recognized that I was writing their story to understand myself better. But like the story about Fishneck, this time I also would feel pulled by the competing demands to tell a story of conflicts and difference that I and readers could learn from and a story of sameness, empathy, and identification with community members whom I consider to be friends. Like the story of Fishneck, I would continue feeling suffocated by the ethical implications of what I owe characters in my story and how to tell it ethically. Issues I hoped I had resolved after writing about the fishing communities seemed just as complex now as ever. I discovered anew that it is easier to talk abstractly about ethics than it is to put an ethical stance into practice; it's easier doing a "mea culpa" about what I should have done in former studies than doing "right" in the one I'm currently working on; it's easier to instruct others who must make ethical decisions in their research than to follow my own advice. I'm not sure I'm any clearer now than before; I still don't have "the answers." But I take some solace in believing that continuing to ask and reflect on ethical questions is more important than coming up with answers (see Wolf, 1992, p. 5; also, Ellingson, 2009, p. 36; Fine et al., 2000).

CHAPTER FOURTEEN

Returning Home and Revisioning My Story

It was, all sensibly, as if the clear matter being still there, even as a shining expanse of snow spread over a plain, my exploring tread, for application to it, had quite unlearned the old pace and found itself naturally falling into another, which might sometimes indeed more or less agree with the original tracks, but might most often, or very nearly, break the surface in other places. —Henry James, *The Golden Bowl*

The sun shines brightly on the poplar, maple, oak, pine, and sourwood trees that surround our summer home in the southeastern United States.[1] Our log cabin sits on the ridge of Hollow Mountain, thirty-five hundred feet above sea level. Looking out the window of my study, I note how fresh and "attended to" the mountainside looks. I feel a sense of physical accomplishment as I recall swinging the long shaft of my Shindaiwa weed eater back and forth over the tall Kentucky 31 Fescue grass on the hillside. It is a feeling I don't get back at my home in Tampa, where Art and I pay hired workers to do much of our yard work.

For a moment, I glance back at my computer. It's time to write. Still, I take a few more minutes to admire the ridge upon ridge of blue mountains in the Nandina Range that rise in the distance, just south of the taller and craggier Lofty Mountains. I breathe in the fresh smell and soft feel of mountain air that whiffs in through the open windows. There's something spiritual about mountains, I think, as I contemplate the souls of dead family members in the mountain peaks and low cumulus clouds. Is this why I'm always pulled back to mountains? Do I hope to reconnect with family and with my roots here?

Art's two-fingered, rapid typing in the loft next to my second-floor study enters my consciousness. It's ironic that both of us, longtime upper-middle-class professors, are writing stories about growing up in working-class families (Bochner, forthcoming). It's hard to escape those roots entirely no matter how much education you have or how successful you become. Some resist their roots, some embrace them. Most, like me, do both and maintain the ambiguous stance of the border crosser (Law, 1995, p. 6).

I sit up tall to relieve the strain on my neck and back, readying myself to compose and type this final chapter. It seems appropriate to write this book here, in a small-town, southern community in the mountains. With this book, I have revised and re-visioned my life and work, and now find myself circling back to where I began.

A Small-Town Community

Forsythia County is relatively homogeneous, made up primarily of white, southern Baptists and other evangelical Protestant religions.[2] In 2005–2006, approximately thirty-two thousand people lived in the county, with thirty-five hundred residing in Mapleton, the county seat. Approximately ninety-six percent of residents in the county are White, non-Hispanic. Blacks make up about one and a half percent, persons of Hispanic or Latino origin are just over two percent, and American Indian and Asian people compose less than one-half percent each. Most voted for George W. Bush in 2000 and 2004 and consider themselves conservative Republicans who support the war in Iraq and favor an aggressive unilateral foreign policy to maintain the United States' role as the world's superpower.[3] Sometimes we can go for weeks without seeing a person of color. When we do, they most often are construction workers from Mexico, whom the locals refer to as "the Mexicans."

In 2003–2004, Art and I built a log cabin on a mountain ridge about nine miles outside of the town of Mapleton. The eleven families who live on our mile-long dirt road are primarily Florida transplanted retirees. Two families are local; they, plus three of the transplanted families, are full-time residents; the rest of us are vacationers and "summer people" (West, 2000). All our neighbors are White. With the exception of two schoolteachers, the transplants have conservative and traditionally religious values, though they are not as conservative or as religious as the locals. Art and I are among the youngest people on the road and, along with the local folks, are among the few people still employed. Because Floridians know so little about how to survive in the mountains when they arrive, the locals refer to some of us as "Floridiots," though they don't say that to our faces (see West, 2000).

The people in our small community take care of our road, share a well, and have a strong sense of community support and mutuality. The professorial skills that Art and I bring aren't too practical in terms of surviving in the mountains. We've learned to depend on the locals and our neighbors, who have electrical and other handyman skills. Little by little, Art and I have learned the ways of the mountain and how to get by.

Interspersed among "the summer people," the locals have lived here all their lives, and most of them grew up on this mountain. We're good friends with several families, especially with George and Louise and with Sarah Mae and Bobby and their extended kin, friends, and some of the members of their churches. Church and family are the center of this southern, rural community and locals often invite us to church. Though we don't go, we do sometimes attend family and church-related events.

Once you're friends with the locals, they will do anything for you—that is, if you're White and assumed to be Christian (or at least not anti-Christian), heterosexual, and non–drug using. It helps if you don't drink alcohol, don't make too much of global warming, and don't point out when people are being environmentally incorrect. You also best keep quiet about Hillary Clinton, abortion, and sex education, the last a topic that regularly is denounced in local newspapers. Smoking or chewing tobacco, owning and shooting a gun, hunting, canning, and gardening mark you as acceptable. The locals often do work for us and frequently have gotten us out of trouble—when we've been stranded in snow, discovered what we thought was a poisonous snake in our yard, lost power, or needed the name of a reliable person to call for house and car repairs. In return, we pay promptly and rarely complain about the quality or price of the work, are responsible and friendly neighbors, and support the local economy and volunteer associations.

In town are some organic farmers, people who love nature and have moved in during the last twenty years. Many of them go to the Unitarian church and participate in the local, organic tailgate market, which we go to most Saturday mornings for local produce and home-baked and canned goods. We are friends with a gay couple who live on a road near us. They don't advertise that they are gay, but when they ride together on their four-wheeler, one man's arms tight around the other, the locals know. They call the man on the back "the wife." These two men recently opened a restaurant together in town. Though some don't like gay people owning local businesses and frown on the first open bar in town, lines form outside the restaurant every night and every Sunday afternoon after church well before the restaurant opens for business. Those who won't go to this restaurant because it has a bar are losing the battle to those who want liquor available.

Just twenty minutes away is Severn, a small university town and the site of a university with a population of ten thousand students, mostly local. We go to a restaurant in Severn for brunch every Sunday. Since the local newsstand is closed on Sunday, we always hope to get one of the ten or so copies of the *New York Times* delivered to the area, available in a nearby grocery store. Sometimes when we arrive, the papers are sold out and other times they haven't yet arrived. Those mornings we read the free weekly *Forsythia County News*. Occasionally we've gotten the *Times* through the mail, but then we have to wait until Monday afternoon for the Sunday paper and we don't get to read it at Sunday brunch. We often see gays and lesbians in Severn—almost all White—but they don't seem to venture too often to the Mapleton side of the mountain. Hikers and nature lovers frequent the bookstores, outfitters, cafés, and restaurants in the small town.

Just an hour away is Concord, a city of over seventy thousand people full of counterculture and diversity and beautifully situated in the mountains.[4] With its upscale crafts stores, brand-name stores, current and controversial movies, arts and crafts festivals, coffee bars and ethnic restaurants, Concord offers an escape from the rural Wal-Mart and Lowe's living of Mapleton and the small towns nearby. The costs of those advantages are city traffic, congestion, and high prices. Many Mapleton locals go to

Concord often for medical care. So far, we go for the cultural attractions, for items we need that Wal-Mart doesn't provide, to make use of the nearest airport, and to visit Art's twin sister and brother-in-law, who have relocated there from New York. We only recently have begun thinking about how important it is to have good medical care near where you live.

Art and I spend summers and school vacations in Mapleton and are part of those who journey back and forth on the interstate between Florida and the mountains. Locals and retired people in Mapleton often ask when we're going to retire and live full-time in the mountains. It's a status symbol to retire early. "We like our jobs," we reply. "We plan to work another decade." At sixty-two (Art) and fifty-seven (Carolyn), we aren't much younger than the people who ask, which leads the retired people to look at us in disbelief, as if to say, "Why would you want to do that?" The locals just assume that, similar to all the other transplants, our goal is to get out of congested, dirty, crime-ridden, and hurricane-prone urban Florida and retire in their serene neck of the woods as soon as possible. What we don't say is that we do not want to live year-round in Mapleton. There's too much we'd miss—university life, our Tampa friends, cultural diversity, progressive politics, academic discourse, film, art, music, and warm winters, to start.

But we love living in the mountains in the summers and visiting here whenever we have a holiday. Initially we wondered if living in two places, what Jordan (2008) calls "living a distributed life," would make our lives feel too disjointed. There are inconveniences to be sure: the slow satellite service that is the only way to get broadband connections for our computers, books left in Tampa that we need for our writing, the added chaos of transitioning between two places, and the shrinkage of time for our network of friends in Tampa (see Jordan, 2008). But so far, we've found that having the varied lives that two locations allow (perhaps demand) has more upsides than down.

One upside is that we get to experience the excitement of change, yet it is mixed with the security of the familiar, since we return to a place that has been designed by us for our comfort and contains familiar possessions (see also Jordan, 2008). Satellite internet, satellite TV, and cell phones connect us to the larger world and provide a degree of continuity with our urban, liberal, professorial lives in Tampa. We are able to write without interruption and stay connected to our graduate students, activities that, similar to our lives in Tampa, occupy many hours most days. Much of the rest of our life in Mapleton, though, is quite different from the life we lead in Tampa. In Mapleton, we participate in different activities with a larger network of people who are quite different from each other, confront new situations, and learn new things. We think this variety makes us more interesting to ourselves and to each other.

In Mapleton, we are much more likely than in Tampa to involve ourselves jointly in non-academic projects. We spend more time in nature, talking and socializing with neighbors and friends, working around the house and in the garden, and learning how to be more self-sufficient. Not only do I mow the mountainside with my gas weed eater, we landscape our property with trees and plants, and we fertilize and spray for insects and fungus. We spread mulch, paint the railings, rake the gravel, install drainpipe, and attempt minor house repairs, sometimes with the help of neighbors.

We look forward to walking in our garden several times a day and admiring the dahlias, roses, gladiolas, coneflowers, castor bean plants, daylilies, coreopsis, irises, forsythia, daffodils, crocus, hollyhock, sunflowers, Rose of Sharon, and numerous trees—Japanese maple, cherry, apple, and pear, along with various kinds of spruce, pine, hemlock, and cedar—that we have planted and nourished. Almost every night we walk with the dogs on a path beside our home that winds down our mountain; occasionally we ride around Hollow Mountain in our 1997 Jeep Wrangler, with the dogs' noses sniffing out of the open top, and look for new trails to explore. In either case, the dogs run free and chase tennis balls that Art throws down the mountainside. Buddha can retrieve a ball no matter how far it is thrown. Sunya paces herself, now that she is older, but we marvel at how fit she remains as she nears thirteen years of age.

Sometimes Art and I take day hikes in the nearby forests or in the nearby national park. Once each summer we hike to a sixty-six-hundred-foot-high mountain, eight miles up and six miles down, with two friends from our university in Tampa who have moved to Mapleton. We spend the night in cabins heated by propane lanterns and eat food carried up by llamas and prepared on site.

Late evenings back at home, we often sit for hours on our back porch looking out at the mountains and watching the sun go down, the lights in town come on, and the color light show begin. We stop work earlier and spend more time on dinner here than we do in Tampa. We drink more wine—though not large amounts—and eat more appetizers—occasionally more than we should. Usually the additional physical activity makes it all come out even, so that we maintain our normal weight.

Several times a week, we have company, visit neighbors, or sit on our front porch and welcome drop-by visitors, activities we too rarely experience in Tampa.

Good Neighbors: Dropping By/Giving Gifts/Helping Out

"Anybody home?" we yell, as we walk up onto our neighbors' front porch.

"Come in," says George, from his La-Z-Boy. Art and I open the screen door, enter, and take our seats, me on the maroon velveteen couch beside Louise, and Art in the matching plush chair next to George. "Louise, get them a drink," George says. Without a word, Louise gets up and fixes us some sweet ice tea.

"Better not. We haven't eaten yet," I say to Louise's offer of home-baked black walnut cake. "We haven't had dinner yet."

"I'll wrap up two pieces for you to take home," Louise says, and I nod.

"When did you'ns get home? " Louise asks. I tell her we arrived the night before, delighted that she thinks of our cabin here as our home.

Art and George talk about real estate, scraping gravel roads, putting in house places, house repairs, and the new development going in behind our mountain. Occasionally they comment on the politics being discussed on Fox News, which, as always, blares loudly in the background. Their conversations are punctuated by George's spitting his Skol tobacco juice into a covered plastic cup he keeps on an endtable beside his chair. Louise and I talk about shopping, babies, home housewares parties, canning, cooking, and who's sick and laid up. Our conversations are punctuated by Louise's draws on her ever-present Winston Light cigarette. Though she holds the cigarette away from me, the smoke curls around her and permeates my clothes and nose.

I try to listen to both conversations at once. Occasionally I throw in a comment to Art and George's conversation, but then return quickly to the conversation that Louise and I are having. If Louise and I don't hold our own conversation, George and Art usually dominate the talk. I often am amazed at the traditional gender roles and expectations here. Is it only a coincidence that I use Art's last name when calling for repairs or making appointments in Mapleton, when almost all our services in Tampa are listed under my last name? Though I don't say so or act like it is the case, the truth is that I'm far more interested in house repairs, roads, developments—and politics—than in babies, housewares, and canning.

Perhaps I took in more than I think from growing up in my father's construction business. These interests were piqued once I met George, who appeals greatly to my masculine side. Although I am usually responsible for house maintenance for both our houses and more interested in the local construction business than Art is, initially George talked primarily to Art about the work we needed him to do. Over the years, though, I have noticed that he turns to me more often.

Art and I first talked to George about ten years before when he was working mountain roads near where we had rented a house on Hollow Mountain for a month during the summer. The next time we visited Mapleton, Art and I signed a preliminary contract to buy a piece of land on a nearby mountain range. Before we finalized the deal, we called George, who was described by several people as "the best dirt man in town," to talk with us about building a road up to the property. When George arrived in his pickup, we were surprised that it was the same George we had met earlier. Looking up a very steep cliff of the land we were considering, George rubbed his chin for a minute, then said in his southern drawl, "Now I don't mean you'ns no disrespect, but it's going to cost you near as much to put in a road as it is to build your house." I fell for his wealth of knowledge immediately. When he suggested that he could show us much better land, we trusted him right away.

We spent most of the day with George back on Hollow Mountain, where he lived, on the same road as the house we had rented several times, and, coincidentally, where we had considered buying property earlier. We both noted that all roads seemed to take us back to Hollow Mountain. George helped us buy several pieces of property, one of which was on the road named for him and only about a thousand yards from his house. That is where we built our cabin. We have had a friendship and business relationship with George ever since and value his opinion about local culture, especially surviving the mountains and buying property.

"Get them some of the beets and green beans you canned," George says to Louise, when we stand up to leave.

On the way home, we pass neighbors David and Anne, who are headed to town. Art stops the car and we talk through the open windows. "Are your dahlias blooming yet?" David asks, and Art goes into a litany of what's blooming where and when. "Need anything from the store?" Anne asks. We shake our heads no and continue talking. Another neighbor pulls up and waits patiently to pass by David and Anne. Nobody ever seems in a hurry here.

Next evening, while we are working in the garden, neighbors Rachel and Ray drive by. When they see us, they slow down and wave. When we walk toward their car, they stop, and we catch up on the local news. They are returning from a Confederate reenactment in town. We decline their invitation to join them later for "Pickin' on the Square," popular Saturday-night entertainment in Mapleton. Then, "I see your gladiolas are in bloom," says Rachel, looking over at the red and purple blaze of color.

"Here are some dahlias for you," Art says, handing several pots to her. "We grew them from our own tubers. See, they're just starting to poke through the dirt."

"Thanks," says Rachel. "We're going to Concord tomorrow to Sam's. Do y'all need anything?"

"No, we're fine. Hey, that strawberry jam you left on our porch was delicious," I say.

"Glad you enjoyed it," says Ray.

"What should we bring to dinner Saturday night?" asks Rachel.

"I'm making pasta with homemade tomato sauce, from the tomatoes and peppers we got at the U-pick-um farm. David and Ann and Glenn and Marilyn are bringing side dishes. Why don't you bring dessert?"

Rachel nods. "Guess we better be on our way," Ray says. When we don't say "stay awhile," they take off down the road while we hold onto our barking dogs.

Those who "drop by" often bring gifts. It is common to find local produce or other presents, such as Ray and Rachel's jam, on our porch, or birthday cards and other acknowledgments of special occasions in mailboxes. Likewise, whenever we go to the U-pick-um farm, the Saturday tailgate market, or the local produce stand some miles away, we always get extra and deliver it to many of our neighbors. At those times, we drop by unannounced. After all, who doesn't have a few minutes to chat and eat a fresh peach?

Once in the house, we hear a horn beep, and we know Anne and David are returning from the store. We wave from the kitchen window. As soon as we finish dinner, another horn beeps. Looking out, we see Louise and George standing by their red pickup. When we go outside to greet them, George pulls a bag from the back of the pickup. "Some beans and squash," George says, "from our garden."

About that time, Slim, a mid-sixties man who grew up in Hell's Kitchen in New York City, walks by with his bulldog. I restrain Sunya, until Slim, who has characteristics of a dog whisperer, says, "Let her go. They'll be fine." I do, and they are.

"I haven't been feeling good," Slim says, adjusting the oxygen hose from his portable tank that has become his constant companion. We talk for a while about Slim's health. When he walks down the road, we all wonder aloud how long Slim will be able to take his daily walks. His health has deteriorated greatly since the death of his wife from cancer a few months before. He is a fixture on our road, someone I look forward to seeing every day.

"We took him some dinner last night," George says, "because we know how hard it is for him to cook." Everyone who lives on the road has been working as a community to make sure Slim has enough food and money for other necessities. Slim reciprocates in ways that he can. Last time I saw him, he gave me a "good luck" rock and a piece of driftwood that looked like an animal head. When we're not here, he checks around our house for us.

This southeastern mountain culture is a drop-by and gift-giving culture, which, along with mutual aid, are important aspects of being neighborly.[5] "Drop by sometime. Don't be a stranger," people say all the time, and mean it. In my twenty-seven years in Tampa, I only rarely have dropped by anyone's house without advance warning and only rarely has someone dropped by ours without planning ahead. In Mapleton, dropping by is a common practice. Art and I have learned to be more flexible about controlling our time and more spontaneous in our sociability. But drop-bys usually aren't a problem because there seem to be many unspoken rules that ensure people aren't intruding.

For example, drop-bys usually blow the horn outside your home. If you don't come out, they drive away. If you do come out, they stay in the car or stand beside it to talk. They come in on the porch or the home only when invited, and then are careful not to stay too long. Art and I have learned to follow these unspoken norms as well.

Sometimes a visit is unplanned on both sides. Like Rachel and Ray in the scene above, people see you outside as they drive by. Sometimes we wave or yell greetings to neighbors as we walk down the road, and they come out on the porch to talk or invite us in. These drop-bys can happen at any time, though people try not to invade your privacy.

Dropping by someone's house for an extended visit involves more unspoken norms than a short visit. For example, our neighbors have figured out that, though we are home during the day, this is our writing time. So they are not likely to drop by then. Likewise, we normally don't visit George during working hours, even if he is working around his home, though we might stop by while he's taking a lunch break. If we see that someone we want to visit has company, we usually forgo a drop-by, as do our neighbors. Some times are more conducive than others for drop-bys. For example, drop-bys are expected in the evening after supper, often on Saturday nights, and more often on Sunday afternoons, which is considered the best day to "go visiting." Art and I always try to pick up cues to make sure we're not intruding; for example, we note if people are dressed to go out, if they're watching an important TV program (such as NASCAR racing), or if they are going to a church meeting.

We moved to the mountains to "get away," and ironically we have less privacy and more sociability here than we do in Tampa. When we first considered moving to the mountains, I thought I wanted a house on a deserted road—"the more isolated the better," I said—and I fantasized about the joys of living alone and having lots of space to myself. Though I'm glad for the more than two acres we own and the relative peace and quiet, I'm also happy to have a few neighbors. Our house is near the beginning of the dirt road, and I enjoy socializing when an occasional neighbor drives by to do daily errands.

I also appreciate their looking out for our house when we're away. When we're in Tampa, our Mapleton neighbors call us if anything seems amiss at our cabin or if they see anyone there, and they willingly offer to do favors for us. It's not as easy to arrange such care for our home in Tampa when we're away from it, since our urban neighbors do not value mutual aid in the same way as our backwoods neighbors. We don't even know the names of some of our Tampa neighbors, who rarely peek out of the privacy of their homes and garages and are seldom seen in their front yards. The expected sociability and spontaneity in our Mapleton neighborhood keep me from being too rigid and set in my "go to the study and write" ways.

A Mutual Aid Community: Walkin' the Line

Neighbors eagerly help out in emergencies and often lend a hand to help with a house repair. If someone is building a shed or putting on a roof, other neighbors will drop by to help or watch. If a job needs to be done, people volunteer. This practice is associated with the norms of mutual aid that are an integral part of this community, among the transplanted retirees as well as the locals, and with the norm of community self-sufficiency—don't pay for what you and your neighbors can do yourselves.

When our community well system develops a leak, one of our transplanted neighbors, Glenn, takes it upon himself to find the leak, so we don't have to pay the local well company. Another neighbor calls our house to see if Art or I can "walk the line" with Glenn. "I'd do it if I could," the neighbor says, "but I physically can't." Though I know it will be treacherous, with the possibility of running into snakes or other creatures in the overgrown brush, I volunteer. It feels important to do my part for the community. I also realize I am one of the few people on the road, with the exception of the locals, who easily can walk down the mountain.

Though it is summer, I put on my long-sleeved shirt, hiking boots, and gloves, and tuck my heavy jeans into my wool socks. I then spray my clothes with Off to protect against chiggers and ticks. When I join Glenn, he is dressed similarly and carries a scythe. He hands me a short-handled shovel, "just in case," he says. Off we go down the mountain, following the water line, with Glenn leading and cutting a path in the tall bushes and blackberry briars. It is hot and a little scary, but I rather enjoy the adventure, and learning from Glenn about water lines, pipes, and well pumps. Though we don't find the water leak that day, we locate it a few days later when a gusher floods another neighbor's lawn.

As we walk, I ask Glenn what he thinks about our getting a surge protector for our cabin, since we've been hit by lightning a few times. "I'll get one next time I'm in town and put it on for you," he says. "I can also get a regulator for your water heater."

"We'll pay you for your labor," I insist.

"Being friends is payment enough," he says. I don't object; I know he means it and will take it as an insult if I insist on paying him.

Killin' Rabbits

When Art and I get back from our walk the next evening, Bobby's blue pickup is parked in our driveway. Bobby is a carpenter and we met him when he helped us build our cabin. He does some handyman work for us now and then, and we often visit with him and his wife, Sarah Mae, who live about a mile from us. "I bet Bobby came to kill the rabbit," Art says.

"You didn't tell me he was going to do that," I say.

"I didn't know for sure he was. I just mentioned the problem we've been having with the rabbits when we were there last night," Art says. "I guess you missed that conversation."

Rabbits have been eating our plants. First, the hostas disappeared, then the hollyhocks. Then the critters started nibbling the roses—not nibbling; they took down several large, six-foot-tall canes. Now they had started on Art's prized dahlias, eating the shoots of the little plants we grew in pots. This was all-out war. We tried every home remedy known to gardeners—hot pepper of various kinds and blends, garlic, dog hair, human hair, blood meal and other chemicals from the local nurseries, even my urine. Each solution seemed to attract rather than repel the rabbits. Chicken-wire fences helped a bit, but it was impossible (and aesthetically unattractive) to fence in our whole property. Our morning walks in the garden had become depressing as we saw the latest stalks and flowers on the ground, and our evening work sessions now consisted of pulling up dead and dying plants more than anything else.

"The only sure solution is a gun," said the locals, which we had, until now, refused.

"Look, Bobby and Sarah Mae are sitting on our back porch," I whisper to Art, as we pull in behind their blue pickup. Without making a sound, we get out of the car, tiptoe into the house, and lock the dogs in the back bedroom to keep them quiet. We join Bobby and Sarah Mae on the back porch. Bobby is sitting in a chair, his feet propped up on the lower rung of the railing, with his cocked, twenty-gauge shotgun pointed out over the top railing toward the remains of our hostas. The scene is right out of a Wild West movie. We sit quietly for more than thirty minutes. Occasionally, Sarah Mae and I giggle softly, like two schoolgirls. I enjoy the quiet and watching the sun drop and then the sunlight spread behind the mountain, the colors making the blue of the close mountains appear almost black and forming a halo behind the white puff of forming clouds. The twilight and colors hang in the sky the entire time we're on the porch.

Suddenly, Bobby grabs his gun, walks out into the yard and down the road a short way. A gunshot blasts and soon Bobby appears with a rabbit hanging from his hand, its two front legs and head dangling.

"He's a big one," says Bobby, and everyone starts talking at once as though the mute button has just been released.

"Do you want him for your dogs?" I ask, getting out of my grief-stricken head and into my practical one, as I recall that Bobby threw rabbits he killed into his dog cages one night when we were there. This is survival of the fittest.

"No, my dogs have already eaten," he says.

We leave the dead rabbit on the ground at the mailbox to scare off any other rabbits. The next day I insist that Art put the dead body into a bag and take it to the dump, along with our other garbage. Both of us feel guilty for the murder of the rabbit and for treating it like garbage, but our guilt disappears when our plants revive and we don't see another rabbit the rest of the summer. Surely one rabbit could not have done all that damage. Had the scent of death scared off the others?

Next day, Art says he's going to Wal-Mart to buy Bobby some "bullets, since he won't take money from us."

"You probably should ask for shells," I say laughing, "rather than bullets. Or they'll know you are a Floridiot."

The Fourth of July and the Old Rugged Star of David

"Let's go. It'll be fun," I say to Art. "There will be fireworks, and live music, and a potluck dinner. I'll make corn pudding. The food will be great and plentiful. And we'll get to see some of the local culture we usually aren't privy to."

"I don't know if I'll enjoy it," Art says. "They'll all be southern Baptists and I'm not sure I'll fit in."

"Oh, come on. It'll be great ethnography and good food, and some of our neighbors will be there," I urge, as visions of church picnics of my youth float through my memory. "I think it's really nice that they included us."

We have been invited to a Fourth of July picnic at Bobby and Sarah Mae's daughter's house. Art finally agrees to go, and neighbors Ray and Rachel pick us up the next day at five p.m. We drive way out into the country, then park and walk up a dirt road to the picnic. More than a hundred people are there, some getting food ready and others sitting in lawnchairs talking and enjoying the end of the day. Several long tables are covered with food. Bobby's grandchildren direct traffic, his son-in-law and daughter welcome newcomers, and his other son-in-law barbecues pork and chicken on a large grill that he pulled behind his car to the picnic.

As we greet the people we know and Bobby introduces us to others, I notice that Art's Jewish star, the one he has worn since his mother died, is hanging outside his shirt. He normally wears it tucked inside. I start to tell him to "fix" it and contemplate tucking it in myself. Then I hesitate. Perhaps he has made a conscious decision to wear it on the outside. I wonder how people will respond to the symbol? To a man wearing a "necklace"? I say nothing. I feel proud that Art's Jewish star is visible for all to see. The star is an important symbol to Art of his Jewishness, and it is important to me as well. Other than with two close friends on our road—the schoolteachers—we have not discussed Art's ethnicity with others in the community, though it has not been our intent to hide it.

On several occasions, Bobby has used the expression "jewing someone down." "Does it bother you?" I ask Art one day after Bobby says it.

"No," he replies.

"Maybe it should," I offer.

"I don't think he says it to insult Jews," Art explains. I raise my eyebrows but say nothing. "I doubt he's ever interacted with another Jewish person," Art continues.

"I've never seen another person in Mapleton who even looks Jewish," I say, deciding that if Art isn't going to make a big deal out of it, then I'm not. The expression grates on me, though not as much as some of the other racist things locals sometimes say. This phrase also reminds me of the way people in Luray, including my father, used to talk, and I feel less judgmental when I remember that.

"Let me put this down," I say, nodding toward the paper bag I hold in both hands, which contains my still-warm corn pudding wrapped in a kitchen towel. I take my white CorningWare bowl out of the bag and place it near the other vegetables on one of the tables. I check to make sure that my name is still taped on the bottom, a practice I learned from the church and funeral dinners I attended in Luray. Then I insert the spoon I have brought and cock the glass lid to one side. I note that my contribution blends in with many similar dishes on the table.

Cokes, bottled water, and other soft drinks peek out of ice-filled tubs. When I don't find any diet drinks, I fish out two bottles of water, one for me and one for Art. I am not surprised that there are no alcoholic drinks, though I do think how that wouldn't happen at a party in Tampa. Later, when I finish my drink, I will reluctantly throw my empty bottle into the trash bins with the other trash since there are no containers for recycling bottles.

We place the folding chairs we have brought from home in rows near people from our neighborhood. We sit facing the band, which consists of several men with drums, guitar, and fiddles, and several standing microphones, all on the back of a flat-bed trailer. The trailer is decorated with American flags draped in front and bales of hay along the side. Five men, a group from one of the local churches, sing religious songs with lots of twang.

The lyrics center on sin, death, going home and going to heaven, and Jesus as the savior. Young people from a church group also sing the same kind of songs. I try to enjoy the entertainment, but the singing isn't always on key, they don't sing the songs familiar to me from my Lutheran upbringing, and the overall messages in the songs seem repetitive and don't speak to me.

"There's no passion in the singing," Art says, seeming bored. "It's just reciting."

"That's what you do in church," I say. "You recite."

The band ends with "America" and "My Country 'Tis of Thee," and everyone stands and sings along, hands over hearts. The preacher then gives a benediction, which includes a blessing for President Bush and our country.

On cue, after the blessing, everyone moves en masse to the food line. We move with them. I look forward to eating all the familiar food of my youth. Along with the pulled pork and chicken are pots of green beans with ham hock, green bean casseroles, various corn puddings, squash casseroles, candied sweet potatoes, scalloped potatoes, black-eyed peas; chili, baked beans, and other dishes flavored with hamburger; corn bread, biscuits, rolls, and hamburger buns for the barbecue; pasta, macaroni, potato, and molded and jellied fruit salads; relishes and deviled eggs; all kinds of cakes, rhubarb, apple, and other fruit pies, brownies, and Jell-O desserts. I pile as much as I can on the sturdy, disposable plastic plate.

As Art bends over to scoop out some mashed potatoes, his necklace swings freely. He notices and tucks the Star of David into his shirt. "I liked it out," I say quietly, "though I understand that you don't want to be too conspicuous." He shrugs, and I turn to talk to other people. At the end of the line, we place money in a donations jar to help finance the fireworks we will see later.

When we both go back for seconds, Art and I quietly note to each other that the food is somewhat bland, compared to what we are used to. "That's because they only season with salt, pepper, onion, and fatback," I say, thinking of the spicy Thai and other ethnic food we consume often in Tampa. On my second trip, I ask Sarah Mae which green beans are hers, but her quiet nod toward her pot makes me think that might not be an acceptable question to ask, at least not publicly. I guess you aren't supposed to acknowledge that you might prefer one person's cooking over another's, though Bobby has said before that he eats exclusively his wife's cooking at potlucks. After a second helping of green beans, I fill my plate with a variety of the well-sweetened pies and cakes, reminiscent of the desserts my Aunt Florence made every Saturday.

The next day I ask Art why he felt the need to hide his Star of David when it is such an important Jewish symbol. He replies, "You're making the act more intentional than it was. I simply noticed the necklace and put it inside my shirt, where I usually wear it. It wasn't that conscious."

"Are you sure? It seemed pretty conscious to me."

"Most of the people there didn't know what it means anyway."

"Probably true," I say. "They'll just think it's strange that a man is wearing a necklace."

"The reason I wear it has less to do with it being a Jewish symbol and more because of my mother," Art explains. "I got it right after she died . . ."

"I know. I gave it to you."

He nods. "And I've worn it constantly ever since. Wearing it makes me feel connected to her."

"That's nice," I say. "Like my mother's wedding ring." I twist the gold band on my finger.

"You know," I continue, "part of what interests me is trying to figure out why I didn't become one of the people at that party last night. Although while I was in Luray, I was like them."

"No, you weren't," says Art. "You couldn't have been. There was a part of you that didn't really absorb the ideology or believe it."

"That's not true," I say. "I believed all of it wholeheartedly, at least for a while. When you live inside the ideology, you do. You don't know there is an 'it' you're inside of, or that there is any other way to believe."

"You were into church like they are?" Art asks.

"Sure was. It was my only social life until high school. Besides, I didn't know not to be into church. 'Good' people were into church—no matter what they did the rest of the week. I didn't know it was possible to think any differently until I went to college."

"Education makes a difference, along with interacting with people different from you. Most of the people at the picnic haven't traveled beyond a ten-mile radius of where they grew up, except to hunt deer."

"That's true," I respond. "And that's why I think our relationship with them can have an impact. That's what happened to me at college—I met people different from me. These kids don't aspire to go to college, other than the local junior college, and they're not going to meet people there who are different. I desperately wanted to go away from home to college. What made me want to do that?" I ask. "In high school I was mesmerized with learning about the world and how people thought and felt. I was good at school and I wanted more of it. I wanted to learn new things and have new experiences," I say, answering my own question.

"I never really understood the role that religion played once you went to college, though we've talked some about it," Art says.

"The first year at college I went to church sometimes, to a very progressive Lutheran church, and to some youth meetings. I think I was just homesick and looking to belong to something. I remember thinking for about a week then that I had been saved—actually I wrote a note to the minister and said that I had accepted Jesus as my savior. I just got that idea one day and decided it was true. The minister didn't respond. And the idea didn't hold; it didn't feel real to me. No doubt I was affected by the sociology courses I was taking—for example, Marx's [1844] idea of religion being the opiate of the masses and Durkheim's [1912/1965] notion of religion being produced by society. It was hard not to be aware that I was socially constructing this belief to make me feel better. After taking a survey of religion class, I stopped going to church entirely, and I haven't gone back since, except when I visited my mother. Now I wouldn't give up our Sunday mornings relaxing and reading the paper to attend church, though sometimes I miss belonging to a group outside of those we form at work."

"That would be hard, wouldn't it? Those Sunday mornings get me through the week. At the picnic, I couldn't help watching the kids and thinking about how much they're missing," Art says.

"Who is to say our lives are better than theirs?" I ask.

"I'm not saying it's better for everyone. Only that I can't fathom such an unreflective life, one free of thoughtful contemplation," Art says.

"I can't either, but that doesn't mean I want to put down how they live."

"Sometimes belief systems are dangerous," Art replies. "Their belief is based on faith and the expectation of going to heaven. Everything in their lives boils down to religion. They just believe what the minister says to believe. But that means they don't think about how so much of the violence and killing in the world and in history has been done in the name of religion."

"It is simple, isn't it?" I ask. "All you have to do is believe. That's really all that's required of you." Art nods. "But you know that a lot of Americans hold to those values."

"Yes, and that leads to some of the problems we have," Art proclaims.

"My parents would have loved the picnic," I say defensively. "There isn't that much difference—if any—between my family and the people there last night. Just look at my sister, who is heavily involved in an evangelical church in Mississippi, one where they speak in tongues. She goes to church several times a week. My parents weren't as evangelical as the locals, or as my sister, but still they believed basically the same things. Sometimes I wonder how different I really am from the locals."

"Oh, you're different all right," Art replies, nodding his head for emphasis. "You read, you think and question, and you definitely need intellectual stimulation."

Love Thy Neighbor—If He's White

"How many Black students are in your school?" I ask Sarah Mae, who works in an elementary school as a teacher's aide.

"One," she answers, rocking back and forth in her favorite rocker. Art and I are visiting Bobby and Sarah Mae on their front porch.

"So why do you think there aren't more Blacks living here?" I ask Bobby.

"They know we don't want them here," Bobby says. "We don't like niggers."

"Bobby, I don't like it when you talk that way."

"Well, that's the truth. We don't like niggers." I note that Sarah Mae laughs when Bobby uses the N-word, but I also note that she never says it herself.

"My boss is a Black man, a wonderful man," I say, trying to challenge Bobby gently but firmly. I don't try to explain that the man I am talking about is dean of the college—that would be going too far.

"I wouldn't tell anybody that, if I was you."

"Why not?"

He rolls his eyes. I sigh deeply and rock faster.

"I only met one colored man that was any good," he says.

"Who was that?" I ask, hopeful that at least there is one and that at least he has used "colored" instead of the N-word.

"He was in the funeral home. The only good nigger is a dead nigger."

I sigh again. This is hopeless. How can I be friends with someone who thinks this way? My only hope is that there will be change in the next generation, I think, as I recall Bobby's daughter reprimanding him for using the N-word. "I don't teach my children to talk that way," she had said to Bobby one day. "And I don't want you using that word around them."

Several months later, while teaching a class on "Race, Class, and Emotions," I have the following dream.

Art and I are talking, when two Black men approach. One of them has a gun. I am frightened. But then I notice that Bobby, our mountain neighbor, is also in the dream. He leaves the scene for a moment and I know he is going to his pickup for his gun. I am glad he is there. He will know what to do. The Black man continues pointing his gun at Art. It is not clear what he wants or how we can appease him. I am afraid to say anything. Art does not speak either. Suddenly Bobby shoots into the air. "Drop your gun," Bobby says, and I think that he has given ample warning. The two Black men don't even flinch. The man with the gun starts squeezing the trigger; the gun points directly at Art's head. I tense; so does Art. Bobby fires and the man with the gun falls to the ground. I am relieved when I wake up, but confused and upset by the images.

My voice shakes as I tell the class this dream and describe to them the conversation I had with Bobby. I fear how the students might interpret the dream and me for having it and for being friends with someone who says such racist things. "Does this dream represent my desire for white privilege?" I ask. They listen attentively. "Do I not say more to Bobby, because I don't want to give up the advantage my membership in the 'White club' affords me, which is protection by people like Bobby?" I ask, and a spirited discussion follows about White privilege.

A few days later, our class watches the movie *Crash*. The racist cop in the movie stops a Black couple who appeared to be interracial and to be having oral sex while driving in a car. The cop humiliates the couple by fondling the light-skinned Black woman as he searches her, while her husband looks on, afraid to do anything about it because the cops have guns and might use them. But the cop is more than a racist cop; he also is a complex character who lovingly takes care of his elderly father. Then later in the movie, the same cop risks his life to save the same Black woman when she is in a wreck and the car is about to explode.

This movie makes me think of Bobby. Bobby, like the cop, also is a complex character. He speaks racist language unreflectively. What he learned as a kid resurfaces. But I believe he would save a Black woman from a burning car as well. I have to believe that or how can I justify being friends with him? I also have to believe that he would have thought and felt differently had he been born and raised in a different environment and had different experiences. I believe the same about my parents. We aren't born with these prejudices. They originate in our families and are modified by our life experiences.

That's how I justify caring so much about a man who holds racist beliefs and makes racist comments. I hate the parts of him that are racist, but I don't hate him. I want to change him, but I don't know how and I don't want to risk losing him as a friend.

Gender Politics

"Hillary won't get elected. No way. A woman can't run the country," says George, as Art and I are walking out the door after a visit at George's house.

"Why do you say that?" I ask.

"It says so in the Bible," he responds, getting up out of his chair and holding the door open for us.

"What does it say?" I ask.

"It says that men are to be the leaders and women are to be obedient and submissive to men."

"The Bible was written and passed down a long time ago," I say. "Do you believe everything the Bible says?"

"Yes I do."

"What about . . ."

"Let's go," Art interrupts, pulling me out the door.

"Why didn't you let me finish?" I ask when we're in the car.

"You can't win that argument," Art says. "You're not going to change George's mind."

"How can we be friends with someone who thinks that?" I explode. "He says that even Huckabee isn't conservative enough for him. How can you get any more conservative? Huckabee's a southern Baptist."

"George says Huckabee's not the right kind of southern Baptist, because he didn't join up with the conservatives who rebelled against the liberal wing at the southern Baptist convention back in the seventies."

"Liberal southern Baptists? Isn't that an oxymoron?"

On the way home, driving by the "Vote for Bush and Cheney" sign in a neighbor's yard incites my rage again. "I hate that damned sign," I say. "It's been up now for four years."

"I'm going to steal it one of these days," Art chimes in. "Enough already."

"They'd know who took it," I reply.

"You're probably right," Art says, "since we're two of the four liberals on the road."

"Just wait until we put up our Obama or Clinton signs," I say. We both chuckle at the image. Several months later, after the Democratic primary, we proudly wear our Obama T-shirts and caps and put Obama stickers on the bumpers of our cars.

Just Say No to Global Warming

The owner at the local nursery always greets us warmly and spends hours talking to us about plants and trees—what to buy and how to solve problems. We've come to rely on him. "We lost all three of our Japanese maples," Art tells him.

"First it was the warm spring and then the deep freeze in April. The combination got them. Worst I've ever seen," the nursery owner says.

"And with global warming, it's just going to keep on happening," Art says. I look at him, surprised he has brought up this topic.

"Well, there was an ice age too. This is no different. There's no global warming. The weather gets colder, then it gets warmer. There are cycles. That's all," the nursery owner replies.

How can we support the business of someone who thinks that?

The Mexicans: Brown Skin and Hard Workers

"The Mexicans should go back where they came from," George says as we sit talking on his porch in 2006. "They're ruining the local economy. A White man can't get a job around here now."

George's attitude reflects the opinion of many of the locals, who are having to get used to seeing brown faces all over the county now. Yesterday I had noticed that George drove slowly by our house while some Mexican workers were putting in a path of large stones down our hill. I was concerned that George might be upset that we didn't give him the work, though Art disagreed and said that this wasn't the kind of thing that George could do easily. After George's comments, I'm not so sure that Art is right.

"They can if they'll work for the same wages," Art replies to George.

"That's hard," says George, "because the illegal Mexicans are paid under the table and they don't have to pay taxes.

"Seems to me that's the fault of the companies that hire them then," Art says, thinking but not saying that the locals follow the same business practices as the Mexicans.

"They get free medical care that we have to pay for and they live together sometimes a dozen or more in the same house," George replies, ignoring Art's comment.

"We had some Mexican men do work at our house yesterday. We had hired a company that employed Mexican workers," I say. "They did really good work. We're very pleased." George doesn't reply.

A year later, George hires a Mexican man to mow his mountainside. "He's really good," George says to us. "Works hard and doesn't even take a break. He gets $10 an hour. You should come see what he did on our hill."

I note to Art that we gladly pay George $20 an hour to do similar kinds of things for us.

Another year passes and in 2008, Bobby and other contractors in the area have hired Mexican workers on their work crew. George now pays the man who cleans his mountainside $20 an hour and recommends him to others. Everyone talks about what good workers the Mexicans are, and many frequent the Mexican restaurants that now dot the area.

Sharing Lives: The Mundane and the Extraordinary

Out for a walk, I hesitate halfway up Louise's driveway, stand and watch her pushing and pulling the small powered lawn mower. She hasn't seen me yet. Maybe I shouldn't disturb her. Suddenly Louise waves. Is it a half-hearted wave? I can't read the expression on her face. She keeps mowing and I walk to the top of the driveway, then stop, look around, and try to appear like I don't mind waiting, which I don't. I'll just stay a minute, I decide, say hello, and leave. After a few more pushes, Louise motions toward the porch and shouts, "I'll be done in a minute."

Good. This way I won't interfere with her work, and we'll have a longer, more relaxed visit when she's finished mowing. I walk around admiring her daylilies, calla lilies, roses, and Rose of Sharon bushes. Louise has a green thumb and an intuitive understanding of plants. "You just put them in the ground," she had said the day before, when George pulled a Rose of Sharon out of the ground by the roots for us to take home.

"Your flowers are gorgeous," I say, when Louise turns off the motor.

She nods. "Come sit on the porch," she says, motioning again toward the two big rocking chairs here. She wipes the sweat from her face with a tissue she pulls from her bra.

"Next Thursday I'm having a housewares party. I want you to come," Louise says as soon as we sit down.

"Oh good. I'd love to." I've heard a lot about these parties and I think they must be similar to Tupperware parties, the private home buying parties from my childhood.

"I'll get you the catalogues," she says. I follow her into her house, where she shows me her many purchases from the last party her daughter had the week before. "You can take the catalogues home and look at them before you come." She hands me two catalogues and three circulars.

"Thanks. I'm sure I'll find all kinds of things I want," I say.

"I'll get free gifts for everything that I sell," Louise says, "and gifts for just having the party. Plus anything I buy is discounted. I just have to bring some refreshments. It's at another woman's house."

As I flip through the catalogues, I'm disappointed that the merchandise seems similar to what I might find in a K-Mart circular, except that it's about triple the price. I'll still have to buy something, I tell myself, and anyway it will be an interesting experience.

When I do attend the next week, I find the experience as disappointing as the merchandise. Seven or eight women sit in a circle and look through the same catalogues I've already looked through, then check out the merchandise stacked around the room on "for sale" shelves. Most of the conversation is about what we will buy. I reluctantly buy a candle and holder for $69. The other women buy numerous items. Then we quickly have some soda and cookies, and go home. I don't even take the candleholder out of the box when it arrives.

"How have you been?" I ask Louise when we return to the porch. I wonder if something is wrong since she's not as lively as usual.

"My niece is sick. She's got cancer, really bad."

"Oh, I'm so sorry," I say. "What kind of cancer?"

"In her knee. Just found out yesterday. It's the fast-movin' kind, they say." Louise has a vacant look in her eyes and her voice shakes a little.

"That's awful," I say, not sure what else is appropriate.

"She's got to have chemo and radiation every other day for three months."

"Where will she have it?" I ask.

"In Concord."

"So somebody will have to take her each time?" I think of what a life-stopper that would be—having cancer and having to go forty miles to Concord that often.

"Yes, somebody will." She looks pensive. "It only takes an hour or so to get there, but you end up spending the whole day. Yes, might as well say a whole day."

We sit in silence. Then, "Does she have children?" I ask.

"Two little kids, one not even walkin' yet."

"Oh my."

Louise shakes her head. "I know she's worried about them."

"Who will keep them?"

"I don't know. Her husband will have to keep working. He does maintenance at the hospital."

Louise looks straight ahead, her mouth closed tight, shaking her head as though she doesn't have a solution. I'm glad I don't know the people she is talking about; otherwise, I'd feel I should volunteer to drive the woman to Concord at least once. I remember how Art stopped everything he was doing recently to drive our neighbor Dave to Concord when he was having a medical problem and his wife was babysitting their granddaughter. It is important to help people in need.

"That's really hard," I say, returning to my conversation with Louise.

"They're starting the chemo right away, even before they do surgery to take out the tumor. It's the fast-growin' kind, so they don't want to wait. They found all this from an X-ray. Now they're doing tests to see if it's spread anywhere else."

I waver back and forth between feeling for this person I don't know—don't even know her name—and keeping my distance. But when I look at Louise, I can't help but feel sad. Her pain is written all over her body, the way her shoulders are slumped, her head lowered, her stare vacant. Louise sighs deeply and rests her chin on her fist.

Louise just lost her brother-in-law a few weeks ago, and now this. When George's brother died, I left two dishes of corn pudding on their kitchen table. "One is for you," my note said, "and the other is for George's brother's family." I didn't know his brother, but it seemed right to honor their loss in this way. I knew from having attended funerals in Luray that sharing food is important.

"I have a student who had cancer in her knee and then it spread to her bones," I say.

Louise turns toward me, listening intently, waiting . . . then, "That's what they're checking for, to see if it's spread to her bones. It's the fast-growin' kind," she says again.

"My student's doing fine now," I hurry to assure. What I don't know then is that several months later she will have to have her leg amputated.

"Doctor said this would be the hardest year of her life," Louise says. "He told her to get prepared."

"My student had a hard time," I say, "and had several knee replacements, but she can ride a bike and get around well now."

"I hope my niece gets to be that good," Louise says. "She's only thirty-six. Same age as my daughter."

"When did you find this out?" I ask.

"My brother called to tell us last night. My brother never shows emotion," she says. "That's just the way he is. But last night he just sobbed on the phone. I couldn't believe he was in that shape. He just said, 'She's only thirty-six and I don't think there's anything that can help her, except prayer.'"

We sit silently for a few minutes. I feel close to Louise. It doesn't seem right to offer platitudes, especially ones that I don't believe.

"How's your daughter-in-law?" I ask after a while. "What did the doctor tell her?"

"He put her on fertility drugs," she replies. "That girl wants a baby more than anything."

"I had a friend who had fertility treatments and then had her egg fertilized in a dish by the sperm. It finally worked, but talk about expensive." I don't tell her my friend is a lesbian.

I think about how often I tell Louise about friends. I offer my experience to try to make her feel better and to note commonalities between her life and mine, similar to the reasons I write autoethnography. I try to stay away from topics she won't relate to or with which she'll disagree because I want us to relate to each other as friends. I want her to be my friend and I want to be hers.

"Is that George?" I ask when I see a white truck pull up.

"No, that's Junior [her son]. He's been working all day with George. Now he's got to go to work at the factory. He hates being inside there," Louise says. "It nearly kills him. He'd rather be outside working with his daddy. But he stays because he gets health insurance there."

"Hi, Junior," I say, as he walks up the drive. Junior nods.

"Where's your daddy?" Louise asks.

"Still up on the mountain scraping roads," he replies.

"I don't know how you work two jobs," I say.

He shrugs. "Ain't nothin.'"

"He's going to work hisself to death," Louise says. "His daddy too. I tell George to slow down, but he don't. One of these days somethin's goin' to slow him down. He'd rather be workin' than doing anything. Never rests. Won't take a vacation. He'll be workin' when he dies."

"Guess you're not gonna get that vacation this summer," I say, noticing the southern twang that reappears in my voice when I talk to Louise.

"Guess not," she says, with no particular expression.

"I better get down the road," I say. "It looks like rain."

"We need it," Louise says. "The ground's dry."

We sit for a moment in silence and I think of how comfortable I am sitting on Louise's porch, happy listening to the stories of her life, and content to share in her grief, her day-to-day life, and the hopes and dreams of her family. Our deepest concerns aren't really that different, I think.

"I'm going to go look at my lilies," Louise says.

I know this is an invitation for me to accompany her, and I do. "Are your dahlias blooming yet? Ours are gorgeous."

"The red one is in full bloom. Look," she says, walking to the edge of the porch and pointing.

Meta-Autoethnography: Thinking Ethically

I am surprised, though I shouldn't be, that the ethical dilemmas and relational responsibilities present in my study of Fisher Folk revisit me as I write these stories about my life in the mountains. As I feel and think my way through these issues, I also listen to how other seasoned ethnographers respond as they read this chapter and discuss my work with me. The voices in my head go something like this.

Alter Ego: I can tell you've been thinking a lot about writing this chapter. You haven't been sleeping well lately, have you?

EGO: No, I haven't. I've been thinking day and night about the ethics of writing these stories about the mountain folk and I've written pages and pages about all this. I feel compelled to include these stories, since they're the best way I know to demonstrate the life I live in the mountains, both the pulls to be there and the moral conflicts I face when I am there. Exploring this mountain community, and my part in it, is an important component of my "revision," and how I position myself now in terms of my past, present, and future.

ALTER EGO: I sense there's a "but"?

EGO: [nods] But there's the lingering question of whether I have the right to write about others without their consent, especially when what I say shows them complexly and includes some of their prejudices as well as their positive qualities. I also worry about the effect these stories might have on the mountain folks and on my relationships with the people there.

ALTER EGO: Why not leave out those stories that are difficult, as Laurel Richardson [personal communication] suggested when she read this chapter? "Tell the reader you just can't say those things right now," she said, "because this is where you live and you've had so many consequences for your sharing others' lives that you're not settled about what to do."

EGO: That's probably what Laurel would do and the practice she's followed in writing some of her family stories in the past [Ellis, 2004, p. 173; but see Richardson, 2007]. It's what I did in my childhood stories that began this volume, which left out particular stories and stopped short of spelling out some of the difficulties.

ALTER EGO: So why not follow the same guidelines here with the mountain folk? You make the argument that the messy details you left out about your family were such a small part of who they were and your life there. Isn't that true for the mountain folk as well?

EGO: I've tried to contextualize the difficulties within the mountain folks' everyday lives, feeling worlds, and love of family and community. But I don't know how I can tell this story without the messiness.

ALTER EGO: I guess it's easier to write about other peoples' families than about your own, especially when what you have to say is negative.

EGO: None of the writing and decision making is easy. Even if I were willing to take out the problematic stories, how would I decide which ones are problematic? And problematic to whom? Would I omit the stories about racism, in particular, which I predict many readers will see as most condemning? Or the ones where Art and I talk about their bland food, bad singing, and my lack of interest in babies and housewares, which readers probably won't think about much at all? My guess is that George and Bobby won't care much that I tell stories about the things they say that we consider to be racist, sexist, and homophobic. They often say those in public situations. They might even see this as a way to get their beliefs out in the world. . . .

ALTER EGO: Maybe, but you might be wrong about that. You only know that they say those things in front of family and to you and Art. You don't know how they talk when you're not around. Maybe they only say these things in front of people they trust, and they trust you and Art. After all, you've known both of them almost ten years now.

EGO: Sometimes I wonder if they say these things to get my goat. It might be their way to critique our progressive politics without simply saying that we're wrong and they're right.

ALTER EGO: Or maybe saying these things to you is their way of trying to convert you to their way of thinking, since other than your liberal values, they really do seem to like you.

EGO: You're right, I don't know.

ALTER EGO: But you do know that *you* see these values as wrong and destructive, and you know that most of your readers will see them that way as well. It's different when the locals say it and when you put it in a book for all to read and judge.

EGO: You're right again. But I think the mountain people, including George and Bobby, will be most offended by our comments about their politics, religion, and simple faith. And Louise and Sarah Mae will be disappointed about how I perceive their food, the things they buy, and the conversations we have. They all might wonder whether we appreciate their hospitality, which we do, or respect their values, much of which we actually see as positive expressions of the place of community and family in their lives. Maybe I could leave out my comments about bland southern cooking, though I think it is significant that my tastes are different from theirs. I remember loving that food when I was growing up. And I realize it's only bland to us. For them, if it's fried with fatback and lots of salt and butter, well, that makes it tasty. I'm sure the mountain people will think I'm weird for not feeling immersed in talk about babies and housewares, but they will have to deal with that. It comes down to experience. Babies have not been part of my life as they have in theirs.

ALTER EGO: Um, it is complex, isn't it? But if you don't ever put in the critical stuff, then are you really an "interpretive ethnographer"? Is what you write really an ethnography?

EGO: Good questions, which make me think about what we owe readers[6] and ourselves. As interpretive and critical ethnographers, we are responsible for providing a complex portrayal and interpretation of the communities we study, including our place in them.

ALTER EGO: But that doesn't take us off the hook for what we owe participants. If you don't want to omit stories, then don't you still need to consider which ones to take back to those you write about to get approval or feedback? All of them? Only the ones that participants might see as problematic or hurtful? Those that readers might condemn? That you, the author, worry about or see as negative?

EGO: Just how far do we take the idea of getting permission and approval for what we write? Do we need permission to write everything about anybody? Should I get permission from every character who appears in this book, no matter how minimal? If we take this practice to the extreme, we won't be able to write honestly or critically about anything, including our own lives, maybe especially including our own lives. Don't I have the right to write about myself?

ALTER EGO: [*ignoring the question that has been hashed and rehashed to death*] I want to return to your decision not to write openly about some of the complexities in your own family's life. Do they deserve protection more than the mountain people?

EGO: Though I felt protective of my family and thought it unnecessary to dwell on the traumatic details, I did decide it was important to give readers indications of the messiness in order to tell an honest account. In the case of the mountain people, the messy details are accompanied by stories demonstrating positive values in the community. Just as critics overlooked the positive aspects of my portrayal of my mother in my story about my brother's death, I think it's easy to do the same thing here. The stories I included here were important for signifying issues I'm trying to work out for myself now and they are integral to my place in this community, to who I've been and can become, and to understanding how I am revising my story. The stories about values are particularly crucial, I think.

ALTER EGO: I worry that the comments you make about individuals will be taken as representing the southern mountain culture as a whole. Not everyone thinks the same as George and Bobby, for example, who are outspoken in their views.

EGO: I know they don't. The younger generations, for example, are not as prejudiced as the older generation. The people who have moved in from other states are not as conservative as the locals. Nevertheless, racism, sexism, and homophobia are prevalent in the local culture.

ALTER EGO: Are you ambivalent about the mountain people? Is that what we're seeing in the stories?

EGO: I'm not ambivalent about them; I am ambivalent—well, actually critical— about some of their beliefs. In the mountains, I have to confront values very different from mine, yet these are values I embraced growing up. So it's like I'm confronting the different parts of myself here—especially the Luray girl vs. the university professor.

ALTER EGO: So this story is really as much about you as about them?

EGO: More, I think. The ethnography was really accidental.[7] Sometimes it's pretty eerie to experience with the mountain people that strange familiarity of who I used to be, to feel I understand how they're thinking and what it's like to live inside their belief system. I'm talking understanding from the outside; I could never actually live like that again. Other times, I watch them and I feel so different. I can't find the Luray girl; I don't want to find her.

ALTER EGO: Doesn't this value conflict make you want to run from the mountains?

EGO: If that was all I experienced there, then I wouldn't want to spend much time in the mountains. What happens, though, is that I get attracted to their sense of community, blend of mutual aid and self-sufficiency, importance they place on family and friendship, and their inclination to live more spontaneously in the moment than I do, yet be more laid-back about it—and that Luray girl sticks out her head again and starts speaking with a southern accent.

ALTER EGO: And you're attracted to the beauty of the area and being in nature.

EGO: Yes, that's the biggest pull, for sure.

ALTER EGO: The way you're pulled back to the mountains is intriguing. On most counts you are comfortable and happy in your life as a professor and you live a comfortable upper-middle-class professional life.

EGO: Richard Russo, in an interview, said something about his small-town upbringing that spoke to me: "I've always had the feeling that part of me left. I mean, the Richard Russo who grew up and became a novelist is one person. But I've always had the distinct feeling that there was a ghost version of myself still living back in that place that's still so real in my imagination and that I've been telling fibs about all this time" [NPR, 2007]. This passage describes how I feel, and how many people who have moved from working-class to academic lives feel.

ALTER EGO: So, can't you write about those tensions without writing about identifiable mountain folk?

EGO: I don't know how to do that. I don't think I (or anyone really) can do that.

ALTER EGO: Norman Denzin manages just that in his work on the Wild West and his rural community in Montana where he has his summer home [for example, Denzin, 2003, 2008b]. He doesn't include recognizable people in his stories, other than himself and a few family members and public figures. Instead he focuses on places, events, symbols, signs, historical events, fictional dialogues and performances with unnamed narrators and numbered voices that stand in for historical societies, dignitaries, school board members, Native Americans, ranchers, and White people.

EGO: That's an interesting solution, but I don't think I'd be comfortable writing that way.

ALTER EGO: Chris Poulos [2008a] also writes about family without revealing exactly who he is writing about. He purposely leaves characters nameless and identifies them by their roles. For example, readers aren't sure whether the "father" in the story refers to Chris's father's father, his own father, or himself as a father to his sons. "Father" does not always refer to the same person, even within the same story.

EGO: I find that style fascinating, but it means the plot has to be fragmented and discontinuous and the details somewhat undeveloped.

ALTER EGO: True, but this approach works for Chris's purpose of taking the focus off a particular family and particular family members and showing that these stories are about all of us [Poulos, 2008a, p. 65].

EGO: It does. But the way I like to tell stories—where real people in specific places have conversations with each other (and with me) and do concrete things together, where the same characters appear in different scenes over time and a plot develops—presents problems not solvable by the techniques Denzin and Poulos use.

ALTER EGO: Are you sure you're not just wedded to this account because it's such a good way to loop back to your family and childhood and the stories you're written before, add to the revisions, and complete the circle?

EGO: I've asked myself that question many times. For sure I don't want to give up this late in the writing process the plot that holds this book together.

ALTER EGO: If you don't want to give it up, you could resolve the ethical conflicts by having a conversation with the mountain folks before publishing this, as Laurel suggested. Didn't she recommend that you have George over for some lox and bagels and conversation?

EGO: Yes, she did. That made me laugh. George and Louise won't eat at my house. They came to a party one time and didn't eat anything. George won't even drink our water. He told me he only likes to eat Louise's cooking. Only thing I think he's ever eaten that I cooked is the corn pudding I took him, but I didn't see him eat that. I know he wouldn't eat lox and bagels. Neither would Bobby and Sarah Mae. They're meat-and-fried-potatoes folks.

ALTER EGO: So how do you justify not taking these stories back to the mountain folk? Aren't you worried that the same thing will happen here that happened in *Fisher Folk*?

EGO: Oh yes. This is on my mind all the time. And this time it could be much worse. I only visited in the fishing communities. We have a home in the mountains and we're part of the community. I often imagine sitting on the porch with Louise and George, or with Bobby and Sarah Mae, and I wonder how I'll feel knowing I've written these stories.

ALTER EGO: And . . . ?

EGO: And then I think about how I'll feel sitting on the porch if I've confronted them with these stories. That's the part that doesn't make sense. If I think these stories might be painful, then why would I want to give them to the mountain people and make them deal with the things I say?

ALTER EGO: So you're going to take your chances, like you did with the Fisher Folk?

EGO: I didn't take my chances with the Fisher Folk. Back then, I didn't think about these ethical issues beforehand. I just wrote the stories and put them out there.

ALTER EGO: And the difference now?

EGO: This time I'm thinking the issues through as well as I can, and I'm willing to take responsibility for what I write and face whatever happens if the mountain people read my stories. There's a part of me that would be happy if the mountain people did know more about me and Art. Most of the locals have no idea what Art and I do, who we really are, or what we think, other than that we are political liberals, which we don't talk about much with anybody other than George and two former teachers who live on the road. It's not that we're trying to hide aspects of ourselves, as I did in Fishneck so long ago; it's more that almost no one ever asks, or even thinks to ask. Part of that comes from their not having attended college, but sometimes I wish they'd ask me questions about my life like I ask them questions about theirs. I'd like to be able to show more of the different parts of myself there. They're not introspective or inquiring like people in our university community.

ALTER EGO: But that's not who they are. You say yourself that they talk about the everyday, in-the-moment kind of stuff, more than anything else, as your parents did. And that's part of what you like about them. You're not saying you're smarter than they are, are you?

EGO: Not at all. They know a whole lot more about survival and the material world, such as construction and property maintenance, than I ever will. I often feel kind of stupid when faced with their knowledge. I am attracted to their practical knowledge at the same time I am repulsed by their narrow perspectives about how life should be lived.

ALTER EGO: Don't you sometimes think about how they see you? You don't know much about the material world and you spend your days tied to your computer when you could be outside doing real work, such as tending the house or yard, or enjoying the day.

EGO: But how different are George and Bobby really? They also are tied to their work, just like we are.

ALTER EGO: But what they're doing is considered "real work"—taking care of the material world.

EGO: While the kind of work we do is work that they think people can't wait to retire from.

ALTER EGO: Exactly. My guess is that they think you're dumber than most Floridiots.

EGO: You mean in the sense that other Floridiots may not know anything, but at least they retire and take life easy and do their own home maintenance.

ALTER EGO: Yes. And besides you don't go to church and you haven't been saved . . .

EGO: And we're crazy liberals on top of it.

ALTER EGO: Given all that, maybe what you write here won't surprise them. Sometimes I wonder if you're trying too hard to figure out all the ethical issues. Tony Adams [personal communication] says that having a discussion with colleagues about ethical issues, including how one feels about not talking about particular ethical issues with respondents—what you're doing here—is what's important, not necessarily deciding which or whose ethics are better. Don't you also have to think about having ethical relationships with the mountain people in terms of talking with them about beliefs and prejudices you find harmful? Tony says that's also a part of relational ethics.

EGO: That's what I've been doing with George and Bob. I have been working on both of them, gradually, gently, and lovingly, to try to get them to think about race, gender, sexual orientation, and ethnicity in more complex ways.

ALTER EGO: If I might interrupt this flow for a minute, I have to point out that you rarely talk about impacting the women's views. Why is that?

EGO: Yes, I noticed that as we were talking. The women rarely say anything about these issues. They tend to let their men speak for them, and I think they also tend to take on the views of the men in their lives. Or, at least, they follow the credo not to challenge their husband's point of view.

ALTER EGO: Wouldn't showing all of them this chapter force all of them to confront your views and give women a space to assert theirs?

EGO: You don't know this culture. I fear that showing them what I have written would be perceived as my trying to force them to read and respond. Confrontation might make them dig in, even write me off. That kind of pressure might ruin anything that I've managed to accomplish. In southern culture, you're supposed to "play nice." Confrontation tends to lead to fistfights or ignoring each other, not change.

ALTER EGO: But what if the locals get hold of this manuscript?

EGO: Then whether they read this or not, whether they choose to talk about it with me or not ... well, those will be their decisions. And, under those conditions, I'm willing and ready to have those conversations. Some of them anyway.

ALTER EGO: What do you mean?

EGO: I think their knowing some of the things I write about myself in this book will be more problematic than anything I said about them. They will be very judgmental about my abortion and my having had a relationship with a Black man, for example, and other ways I live my life. I'm not sure I want to, or should be forced to, have those conversations.

ALTER EGO: That makes me think ...

EGO: Yes ...

ALTER EGO: That yes, you have to think about yourself here as well as the mountain people. But there also are other people you have to think about as well.

EGO: You mean Art? [Alter Ego nods.] I have thought about him. That's why I've made sure that he has read several versions of this chapter and had input.

ALTER EGO: Ummmm, interesting. Still, he is more of the "bad cop" in the text.

EGO: [laughs] That's because he's more of the bad cop in real life. But seriously, I am concerned that he is implicated in what I say here, and he has to live in the community too, so I want what I say here to be okay with him. Laurel picked up the complexities when she first read this chapter. "Art's involved here too," she said. "I am really concerned that the mountain folk will say, 'Ah, just like a Jew and Jew-lover ... deceitful, can't be trusted, and so on.'" That got me thinking. Will Art suffer more than I from what I write because he is Jewish? He doesn't say much directly to the mountain folk in this text, but his opinion about some aspects of the culture, such as the religion, is stronger than mine. Mine is softened by growing up in the rural south and being related to family who believe similarly. I don't want to hurt the mountain people or lose our place in the community and our friendships; nor do I want the mountain people (or readers) to think I don't value or am condemning their culture. I wouldn't be living there if that were the case ...

ALTER EGO: Though don't you and Art sometimes feel you are fish out of water?

EGO: [*laughs*] Yes, we say that often, but both of us—not just me—are attracted to our lives there, the beauty of the area, and the warmth of the people. We're often happier in the mountains than we are in Tampa, though I don't know how much of that is the sense that we are on vacation in the mountains and returning to our more structured work world when we go to Tampa.

ALTER EGO: So do the benefits of writing and sharing these stories outweigh the risks?

EGO: I hope so. I think this chapter suggests how others might examine and think about revising their lives, even when the process is difficult. Living in this community takes me back to Luray in interesting ways, reminding me of what I didn't value about small-town southern communities but also reminding me of my connection there and what I did appreciate about the community and my family. Sometimes when Art and I are having breakfast at one of the local restaurants, I look at the men gathered around the bar smoking and having coffee—all you can drink for a dollar—or a two ninety-nine breakfast special, and it's like I'm seeing my dad in the diner in Luray. I think it's important for readers to see that I haven't just escaped my past and become an upper-middle-class professional. I'm still struggling to define myself, trying to understand my past, as I continue to strongly resist certain elements of it. I'm hoping these stories touch readers and lead them to think about the trajectory of their lives, who they have become, and how our stories of the past contribute to our stories of our present and future. There is value in re-storying/revising ourselves rather than uncritically accepting for ourselves the stories we have constructed in the past.

I'm trying to consider who I have become, but I'm also thinking about what it means to interact with people holding values different from mine. George and Bobby are the epitome of that for me in terms of politics, gender, ethnicity, race, abortion, the environment, religion—issues that are important to me. Yet we also share many values—the value of community and family, love and mutual support, neighborliness, responsibility, being true to your word, hard work, doing and contributing your share, and fairness, to start. I guess that's how I can be friends with them, because I recognize those common values. I also recognize our common humanity—the pain of loss and human suffering, for example.

ALTER EGO: Which brings me back to your point about interacting with people with different values. It also seems important in the polarized political climate today to be able to have relationships across these boundaries of conservative and liberal values.

EGO: I think that's true. Maybe relating to George and Bobby is my contribution to Barack Obama's audacity to hope that we can talk across divides. Equality in race, gender, ethnicity, sexual orientation, and economic opportunity are core values to me. Sometimes I think I don't want anything—or shouldn't want anything—to do with anyone who doesn't feel the same way. But knowing local people in Mapleton has made me think about how and why fundamentalist conservatives put their world together the way they do. It also has made me think more deeply about my own family and background. Sometimes

I think the best I can do is to love people who think differently, and lovingly explain my position and listen to and ask questions about theirs. I'd like to be able to have more open conversations about all this. Just so I don't have to watch Fox News every night.

ALTER EGO: How about NASCAR?

EGO: Oh my, please. That would be worse than my mother's soaps. [*Their laughter blends into one loud hoot.*]

ALTER EGO: So how to end this?

EGO: There is no ending. As Laurel and I agreed after she read an earlier version of this chapter, eventually we do what we do, and we do it hoping that it will turn out for the best, and we accept that we are responsible for our choices. Then we ask more questions of ourselves and push ourselves to think broader and deeper.

ALTER EGO: Didn't Chris Poulos [personal communication] say that "it is my calling to tell *my* story as I come to know it, through my experiences, through my encounters with others, and through the process of writing it," while at the same time "being sensitive to the needs and concerns of others"?

EGO: Yes, and he also said that "[t]o tell the story may well be the *only* ethical thing to do" in the sense that telling the story allows us to follow "the mystery of human life" [Poulos, 2008a, p. 65].

ALTER EGO: I found it interesting along those lines that Laurel reread *Fisher Folk* for the panel on your work at SSCA [Southern States Communication Association, 2008] and said that she thought it perverse that such a bad fuss was made about it all.

EGO: Ha, perhaps I was the one who kicked up all the controversy by writing so much about the ethics of that research. Maybe I'm doing the same thing here. Still, I can't help but wonder if this ending will disappoint people who have spoken favorably about the depth of my ethical introspection [Denzin, 2008b; Frentz, 2008a; Pelias, 2008; Poulos, 2008b]. Have I gone far enough? Taken the easy way out? Made the right decisions?

Upon reading an earlier draft of this chapter, Lisa Tillmann [personal communication] wrote that she was not convinced that the insights I had in this chapter warranted the risk that publication of these stories might bring "unwanted exposure to my neighbors and irreparable damage to my relationships with them." She didn't think I had lived up to the promise of the "Returning to the Field" [Ellis, 1995b] piece I wrote about my work with the Fisher Folk. That really stopped me in my tracks. I made a lot of changes after that, but it's up for grabs whether I have fulfilled my promise or not.

ALTER EGO: Promises are made in a context. "Returning to the Field" did not resolve the tension an ethnographer feels between telling the truth and acting honorably and sensitively toward your informants. Mainly it acknowledged the tensions, which are present and depend on many local considerations. I think you've tried to think through all those here.

EGO: Hey, thanks. I hope so. Whatever the case, I trust that this chapter will at least serve to keep this conversation going among all of us doing ethnographic research.

ALTER EGO: It's an ongoing process, isn't it?

EGO: Yes, who I am is unfinished and in motion, as a researcher and writer, and as one who lives in the city among progressives and in the mountains among conservatives. My relationship with the mountain people is still becoming and who and what we are and can be to each other is still in process [Ceglowski, 2000]. The same is true of my relationship with readers and the way I make ethical decisions. These stories are revisions, yet once again they risk being frozen frames—though many of the images have not come clearly into focus yet.

ALTER EGO: Perhaps they never will. But you go on anyway. [*Ego nods.*]

Ethical Revision

In the last revision of this chapter in summer 2008, I reluctantly use pseudonyms for all places and people and change as many identifying characteristics as I can without changing meaning. I add fictional characters to make it more difficult and confusing for locals to identify particular people in this story[8] and for outsiders to recognize the place, though, as in all ethnography, with some effort it is possible to determine where it is located. Though I use fictional devices and camouflage identities, this chapter is based solely on my experiences. I do not know if these changes help my case for writing ethically, or if they simply provide unnecessary window dressing.

Epilogue: Old Paths/New Paths

The summer is fading away now. I can see a hint of red in the sweet gum trees outside my study window and in the burning bushes that follow our property line along the dirt road in the front. Already a few brown leaves float to the ground, reminding me that autumn is not far behind. The crepe myrtle and dahlias are in bloom and Art and I are sad to be missing so many of them—particularly the late-blooming Envy and Bodacious dahlias we have come to love. The cicadas sing every night now, their mesmerizing and reverberating sounds only occasionally a bit too loud for sleeping. It's finally raining after a long, dry summer.

Art and I feel enveloped in sadness as we finish winterizing the plants. We spray Merit on our four hemlocks to prevent the wooly adelgid bug from killing them, as it has destroyed most of the hemlocks of the Southern Appalachians. We blanket the front yard with pitchfork after pitchfork of the mulch that George delivered this morning on his flatbed truck. Is this just the adult version of the end-of-summer blues I felt when I was a kid? The end of vacation? It's not as though I don't like my life back in Tampa. I look forward to seeing my friends and students and continuing all the work I do there. What hold does this place have over me?

We head indoors as the black clouds quickly form. The lightning flashes and the thunder claps. We rush to close the windows and unplug all the electronics that aren't on surge protectors, having learned the hard way that we are a lightning rod on this mountain ridge. Then we stand on our back porch and watch the show as the storm moves up the mountain. You can literally see the lines of rain heading our way little by little. The wind begins to howl and then the raindrops start, first on one side of the cabin, then the other. We dash around moving the precariously swaying porch furniture from the west mountain side to the calmer north side, and hold on tight to the swinging French doors as we head back inside.

The rain beats on the side of the cabin, overflowing the gutters on our steep 10/12 pitch roof. The rain pours and pours, like it often does in Florida. In spite of the hurricanes in Florida, somehow it seems more precarious here, perched on top of this ridge where anything can happen. Sunya, our herding dog, sleeps peacefully on the floor beside us, taking it all in stride—even the creaking sounds of the round logs repositioning themselves. Buddha starts to shake, and tries to bury her body first in mine, then in Art's. Art and I react somewhere in the middle, attracted to the danger and fearing it at the same time.

Then suddenly, as quickly as it came, the storm is over, and we decide that we can still go for our evening walk. The rain makes for a muddy trek down the mountain, but since it is the last mountain walk Art and I and the doggies will have for a while, we are determined. As we walk down the mountainside, I try to take it all in, to remember the feel, the smell, the sound, the sight, so that I can call it up in memory in Tampa when I'm thinking about how I can't wait to get back to the mountains. As we walk back up the hill, Art throws the ball for Buddha over and over. When he doesn't throw it fast enough, Buddha pushes the ball with her nose until it rolls down the hill and then she chases it. Art, ever the wordsmith, calls this "master-balling." We laugh, then note that Sunya has slowed down even more over the summer and sometimes doesn't bother to run after the ball at all.

I pick my way carefully up the path, trying not to get any muddier. I see our tracks from the daily trips we have taken up and down this trail all summer. Trying to step in many of the same tracks, I avoid those that are vegetation bare and prefer to step on the fallen leaves, though I know they are slippery. When I try to walk in the same tracks up that I walked down, the newly fallen leaves make some of the impressions difficult to locate and those visible hard to match because of the different angles I place my feet. The trip back cannot be made the same way it was made the first time, or even the time before. The way back up presents a different perspective, even though you are looking at the same things. You realize there is so much there that you barely noticed in prior trips, and, over time, the trees grow taller, new plants take root, the weeds sprout flowers and cease being viewed as weeds, the vines cover old paths, and new paths are carved out between the rocks by the rain and running water.

Nevertheless, my footsteps from before offer a familiarity, a comfort, a sense of continuity much like the seasonal cycles and our regular journeys between the mountains and Tampa. Of course, along with the continuity comes unpredictability—the traffic jams on I-75, water leaks and other repairs waiting in our Tampa home, the late spring freeze, the plant that doesn't come back the next year, the parts of the path now covered over. I breathe in the smells and think how my life, like this landscape, is both a familiar and unpredictable work in progress. I enjoy thinking about how it was, is, and might be; I freeze-frame it at various moments and take a look, a partial look at a life in motion. Sometimes the task seems overwhelming and I wonder whether I miss out on a lot of experience by overanalyzing it. Yet, isn't analysis also part of experience? Isn't that one of the fundamental differences between the mountain culture and the culture of the university?

"Go get it," I yell to Buddha and Sunya as Art hurls a tennis ball out of sight down the mountain. Buddha scurries down the mountain, following the path of the ball and sniffing at each place the ball bounced on the ground as it skimmed along. Sunya scampers behind and stops when she sees that there's no way she can beat Buddha to the ball. Art and I encourage them. "Find it. Find it." Soon Buddha comes up the mountainside with the ball in her mouth, head held high, her body literally bobbing with joy. Sunya follows, huffing. With a burst of energy Sunya tries to steal the ball with her larger jaws, but Buddha stops, moves right and then left, and ducks her head, using her quickness to juke Sunya. Then, suddenly, Buddha stops and lets Sunya take the ball from her mouth and present it to us. It's the elder's privilege. I give them each a cookie.

"So what do you think of my last chapter?" I ask. Art spent part of the day reading and editing it for me.

"I like it," Art replies. "The stories are great. But I wonder about all your concerns about writing ethically, especially your decision to change all the names of places and create fictional characters to take the brunt of your criticism. Autoethnography *is* personal. There's no getting around that. It feels like you're taking the personal out of it. But you've got to let this book go and get on with your life. A story never reaches perfection. No more revisions. Enough already."

"Ah, revisions, they're never done," I say, knowing we will continue talking about all these issues on the ride home.

Art takes my hand and we continue up the road, now in silence, enjoying the walk as always, though now being more careful than we used to be about the steps we take and how fast we climb. I lock up the cabin, while Art gets the dogs settled in the car. When I get into the passenger seat, after going back into the house three times for things we've forgotten, Art has pulled the car to the far side of our cabin. As I breathe a sigh of completion and note the dinner plate–sized dahlia Art has cut and placed between our seats, Johnny Cash's song "The Rose of My Heart" plays on our CD player. Finally, I notice that Art has parked in front of our rose bushes. Johnny sings, "We're the best partners this world's ever seen/Together we're close as can be/But sometimes it's hard to find time in between/To tell you what you mean to me."

As Johnny continues singing about the "rose of his heart" and the "love of his life," Art and I look at each other and tears form on smiling faces as we think about the summer we have just spent walking our path and tending to our garden together.

Meta-Autoethnography: Revision and Memory—A Dream Story[9]

Art and I run for our lives. Unidentified men chase us. The action is fuzzy, as dreams sometimes tend to be. I don't know why we are running or what is going on, though this scene feels like part of a developed plot, such as one you'd see in a Hollywood action film. As I become conscious of the dream, I am aware that Art has headed down a hallway while I have opened a heavy door and run down an empty stairwell, one like you might see in an old university building. Suddenly the door opens on the floor below me, and one of the men who has been chasing us says, "Ha. That was not smart. Don't you know that the first place we'd look would be the stairwell? Don't you go to the movies?" I crouch down in the stairway, covering my head with my arms, wondering how I'm going to get out of this predicament.

As this plot winds through my head, I am between sleep and wakefulness. I resist waking up, much as one might do after passing out, because I am unsure what I will wake up into. Am I really being chased? Should I stay asleep to escape this frightening reality? Or is this scene occurring in my dream world and waking will get me out of it? A voice in my head tells me not to worry because I am the narrator of this experience at the same time I am the person in the experience. It feels like I have caught myself in the process of the dream filling—literally exploding in—my head as I awake. I am creating the dream at the same time I am becoming conscious of it. I feel—for a brief moment anyway—like I can choose to continue sleeping and dreaming or wake up and take my chances. I fear the dream may take on a life of its own once I go back to sleep and I will return to running scared or crouching in the stairwell. This seems an easy decision: wake up! But the dream intrigues me and I do not want to let it go, especially my processing of it. A little more conscious now, I tell myself that if I continue waking up, I can make myself remember and construct the dream and its meaning. But is that as good as the dream itself? These thoughts alter the dream, which quickly begins fading away into the dark.

Now I am immersed in holding on to and letting go of the dream, wondering how much control I might be able to exert over the plot of the dream, wondering how much control I have over sleeping and waking. All of these thoughts now are more intriguing than the dream itself. This "thought play" makes the dream recede farther and wakefulness take over, until I now locate myself in my bed rather than in the stairwell. I doubt I could get back there even if I tried. Instead, I concentrate on remembering—and reconstructing—the dream process.

I smile in my half-awake state, thinking that this dream is similar to the book I am writing. Sometimes the plot just happens, seemingly on its own, and my typing fingers rush to catch up; other times I am aware of myself selecting from my memory bank and interacting with what I find there to create a plot that is in harmony with my memory.

Excited by the similarities between my book and my dream, I consider getting up for a pen and paper so I might write down this dream before it disappears. I open one eye for a brief moment, then decide that I don't want to interrupt this perfect state of mind and relaxation—I love being half awake and half asleep, which staying in bed affords me. I also don't want to wake up Art or the dogs, who I know also enjoy their morning naps. Why disturb this perfect moment to record it?

Sunya sighs from her bed in the corner, Buddha snuggles closer to my body, and I wrap myself around Art, who doesn't move. I let the story I have told above float in my head as I, on the one hand, vow to remember it yet, on the other, acknowledge that I am willing to relinquish it if necessary. We all doze for a few more hours.

I recall the dream when I sit down at my computer in the afternoon and pick up one of Chris Poulos's (2008a) articles to read for the last chapter of this book. Then the dream story comes flooding back, and I type and interpret what I remember, organizing the chaotic details into a linear story that resonates with my memory. Are these my memories from then or from now? Are these the interpretations I had now or before? And if before, were they during or immediately after the dream? I don't know what I have forgotten or when I forgot it, or how much of the story above really happened, was plucked from my memory, constructed in the remembering and writing process, or imagined (see Tullis Owen et al., in press).

Intrigued, I take some books off my shelf and begin reading about memory: "The nature of memory is to mix imagination and fact" and the best strategy is to "admit to the tension—not to cover it up," says Larson (2007, p. 25). The past is "much affected by the present moment," says Woolf (1985, p. 75) and "since my present is always in motion, my past itself changes too—*actually changes*—while the illusion created is that it stays fixed" (Mandel, 1981, p. 77; see also Larson, 2007, p. 34). "[My] memory supplies what I had forgotten, so that it seems as if it were happening independently, though I am really making it happen" (Woolf, 1985, p. 67). "What one forgets is as important—if not more so—as what one remembers" (Woolf, 1985, p. 69). "There is no fixed truth of the past to which we can gain access; everything we say and mean and make of the past is a form of revision" (Bochner, 2007, p. 206).

My mind is so full, I've forgotten about the action dream itself. Who are we running from? Why do Art and I go in different directions? And what have I been caught doing? I could write a book about this dream alone.

That's the way of memory . . . and personal storytelling. Revision(ing) is crucial.

Notes

Notes to the Introduction

1. For more information on "going meta," see Simons (1994). Simons defines *going meta* as "to provide a strategic, reflexive, frame-altering response to another's prior message or messages, or to a shared message context" (p. 469). The term *meta-communication*, or communication about communication, is frequently used to signify that which frames, alters a frame, provides multiple frames, or contextualizes messages to help participants understand a communicative event. See also Bateson (1972); Bochner & Krueger (1979); Goffman (1974, 1981); Watzlawick, Bavelas, & Jackson (1967); Wilmot (1980).

2. Davies and Davies (2007, p. 1157) use the term "texts in motion."

3. Thanks to Art Bochner for this idea; see also Richardson (1997).

Notes to Chapter 1

1. Though my older brother is named Art, I call him Arthur in this book so as not to confuse him with my partner, who also is named Art.

2. Thanks to Ruth Spitler for sharing her memories of The Store.

3. More than two decades later, my friend would discover that her parents were Jewish and had escaped from Germany during the Holocaust. But while they lived in Luray, the whole family attended a Baptist church and kept their ethnicity secret.

4. Written July 2008.

5. See, for example, Rambo Ronai (1995) and Karr (1995). Birkerts (2008, p. 145) contrasts traumatic memoirs with lyric memoirs. Lyric memoirs, such as the one I write here, "are undertaken contemplatively, often in a spirit of curiosity, and are bent on recovering the felt core of early experience, implicitly searching out the persistence of the self over time," while trauma-based accounts are "private salvage" operations, reflecting on and trying to compensate for the "destruction" and "rupture."

Notes to Chapter 2

1. I never understood, and nobody seemed able to tell me, why Washington, D.C., which was across a mountain range and ninety miles east in a large metropolitan area, was always referred to as "down in the country." Growing up, I had a strange image of D.C. as full of crooked politicians who lived on large farms! I recall visiting there only once or twice during high school with a group to see a movie. I'm not sure now if I saw *My Fair Lady*, *The Sound of Music*, or *Gone with the Wind* there; I do remember seeing all three during high school.

2. Portions of this text are adapted from Ellis (1997, pp. 117–119).

3. This text is adapted from Ellis (1995d, pp. 147–167).

4. As I look back on this event from my position now, I am aware of my "othering of the exotic," and I refrain from changing my prose since I want to stay faithful to the way I perceived Grady at that point. See, for example, Villenas (2000).

5. According to http://www.epodunk.com/cgi-bin/popInfo.php?locIndex=8954

6. http://www.tampabay.org/press.asp?rls_id=1384&cat_id=1

Notes to Chapter 3

1. See Ellis (1998) and also Chapter 10 in this volume.
2. Portions of this text are adapted from Ellis (1995b, pp. 5–7 and 1997, pp. 121–126).
3. These vignettes are adapted from Ellis (1986).
4. Ellis (1986, pp. 121–122).
5. Ellis (1986, p. 30).
6. Ellis (1986, pp. 80–81).
7. This text is adapted from a longer paper entitled "Emotional and Ethical Quagmires in Returning to the Field" (Ellis, 1995b).
8. See Ellis (1995b) for a more detailed version of this story.
9. Though this event happened in 1989, it was not written and published until 1995.
10. See Ellis (1995b) for an extended discussion of these issues.

Notes to Chapter 4

1. See Ellis (1995a) for the detailed story.
2. Portions of the above text are adapted from Ellis (1997, pp. 124–126) and Ellis (1995a, pp. 7–9).
3. See Ellis (1995a) for details of this process; see also Ellis (2000).
4. These excerpts come from Ellis (1995a).
5. This text is adapted from Ellis (1995a, pp. 49–53, 63).
6. This text is adapted from Ellis (1995a, pp. 53–56).
7. This text is adapted from Ellis (1995a, pp. 287–289).
8. Portions of this text are adapted from Ellis (2000, pp. 303–304).

Notes to Chapter 5

1. Portions of this text are adapted from Ellis (1995a, pp. 304–306).
2. This text is an edited and condensed version of Ellis (1991a).
3. Denzin's (1984, 1985, 1987) work is an exception in its emphasis on lived experience. Following Derrida (1978), Denzin (1988) takes the position that one cannot study lived experience directly, but can only study the texts that express that lived experience.
4. For example, Armon-Jones (1986, p. 46) approaches emotions from a constructionist and phenomenological perspective, but then concludes that emotion can "be adequately characterized without appealing to qualia or to physiological factors as necessary constituents of the total emotion event." She reaches this conclusion because she sees subjective feeling as implying irreducibility and having individualistic implications (see also Harré, 1986).
5. Camic (1986) discusses the exclusion of the concept of habit by sociologists as a result of their revolt against behaviorism. He notes that sociologists rejected the Watsonian approach that "made habit virtually everything in social life" (p. 1072). But, instead of restating the position that habit is a part of social action, they then rejected habit completely. The same is true of introspection.
6. Cooley (1926), in particular, advocated "sympathetic introspection," a process by which one comes to understand others by sympathetically ascribing to them one's own response in similar situations. Compare also Dilthey's (1900/1976) "symbolic understanding"; Weber's (1949) "verstehen"; MacIver's (1931) "sympathetic reconstruction"; Schwartz & Schwartz's (1955) "sympathetic identification"; and Znaniecki's (1934) "humanistic coefficient" among others.
7. See, however, Evert and Bijkerk (1987) where the therapist and patient introspect about their experiences in therapy.
8. This text is adapted from Ellis (1995a, pp. 307–308, 318–323); Ellis (1997, pp. 127–132); and Ellis (1996b, pp. 155–163).
9. Portions of this text are adapted from Ellis (2004, pp. 54–57). Art Bochner and Carolyn Ellis gave the original performance, from which this text is excerpted, in the Dow Visiting Scholars Program

at Saginaw Valley State University in 1999. The talk was entitled "Talking Over Ethnography: A Dialogue on Intersecting Life and Work."

10. Weinstein (1963, 1969).

11. See Ellis (1996b, pp. 168–173) for an extended discussion of this topic.

12. This text is adapted from Ellis (1995a, pp. 334–337).

13. But see Rosenblatt (1996) who argues that grief occurs over a lifetime.

14. See Moss and Moss (1996) who discuss triadic relationships between people and their current and deceased spouses.

Notes to Chapter 6

1. This text is adapted from Ellis (1993, pp. 711–730).

Notes to Chapter 7

1. Sherryl Kleinman is a professor of sociology at University of North Carolina, Chapel Hill. She published this essay in *The Sociological Quarterly*, copyright 1993 (Vol. 34, no. 4, pp. 731–733). This article is reprinted with permission from Blackwell Publishing.

2. Art Bochner is a professor of communication at University of South Florida. This work was published in J. Paul (ed.), *Introduction to the Philosophies of Research and Criticism in Education and the Social Sciences*, 1st edition, copyright 2005, pp. 268–273. This chapter is reprinted by permission of Pearson Education, Inc., Upper Saddle River, NJ. See Bochner (2005a) and also Bochner (2005b).

3. For example, see eight responses in Paul (2005).

4. For example, Left Coast Press, Inc.: *Writing Lives: Narrative Ethnography*; AltaMira: *Crossroads in Qualitative Inquiry*; AltaMira: *Ethnographic Alternatives*.

5. For example, Angrosino (1998); Ellingson (2005); Charlés (2007); Foster (2007); Frentz (2008b); Holman Jones (2007); Pelias (2004); Poulos (2008b); Richardson (2007); Tillmann-Healy (2001).

6. For example, Berger & Quinney (2004); Bochner & Ellis (2002); Clair (2003); Ellis & Bochner (1996); Ellis & Flaherty (1992); Hertz (1996); Reed-Danahay (1997); Roth (2005); Vaz (1997). See also Knowles & Cole (2008); Levy (2009); Liamputtong & Rumbold (2008).

7. For example, *Qualitative Inquiry, Journal of Contemporary Ethnography, Symbolic Interaction, Cultural Studies—Critical Methodologies, Journal of Loss and Trauma, Studies in Symbolic Interaction, International Review of Qualitative Research*.

8. For example, Arts-Based Education Research Conference (Bristol, UK), National Communication Association's Ethnography Division, International Congress of Qualitative Inquiry, American Educational Research Association, Society for the Study of Symbolic Interaction, QUIG: Conference on Interdisciplinary Qualitative Studies, Canadian International Qualitative & Ethnographic Research Conference, The Bournemouth Qualitative Research Conference, Reflective Practice Conference, and Association of Qualitative Research in Australia.

9. See, for example, Lehman et al. (1987), Sanders (1982), and the literature review in Carr et. al. (2001). Findings are inconsistent across studies, depending on the variables and populations examined. Results are more complex than the common claim that loss from sudden death is more intense and prolonged than loss from long-term illness. For example, Sanders's (1982) study of loss of family members showed an internalized emotional response in the sudden-death group that led to prolonged physical stress, while the long-term chronic illness group experienced dejection, loneliness, and frustration though no prolonged physiological component. The research of Carr et al. (2001) suggests that the protective effects of anticipated death on survivors' mental health may be overstated. Also, these studies often report on grief experiences shortly after the loss and again at intervals of a few years, so it is unclear how relevant they are to my experiences of grief more than twenty-five years after the loss. Reports of grief so long after a loss commonly have been thought of as "pathological" or "unresolved" rather than viewed as a healthy response to loss of a loved one and a way of maintaining relationships with those we love. See articles in Stroebe et al. (1993) that summarize pathological and normal grief. See articles in Klass et al. (1996), in

particular Silverman & Klass (1996), which discuss grief that occurs over a lifetime. Rosenblatt (1996), for example, describes loss as a "sequence over our lifetime of new losses or new realizations of loss" and he studies grief up to fifty years after the loss (pp. 49–50).

10. Thanks to Lisa Tillmann for this insight.

11. I also am aware that my father does not have a large role in this metastory (or this book) either. I'm not sure why, other than that my father has been dead since 1987, now more than twenty years. Thus our relationship did not have time to go through the changes after Rex's death that my relationship with my mother did. I remember how affectionate and hard-working my father was, his desire for fun and adventure, his love for his job and making a living, and his need for love, especially when he was drinking alcohol. Though there is plenty to write about that relationship, I do not need to analyze our connection relative to Rex's death. Thus, I will save this analysis for another time.

12. Looking back now, I remember that guilt was eschewed in the counterculture of the sixties in which I came of age. I wonder what impact, if any, that culture had on Sherryl's Jewish-inspired feeling of guilt. Or on the lack of feelings of guilt in my own life.

13. I will later come to see in a story I wrote, entitled "Speaking of Dying" (Ellis, 1995c), how tricky it is for the outer circle of people as well, who may not be allowed into the "inner circle" of dying. See Chapter 10.

14. See Chapter 8 in this volume.

Notes to Chapter 8

1. This text is adapted from Ellis (1996a, pp. 240–243).

2. This text is adapted from Ellis (2001, pp. 598–616).

3. Those who have researched the role of soap operas in people's lives note that soap operas create "parallel lives" (Porter, 1982) for viewers and provide a sense of belonging and companionship, especially for the lonely (Brown, 1994). They provide a "pseudo-reality" (Ang, 1996) in that the characters become a part of our lives and our memories (Hobson, 1982). The people on the screen become our friends and allow us to escape our own lives as we get involved in theirs (Ang, 1996). Soap operas give us a moment of catharsis (Kilborn, 1992) in which we can feel for the characters and let out our emotions at an aesthetic and safe distance from actual events. They provide "ritual pleasure" (Brunsdon, 1984) and exciting cliffhangers as we look forward to our time together and seeing how their lives unfold (see, also, Lewis, 1997).

4. It's interesting that in the context of critiquing autoethnography, several poststructuralist readers have criticized this published piece for not offering more complexity. Gannon (2006), for example, notes that I leave little space for my mother and, in contrast to my eschewing more complexity in my tale, she suggests that a poststructural autoethnography "might embrace multidimensionality, might aim to construct texts that are not easily ingested, that turn around and around so that we are encouraged (or forced or led) to a place of thinking differently and with more complexity about the world and our places within it" (p. 488). Jackson and Mazzei (in press) question my need to "tidy the ending" to this story. They ask about the various ways I might have "recast my easy and comfortable reading," in particular the possible alternative readings of my mother, our relationship, and the narration of my own "I." Additionally, Frentz (2008) suggests that this piece would benefit from a more coconstructed narrative where my mother would tell her own story. These are interesting issues that make me consider how many ways there are to tell and read a story.

5. See Hedtke and Winslade (2004), who after Myerhoff (1982), White (1988), and Epston and White (1992), discuss "re-membering" and membership in terms of the "club" of significant people in a person's life. These researchers suggest that people remain part of that club in a narrative form even after they die as long as they are remembered. They continue to be part of the current constructed reality.

Notes to Chapter 9

1. For a fuller discussion of these topics, see Ellis (2004, pp. 71–72, 77); Bochner & Ellis (1992, 1995); Ellis & Berger (2001).

2. This text is adapted from Ellis & Bochner (1992, pp. 79–101).

3. The guilt I acknowledge about having an abortion is interesting in light of the arguments I make in Chapter 7 about the lack of guilt I felt in the matter of my brother's death.

4. According to Finer and Henshaw (2005), from 1973 to 2002, more than forty-two million legal abortions occurred among American women.

5. See Ellis (2004, pp. 77–85) for a fuller discussion of this topic. I also note that I have not been able to write about the deaths of our dogs, though I have tried. I found reliving their deaths too painful. I also have not written about the dying and death of my mother in any detail for the same reason. I felt concern that the details of the stories were too intimate for publication and they made me feel more vulnerable than I was comfortable being at the time.

6. This text is adapted from Ellis (2004, pp. 82–85).

7. Paraphrased from memory; see also Ehrenreich (2004). Additionally, in 2004, a t-shirt was designed and sold on a Soap Box website that read, "I had an abortion." The website explained the t-shirts as "part of a project to tell the truth: that women might be sorry to need an abortion, but they aren't sorry that they had access to one" (Swift, 2007, p. 59). According to a Planned Parenthood website, "The t-shirt is an affirmation that abortion is not shameful" (http://www.ppaction.org/planned-parenthoodlam/notice-description.tcl?newsletter_id=2902061).

8. Cohen is summarizing the position of Exhale, an organization formed in 2000 for the purpose of helping in a nonjudgmental context women and their partners who have had abortions.

9. Kelly Clark/Keefe's (2007) presentation read in part:
"Drawing on, through and about my body's memories of pregnancy, miscarriage, birth, and the simultaneity of motherhood/professorhood, I am exploring, naming, and beginning to theorize the generative space, the burgeoning silence between my method as linguistically-based and my method as pictorially-based. *Mnemosyne* provokes this highly politicized space; one where class, gender, and the body are initially stripped of language, allowing a metaphoric, symbolic, pictorial model to be brought to bear on feminist methodologies. Blending color, laying line, my hand moves to the sensorial rhythms of stretching skin and ligaments, the taste of fluctuating hormones, the sight of a text-saturated academe, and the smell of baby wipes commingling with dry-erase markers. While invoking *Mnemosyne*, I sense the alchemy of matter-with-form, an inclusion of the feminine as intelligible—even, perhaps, a symbolic methodological birth intended to transgress the Cartesian masculinization of thought (Bordo, 1986) and the communicentric bias in knowledge production (Gordon, Miller & Rollock, 1990). *Mnemosyne* courts Luce Irigaray (1991): 'And what is that terror awaiting them in the shadow . . . that peril of water coming from sky and land? And that horror they feel for the sea when she sheds all masks and refuses to be calm, polite, and submissive to the sailors' direction?' (p. 51)
"Irigaray's allegory of woman as water; as woman who, at once, experiences oppression *and* liberatory potential, signals the central site of intrigue and deconstructive energy for examining my methodological subjectivity. Flowing from my reflexive positioning of motherhood/professorhood + researcher/researched, the textual and pictorial introspections of an embodied, social, and psychical subject are enacted—disrupting and antagonizing the binary between a 'self' that can look 'at' and a 'self' that can look 'in.'" (pp. 9–10)
See also Clark/Keefe (in press).

Notes to Chapter 10

1. Examples of the recent critiques of autoethnography abound. See Anderson (2006), Atkinson (2006), and Charmaz (2006) for critiques from a social science perspective; Clough (2000a and b), Gannon (2006), and Jackson & Mazzei (in press) for critiques from a poststructuralist perspective; Gingrich-Philbrook (2005) for a critique from an aesthetic/literary perspective. In addition, see also Buzard (2003) for a claim that autoethnography is undertheorized; Coffey (1999) and Madison (2006) for claims that autoethnography is self-indulgent and navel-gazing; Tierney (2002) for a claim that autoethnography is a move away from praxis and engaged social criticism and from trying to

understand the other. See also specific critiques of Ellis (2004), such as those by Maguire (2006) and Moro (2006); and see Holt (2003), Mykhalovskiy (1996), and Sparkes (2002), who discuss critical reviews of their autoethnographic projects. Of course, with this list, I have omitted the many positive reviews and responses to autoethnography that exist in the literature.

2.   For example, see Berry (2006), who writes intriguingly about ways—sometimes negative—that autoethnography affects audience members.

3.   Take, for example, a few of the social problems–oriented personal narratives published in the last decade: Angrosino's (1998) book on transforming the belittling perceptions of adult mentally retarded people; Frank's (1991) memoir of his own illness in which he encourages us to take a more active part in our illnesses; Tillmann-Healy's (2001) autoethnographic account of developing gay-straight friendships in which she uses her own marriage as an exemplar for crossing boundaries between straight and gay culture; Richardson's (1997) use of her own experience as a critical inquiry into the need to change the university culture; (Rambo) Ronai's (1995) personal exploration of her own sexual abuse and how her experiences relate to social policy; Gray and Sinding's (2002) performative ethnography that employs the performance of personal stories by survivors of breast cancer to alter the community's (laypeople and medical personnel) images of survivors; Ellingson's (2006) work on communicating among team members in an oncology clinic; Foster's (2006) work on hospice volunteers and communicating at end of life. See also Charlés (2007), Frentz (2008b), Nettles (2008), Poulos (2008c), Rushing (2006)—all in the *Writing Lives: Ethnographic Narrative Series* from Left Coast Press, Inc. These are only a few examples of how autoethnography and personal narrative address and contribute to social action and social change.

Other autoethnographies are more consciously political in nature. For example, Denzin includes autoethnographic writing in *Flags in the Window* (2007), his record of his (and others') reactions to the Bush Administration and the war in Iraq. In *Searching for Yellowstone*, Denzin (2008c) examines the cultural meaning of icons that represent and subjugate Native Americans in the American West. In *Writing in the San/d: Autoethnography among Indigenous Southern Africans*, Keyan Tomaselli (2007) and other South Africans study South African Bushman, who are activists engaged in cultural tourism rather than hunter-gatherers, and who critique modernity. In Tillmann-Healy's (2007) later work, the author accompanies gay men to their homes and communities of origin; her hope is to understand family dynamics surrounding having a gay family member and to examine and undermine structures of inequality and oppression.

4.   See, for example, Polletta (2006), who argues for the value of storytelling as a catalyst in social movements and social change and as an analytic tool.

5.   I make this move fully recognizing that it is a luxury to do so. Scholars new to autoethnography and graduate students have to be able to respond to all these positions. Some are devastated the first time they are confronted with these responses, especially if the confrontation is heated. A number of debates do exist about issues in autoethnography. For example, see the special issue of *Journal of Contemporary Ethnography* (2006, no. 4) on analytic autoethnography.

6.   This text is adapted from Ellis (1998, pp. 517–537).

7.   Writing this story helped me understand what was missing for me in Goffman's work. Goffman presents others' selves, but not his own. In actuality, he is all over his descriptions in the role of the all-knowing and disappearing researcher, though he doesn't acknowledge being there. We see through his eye, but we don't feel though his heart. Goffman talks about emotions only in terms of how people try to *appear* to feel (Hochschild, 1979), which he determines from their actions, gestures, looks, and words—in sum, their performances. Hochschild (1979) goes a step further and examines how people *try* to make themselves feel. My goal is to examine the lived experience of feelings—how people experience their feelings—through a narrative that opens up to readers my inner life and my participation with others and invites readers to examine their emotional responses in the process.

8.   This text is shortened and adapted from Ellis (1995c, pp. 73–81).

9. This is similar to Nancy Mair's (1996) discussion of "non-disabled" and disability activists' use of the phrase "temporarily able-bodied" to point out that the boundaries between able-bodied and disabled are permeable and that all of us, if we live long enough, will pass through them.

10. In her dissertation about her high school classmates now in their sixties, Mary Poole (2008) discusses in detail baby boomers' attitudes toward accumulated losses and dying and death.

Notes to Chapter 11

1. See Ellis (2002c, pp. 377–378).

2. This text is adapted from Ellis (2002c, pp. 375–394).

3. This text is adapted from Ellis (2002b, pp. 42–47).

4. This text is adapted from Ellis (2002c, pp. 394–400).

5. This text is adapted from Ellis (2002c, pp. 400–403).

6. I recognize that this is not always the case. Some have argued that at least in some situations, it might be best to repress what has happened to us, rather than replay it over and over (Slater, 2003). Others speak of the pain of remembering and the role of silence in healing (Woodstock, 2001).

7. This text is adapted from Ellis (2002c, pp. 404–409).

8. See Ellis (2003) for a story of tending Mom's grave.

9. Barack Obama's speech to Virginia's Jefferson-Jackson Dinner, Richmond, Virginia, given February 9, 2008, recorded February 10, 2008.

Notes to Chapter 12

1. See Ellis (2004) for details.

2. This text is adapted from Ellis (2004, pp. 272–282).

3. Lauren Slater (2003) makes the case that for some of us some of the time, it might be better to actively repress our traumas and concentrate on doing rather than reflecting.

4. Loseke (2001); Donileen Loseke, personal communication; see also A. Berger (1997).

5. See Fox (1996), who argues that understanding child abuse requires considering the perspectives and agency of children as well as adults; also see Lempert (1996, 1994); Loseke (2001).

6. This text is adapted from Ellis (2004, pp. 282–283).

Notes to Chapter 13

1. This text is adapted from Ellis (2007b) and is an offshoot of a larger paper I wrote about these issues in Ellis (2007a).

2. Jackie is a composite character. Other characters mentioned in this story represent actual students. All conversations come from remembered experiences, though they did not necessarily occur in the time, place, or order in which I present them here.

3. See Slater (2003), who makes a case for considering the potential beneficial aspects of repression.

4. See Chapter 1 in this book.

5. Thanks to Ron Pelias for discussing this idea with me and leading me to this reference.

6. See Poulos (2008c).

Notes to Chapter 14

1. I use pseudonyms for all places and people (with the exception of Art and me, and other family members) and camouflage as many identifying characteristics as reasonable. Of course, those who know Art and me well will know where our summer home is located, but pseudonyms help to protect the identities of the mountain people and the specific locality of the culture from general readers.

2. Access information deleted to protect identity of county.

3.   According to unofficial vote totals for 2004, Bush received 9,400 votes and John Kerry received 5,461 votes in Forsythia County. Access information deleted to protect identity of county.

4.   Concord's population is 17.6 percent Black and 3.8 percent Hispanic. Access information deleted to protect identity of location.

5.   See, for example, Hicks (2004, p. 148). Putnam (2000, pp. 98–100) reports that Americans still socialize together but that social visits with friends and neighbors have decreased by one-third to one-half between the mid-1970s and 2000 (pp. 105–107).

6.   See Josselson (1996) on what we owe readers.

7.   See Poulos (2008c).

8.   See Tolich (2004) on issues of internal confidentiality.

9.   See Poulos (2006) on dream stories.

References

Abrahams, R. (1986). Ordinary and extraordinary experience. In V. Turner & E. Bruner (Eds.), *The anthropology of experience* (pp. 45–72). Urbana: University of Illinois Press.

Adams, T. (2006). Seeking father: Relationally reframing a troubled love story. *Qualitative Inquiry, 12*(4), 704–723.

Adams, T. E. (2008). Learning, living, and leaving the closet: Making gay identity relational. Unpublished doctoral dissertation, University of South Florida, Tampa.

Adler, N., David, H., Major, B., Roth, S., Russo, N., & Wyatt, G. (1990). Psychological responses after abortion. *Science, 248*(4951), 41–44.

Adler, P., & Adler, P. A. (1980). Symbolic interactionism. In J. Douglas, et al. (Eds.), *Introduction to the sociologies of everyday life* (pp. 20–61). Boston: Allyn and Bacon.

Adler, P., & Adler, P. A. (1987). The past and the future of ethnography. *Journal of Contemporary Ethnography, 16,* 4–24.

Anderson, L. (2006). Analytic autoethnography. *Journal of Contemporary Ethnography, 35,* 373–395.

Anderson, R. (1968). I never sang for my father. In O. Guernsey, Jr. (Ed.), *The best plays of 1967–1968* (pp. 277–298). New York: Dodd, Mead, and Company.

Ang, L. (1996). *Watching Dallas.* London: Routledge.

Angrosino, M. (1998). *Opportunity House: Ethnographic stories of mental retardation.* Walnut Creek, CA: AltaMira Press.

Anspach, R. R. (1979). From stigma to identity politics: Political activism among the physically disabled and former mental patients. *Social Science and Medicine, 13A,* 765–772.

Archibald, R. (2001, October 21). For artists who lived near towers, disaster brings its own palette. *New York Times,* p. B10.

Armon-Jones, C. (1986). The thesis of constructionism. In R. Harré (Ed.), *Social construction of emotions* (pp. 32–56). New York: Basil Blackwell.

Arnett, R. C. (2002). Paulo Freire's revolutionary pedagogy: From a story-centered to a narrative-centered communication ethic. *Qualitative Inquiry, 8*(4), 489–510.

Arras, J. (1997). Nice story but so what? In H. Nelson (Ed.), *Stories and their limits: Narrative approaches to bioethics* (pp. 65–90). London: Routledge.

Atkinson, P. (2006). Rescuing autoethnography. *Journal of Contemporary Ethnography, 35,* 400–404.

Attig, T. (2001). Relearning the world: Making meaning and finding meanings. In R. Neimeyer (Ed.), *Meaning reconstruction & the experience of loss* (pp. 33–54). Washington, DC: American Psychological Association.

Averill, J. (1974). An analysis of psychophysiological symbolism and its influence on theories of emotion. *Journal for the Theory of Social Behaviour, 4,* 147–190.

Averill, J. (1986). The acquisition of emotions during adulthood. In R. Harré (Ed.), *The social construction of emotions* (pp. 98–118). New York: Basil Blackwell.

Baerger, D., & McAdams, D. (1999). Life story coherence and its relation to psychological well-being. *Narrative Inquiry, 9,* 69–96.

Bakan, D. (1954). A reconsideration of the problem of introspection. *Psychological Bulletin, 51,* 105.

Bakhtin, M. (1984). *Problems of Dostoevsky's poetics* (C. Emerson, Ed. & Trans.). Minneapolis: University of Minnesota Press.

Barry, J. (2007, April 30). Women's regrets become part of debate on abortion. *St. Petersburg Times,* Section A, pp. 1, 10.

Bateson, G. (1972). *Steps to an ecology of mind.* New York: Ballantine.

Bateson, G., Jackson, D. D., Haley, J., & Weakland, J. H. (1956). Toward a theory of schizophrenia. *Behavioral Science, 1,* 251–264.

Bazelon, E. (2007, January 27). Is there a post-abortion syndrome? *New York Times Magazine,* pp. 41–47, 62, 66, 70.

Becker, G. (1998). *Disrupted lives: How people create meaning in a chaotic world.* Berkeley and Los Angeles: University of California Press.

Becker, H. (1994). FOI POR ACASO: Conceptualizing coincidence. *The Sociological Quarterly, 35,* 183–194.

Becker, H., McCall, M., & Morris, H. (1989). Theatres and communities: three scenes. *Social Problems, 36,* 93–116.

Bedford, E. (1986). Emotions and statements about them. In R. Harré (Ed.), *The social construction of emotions* (pp. 15–31). New York: Basil Blackwell.

Benjamin, W. (1968). What is epic theater? In W. Benjamin, *Illuminations* (H. Arendt, Ed., H. Zohn, Trans.: pp. 149–150). New York: Harcourt, Brace & World.

Berger, A. (1997). *Narratives in popular culture, media, and everyday life.* Thousand Oaks, CA: Sage.

Berger, P. L., & Luckmann, T. (1967). *The social construction of reality.* New York: Doubleday: Anchor.

Berger, R. J., & Quinney, R. (Eds.) (2004). *Storytelling sociology: Narrative as social inquiry.* Boulder, CO: Lynne Rienner.

Bergum, V. (1998). Relational ethics. What is it? *In Touch,* 1. Retrieved February 10, 2005, from http://www.phen.ab.ca/materials/intouch/vo11/intouch1–02.html

Berry, K. (2006). Implicated audience member seeks understanding: Reexamining the "gift" of autoethnography. *International Journal of Qualitative Methods, 5*(3). Retrieved February 7, 2008, from http://www.ualberta.ca/~iiqm/backissues/5_3/HTML/berry.htm

Berscheid, E. (1983). Emotions. In H. Kelly, E. Berscheid, A. Christensen, J. Harvey, T. Huston, G. Levinger, E. McClintock, A. Peplau, & D. R. Peterson (Eds.), *Close relationships* (pp. 110–168). San Francisco: Freeman.

Bertaux-Wiame, I. (1981). The life history approach to the study of internal migration. In D. Bertaux (Ed.), *Biography and society: The life history approach in the social sciences* (pp. 249–265). Beverly Hills, CA: Sage.

Birkerts, S. (2008). *The art of time in memoir: Then, again.* St. Paul, MN: Graywolf Press.

Black, P. (1982, March 28). Abortion affects men too. *New York Times Magazine,* pp. 76–94.

Bochner, A. P. (1981). Forming warm ideas. In C. Wilder & J. Weakland (Eds.), Rigor and imagination: Essays in honor of Gregory Bateson (pp. 65–81). Palo Alto, CA: Praeger.

Bochner, A. P. (1994). Perspectives on inquiry II: Theories and stories. In M. Knapp & G. Miller (Eds.), *Handbook of interpersonal communication* (pp. 21–41). Thousand Oaks, CA: Sage.

Bochner, A. P. (1997). It's about time: Narrative and the divided self. *Qualitative Inquiry, 3,* 418–438.

Bochner, A. P. (2001). Narrative's virtues. *Qualitative Inquiry, 7,* 131–157.

Bochner, A. P. (2002a). Love survives. *Qualitative Inquiry, 8,* 161–169.

Bochner, A. P. (2002b). Perspectives on inquiry III: The moral of stories. In M. Knapp & G. Miller (Eds.), *Handbook of interpersonal communication,* 3rd ed. (pp. 73–101). Thousand Oaks, CA: Sage.

Bochner, A. P. (2005a). Interpretive and narrative on the Ellis study. In J. Paul (Ed.), *Introduction to the philosophies of research and criticism in education and the social sciences* (pp. 268–273). Upper Saddle River, NJ: Pearson Education, Inc.

Bochner, A. P. (2005b). Surviving autoethnography. *Studies in Symbolic Interaction, 28,* 51–58.

Bochner, A. P. (2007). Notes toward an ethics of memory in autoethnography. In N. Denzin & M. Giardina (Eds.), *Ethical futures in qualitative research: Decolonizing the politics of knowledge* (pp. 197–208). Walnut Creek, CA: Left Coast Press, Inc.

Bochner, A. P. (forthcoming). *Researchers as storytellers: The narrative turn in the human sciences.* Walnut Creek, CA: Left Coast Press, Inc.

Bochner, A. P., & Ellis, C. (1992). Personal narrative as a social approach to interpersonal communication. *Communication Theory, 2,* 165–172.

Bochner, A. P., & Ellis, C. (Eds.) (2002). *Ethnographically speaking: Autoethnography, literature, and aesthetics.* Walnut Creek, CA: AltaMira.

Bochner, A. P., & Ellis, C. (2006). Communication as autoethnography. In G. Shepherd, J. St. John, & T. Striphas (Eds.), *Communication as . . . : Perspectives on theory* (pp. 110–122). Thousand Oaks, CA: Sage.

Bochner, A., Ellis, C., & Tillmann-Healy, L. (1997). Relationships as stories. In S. Duck (Ed.), *Handbook of personal relationships*, 2nd ed. (pp. 307–324). New York: John Wiley and Sons.

Bochner, A. P., Ellis, C., & Tillmann-Healy, L. (1998). Mucking around looking for truth. In B. Montgomery & L. Baxter (Eds.), *Dialectical approaches to studying personal relationships* (pp. 41–62). Mahwah, NJ: Lawrence Erlbaum Associates.

Bochner, A. P., & Krueger, D. L. (1979). On inscrutable epistemologies and muddled concepts. In D. Nimmo (Ed.), *Communication yearbook 3* (pp. 197–211). New Brunswick, NJ: Transaction Books.

Bogdan, R., & Taylor, S. (1989). Relationships with severely disabled people: The social construction of humanness. *Social Problems, 36,* 135–148.

Bonavoglia, A. (1991). *The choices we made: Twenty-five women and men speak out about abortion.* New York: Random House.

Bordo, S. (1986). The Cartesian masculinization of thought. *Signs, 11,* 439–456.

Boring, E. (1953). A history of introspection. *Psychological Bulletin, 50,* 169–189.

Bower, G. H. (1981). Mood and memory. *American Psychologist, 36,* 129–148.

Boylorn, R. (2008). *Southern black women: Their lived realities.* Unpublished doctoral dissertation, University of South Florida.

Branaman, A. (1997). Goffman's social theory. In C. Lemert & A. Branaman (Eds.), *The Goffman reader* (pp. xiv–xxxii). Cambridge, MA: Blackwell.

Brody, H. (1987). *Stories of sickness.* New Haven: Yale University Press.

Brooks, M. (2006). Man-to-man: A body talk between male friends. *Qualitative Inquiry, 12*(2), 185–207.

Brown, M. E. (1994). *Soap opera and women's talk.* London: Sage.

Bruner, E. (1986a). Experience and its expressions. In V. Turner & E. Bruner (Eds.), *The anthropology of experience* (pp. 3–30). Urbana: University of Illinois Press.

Bruner, E. (1986b). Ethnography as narrative. In V. Turner & E. Bruner (Eds.), *The anthropology of experience* (pp. 130–155). Urbana: University of Illinois Press.

Brunsdon, C. (1984). Writing about soap opera. In L. Masterman (Ed.), *Television mythologies* (pp. 82–87). London: Comedia.

Buzard, J. (2003). On auto-ethnographic authority. *The Yale Journal of Criticism, 16,* 61–91.

Buzzanell, P. M. (2004). Revisiting sexual harassment in academe: Using feminist ethical and sensemaking approaches to analyze macrodiscourse and micropractices of sexual harassment. In P. M. Buzzanell, H. Sterk, & L. H. Turner (Eds.), *Gender in applied contexts* (pp. 25–46). Thousand Oaks, CA: Sage.

Cahill, S., & Eggleston, R. (1995). Reconsidering the stigma of physical disability: Wheelchair use and public kindness. *The Sociological Quarterly, 36,* 681–698.

Camic, C. (1986). The matter of habit. *American Journal of Sociology, 91,* 1039–1087.

Cannella, G., & Lincoln, Y. (2004). Epilogue: Claiming a critical public social science—Reconceptualizing and redeploying research. *Qualitative Inquiry, 10*(2), 298–309.

Carlisle, J. (1985). *Tangled tongue: Living with a stutter.* Toronto: University of Toronto Press.

Carlson, R. (2007). *Ron Carlson writes a story.* St. Paul, MN: Graywolf Press.

Carr, D. (1986). *Time, narrative, and history.* Bloomington: Indiana University Press.

Carr, D., House, J., Wortman, C., Nessse, R., & Kessler, R. (2001). Psychological adjustment to sudden and anticipated spousal loss among older widowed persons. *The Journals of Gerontology Series B: Psychological Sciences and Social Sciences, 56,* S237–S248.

Carter, S. (2002). How much subjectivity is needed to understand our lives objectively? *Qualitative Health Research, 12*(9), 1184–1201.

Casey, J. G. (2005). Diversity, discourse, and the working-class student. *Academe Online. AAUP Publications and Research.* Retrieved October 2, 2007, from http://ww.aup.org/AAUP/pubsres/academe/2005/JA/Feat/ase.htm

Caughey, J. (1982). Ethnography, introspection, and reflexive culture studies. *Prospects, 7,* 115–139.

Ceglowski, D. (2000). Research as relationship. *Qualitative Inquiry, 6,* 88–103.

Charlés, L. (2007). *Intimate colonialism: Head, heart, and body in West African development work.* Walnut Creek, CA: Left Coast Press, Inc.

Charmaz, K. (2006). The power of names. *Journal of Contemporary Ethnography, 35,* 396–399.

Charon, J. (1985). *Symbolic interactionism: An introduction, an interpretation, an integration* (2nd ed.). Englewood Cliffs, NJ: Prentice-Hall.

Christians, C. (2000). Ethics and politics in qualitative research. In N. Denzin & Y. Lincoln (Eds.), *Handbook of qualitative research,* 2nd ed. (pp. 133–155). Thousand Oaks, CA: Sage.

Cicourel, A. (1974). *Theory and method in a study of Argentine fertility.* New York: John Wiley and Sons.

Clair, R. (Ed.). (2003). *Expressions of ethnography: Novel approaches to qualitative methods.* Albany: SUNY Press.

Clanton, G., & Smith, I. (1977). *Jealousy.* Englewood Cliffs, NJ: Prentice-Hall.

Clark/Keefe, K. (2007). Invoking Mnemosyne: A feminist automethodography of embodying inquiry through becoming mom, performing professor, and painting the meaning of memory. Paper given at the International Congress of Qualitative Inquiry. Champaign/Urbana, Illinois.

Clark/Keefe, K. (in press). *Invoking Mnemosyne: Art, memory and the uncertain emergence of a feminist embodied methodology.* Rotterdam, the Netherlands: Sense Publishers.

Clifford, J. (1986). Introduction: Partial truths. In J. Clifford & G. Marcus (Eds.), *Writing culture: The poetics and politics of ethnography* (pp. 1–26). Berkeley: University of California Press.

Clough, P. (2000a). *Autoaffection: Unconscious thought in the age of teletechnology.* Minneapolis: University of Minnesota Press.

Clough, P. (2000b). Comments on setting criteria for experimental writing. *Qualitative Inquiry, 6,* 278–291.

Coffey, A. (1999). *The ethnographic self.* London: Sage.

Cohen, S. (2006). Abortion and mental health: Myths and realities. *Guttmacher Policy Review, 9,* 8–11, 16.

Coles, R. (1989). *The call of stories: Teaching and the moral imagination.* Boston: Houghton Mifflin.

Collins, J. (2004, February 19). Integration pushes Luray High School to its first state title in '67. *Page News and Courier,* B1–B2.

Condit, C. M. (1990). *Decoding abortion rhetoric: Communicating social change.* Urbana: University of Illinois Press.

Conquergood, D. (1990). *Rethinking ethnography: Cultural politics and rhetorical strategies.* Paper presented at the Temple Conference on Discourse Analysis, Temple University.

Cooley, C. H. (1902). *Human nature and social order.* New York: Scribner's.

Cooley, C. H. (1926). The roots of social knowledge. *American Journal of Sociology, 32,* 59–79.

Coulter, J. (1986). Affect and social context: Emotion definition as a social task. In R. Harré (Ed.), *The social construction of emotions* (pp. 120–135). New York: Basil Blackwell.

Crapanzano, V. (1970). The writing of ethnography. *Dialectical Anthropology, 2,* 69–73.

Crites, S. (1971). The narrative quality of experience. *Journal of the American Academy of Religion, 39,* 291–311.

Curry, E. A. (2005). Communication collaboration and empowerment: A research novel of relationships with domestic violence workers. Unpublished dissertation. Department of Communication, University of South Florida, Tampa.

Curry, E., & Walker, D. (Eds.). (2002). *Many faces, many voices working against domestic violence: The CASA story of stories.* St. Petersburg, FL: CASA.

Daly, K. (1997). Re-placing theory in ethnography: A postmodern view. *Qualitative Inquiry, 3,* 343–365.

Davies, B., & Davies, C. (2007). Having, and being had by, 'experience': Or, 'experience' in the social sciences after the discursive/poststructuralist turn. *Qualitative Inquiry, 13,* 1139–1159.

Davis, C. S. (2005). A future with hope: The social construction of hope, help, and dialogic reconciliation in a community children's mental health system of care. Unpublished Ph.D. dissertation. Department of Communication, University of South Florida, Tampa.

Davis, C. S. (2006). Sylvia's story: Narrative, storytelling, and power in a children's community mental health system of care. *Qualitative Inquiry, 12*, 1220–1243.

Davis, C. S., & Ellis, C. (2008). Emergent methods in autoethnographic research: Autoethnographic narrative and the multiethnographic turn. In S. Hess-Biber & P. Leavy (Eds.), *The handbook of emergent methods* (pp. 283–302). New York: Guilford Press.

Davis, C. S., & Salkin, K. A. (2005). Sisters and friends: Dialogue and multivocality in a relational model of sibling disability. *Journal of Contemporary Ethnography, 34*, 206–234.

Davis, C. S., Ellis, C., Myerson, M., Poole, M., & Smith-Sullivan, K. (2006). The menopause club: Five hot middle-aged women talk about their bodies. Paper presented at National Communication Association, San Antonio, TX.

Davis, K. (1936). Jealousy and sexual property. *Social Forces, 14*, 395–405.

Davitz, J. (1969). *The language of emotion.* New York: Academic Press.

Denzin, N. K. (1971). The logic of naturalistic inquiry. *Social Forces, 50*, 166–182.

Denzin, N. K. (1984). Toward a phenomenology of domestic family violence. *American Journal of Sociology, 90*, 483–513.

Denzin, N. K. (1985). Emotion as lived experience. *Symbolic Interaction, 8*, 223–240.

Denzin, N. K. (1987). *The alcoholic self.* Beverly Hills, CA: Sage.

Denzin, N. K. (1988). The narrative undoing of interactionism. Presented to the 1988 Annual Meetings of the Society for the Study of Symbolic Interaction.

Denzin, N. K. (1989). *Interpretive interactionism.* Newbury Park, CA: Sage.

Denzin, N. K. (1990). Harold and Agnes: A feminist narrative undoing. *Sociological Theory, 8*, 198–216.

Denzin, N. K. (1991). On understanding emotion: The interpretive-cultural agenda. In T. Kemper (Ed.), *Research agendas in the sociology of emotions* (pp. 85–116). Albany, NY: SUNY Press.

Denzin, N. K. (1997). *Interpretive ethnography: Ethnographic practices for the 21st century.* Thousand Oaks, CA: Sage.

Denzin, N. K. (2003). *Performance ethnography: Critical pedagogy and the politics of culture.* Thousand Oaks, CA: Sage.

Denzin, N. K. (2007). *Flags in the window: Dispatches from the American war zone.* New York: Peter Lang.

Denzin, N. K. (2008a). Interpretive biography. In J. G. Knowles & A. Cole (Eds.), *Handbook of the arts in qualitative research.* Thousand Oaks, CA: Sage.

Denzin, N. K. (2008b). Living in the postmodern West: Notes on Carolyn. Paper presented at the Southern States Communication Association, Savannah, GA.

Denzin, N. K. (2008c). *Searching for Yellowstone.* Walnut Creek, CA: Left Coast Press, Inc.

Derrida, J. (1978). *Writing and difference.* Chicago: University of Chicago Press.

DeSalvo, L. (2000). *Writing as a way of healing: How telling our stories transforms our lives.* Boston: Beacon Press.

Dilthey, W. (1976). *Selected writings* (H. P. Rickman, Ed & Trans). Cambridge: Cambridge University Press. (Original work published in 1900.)

Dinesen, I. (1992). *Out of Africa.* New York: Modern Library.

Dougherty, D., & Atkinson, J. (2006). Competing ethical communities and a researcher's dilemma: The case of a sexual harasser. *Qualitative Inquiry, 12*(2), 292–315.

Douglas, J. (1977). Existential sociology. In J. Douglas & J. Johnson (Eds.), *Existential sociology* (pp. 3–72). Cambridge: Cambridge University Press.

Durkheim, E. (1912/1965). *The elementary forms of the religious life* (new translation by Karen E. Fields). New York: The Free Press.

Ehrenreich, B. (2004, July 22). Owning up to abortion. *New York Times.* Retrieved July 11, 2007, from http://query.nytimes.com/gst/fullpage.html?res=9F01E6DF1F3AF931A15754C0A9629C8

Elbow, P. (1973). *Writing without teachers.* New York: Oxford University Press.

Elias, M. (2001, October 25). Attack aftermath ravages fragile emotions. *USA Today*, 5D.

Ellingson, L. (2005). *Communicating in the clinic: Negotiating frontstage and backstage teamwork.* Cresskill, NJ: Hampton Press.

Ellingson, L. (2009). *Engaging crystallization in qualitative research*. Thousand Oaks, CA: Sage.

Ellis, C. (1986). *Fisher folk: Two communities on Chesapeake Bay.* Lexington: The University Press of Kentucky.

Ellis, C. (1989). "What are you feeling?": Issues in introspective method. Paper presented at American Sociological Association, San Francisco, CA.

Ellis, C. (1991a). Sociological introspection and emotional experience. *Symbolic Interaction, 14,* 23–50.

Ellis, C. (1991b). Emotional sociology. *Studies in Symbolic Interaction, 12,* 123–145.

Ellis, C. (1993). "There are survivors": Telling a story of sudden death. *Sociological Quarterly, 34,* 711–730.

Ellis, C. (1995a). *Final negotiations: A story of love, loss, and chronic illness.* Philadelphia: Temple University Press.

Ellis, C. (1995b). Emotional and ethical quagmires in returning to the field. *Journal of Contemporary Ethnography, 24*(1), 711–713.

Ellis, C. (1995c). Speaking of dying: An ethnographic short story. *Symbolic Interaction, 18,* 73–81.

Ellis, C. (1995d). The other side of the fence: Seeing black and white in a small, southern town. *Qualitative Inquiry, 1*(2), 147–167.

Ellis, C. (1996a). Maternal connections. In C. Ellis & A. Bochner (Eds.), *Composing ethnography: Alternative forms of qualitative writing* (pp. 240–243). Walnut Creek, CA: AltaMira Press.

Ellis, C. (1996b). On the demands of truthfulness in writing personal loss narratives. *Journal of Personal and Interpersonal Loss, 1,* 151–177.

Ellis, C. (1997). Evocative autoethnography: Writing emotionally about our lives. In W. Tierney & Y. Lincoln (Eds.), *Representation and the text: Re-framing the narrative voice* (pp. 116–139). Albany: SUNY Press.

Ellis, C. (1998). I hate my voice: Coming to terms with minor bodily stigmas. *The Sociological Quarterly, 39,* 517–37.

Ellis, C. (2000). Negotiating terminal illness: Communication, collusion, and coalition in caregiving. In J. Harvey and E. D. Miller (Eds.), *Loss and trauma: General and close relationship perspectives* (pp. 284–304). Philadelphia: Brunner-Routledge.

Ellis, C. (2001). With mother/with child: A true story. *Qualitative Inquiry, 7,* 598–616.

Ellis, C. (2002a). Being real: Moving inwards to social change. *Qualitative Studies in Education, 15,* 399–406.

Ellis, C. (2002b). Take no chances. *Qualitative Inquiry, 8,* 42–47.

Ellis, C. (2002c). Shattered lives: Making sense of September 11th and its aftermath. *Journal of Contemporary Ethnography, 31,* 375–410.

Ellis, C. (2003, May). Grave tending: With mom at the cemetery. *Forum Qualitative Sozialforschung/ Forum: Qualitative Social Research, 4*(2). Retrieved July 9, 2008, from http://www.qualitative-research.net/fqs-texte/2–03/2–03ellis-e.htm

Ellis, C. (2004). *The ethnographic I: A methodological novel about autoethnography.* Walnut Creek, CA: AltaMira Press.

Ellis, C. (2006). On not telling family secrets. Unpublished manuscript, University of South Florida, Tampa.

Ellis, C. (2007a). Telling secrets, revealing lives: Relational ethics in research with intimate others. *Qualitative Inquiry, 13*(1), 3–29.

Ellis, C. (2007b). 'I just want to tell MY story': Mentoring students about relational ethics in writing about intimate others. In N. K. Denzin & M. Giardina (Eds.), *Ethical futures in qualitative research: Decolonizing the politics of knowledge* (pp. 209–228). Walnut Creek, CA: Left Coast Press, Inc.

Ellis, C., & Berger, L. (2002). Their story/my story: Including the researcher's experience in interviews. In J. Gubrium & J. Holstein (Eds.), *Handbook of interview research: Context and method* (pp. 849–75). Thousand Oaks, CA: Sage.

Ellis, C., & Bochner, A. P. (1992). Telling and performing personal stories: The constraints of choice in abortion. In C. Ellis & M. Flaherty (Eds.), *Investigating subjectivity: Research on lived experience* (pp. 79–101). Newbury Park, CA: Sage.

Ellis, C., & Bochner, A. P. (Eds.) (1996). *Composing ethnography: Alternative forms of qualitative writing.* Walnut Creek, CA: AltaMira Press.

Ellis, C., & Bochner, A. (1999). Talking over ethnography: A dialogue on intersecting life and work. Address given at Saginaw Valley State University, Dow Visiting Scholars Program.

Ellis, C., & Bochner, A. P. (2001). Autoethnography, personal narrative, reflexivity: Researcher as subject. In N. Denzin & Y. Lincoln (Eds.), *Handbook of qualitative research*, 2nd ed. (pp. 733–768). Thousand Oaks, CA: Sage.

Ellis, C., Bochner, A., Denzin, N., Lincoln, Y, Morse, J., Pelias, R, & Richardson, L. (2007). Talking and thinking about qualitative research. In N. K. Denzin & M. D. Giardina, *Ethical futures in qualitative research: Decolonizing the politics of knowledge* (pp. 229–267). Oxford: Berg Publishers.

Ellis, C., & Flaherty, M. (Eds.). (1992). *Investigating subjectivity: research on lived experience* (pp. 125–137). Newbury Park, CA: Sage.

Ellis, C., Kiesinger, C. E., & Tillman-Healy, L. M. (1997). Interactive interviewing: Talking about emotional experience. In R. Hertz (Ed.), *Reflexivity and voice* (pp. 119–149). Thousand Oaks, CA: Sage.

Ellis, C., & Weinstein, E. (1986). Jealousy and the social psychology of emotional experience. *Journal of Social and Personal Relationships, 3*, 337–357.

Epston, D., & White, M. (1992). *Experience, contradiction, narrative and imagination.* Adelaide, Australia: Dulwich Centre Publications.

Ericsson, K. A., & Simon, H. (1980). Verbal reports as data. *Psychological Review, 87*, 215–251.

Ericsson, K. A., & Simon, H. (1984). *Protocol analysis.* Cambridge: The MIT Press.

Ernaux. A. (1991). *A woman's story.* (T. Leslie, Trans.) New York: Ballentine.

Etherington, K. (2005). Writing trauma stories for research. *Lapidus Quarterly, 1*(2), 25–31.

Etherington, K. (2007). Ethical research in reflexive relationships. *Qualitative Inquiry, 13*, 599–616.

Evert, K., & Bijkerk, I. (1987). *When you're ready.* Walnut Creek, CA: Launch Press.

Fasching, D. J., & deChant, D. (2001). *Comparative religious ethics: A narrative approach.* Oxford: Blackwell.

Fine, M. (1994). Working the hyphens: Reinventing self and other in qualitative research. In N. Denzin & Y. Lincoln (Eds.), *Handbook of qualitative research*,1st ed. (pp. 70–82). Thousand Oaks, CA: Sage.

Fine, M., Weis, L., Weseen, S., & Wong, M. (2000). For whom? Qualitative research, representations and social responsibilities. In N. Denzin & Y. Lincoln (Eds.), *The handbook of qualitative research* (2nd ed.) (pp. 107–132). Thousand Oaks, CA: Sage.

Finer, L. B., & Henshaw, S. K. (2005). *Estimates of U.S. abortion incidence in 2001 and 2002.* The Alan Guttmacher Institute. Retrieved May 25, 2006, from http://wwwguttmacher.org/pubs/2005/05/18/ab_incidence.pdf

Foster, E. (2007). *Communicating at the end of life.* Mahwah, NJ: Lawrence Erlbaum.

Fox, K. (1996). Silent voices: A subversive reading of child sexual abuse. In A. Bochner & C. Ellis (Eds.), *Composing ethnography: Alternative forms of qualitative writing* (pp. 330–356). Walnut Creek, CA: AltaMira Press.

Francke, L. (1978). *The ambivalence of abortion.* New York: Random House.

Frank, A. (1991). *At the will of the body: Reflections on illness.* Boston: Houghton Mifflin.

Frank, A. (1995). *The wounded storyteller: Body, illness, and ethics.* Chicago: University Press of Chicago.

Frank, A. (2004). Moral non-fiction: Life writing and children's disability. In P. J. Eakin (Ed.), *The ethics of life writing* (pp. 174–194). Ithaca, NY: Cornell University Press.

Frank, A. (2005). What is dialogic research, and why should we do it? *Qualitative Health Research, 15*, 964–974.

Frank, G. (1988). Beyond stigma: Visibility and self-empowerment of persons with congenital limb deficiencies. *Journal of Social Issues, 44*, 95–115

Freadman, R. (2004). Decent and indecent: Writing my father's life. In J. P. Eakin (Ed.), *The ethics of life writing* (pp. 121–146*).* Ithaca, NY: Cornell University Press.

Freeman, M. (1998). Mythical time, historical time, and the narrative fabric of self. *Narrative Inquiry, 8*, 27–50.

Frentz, T. (2008a). The ethics of telling. Paper presented at the Southern States Communication Association, Savannah, GA.

Frentz, T. (2008b). *Trickster in tweed: The quest for quality in a faculty life.* Walnut Creek, CA: Left Coast Press, Inc..

Freud, S. (1914/1984). On narcissism: An introduction. In A. Richards (Ed.), *On metapsychology: The theory of psychoanalysis, Vol. 11* (pp. 59–98). New York: Penguin.

Gagnon J. (1990). Conversations in the self. Paper presented at the SSSI Stone Symposium, St. Petersburg, FL.

Gannon, S. (2006). The (im)possibilities of writing the self-writing: French poststructural theory and autoethnography. *Cultural Studies–Critical Methodologies, 6,* 474–495.

Geertz, C. (1973). *The interpretation of cultures.* New York: Basic Books.

Geertz, C. (1983). *Local knowledge: Further essays in interpretive anthropology.* New York: Basic Books.

Geist, P., & Miller, M. (1998). What's in a name? The ethics and politics of nom de plume. Paper presented at the National Communication Association, New York.

Gergen, K. (1997). *Realities and relationships: Soundings in social construction.* Cambridge, MA: Harvard University Press.

Gilligan, C. (1982). *In a different voice: Psychological theory and women's development.* Cambridge, MA: Harvard University Press.

Gingrich-Philbrook, C. (2005). Autoethnography's family values: Easy access to compulsory experiences. *Text and Performance Quarterly, 25,* 297–314.

Glaser, B., & Strauss, A. (1967). *Discovery of grounded theory: Strategies for qualitative research.* Mill Valley, CA: Sociology Press.

Goff, T. W. (1980). *Marx and Mead: Contributions to a sociology of knowledge.* London: Routledge and Kegan Paul.

Goffman, E. (1956). Embarrassment and social organization. *American Journal of Sociology, 62,* 264–271.

Goffman, E. (1959). *The presentation of self in everyday life.* Garden City, NY: Doubleday/Anchor Books.

Goffman, E. (1963). *Stigma: Notes on the management of spoiled identity.* Englewood Cliffs, NJ: Prentice-Hall.

Goffman, E. (1967). *Interaction ritual: Essays on face-to-face behavior.* New York: Pantheon Books.

Goffman, E. (1971). *Relations in public: Microstudies of the public order.* New York: Basic Books.

Goffman, E. (1974). *Frame analysis.* New York: Harper and Row.

Goffman, E. (1981). *Forms of talk.* Philadelphia: University of Pennsylvania Press.

Goldner, V., Penn, P., Sheinberg, M., & Walker, G. (1990). Love and violence: Gender paradoxes in volatile attachments. *Family Process, 29,* 343–64.

Goodall, H. L. (2006). *A need to know: The clandestine history of a CIA family.* Walnut Creek, CA: Left Coast Press, Inc.

Goode, E. (2001, November 6). Traumatic moments end, but the reminders linger. *New York Times,* pp. D1, D7.

Goodman, W. (1994, June 19). Television, meet life. Life, meet TV. *New York Times,* Section 4, pp. 1, 6.

Gordon, E. W., Miller, F., & Rollock, D. (1990). Coping with communicentric bias in knowledge production in the social sciences. *Educational Researcher, 19,* 14–19.

Gordon, S. (1989). Institutional and impulsive orientations in selectively appropriating emotions to self. In D. Franks & E. McCarthy (Eds.), *The sociology of emotions: Original essays and research papers* (pp. 115–135). Greenwich, CT: JAI Press.

Gouldner, A. (1970). *The coming crisis of Western sociology.* New York: Avon Books.

Grafanaki, S. (1996). How research can change the researcher: The need for sensitivity, flexibility and ethical boundaries in conducting qualitative research in counselling/psychotherapy. *British Journal of Guidance and Counselling, 24*(3), 329–338.

Gray, R., & Sinding, C. (2002). *Standing ovation: Performing social science research about cancer.* Walnut Creek, CA: AltaMira Press.

Greenspan, H. (1998). *On listening to Holocaust survivors: Recounting and life history.* Westport, CT: Praeger.

Grover, S. (1982). A re-evaluation of the introspection controversy: Additional considerations. *Journal of General Psychology, 106*, 205–212.

Guillemin, M., & Gillam, L. (2004). Ethics, reflexivity, and 'ethically important moments' in research. *Qualitative Inquiry, 10*(2), 261–280.

Hahn, H. (1985). Towards a politics of disability: Definitions, disciplines, and policies. *Social Science Journal, 22*, 87–105.

Harré, R. (1986). An outline of the social constructionist viewpoint. In R. Harré (Ed.), *The social construction of emotions* (pp. 2–14). New York: Basil Blackwell.

Harry, B. (2005). Race, ethnicity, and gender on the Ellis study. In J. Paul (Ed.), *Introduction to the philosophies of research and criticism in education and the social sciences* (pp. 273–276). Upper Saddle River, NJ: Pearson Education, Inc.

Hauerwas, S. (1990). *Naming the silence: God, medicine, and the problem of suffering.* Grand Rapids, MI: William B. Eerdmans.

Hayano, D. (1979). Auto-ethnography: Paradigms, problems, and prospects. *Human Organization, 38*, 99–104.

Hedtke, L., & Winslade, J. (2004). *Re-membering lives: Conversations with the dying and the bereaved.* Amityville, NY: Baywood Publishing Co.

Henry, J. (1971). *Pathways to madness.* New York: Random House.

Henshaw, S. K. (1998). Unintended pregnancy in the United States. *Family Planning Perspectives, 30*, 24–29 & 46.

Hertz, R. (Ed.) (1996). *Qualitative Sociology, 19.* (Special issue: Ethics, reflexivity and voice.)

Hicks, G. (2004). *Small town.* New York: Fordham University Press.

Hinkle, R., & Hinkle, G. (1954). *The development of modern sociology: Its nature and growth in the United States.* New York: Random House.

Hoagland, T. (2003). Negative capability: How to talk mean and influence people. *American Poetry Review, 32*(March/April), 13–15.

Hobson, D. (1982). *Crossroads: The drama of a soap opera.* London: Methuen.

Hochschild, A. (1979). Emotion work, feeling rules and social structure. *American Journal of Sociology, 85*, 551–575.

Hochschild, A. (1983). *The managed heart.* Berkeley: University of California Press.

Hochschild, A. (1990). Ideology and emotion management: A perspective for future research. In T. Kemper (Ed.), *Research agendas in the sociology of emotions* (pp. 117–142). Albany, NY: SUNY Press.

Holman Jones, S. (2005). Autoethnography: Making the personal political. In N. Denzin & Y. Lincoln (Eds.), *Handbook of qualitative research*, 2nd ed. (pp. 763–792). Thousand Oaks, CA: Sage.

Holman Jones, S. (2007). *Torch singing: Performing resistance and desire from Billie Holiday to Edith Piaf.* Walnut Creek, CA: AltaMira Press.

Holt, N. (2003). Representation, legitimation, and autoethnography: An autoethnographic writing story. *International Journal of Qualitative Methods, 2*(1), Article 2. Retrieved February 7, 2008, from http://www.ualberta.ca/~iiqm/back issues/2_1final/html/holt.html

Irigaray, L. (1991). *Marine lover of Friedrich Nietzsche.* New York: Columbia University Press.

Jackson, A., & Mazzei, L. (in press). Experience and "I" in autoethnography: A deconstruction. *International Review of Qualitative Research.*

Jackson, M. (1989). *Paths toward a clearing: Radical empiricism and ethnographic inquiry.* Bloomington: Indiana University Press.

Jackson, M. (1995). *At home in the world.* Durham, NC: Duke University Press.

Jago, B. (2002). Chronicling an academic depression. *Journal of Contemporary Ethnography, 31*(6), 729–757.

James, W. (1981). *The principles of psychology, Vols. I and II.* London: Macmillan. (Original work published in 1890.)

Janoff-Bulman, R. (1992). *Shattered assumptions: Towards a new psychology of trauma.* New York: The Free Press.

Janoff-Bulman, R., & Frantz, C. (1996). The loss of illusions: The potent legacy of trauma. *Journal of Personal and Interpersonal Loss, 2,* 133–150.

Janoff-Bulman, R., & Timko, C. (1987). Coping with traumatic life events: The role of denial in light of people's assumptive worlds. In C. R. Snyder & C. Ford (Eds.), *Coping with negative life events: Clinical and social psychological perspectives* (pp. 135–159). New York: Plenum.

Jezer, M. (1997). *Stuttering: A life bound up in words.* New York: Basic Books.

Johnson, J. (1975). *Doing field research.* New York: The Free Press.

Jordan, B. (2008). Living a distributed life: Multi-locality and working at a distance. In Meerwarth et al. (Eds.), Mobile work, mobile lives: Cultural accounts of lived experiences. *NAPA Bulletin #30.* Berkeley: University of California Press. Retrieved March 4, 2008, from http://www.lifescapes.org/Papers/NAPA-gj-paper.doc

Josselson, R. (1996). On writing other people's lives: Self-analytic reflections of a narrative researcher. In R. Josselson (Ed.), *Ethics and process in the narrative study of lives, Vol. 4* (pp. 60–71). Thousand Oaks, CA: Sage.

Journal of Contemporary Ethnography (2006, August). Special issue on analytic autoethnography, 35(4).

Jules-Rosette, B. (1975). *African apostles: Ritual and conversion in the church of John Maranke.* Ithaca, NY: Cornell University Press.

Karr, M. (1995). *The liars' club: A memoir.* New York: Viking.

Kemper, T. (1981). Two approaches to the sociology of emotions. *American Journal of Sociology, 87,* 336–362.

Kiesinger, C. (2002). My father's shoes: The therapeutic value of narrative reframing. In A. P. Bochner & C. Ellis (Eds.), *Ethnographically speaking: Autoethnography, literature, and aesthetics* (pp. 95–114). Walnut Creek, CA: AltaMira.

Kilborn, R. (1992). *Television soaps.* London: B. T. Batsford.

Klass, D., Silverman, D. & Nickman, S. (Eds.) (1996). *Continuing bonds: New understanding of grief.* London: Taylor and Francis Group.

Kleinman, S. (1993). Culturally speaking: Carolyn Ellis' "There are survivors." *The Sociological Quarterly, 34,* 731–733.

Knowles, J. G., & Cole, A. (Eds.). (2008). *Handbook of the arts in qualitative research.* Los Angeles: Sage Pubs.

Kohut, H. (1959). Introspection, empathy, and psychoanalysis: An examination of the relationship between mode of observation and theory. *Journal of the American Psychoanalytic Association, 7,* 459–483.

Kotarba, J. (1983). *Chronic pain: Its social dimensions.* Beverly Hills, CA: Sage.

Krieger, S. (1984). Fiction and social science. In N. Denzin (Ed.), *Studies in symbolic interaction, Vol. 5* (pp. 269–286). Greenwich, CT: JAI.

Krieger, S. (1985). Beyond 'subjectivity': The use of the self in social science. *Qualitative Sociology, 8,* 309–324.

Krieger, S. (1991). *Social science and the self: Personal essays on an art form.* New Brunswick, NJ: Rutgers University Press.

Langellier, K. (1989). Personal narrative: Perspectives on theory and research. *Text and Performance Quarterly, 9,* 243–276.

Larson, T. (2007). *The memoir and the memoirist: Reading and writing personal narrative.* Athens, OH: Swallow Press.

Law, C. L. (1995). Introduction. In C. Dews and C. Law (Eds.), *This fine place so far from home: Voices of academics from the working class* (pp. 1–12). Philadelphia: Temple University Press.

Leavy, P. (Ed.). (2009). *Method meets art: Arts-based research practice.* New York: The Guilford Press.

Lehman, D., Wortman, C., & Williams, A. (1987). Long-term effects of losing a spouse or child in a motor vehicle crash. *Journal of Personality & Social Psychology, 52,* 218–231.

Lempert, L. (1994). A narrative analysis of abuse. *Journal of Contemporary Ethnography, 22,* 411–441.

Lempert, L. (1996). Women's strategies for survival: Developing agency in abusive relationships. *Journal of Family Violence, 11,* 269–289.

Lewis, C. S. (1963). *A grief observed*. Greenwich, CT: Seabury Press.

Lewis, J. D. (1979). A social behaviorist interpretation of the Meadian 'I.' *American Journal of Sociology, 85*, 261–287.

Lewis, P. (1997). Why are soap operas so popular? Retrieved April 11, 2007, from http://www.aber. ac.uk/media/Students/pj19601.html

Liamputtong, P., & Rumbold, J. (Eds.). (2008). *Knowing differently: Arts-based and collaborative research methods*. New York: Nova Science Publishers, Inc.

Lifton, R. J. (1967). *Death in life: Survivors of Hiroshima*. New York: Simon & Schuster.

Lifton, R. J. (1986). *The Nazi doctors: Medical killing and the psychology of genocide*. New York: Basic Books.

Lifton, R. J. (1988). Understanding the traumatized self: Imagery, symbolization, and transformation. In J. Wilson, Z. Harel, & B. Kahana (Eds.), *Human adaptation to extreme stress: From the Holocaust to Vietnam* (pp. 7–31). New York: Plenum Press.

Lincoln, Y. (1995). Emerging criteria for quality in qualitative and interpretive research. *Qualitative Inquiry, 1*(3), 275–289.

Lincoln, Y. (2005). Constructivism on the Ellis study. In J. Paul (Ed.), *Introduction to the philosophies of research and criticism in education and the social sciences* (pp. 267–268). Upper Saddle River, NJ: Pearson Education, Inc.

Linden, R. (1993). *Making stories, making selves: Writing sociology after the Holocaust*. Columbus: The Ohio State University Press.

Lopate, P. (1994). *The art of the personal essay: An anthology of the form, from Seneca and Plutarch to the present*. New York: Doubleday.

Loseke, D. (2001). Lived realities and formula stories of "battered women." In J. Gubrium and J. Holstein (Eds.), *Institutional selves: Troubled identities in a postmodern world* (pp. 107–126). New York: Oxford University Press.

Louis, M. (1980). Surprise and sensemaking: What newcomers experience in entering unfamiliar organizational settings. *Administrative Science Quarterly, 25*, 226–251.

Lubrano, A. (2004). *Limbo: Blue collar roots, white collar dreams*. New York: Wiley.

MacIntyre, A. (1981). *After virtue: A study in moral theory*. Notre Dame, IN: University of Notre Dame Press.

MacIver, R. M. (1931). Is sociology a natural science? *American Journal of Sociology, 25*, 25–35.

Madison, D. S. (2006). The dialogic performative in critical ethnography. *Text and Performance Quarterly, 26*, 320–324.

Maguire, M. (2006). Autoethnography: Answerability/responsibility in authoring self and others in the social sciences/humanities. Review essay: Carolyn Ellis (2004). The ethnographic I: A methodological novel about autoethnography. *Forum Qualitative Sozialforschung/Forum: Qualitative Social Research*. Retrieved December 12, 2007, from http://www.qualitative-research.net/fqs-texte/2–06/06-2-16-e.htm

Mairs, N. (1993, February 21). When bad things happen to good writers. *New York Times Book Review*, pp. 1, 25–27.

Mairs, N. (1994). *Voice lessons: On becoming a (woman) writer*. Boston: Beacon Press.

Mairs, N. (1996). *Waist-high in the world: A life among the nondisabled*. Boston: Beacon Press.

Malcolm, J. (1990). *The journalist and the murderer*. New York: Knopf.

Mandel, B. J. (1981). The past in autobiography. *Soundings: An interdisciplinary journal, 64*, 75–92.

Mandler, G. (1984). *Mind and body: Psychology of emotion and stress*. New York: Norton.

Marcus, G. (1994). What comes (just) after 'post'? The case of ethnography. In N. Denzin & Y. Lincoln (Eds.), *Handbook of qualitative research* (pp. 563–574). Thousand Oaks, CA: Sage.

Marx, K. (1844). *A contribution to the critique of Hegel's Philosophy of Right, Deutsch-Französische Jahrbücher*, February.

Marzano, M. (2007). Informed consent, deception and research freedom in qualitative research: A cross-cultural comparison. *Qualitative Inquiry, 13*, 417–436.

Mason, J. (1996). *Qualitative researching*. London: Sage.

McClowry, S. G., Davies, E. B., Kulenkamp, E. J., & Martinson, I. M. (1987). The empty space phenomenon: The process of grief in the bereaved family. *Death Studies, 11,* 361–374.

McDonnell, K. (1984). *Not an easy choice: A feminist examines abortion.* Boston: South End.

McDougall, W. (1922). Prolegomena to psychology. *Psychological Review, 29,* 1–43.

Mead, G. H. (1962). *Mind, self and society: From the standpoint of a social behaviorist.* Chicago: University of Chicago Press. (Original work published in 1934.)

Medford, K. (2006). Caught with a fake ID: Ethical questions about *slippage* in autoethnography. *Qualitative Inquiry, 12,* 853–864.

Meltzer, B., Petras, J., & Reynolds, L. (1975). *Symbolic interactionism: Genesis, varieties and criticisms.* London: Routledge and Kegan Paul.

Merleau-Ponty, M. (1964). *Signs.* (R. C. McCleary, Trans.). Evanston, IL: Northwestern University Press.

Messer, E., & May, K. (1989). *Back rooms: An oral history of the illegal abortion era.* New York: Simon & Schuster.

Mill, J. S. (1879). *A system of logic* (10th ed.), Book V. On the logic of the moral sciences. London: Longmans, Green, and Co.

Mills, C. W. (1959). *The sociological imagination.* London: Oxford University Press.

Montaigne, M. de. (1973). Selections from the essays. (D. M. Frame, Ed. and Trans.). Arlington Heights, IL: AHM Publishing.

Morgan, C., & Averill, J. R. (1992). True feelings, the self, and authenticity: Social perspectives. In D. Franks and V. Gecas (Eds.), *Social perspectives on emotion,* Vol. 1 (pp. 95–123). Greenwich, CT: JAI Press, Inc.

Moro, P. (2006). It takes a darn good writer: A review of *The Ethnographic I. Symbolic Interaction, 29,* 265–270.

Moss, M., & Moss, S. (1996). Remarriage of widowed persons: A triadic relationship. In D. Klass, D. Silverman, & S. Nickman (Eds.), *Continuing bonds: New understanding of grief* (pp. 163–178). London: Taylor and Francis Group.

Myerhoff, B. (1978). *Number our days.* New York: Simon & Schuster.

Myerhoff, B. (1982). Life history among the elderly: Performance, visibility and remembering. In J. Ruby (Eds.), *A crack in the mirror: Reflexive perspectives in anthropology* (pp. 99–117). Philadelphia: University of Pennsylvania Press.

Mykhalovskiy, E. (1996). Reconsidering table talk: Critical thoughts on the relationship between sociology, autobiography and self-indulgence. *Qualitative Sociology, 19,* 131–151.

Nettles, K. (2008). *Guyana diaries: Women's lives across difference.* Walnut Creek, CA: Left Coast Press, Inc.

Noblit, G. (2005). Critical theory on the Ellis study. In J. Paul (Ed.), *Introduction to the philosophies of research and criticism in education and the social sciences* (pp. 276–279). Upper Saddle River, NJ: Pearson Education, Inc.

Noddings, N. (1984). *Caring, a feminine approach to ethics & moral education.* Berkeley: University of California Press.

Noddings, N. (2005). Pragmatisim on the Ellis study. In J. Paul (Ed.), *Introduction to the philosophies of research and criticism in education and the social sciences* (pp. 265–266). Upper Saddle River, NJ: Pearson Education, Inc.

NPR (2007, October 1). Richard Russo's small-town America. Morning Edition. Retrieved April 20, 2008, from http://www.npr.org/templates/story/story.php?storyId=14806290

Obama, B. (2006). *The audacity of hope.* Bethel, CT: Crown Publishing House.

Olesen, V. (2000). Feminisms and qualitative research at and into the millennium. In N. Denzin & Y. Lincoln (Eds.), *Handbook of qualitative research* (2nd ed.) (pp. 215–256). Thousand Oaks, CA: Sage.

Paget, M. (1990). Performing the text. *Journal of Contemporary Ethnography, 19,* 136–155.

Parry, A. (1991). A universe of stories. *Family Process, 30,* 37–54.

Patterson, O. (2006, December 30). The last race problem. *New York Times.* Retrieved September 27, 2007, from http://select.nytimes.com/2006/12/30/opinion/30patterson.html

Paul, J. (Ed.). (2005). *Introduction to the philosophies of research and criticism in education and the social sciences.* Upper Saddle River, NJ: Pearson Education, Inc.

Peirce, C. S. (1958). *Collected papers of Charles Sanders Peirce, Vols. 7 and 8*. (C. Hartshorne, Ed. and P. Weiss, Trans.). Cambridge, MA: Belknap Press of Harvard University Press.

Pelias, R. (2004). *A methodology of the heart: Evoking daily and academic life*. Walnut Creek, CA: Alta-Mira Press.

Pelias, R. (2008). The ethics of Carolyn Ellis. Paper presented at the Southern States Communication Association, Savannah, GA.

Pelto, P. J. (1968). The study of man: The differences between 'tight' and 'loose' societies. *Transaction, 5*, 37–40.

Pennebaker, J. (1990). *Opening up: The healing power of expressing emotions*. New York: Guilford Press.

Perry, J. (1996). Writing the self: Exploring the stigma of hearing impairment. *Sociological Spectrum, 16*, 239–261.

Perry, J. (2001). Sibling relationships and care of parents: Deconstructing memoirs and personal narratives. Unpublished Ph.D. dissertation, Department of Communication, University of South Florida, Tampa.

Petchesky, R. (1990). *Abortion and woman's choice: The state, sexuality and reproductive freedom*. Boston: Northeastern University Press.

Petrunik, M., & Shearing, C. (1983). Fragile facades: Stuttering and the strategic manipulation of awareness. *Social Problems, 31*, 125–138.

Philipsen, G. (1975). Talking like a man in Teamsterville. *Quarterly Journal of Speech, 67*, 13–22.

Polkinghorne, D. (1983). *Methodology for the human sciences: Systems of inquiry*. Albany, NY: SUNY Press.

Polkinghorne, D. (1988). *Narrative knowing and the human sciences*. Albany, NY: SUNY Press.

Polletta, F. (2006). *It was like a fever: Storytelling in protest and politics*. Chicago. University of Chicago Press.

Poole, M. (2008). The class of '65: Boomers at sixty recall turning points that shaped their lives. Unpublished dissertation. University of South Florida, Tampa.

Porter, D. (1982). Soap time: Thoughts on a commodity art form. In H. Newcomb (Ed.), *Television: The critical view*, 3rd ed. (pp. 122–131). New York: Oxford University Press.

Poulos, C. (2006). The ties that bind us, the shadows that separate us: Life and death, shadow and (dream) story. *Qualitative Inquiry, 12*, 96–117.

Poulos, C. (2008a). Narrative conscience and the autoethnographic adventure: Probing memories, secrets, shadows, and possibilities. *Qualitative Inquiry, 14*, 46–66.

Poulos, C. (2008b). The Ethnographic I and a relational ethic of practicing ethnography. Paper presented at the Southern States Communication Association. Savannah, GA.

Poulos, C. (2008c). *Accidental ethnography: An inquiry into family secrecy*. Walnut Creek, CA: Left Coast Press, Inc.

Punch, M. (1994). Politics and ethics in qualitative research. In N. Denzin & Y. Lincoln (Eds.), *Handbook of qualitative research* (pp. 83–97). Thousand Oaks, CA: Sage.

Putnam, R. (2000). *Bowling alone*. New York: Simon & Schuster.

Quinney, R. (1991). *Journey to a far place: Autobiographical reflections*. Philadelphia: Temple University Press.

Quinney, R. (1996). Once my father traveled west to California. In C. Ellis & A. Bochner (Eds.), *Composing ethnography* (pp. 357–382). Walnut Creek, CA: AltaMira Press.

Radford, J. (1974). Reflections on introspection. *American Psychologist, 29*, 245–250.

Rambo, C. (2005). Handing IRB an unloaded gun. Unpublished manuscript. University of Memphis, Memphis, TN.

(Rambo) Ronai, C. (1995). Multiple reflections of child sex abuse: An argument for a layered account. *Journal of Contemporary Ethnography, 23*, 395–426.

Reason, P. (1993). Reflections on sacred experience and sacred science. *Journal of Management Inquiry, 2*(3), 273–283.

Reed-Danahay, D. (1997). *Auto/ethnography: Rewriting the self and the social*. Oxford: Berg.

Reinharz, S. (1979). *On becoming a social scientist*. San Francisco: Jossey-Bass.

Richardson, L. (1990). *Writing strategies: Reaching diverse audiences*. Thousand Oaks, CA: Sage.

Richardson, L. (1992a). The consequences of poetic representation: Writing the other, rewriting the self. In C. Ellis & M. Flaherty (Eds.), *Investigating subjectivity: Research on lived experience* (pp. 125–137). Thousand Oaks, CA: Sage.

Richardson, L. (1992b). Trash on the corner: Ethics and technology. *Journal of Contemporary Ethnography*, 21, 103–119.

Richardson, L. (1996). Speech lessons. In C. Ellis & A. Bochner (Eds.), *Composing ethnography* (pp. 231–239). Walnut Creek, CA: AltaMira Press.

Richardson, L. (1997). *Fields of play: Constructing an academic life.* New Brunswick, NJ: Rutgers University Press.

Richardson, L. (2007). *Last writes: A daybook for a dying friend.* Walnut Creek, CA: Left Coast Press, Inc.

Richardson, L. (2008). Comments on *Fisher Folk.* Paper presented at the Southern States Communication Association, Savannah, GA.

Riessman, C. K. (1990). *Divorce talk: Women and men make sense of personal relationships.* New Brunswick, NJ: Rutgers University Press.

Riskind, J. H. (1999). The psychology of looming vulnerability: Its relationships to loss. *Journal of Personal and Interpersonal Loss,* 4, 25–46.

Rochford, E. B. (1983). Stutterers' practices: Folk remedies and therapeutic intervention. *Journal of Communication Disorders,* 16, 373–384.

Rodriquez, R. (1983). *Hunger of memory: The education of Richard Rodriguez.* New York: Bantam.

Rorty, R. (1982). *Consequences of pragmatism.* Minneapolis: University of Minnesota Press.

Rorty, R. (1989). *Contingency, irony, solidarity.* Cambridge: Cambridge University Press.

Rorty, R. (1991). *Essays on Heidegger and others.* Cambridge: Cambridge University Press.

Rosaldo, M. (1984). Toward an anthropology of self and feeling. In R. Shweder & R. Levine (Eds.), *Culture theory: Essays on mind, self, and emotion* (pp. 137–157). Cambridge: Cambridge University Press.

Rosaldo, R. (1989). *Culture and truth: The remaking of social analysis.* Boston: Beacon Press.

Rosenberg, M. (1988). Self-concept research: A historical overview. Revised version of a paper presented at the Southern Sociological Society, Nashville, TN.

Rosenblatt, P. (1996). Grief that does not end. In D. Klass, D. Silverman, & S. Nickman (Eds.), *Continuing bonds: New understanding of grief* (pp. 45–58). London: Taylor and Francis Group.

Rosenwald, G. (1992). Conclusion: Reflections on narrative understanding. In G. Rosenwald & R. Ochberg (Eds.), *Storied lives: The cultural politics of self-understanding* (pp. 265–289). New Haven, CT: Yale University Press.

Rosenwald, G., & Ochberg, R. (Eds.). (1992). *Storied lives: The cultural politics of self-understanding.* New Haven, CT: Yale University Press.

Ross, D. (1979). The development of the social sciences. In A. Olesen & J. Voss (Eds.), *The organization of knowledge in modern America, 1860–1920* (pp. 107–138). Baltimore: Johns Hopkins University Press.

Roth, W. M. (Ed). (2005). *Auto/biography and auto/ethnography: Praxis of research method.* Rotterdam: Sense Publishers.

Rubin, S. S. (1996). The wounded family: Bereaved parents and the impact of adult child loss. In D. Klass, D. Silverman, & S. Nickman (Eds.), *Continuing bonds: New understanding of grief* (pp. 217–232). London: Taylor and Francis Group.

Rushing, J. H. (2006). *Erotic mentoring: Women's transformations in the university.* Walnut Creek, CA: Left Coast Press, Inc.

Sanders, C. M. (1979–80). A comparison of adult bereavement in the death of a spouse, child, and parent. *Omega: Journal of Death & Dying,* 10, 303–20.

Sanders, C. M. (1982). Effects of sudden vs. chronic illness death on bereavement outcome. *Omega: Journal of Death & Dying,* 13, 227–241.

Sarbin, T. (1986). Emotion and act: Roles and rhetoric. In R. Harré (Ed.), *The social construction of emotions* (pp. 83–97). New York: Basil Blackwell.

Scarry, E. (1985). *The body in pain: The making and unmaking of the world.* New York: Oxford University Press.

Scheff, T. (1983). Toward integration in the social psychology of emotions. *Annual Review of Sociology,* 9, 133–54.

Scheff, T. (1985). Universal expressive needs: A critique and a theory. *Symbolic Interaction, 8,* 241–262.

Schwartz, M., & Schwartz, C. (1955). Problems in participant observation. *American Journal of Sociology, 60,* 343–354.

Scott, R. (1970). The construction of conceptions of stigma by professional experts. In J. Douglas (Ed.), *Deviance and respectability: The social construction of moral meanings* (pp. 255–290). New York: Basic Books.

Scott-Hoy, K. (2002). What kind of mother ... ? An ethnographic short story. *Qualitative Inquiry, 8*(3), 273–279.

Shames, L., & Barton, P. (2004). *Not fade away: A short life well lived.* New York: Harper Perennial.

Sharf, B. (1993). Reading the vital signs: Research in health care communication. *Communication Monographs, 60,* 35–41.

Shelton, A. (1995). Foucault's Madonna: The secret life of Carolyn Ellis. *Symbolic Interaction, 18,* 83–87.

Sherwood, S., Smith, P., & Alexander, J. (1993). The British are coming ... again!: The hidden agenda of "cultural studies." *Contemporary Sociology, 22,* 370–375.

Shott, S. (1979). Emotion and social life: A symbolic interactionist analysis. *American Journal of Sociology, 84,* 1317–1333.

Silverman, P. R., & Klass, D. (1996). Introduction: What's the problem? In D. Klass, D. Silverman, & S. Nickman (Eds.), *Continuing bonds: New understanding of grief* (pp. 3–30). London: Taylor and Francis Group.

Simmel, G. (1950). *The sociology of Georg Simmel* (Compiled and translated by Kurt Wolff). Glencoe, IL: Free Press.

Simons, Herbert (1994). 'Going meta': Definition and political applications. *Quarterly Journal of Speech, 80,* 468–481.

Slate Magazine (2007, March 27–29). Memoir Week: The stories we tell about ourselves. Retrieved July 15, 2008, from http://www.slate.com/id/2162677/

Slater, L. (2003, February 23). Repress yourself. *New York Times Magazine,* pp. 48–53.

Slattery, P., & Rapp, D. (2003). *Ethics and the foundations of education: Teaching convictions in a postmodern world.* Boston: Allyn & Bacon.

Smith, B., & Sparkes, A. (2006). Narrative inquiry in psychology: Exploring the tensions within. *Qualitative Research in Psychology, 3,* 169–192.

Smith, D. (1979). A sociology for women. In J. Sherman & E. Black (Eds.), *The prism of sex: Essays in the sociology of knowledge* (pp. 135–187). Madison: University of Wisconsin Press.

Smith-Sullivan, K. (2008). The autoethnographic call: Current considerations and possible futures. Unpublished dissertation, University of South Florida, Tampa.

Solomon, R. (1984). Getting angry: The Jamesian theory of emotion in anthropology. In R. Shweder & R. Levine (Eds.), *Culture theory: Essays on mind, self, and emotion* (pp. 238–254). Cambridge: Cambridge University Press.

Spence, D. (1982). *Narrative truth and historical truth.* New York: W. W. Norton and Co.

Sparkes, A. (2002). Autoethnography: Self-indulgence or something more? In C. Ellis & A. Bochner (Eds.), *Composing ethnography: Alternative forms of qualitative writing* (pp. 209–232). Walnut Creek, CA: AltaMira Press.

Stacey, J., & Thorne, B. (1985). The missing feminist revolution in sociology. *Social Problems, 32,* 301–316.

Stearns, C., & Stearns, P. (1986). *Anger: The struggle for emotional control in America's history.* Chicago: University of Chicago Press.

Stone, C., & Farberman, H. (1970). *Social psychology through symbolic interaction.* New York: John Wiley and Sons.

Stone, L. (2005). Poststructuralism on the Ellis study. In J. Paul (Ed.), *Introduction to the philosophies of research and criticism in education and the social sciences* (pp. 281–283). Upper Saddle River, NJ: Pearson Education, Inc.

Stroebe, M., Strobe, W., & Hansson, R. (1993). *Handbook of bereavement: Theory, research, & intervention.* Cambridge: Cambridge University Press.

Stryker, S. (1981). Symbolic interactionism: Themes and variations. In M. Rosenburg & R. Turner (Eds.), *Social psychology: Sociological perspectives* (pp. 3–29). New York: Basic.

Sudnow, D. (1978). *Ways of the hand.* Cambridge, MA: Harvard University Press.

Swift, C. L. (2007). "I had an abortion." The rhetorical situation of a Planned Parenthood t-shirt. *Qualitative Research Reports in Communication, 8*, 57–63.

Thoits, P. (1990). Emotional deviance: Research agendas. In T. Kemper (Ed.), *Research agendas in the sociology of emotions* (pp. 180–203). Albany, NY: SUNY Press.

Thomas, D. J. (1982). Interactions. In D. Thomas (Ed.), *The experience of handicap* (pp. 54–70). New York: Methuen.

Thompson, S., & Janigian, A. (1988). Life schemes: A framework for understanding the search for meaning. *Journal of Social and Clinical Psychology, 7*, 260–280.

Tierney, W. G (1993). Introduction: Developing archives of resistance. In D. McLaughlin & W. G. Tierney (Eds.), *Naming silenced lives: Personal narratives and the process of educational change.* New York: Routledge.

Tierney, W. G. (2002). Get real: Representing reality. *Qualitative Studies in Education, 15*, 385–398.

Tillmann, L. (2007). Going home: Gay men's identities, families, and communities. Unpublished manuscript. Orlando, FL.

Tillmann, L. (in press, 2008). Body and bulimia revisited: Reflections on 'A secret life.' *Journal of Applied Communication Research.*

Tillmann-Healy, L. (1996). A secret life in a culture of thinness: Reflections on body, food and bulimia. In C. Ellis & A. Bochner (Eds.), *Composing ethnography: Alternative forms of qualitative writing* (pp. 77–109). Walnut Creek, CA: AltaMira Press.

Tillmann-Healy, L. (2001). *Between gay and straight: Understanding friendship across sexual orientation.* Walnut Creek, CA: AltaMira Press.

Tolich, M. (2004). Internal confidentiality: When confidentiality assurances fail relational informants. *Qualitative Sociology, 27*, 101–106.

Tollifson, J. (2003) *Awake in the heartland: The ecstasy of what is.* Oxford: Trafford Publishing.

Tomaselli, K. (2007). *Writing in the San/d: Autoethnography among indigenous Southern Africans.* Walnut Creek, CA: AltaMira Press.

Tullis Owen, J. A. T., McRae, C., Adams, T. E., Vitale, A. (in press). Truth troubles. *Qualitative Inquiry, 15*(2).

Turner, V. (1986). *The anthropology of performance.* New York: PAJ Publications.

Tyler, S. (1986). Post-modern ethnography: From document of the occult to occult document. In J. Clifford & G. Marcus (Eds.), *Writing culture* (pp. 122–140). Berkeley: University of California Press.

Ulmer, G. (1989). *Teletheory.* New York: Routledge.

Updike, J. (1989). *Self-conscious memoirs.* New York: Fawcett Crest.

Valdez, L. (1997, May 20). Baby-boomer moms send mixed messages to their daughters. *Tampa Tribune,* p. 7.

Van Maanen, J. (1988). *Tales of the field.* Chicago: University of Chicago Press.

Vangelis, L. (2006). Communicating change: An ethnography of women's sensemaking on hormone replacement therapies, menopause, and the Women's Health Initiative. Unpublished dissertation. University of South Florida, Tampa.

Vaz, K. M. (Ed.) (1997). *Oral narrative research with black women.* Thousand Oaks, CA: Sage.

Vidich, A. J., & Bensman, J. (1958). *Small town in mass society: Class, power and religion in a rural community.* Princeton, NJ: Princeton University Press.

Villenas, S. (2000). This ethnography called my back: Writings on the exotic gaze, "othering" Latina, and recuperating xicanisma. In E. St. Pierre & W. Pillow (Eds.) *Working the ruins: Feminist post-structural theory and methods in education* (pp. 74–94). London: Routledge.

Walker, D. C. (2005). Motive and identity in the narratives of community service volunteers. Unpublished dissertation. University of South Florida, Tampa.

Wasielewski, P. (1990). Post abortion syndrome: Emotional battles over interaction and ideology. Unpublished paper.

Waterman, R. H., Jr. (1990). *Adhocracy: The power to change.* Memphis, TN: Whittle Direct Books.

Watson, J. B. (1913). Psychology as the behaviorist views it. *Psychological Review, 20,* 158–177.

Watzlawick, P., Bavelas, J. B., & Jackson, D. D. (1967). *Pragmatics of human communication.* New York: W.W. Norton.

Weber, M. (1949). *The methodology of the social sciences.* (E. Shils & H. Finch, Eds. & Trans.) Glencoe, IL: The Free Press.

Webster, S. (1982). Dialogue and fiction in ethnography. *Dialectical anthropology, 7,* 91–114.

Weick, Karl. (1995). *Sensemaking in organizations.* Thousand Oaks, CA: Sage.

Weinstein, E. A., & Deutschberger, P. (1963). Some dimensions of altercasting. *Sociometry, 26,* 454–466.

Weinstein, E.A. (1969). The development of interpersonal competence. In D. A. Goslin (Ed.), *Handbook of socialization theory and research* (pp. 753–775). Chicago: Rand McNally.

Wentworth, W. M., & Ryan, J. (1992). Balancing body, mind and culture: The place of emotion in social life. In D. Franks & V. Gecas (Eds.), *Social perspectives on emotion* (pp. 25–46). Greenwich, CT: JAI Press, Inc.

West, J. F. (2000). *The summer people.* Boone, NC: Parkway Publishers.

White, M. (1988). Saying hullo again. *Dulwich Centre Newsletter, 2,* 29–36.

Wilmot, W. W. (1980). Metacommunication: A re-examination and extension. In D. Nimmo (Ed.), *Communication yearbook 4* (pp. 61–72). New Brunswick, NJ: Transaction.

Wood, J. (2001). The normalization of violence in heterosexual romantic relationships: Women's stories of love and violence. *Journal of Social and Personal Relationships, 18,* 239–261.

Wood, L. (1986). Loneliness. In R. Harré (Ed.), *The social construction of emotions* (pp. 184–208). New York: Basil Blackwell.

Woodstock, L. (2001). Hide and seek: The paradox of documenting a suicide. *Text and Performance Quarterly, 21,* 247–260.

Wolf, M. (1992). *A thrice told tale: Feminism, postmodernism, and ethnographic responsibility.* Stanford, CA: Stanford University Press.

Woolf, V. (1953). *The common reader.* New York: Harcourt Brace & World.

Woolf, V. (1985). A sketch of the past. In J. Schulkind (Ed.), *Moments of being* (pp. 61–159). San Diego: Harcourt Brace Jovanovich.

Wright, B. A. (1983). *Physical disabilities: A psychosocial approach.* New York: Harper and Row.

Zald, M. (1991). Sociology as a discipline: Quasi-science, quasi-humanities. *American Sociologist, 22,* 165–187.

Zaner, R. (2004). Quiet rooms for troubled voices. *Conversations on the edge: Narratives of ethics and illness* (pp. 1–16). Washington, DC: Georgetown University Press.

Zaner, R. (2007). Narrative and decision. Presentation at National Communication Association, Chicago.

Zimmerman, M. (1977). *Passage through abortion: The personal and social reality of women's experiences.* New York: Praeger.

Znaniecki, F. (1934). *The method of sociology.* New York: Farrar and Rinehart.

Name Index

Subject Index

A
abortion, 198–221
  ambivalences of, 211–19
  emotional/cognitive process of, 211–13
  moral choices of, 204, 205, 211, 213
  politics of, 211, 216, 220
abusive relationships, 295–96. *See also* CASA
  (Collective Action Stops Abuse)
academic tribe, 64–65
academic vocabulary, 63–65
accidental ethnography, 317–18
African-American identity. *See* "Other Side
  of the Fence" (Ellis); race relationships
agency, 291, 296
aging issues, 118, 170, 185, 195–96. *See also*
  "Maternal Connections" (Ellis);
  "With Mother/With Child" (Ellis)
alienation, 47, 64
alleviating conditions, 34
ambiguity, 32, 241
  of authenticity, 74
  of stigma, 241
ambivalence, 47, 108, 150, 241
  as a coping mechanism, 91–93
  concerning family, 141, 150
  in abortion, 211–19
  in stigma, 241
analytic texts, 14, 233n4, 233n5, 246
anticipated loss, 152, 152n9

ashamed/shame. *See* shame/ashamed
assumption of truth, 106, 307, 311, 315
The Audacity of Hope (Obama), 348
authenticity, 74–75, 77
autoethnographic performance, 287–90, 293
autoethnography, 12–13, 16, 146, 151, 196, 216,
  229–32, 299, 304
  critique of, 231–33, 231n1

B
battered women. *See* CASA (Collective Action Stops Abuse)
behaviorism, 100, 100n6, 106
bias in research, 109
bodily experience, 101, 197
bodily stigma, 230, 240–42, 246–48, 256

C
canonical story, 193, 281, 296
CASA (Collective Action Stops Abuse),
  288–99
categorical/categories, 65, 230–31, 241, 248–49
chaos narrative, 257, 259–60, 279
close relationships, 116–18, 154–55, 159–64,
  196, 213
coconstructed interview, 195
coconstructed narrative, 17, 195–96, 186n4,
  213
cognitive distance, 79
cognitive processing, 140, 211, 277

individualism vs. communitarianism, 65–66

inside/outside, 50, 147, 162, 162n13, 255–66. *See also* "of/outside of"

integrity of self, 141, 150

interaction with others, 337–40

interactive focus groups, 195

interactive interviewing, 102–103, 195

interiorized anxiety, 247

interpretive studies, 105

interracial relationships, 47–59, 334. *See also* "Other Side of the Fence," (Ellis)

introspection, 83–84, 96–104. *See also* systematical sociological introspection

IRB (institutional review boards), 310

J

jealousy, 83–84

"jew down," 30–31, 330

Judaism/Jewish identity, 32n3, 275, 330–32, 347

L

lack of resolution, 110

life in motion, 232, 315, 350, 352, 354

life scheme, 277

"like them/not like them," 49, 79

limits to openness, 215

lisp, 230, 238–39, 243–47

literature and ethnography, 105–106, 147, 242–43

lived experience, 62–63, 66, 84–85, 97–99, 102, 104, 109, 213

messiness of, 296–297

looking-glass self, 243

loss, experience of, 85, 117–20

lyric memoirs, 32n5

M

marginalized voices, 213

"Maternal Connections" (Ellis), 166–69, 304

memoirs, 32n5

memory, 304, 352–54

messiness of living, 117

messy texts, 94, 297, 341–43

meta-autoethnography, 12, 14, 18, 303–306

metashame, 242, 248

metastory/metaframe, 158n11

minor bodily stigmas, 234, 240–43

Mnemosyne (Clark/Keefe), 224–26

moral(s)

choice, 145, 147, 204, 213

complexities, 214, 216–20, 341

conversation, 17, 115, 148

dimension, 205

identity, 141

political ideology, 211–13

stories, 148

moral indignation, 211

mother-daughter relationships, 155, 161, 186, 189–90. *See also* "Maternal Connections" (Ellis); "With Mother/With Child" (Ellis)

movement in texts, 16, 140

multidimensionality, 186n4

multiple perspectives, 15, 195

multiplicity of selves, 108

multi-voiced accounts, 195, 197, 304, 310

Muslim identity, 230, 273–77

N

narrative

challenge, 13, 296

continuity, 119, 281

criteria for evaluation, 107, 113

goals of, 97, 107n , 145, 166, 197, 211–13, 289

inquiry, 105, 147–48

meaning, 18, 107–11

memorial function, 153

in politics, 220, 286

as social science, 104, 147

theory and, 147–48

as therapy, 94

truth, 15, 107, 315

W

"With Mother/With Child" (Ellis),
169–85
world view, 154, 257, 282
working-class roots, 64, 123, 143–44, 344
"work the hyphen," 78
writing
as inquiry, 15, 118, 229
"mean," 316
as therapy, 33, 95, 106, 118
usefulness, of, 215, 246, 259, 280, 294, 317

About the Author

Carolyn Ellis is professor of communication and sociology at the University of South Florida. She has published three books—*Fisher Folk: Two Communities on Chesapeake Bay, Final Negotiations: A Story of Love, Loss, and Chronic Illness,* and *The Ethnographic I: A Methodological Novel About Autoethnography*—four edited collections, and numerous articles, chapters, and personal stories. With Arthur Bochner, she coedits the Left Coast book series *Writing Lives: Ethnographic Narratives.* Her work is situated in interpretive and artistic representations of qualitative research and focuses on writing and revising autoethnographic stories as a way to understand and interpret culture and live a meaningful life.